I0897088

# Multidisciplinary Approaches to Crowdfunding Platforms

Carla Sofia Vicente Negrão
*University of Coimbra, Portugal*

João António Furtado Brito
*University of Cape Verde, Cape Verde*

A volume in the Advances in E-Business Research (AEBR) Book Series

IGI Global
PUBLISHER of TIMELY KNOWLEDGE

Published in the United States of America by
IGI Global
Business Science Reference (an imprint of IGI Global)
701 E. Chocolate Avenue
Hershey PA, USA 17033
Tel: 717-533-8845
Fax: 717-533-8661
E-mail: cust@igi-global.com
Web site: http://www.igi-global.com



Library of Congress Cataloging-in-Publication Data

Names: Negrão, Carla Sofia Vicente, 1978- editor. | Brito, João António Furtado, 1978- editor.
Title: Multidisciplinary approaches to crowdfunding platforms / Carla Sofia Vicente Negrão and João António Furtado Brito, editors.
Description: Hershey, PA : Business Science Reference, [2020] | Includes bibliographical references and index. | Summary: “”This book examines the current state of crowdfunding. It also explores challenges, opportunities, and limitations of crowdfunding”--Provided by publisher”-- Provided by publisher.
Identifiers: LCCN 2019049673 (print) | LCCN 2019049674 (ebook) | ISBN 9781799832263 (hardcover) | ISBN 9781799832270 (paperback) | ISBN 9781799832287 (ebook)
Subjects: LCSH: Crowd funding. | Venture capital. | Fund raising.
Classification: LCC HG4751 .M854 2020 (print) | LCC HG4751 (ebook) | DDC 658.15/224--dc23
LC record available at https://lccn.loc.gov/2019049673
LC ebook record available at https://lccn.loc.gov/2019049674

This book is published in the IGI Global book series Advances in E-Business Research (AEBR) (ISSN: 1935-2700; eISSN: 1935-2719)

British Cataloguing in Publication Data
A Cataloguing in Publication record for this book is available from the British Library.

# Advances in E-Business Research (AEBR) Book Series

ISSN:1935-2700
EISSN:1935-2719

Editor-in-Chief: In Lee, Western Illinois University, USA

## MISSION

Technology has played a vital role in the emergence of e-business and its applications incorporate strategies. These processes have aided in the use of electronic transactions via telecommunications networks for collaborating with business partners, buying and selling of goods and services, and customer service. Research in this field continues to develop into a wide range of topics, including marketing, psychology, information systems, accounting, economics, and computer science.

The **Advances in E-Business Research (AEBR) Book Series** provides multidisciplinary references for researchers and practitioners in this area. Instructors, researchers, and professionals interested in the most up-to-date research on the concepts, issues, applications, and trends in the e-business field will find this collection, or individual books, extremely useful. This collection contains the highest quality academic books that advance understanding of e-business and addresses the challenges faced by researchers and practitioners.

## COVERAGE

- Economics of e-business
- Evaluation methodologies for e-business systems
- Semantic Web
- Virtual Collaboration
- E-procurement methods
- Outsourcing and e-business technologies
- E-business technology investment strategies
- E-Marketing
- Intelligent Agent Technologies
- Trust, Security, and Privacy

IGI Global is currently accepting manuscripts for publication within this series. To submit a proposal for a volume in this series, please contact our Acquisition Editors at Acquisitions@igi-global.com or visit: http://www.igi-global.com/publish/.

The Advances in E-Business Research (AEBR) Book Series (ISSN 1935-2700) is published by IGI Global, 701 E. Chocolate Avenue, Hershey, PA 17033-1240, USA, www.igi-global.com. This series is composed of titles available for purchase individually; each title is edited to be contextually exclusive from any other title within the series. For pricing and ordering information please visit http://www.igi-global.com/book-series/advances-business-research/37144. Postmaster: Send all address changes to above address. 

## Titles in this Series

*For a list of additional titles in this series, please visit:*
http://www.igi-global.com/book-series/advances-business-research/37144

***Rural Entrepreneurship and Innovation in the Digital Era***
Sachithra Lokuge (RMIT University, Australia) and Darshana Sedera (Southern Cross University, Australia)
Business Science Reference • © 2021 • 337pp • H/C (ISBN: 9781799849421) • US $195.00

***Advanced Digital Architectures for Model-Driven Adaptive Enterprises***
Vinay Kulkarni (TCS Research, Tata Consultancy Services, India) Sreedhar Reddy (TCS Research, Tata Consultancy Services, India) Tony Clark (Aston University, Birmingham, UK) and Balbir S. Barn (Middlesex University, London, UK)
Business Science Reference • © 2020 • 364pp • H/C (ISBN: 9781799801085) • US $205.00

***Interdisciplinary Approaches to Digital Transformation and Innovation***
Rocci Luppicini (University of Ottawa, Canada)
Business Science Reference • © 2020 • 368pp • H/C (ISBN: 9781799818793) • US $215.00

***Implications and Impacts of eSports on Business and Society Emerging Research and Opportunities***
David J. Finch (Mount Royal University, Canada) Norm O'Reilly (University of Guelph, Canada) Gashaw Abeza (Towson University, USA) Brad Clark (Mount Royal University, Canada) and David Legg (Mount Royal University, Canada)
Business Science Reference • © 2020 • 185pp • H/C (ISBN: 9781799815389) • US $165.00

***Tools and Techniques for Implementing International E-Trading Tactics for Competitive Advantage***
Yurdagül Meral (İstanbul Medipol University, Turkey)
Business Science Reference • © 2020 • 395pp • H/C (ISBN: 9781799800354) • US $225.00

***Handbook of Research on Strategic Fit and Design in Business Ecosystems***
Umit Hacioglu (Istanbul Medipol University, Turkey)
Business Science Reference • © 2020 • 775pp • H/C (ISBN: 9781799811251) • US $295.00

*For an entire list of titles in this series, please visit:*
http://www.igi-global.com/book-series/advances-business-research/37144

IGI Global
PUBLISHER of TIMELY KNOWLEDGE

701 East Chocolate Avenue, Hershey, PA 17033, USA
Tel: 717-533-8845 x100 • Fax: 717-533-8661
E-Mail: cust@igi-global.com • www.igi-global.com

# Editorial Advisory Board

# Table of Contents

# Detailed Table of Contents

Although the crowdfunding (CF) sector is booming, research focusing on motivation of contributors is mainly exploratory and does not propose an analytical model. This chapter aims to propose a typology of differentiated motivations according to the type of CF. The main results, authentic compared to the existing literature, show that types of motivation are not the same depending on the type of CF considered. These findings provide significant practical guidelines for three major actors of a CF process: CF platforms must communicate according to the segmentation resulting from the respective predominant motivations. Project leaders should go beyond the simple utility and inform contributors according to the life of the project and its segmentation and the required technical tools of contribution. Contributors share personal ties and observe how the projects succeed regarding loan with interest; therefore, certain motivations, found in this research, such as pleasure of contributing, living experiences, and supporting creators should not be put forward in all the CF campaigns.



By analysing the operations of a lending crowdfunding platform in Portugal, the investigation aims to study the potential contribution of CF for entrepreneurship and regional development. The results reveal that small organisations are especially prone to use CF as a financing strategy, regardless of their seniority, as well as ventures that have a moderated risk profile. However, coastal regions have been more dynamic on CF use than interior located ventures, since most of the operations were realized on the littoral of the country. The results suggest that interior organisations that use CF could have more financing difficulties that led them to look for new fundraising solutions, since they typically have higher size than coastal located organisations, although the risk rating is quite similar. The CF loans period is also shorter. The average interest rate charged is quite similar between both type of locations, although a higher variability exists in the funding conditions of interior organisations. The average offer per investor is also higher in the interior case.



Thanks to the spread of internet technologies, there has recently been a significant upsurge of innovative forms of human cooperation. In an ecosystem characterized by unsteadiness and parceled relations, crowdfunding has quickly become one of the most popular expression of the new wave of the sharing economy philosophies. Although it is undeniable that the success of crowdfunding has increased during a dramatic financial period, characterized by a wide-ranging credit crunch, we can't interpret this phenomenon just as a fade or as a side effect of the economic crisis. However, through a multidisciplinary approach of analysis and through a qualitative explorative research it will be possible to observe what type of solidarity this system is currently promoting.



This chapter compares two national crowdfunding markets based on their platforms and regulatory legislation on crowdfunding. Spain and France were selected though a cluster analysis since both differ on those characteristics. Mean comparison tests were carried out to estimate differences. Data were based on a survey specifically designed and conducted for this research. While crowdfunding is an internet-powered activity with global accessibility, national boundaries and geographic proximity play a significant role in shaping the performance of crowdfunding platforms. Regarding practical implications, as each country developed its specific legislation, it is concluded that this legislation may boost or hinder the growth of crowdfunding. On the other hand, the different way platforms managed their business does not affect their outcomes in terms of number of projects and funds raised. As a result, although platforms are indispensable as an intermediate agent between funders and investors, they determine neither the number of projects hosted nor the funds raised.



Group lending is a social innovation because the substitution of the guarantee on assets by the collective guarantee of the group of belonging leads to the financial inclusion of the excluded. In a lending group, members who know each other mutually control each other to guarantee repayment of the loan and its circulation among the members. Is the social collateral that supported the development of the offline microcredit to the world level transposable to social lending on the internet?

To answer this question, this chapter aims at determining the factors of mutual supervision and control of the members within the affiliation group and examine the potential of their transposition on the internet. Understanding the conditions for transposing social security is not only a solution to the problem of the unbanked; it is also a source of inspiration for peer-to-peer activities which develop considerably on the internet.



Title III of the Jumpstart Our Business Startups Act (JOBS Act) enacted by the U.S. Congress enables a new crowdfunding source of investment capital for entrepreneurs and a new opportunity for all investors (Regulation CF). Given the information asymmetry, the SEC requires that managers provide information to investors (Form C). Using this information, this research tests whether business attributes, financial risks, and offering characteristics are associated with successful crowdfunding efforts for 277 offerings originating during 2016-2017 and closed as of May 2018. The following attributes are positively correlated with funding success: product idea; prior managerial experience with startups; financial risks reported by management; availability of an independent CPA review; and, especially for companies reporting revenue, accounting risk measurements. Finally, the funding intermediary chosen is important and some were more successful than others. Overall, the results provide new insights concerning characteristics of successful security-based crowdfunding offerings.



In this chapter, the authors first provide an overview of the crowdfunding phenomenon. Through the literature review of crowdfunding success factors in the four models, the authors then summarize that the current entrepreneurial research focused on success factors has failed to sufficiently examine how the power of words would affect crowdfunding. Therefore, the authors propose that non-verbal and verbal cues are crucial to entrepreneurial financing success. Based on the insufficient research related with those cues, especially the non-verbal ones, the authors open an area of study on non-verbal and verbal cues in the entrepreneurial financing process by conducting and writing this chapter.



Crowdfunding is an innovative, creative tool of distance collaborative funding, which can galvanise an optimal number of people to various potentials, including education. The aim is to understand crowdfunding and its implementation in Portugal, focusing on successful projects and exploring its potential use in literacy and educational projects, as an alternative to resources perceived as 'classical'. Successful Portuguese projects in education are still underused and under-reported, despite being great allies to innovative, creative educational entrepreneurs requiring swift responses in a post-pandemic future. Is crowdfunding a way to change education?



In this chapter, the research deals with NGOs and their current weight in state's development and public conditions improvement. The researcher also goes to connect the financial challenging faced by NGOs and how the use of crowdfunding platform is important specifically to solicit funding to start, continue, and expand its works. The chapter will highlight the crowdfunding models suitable for NGOs specifically crowdfunding and NGOs in developing countries with describing crowdfunding policies and regulations. Through that, the researcher helps in shaping best practices based on NGO success stories. This chapter will also review previous studies and statistics as a guide for the researcher to present crowdfunding as a tool for the non-profit sector.

# Foreword

Crowdfunding is a form of crowdsourcing and alternative finance, which enable projects and venture to be funded by raising a minor amount of money from a large number of people. By its characteristics associated with technological innovation makes it nowadays, a highly and hot topic discussed among researchers and academicians in financial economics.

This book enhances the literature on crowdfunding by bringing to light new insights that are considered essential to the new era of financial and innovation. The issues discussed in each chapter demonstrate distinctly the contribution that each researcher presents and the remarkable significance of their research in the real world.

This book not only covers theoretical contributions but also emphasizes empirical and practical experiences. It embodies one of the best contribution to crowdfunding topic around the world and particularly in a small open economy, which in my experience on incipient capital markets I strongly recommend its reading.

Throughout its content, I am certain that this book will have a tremendous incremental impact on practitioners and to those that are researching on crowdfunding.

*António Gonçalves de Andrade*
*Central Bank of Cabo Verde, Cabo Verde*

# Preface

During recent years, the number of crowdfunding platforms has increased in worldwide. Crowdfunding plays an important paper in the global digital economy, however, several projects are unsuccessful. In order to discuss ideas, problems, challenges, and solutions for changes in society and organizations to improve crowdfunding platforms, we prepare this book. Based on studies developed by students, researchers, consultants, and experts in the field and who have knowledge on this subject, this book suggests important aspects of crowdfunding involving a multidisciplinary perspective, including entrepreneurism, economy, management, law, computing, sociology, psychology, education, and communication.

This book has an important role to play in providing knowledge for researchers, experts, and practitioners of crowdfunding platforms in the global digital economy. It also intends to provide guidelines for entrepreneurs, economists, managers, consultants, NGOs, startup policy makers, teachers, psychologists, sociologists, investors, and technology developers.

## ORGANIZATION OF THE BOOK

Through a multidisciplinary approach of crowdfunding platforms, this book comprises 10 chapters/sections which take up important aspects of crowdfunding knowledge construction, addressing different research areas. The contributing authors came from several countries like USA, Portugal, Spain, France, Italy, Cape Verde, Reunion, and Tunisia. Different theories and models are used by the authors. The used methodologies ranged from interpretive to positivist research. A brief description of the content of each chapter is explained in detail below.

The first chapter of this edited book is written by the editors Carla Negrão and João Brito, titled "An Empirical Study on the Determinants of Crowdfunding Success Projects: Kickstarter". They take an interesting approach to investigate determinants of crowdfunding platforms success and they use the data of one of the best know platforms in the world – Kickstarter for this quantitative study.

The second chapter is developed by Laurence Attuel-Mendes, Djamchid Assadi, and Silsa Raymond. The title is as follows "Investors' Motivations in Different Types of Crowdfunding". The emphasis of this chapter is the motivations of the contributors. They propose an analytical model to demonstrate that the types of motivations are not the same for each platform considered. The value of such an approach is demonstrated by the concluding chapter's fascinating discussion.

The third chapter has two authors, Susana Bernardino and José Freitas Santos. The title of this chapter is "Lending Crowdfunding and Regional Development: An Empirical Study". The chapter attempts to examine the potential of lending crowdfunding for regional development and entrepreneurship. Using an exploratory approach, the chapter reports interesting results about lending crowdfunding and suggests that it can be a good option for financing Portuguese organizations.

The fourth chapter is written by Francesca Moretti and the title is "Crowdfunding: A New Type of Solidarity for the Digital Era". The author chose a qualitative explorative research in order to see the type of solidarity of the system is using. This captivating study emphasizes that crowdfunding can be understood as a form of solidarity typical of complex societies and in the potential relationships that can be formed.

The fifth chapter is presented by Amaya Erro-Garcés and Begoña Urien. The title is "Crowdfunding Platforms Dynamics: When Local Connections Matter". The authors present an excellent comparison between crowdfunding platforms in Spain and France. To achieve the objective, they conducted a quantitative analysis. They argue that crowdfunding can be a good mechanism to raise funds for SMEs and entrepreneurs.

The sixth chapter is authored by Djamchid Assadi, Arvind Ashta, and Nathalie Duran. The chapter is titled "An Offline Sharing Economy Innovation Transmissible Online? Exploring the Role of Conformity in the Group Lending". This research focuses on factors of mutual supervision and control of the members within the group and their transposition on the Internet by applying a netnographic approach. It is presented a captivating discussion on the proposed topic.

The seventh chapter is developed by William and Margaret Wright. The title for this chapter is "Characteristics of Successful Securities Crowdfunding Campaigns in the United States". Through quantitative analysis, this study analyzes whether business attributes, financial risks, and offering characteristics are associated with successful security-based crowdfunding. This is an excellent support for the theme of this book.

The eighth chapter has the following authors, Yuanqing Li and Sibin Wu and the title is "The Power of Words in Crowdfunding". Conducting a literature review, the authors defend the effect of non-verbal and verbal behaviors of entrepreneurs on crowdfunding, in a very interesting way. They suggest exploring aspects of verbal communication, for example, language styles (simple or complex; emotional, social or psychological) in the crowdfunding context.

The ninth chapter is written by Isabel Maia. The title shown is “Is Crowdfunding One Way to Pay Education?” This fascinating study purpose to comprehend crowdfunding and its implementation in Portugal, based in successful projects and its possible application in literacy and educational projects. The author suggests that crowdfunding provides advantages of transparency and faster implementation of new ideas and that crowdfunding for educational projects can reduce inequalities.

The tenth chapter is presented by Majdi Hassen and Ibtissem Ouertatani. The title is the following: “Crowdfunding and NGOs”. Even though financial sustainability is among the most critical challenges for an NGO, this study aims to develop a new and innovative approach, using crowdfunding as an alternative source of financing for NGOs. The authors emphasize the importance of crowdfunding to creating a financially sustainable NGO.

This book is a great contribution to the literature in the area, the topics covered, and main ideas provide a captivating read. Very useful for those interested in immersing themselves in reading in crowdfunding.

# Acknowledgment

The editors would like to acknowledge the help of all authors and reviewers of the chapters, for sharing their expertise and contribute to the success of our book.

Special thanks go to the publishing team at IGI Global. This book would not be possible without their professional support.

Finally, the editors want to thank everyone who supported us throughout this project.

## Funding

This work has been funded by national funds through FCT – Fundação para a Ciência e a Tecnologia, I.P., Project UIDB/05037/2020.

*Carla Sofia Vicente Negrão*
*University of Coimbra, Portugal*

*João António Furtado Brito*
*University of Cape Verde, Cape Verde*
*July 2020*

# Chapter 1
# An Empirical Study on the Determinants of Success of Crowdfunding Projects:
## Kickstarter

**Carla Sofia Vicente Negrão**
https://orcid.org/0000-0001-6967-7800
*CeBER, University of Coimbra, Portugal*

**João António Furtado Brito**
*University of Cape Verde, Cape Verde*

## ABSTRACT

*Crowdfunding is a way to finance a project in a short time, but it is not easy to develop a successful project. In this study, the authors investigated success determinants of crowdfunding projects by focusing on different categories and the interaction effect of staff pick and video. The authors used econometric analysis for investigating projects of the crowdfunding platform Kickstarter. They found that the funding goal has a negative influence on the probability of success of the crowdfunding project, but the pledged money has a positive influence on all data and by category. The effect of video for staff pick projects is greater than for non-staff pick projects, in art and comic projects. However, the effect of video for staff pick projects is less than for non-staff pick projects, in craft, fashion, food, games, music, photography, and publishing models. These findings are of high interest for practitioners and researchers in the field and extend the knowledge on crowdfunding platforms in several categories and on interaction effects.*

DOI: 10.4018/978-1-7998-3226-3.ch001

## INTRODUCTION

In recent years, crowdfunding has become a possibility for funding new projects and ventures that have increased on the Internet. Crowdfunding platforms offer an infrastructure that facilitates the founder to publish his/her project, allowing fast diffusion, because it can be available 24 hours a day and reach very high numbers of views. However, developing a project successfully is not easy. According to Nguyen (2019), Kickstarter is the best overall of the eight best crowdfunding sites of 2019. Its Web site was founded in 2009 and to July, 2019, it has 452,256 launched projects, but only 166,592 successfully funded projects, while 282,136 projects were unsuccessfully (Kickstarter, 2019). “Very little is known about the factors driving crowdfunding project success and the associated implications for developing crowdfunding platforms and communities” (Kuppuswamy & Bayus, 2018a, p. 370). Therefore, this chapter addresses the following research question: what influences the success of crowdfunding projects? The chapter aims to analyze the determinants for the success of crowdfunding projects by categories and the interaction effect of staff pick and video. In order to reach these goals, the authors propose an empirical study on the crowdfunding platform Kickstarter, in several categories. It is important to know which determinants support the success of crowdfunding projects, both the platform operators, as well as for project founders and funders or bakers, because they reveal what can attract the most backers and allow to achieve the funding goal. The authors use a holistic understanding of the crowdfunding phenomenon based on a multidisciplinary approach. This paper seeks to contribute to scientific research on crowdfunding, giving determinants of crowdfunding projects including in several categories and the interaction term of staff pick and video. To address the relative lack of knowledge about success factors, we focus on Kickstarter crowdfunding platform in several categories.

This chapter is structured as follows: Subsequent to the introduction, the second section presents the theoretical background and literature review on crowdfunding; the third section describes methods and data analysis; the fourth section provides the results and discussion; finally, the fifth section concludes the chapter and provides a summary of the authors' main findings, the limitations of this study, and future research directions.

## THEORETICAL BACKGROUND AND LITERATURE REVIEW

The research into success covers different terms that have been used to refer to this phenomenon in different disciplines. “Success” is a broad term and therefore conceptualized in different forms. Success is “a matter of opinion and may be related to the degree to which objectives are met or exceeded" (Simpson et al., 2012, p. 272). Several ways have been used to measure this phenomenon, in multiple dimensions and in different disciplines. Success is measured in relation to size (Unger et al., 2011), growth (Negrão, 2018, 2020; Unger et al., 2011), profitability/productivity (Negrão, 2018; Unger et al., 2011), perceived performance (Negrão, 2018), large projects (Cordova et al., 2015), and successful vs. failed or cancelled projects (Frydrych et al., 2014).

## Overview of Crowdfunding

Crowdfunding has originated crowdsourcing (Belleflamme et al., 2014), but various terms for crowdfunding exist in the literature, such as crowdfinancing and crowdinvesting (Tomczak & Brem, 2013). The Cambridge Dictionary (2019) defines crowdfunding as "the practice of funding a project or venture by raising money from a large number of people who each contribute a relatively small amount, typically via the Internet". A crowdfunding platform shares several project proposals with a request for funds and a claim of the proponent´s ability to try to make the project successful and when investors are interested in the proposal they contribute funds (Muller et al., 2013). The people who finance the project are the crowd of people (Ordanini et al., 2011).

Several models of funding the projects are available, they include: Donation-based, reward-based, lending-based, and equity-based crowdfunding. However, it is possible to reach different goals at the same time (Mollick, 2014). In donations-based crowdfunding, donations follow a patronage model and the funder does not expect any direct return for his/her donation, such as in art or humanitarian projects (Mollick, 2014) (e.g., GoFundMe, RocketHub and CrowdRise platform). In reward-based crowdfunding, the participants offer a reward to the backers, which ranges from acknowledgements to the delivery of an initial version of the product/service produced from the money collected in the crowdfunding campaign (Dushnitsky et al., 2016) (e.g., Kickstarter and Indiegogo platform). In the lending-based crowdfunding, the compensation is usually through interest payment (Dushnitsky et al., 2016) (e.g., EstateGuru, Flender, Debitum Network, Grupeer, and Mintos platform). Finally, in equity-based crowdfunding, the entrepreneur sells a specific value of equity or bond-like shares in a company for a small group of investors, using an open call for funding on Internet-based platforms (Ahlers et al., 2015). The compensation is through shares, dividends, and/or voting rights in the financed enterprise (Dushnitsky et al., 2016). In this particular case, examples are, Reinvest24, Bulkestate, Crowdestate, SeedMatch, and Property Partner platforms.

In addition, lending-based and equity-based crowdfunding are viewed as investment models, while reward-based and donation-based crowdfunding are understood as non-investment models (Shneor & Munim, 2019). Dushnitsky et al. (2016) proposed that the crowdfunding activity for these four models changes across countries and distinct national patterns.

However, basically two kinds of fundraising exist: Direct and indirect. Direct crowdfunding occurs if the fundraiser asks for funds directly through his/her own platform or supporters. Instead, indirect crowdfunding occurs when the fundraiser asks for funding to the unknow audience or crowd in an intermediary platform (Tomczak & Brem, 2013).

Initially, the researchers on crowdfunding attempted to explain this phenomenon through conceptual models (Beaulieu et al., 2015; Bruton et al., 2015; Tomczak & Brem, 2013). Other authors published reviews on crowdfunding (Kuppuswamy & Bayus, 2018b; Short et al., 2017). However, research on crowdfunding is only in its infancy (Kuppuswamy & Bayus, 2018a). Burtch et al. (2015) looked at the crowdfunder´s behavior.

Research on crowdfunding has been focused mainly on the influence of objective aspects of the crowdfunding page, such as personal network, project quality, geography (Mollick, 2014), and reward type (Belleflamme et al., 2014). Other studies have been focused on more psychological and sociological factors, such as funder motivation Cholakova et al. (2015) or the influence of entrepreneurs' within-platform social capital (Colombo et al., 2015). Alternatively, Zheng et al. (2014) studied the role of social capital in crowdfunding.

Mamonov & Malaga (2018) and Vismara (2016) focused on success factors in equity-based crowdfunding. Cholakova et al. (2015) explored motivations that determine the investors' decisions. In a theoretical model, Belleflamme et al. (2014) focused on the entrepreneur´s choice. They compared two forms of crowdfunding, namely preordering and profit sharing.

Existing empirical studies have analyzed the success of crowdfunding projects (Colombo et al., 2015; Frydrych et al., 2014; Mollick, 2014) and crowdfunding success for technology projects (Cordova et al., 2015). Lelo de Larrea et al. (2019) explored key drivers for success of restaurant crowdfunding. More recently, Cai et al. (2020) showed an inverted U-shape relation between crowdfunding success and reward-based options and the moderating effect of price differentiation.

## The Kickstarter Platform

Two models in the reward-based crowdfunding are available to fundraising goals: "Keep-It-All" and "All-Or-Nothing" (AON), In the "Keep-It-All" model, the proponent maintains the amount raised, while in the AON model, he/she only keeps the money if the goal is reached (Cumming et al., 2020). For the propose of this study, the researchers chose to use the reward-based crowdfuning platform Kickstarter, and adopted an AON model. In the AON model, the proponent receives money if the amount pledged to a project is equal to or greater than the goal at the end of the funding period; if the campaign is unsuccessful, the pledges are canceled (Colombo et al., 2015). When the goal is not reached, the proponent will not receive any funds. There are different types of rewards, such as a book, a gadget, plants, and tickets.

Kickstarter had crowdfunding campaigns in several categories, including art, crafts, comics, dance, design, fashion, film & video, food, games, journalism, music, photography, publishing, technology, and theater. In addition, the project creation can be done by individuals in the following countries: USA, UK, Canada, Australia, New Zealand, Netherlands, Denmark, Ireland, Norway, Sweden, Germany, France, Spain, Italy, Austria, Belgium, Switzerland, Luxemburg, Hong Kong, Singapore, Mexico, Japan, Poland, Greece, and Slovenia (Kickstarter, 2019).

For more than a decade, several authors have studied Kickstarter. Some authors have focuses on the success factors of crowdfunding. Colombo et al. (2015) showed that the internal social capital the proponents develop within the crowdfunding platform has effect on the success of the campaign. In addition, the capital and the backers obtained in the first days of the campaign mediate this effect. Koch & Siering (2015) centered on project and founder specific aspects of crowdfunding success. Mollick (2014) studied the dynamics of crowdfunding. He showed that personal networks and project quality are related with the success. To extend this study, Zheng et al. (2014) analyzed the impact of an entrepreneur´s social capital on crowdfunding performance in three dimensions (i.e., structural, relational, and cognitive), using a comparative study with projects from Kickstarter in the USA with Demohour in China. They evidenced that the three dimensions have effects on crowdfunding performance, but the predictive power was greater in China than in USA.

Alternatively, Allison et al. (2017) studied a model of persuasion. They found out that education of entrepreneurs is more important if the funders have greater capacity and motivation to make careful assessments. More recently, Gafni et al. (2019) indicated that entrepreneurs' descriptions are important, using three variables for success. They found out that projects that frequently mentioned the entrepreneurs' name have higher success rates, especially art projects. Mollick & Nanda (2016) compared crowds with expert evaluation in theater projects. They showed agreement between the crowd´s and experts´ financing decisions.

Still, in the context of crowdfunding success, Chan et al. (2019) pointed to the importance of the communication through the founders´ language for the contribution behavior of funders. They showed that an increase in money saliency has a negative impact on crowdfunding success, while sustainability orientation has a positive impact. In addition, Lelo de Larrea et al. (2019) investigated determinants of success of restaurant crowdfunding. The principal determinants are community orientation, images, and frequent communication with funders.

Other authors analyzed the dynamics of the backer (Kuppuswamy & Bayus, 2017; Kuppuswamy & Bayus, 2018a). Kuppuswamy & Bayus (2017) showed that the projects receive more backers´ support when they are close to the goal, but, if the goal is reached, the support goes down very much. They suggested that people financially support projects when they believe that their contribution really matters. In addition, when the project is close to the financing deadline, the project is small or the project has limited early support, are factors that moderate the effects of goal proximity. Kuppuswamy & Bayus (2018a) explored the backer dynamics over the project-funding cycle.

In a different line of study, Kim & Hann (2019) analyzed how the difficulty of getting bank loans affects the crowdfunding use by entrepreneur. They showed that a decline in housing prices has a significant impact on crowdfunding. This effect was more significant for areas with low socioeconomic status. In these areas, the increase in crowdfunding projects was influenced by the increase in unsuccessful projects. However, the influence of housing prices on successful projects was significant only in areas with high socioeconomic status. Table 1 illustrates several studies which have been developed on the Kickstarter platform, by author, unit of analysis and number of observations, and dependent variable used.

Researchers have begun to pay attention to several aspects of crowdfunding. The related empirical studies of crowdfunding in Kickstarter have focused on all data or some categories of projects, and have used various dependent variables. However, the success usually consists in the project being funded because the goal has been achieved. Normally, the literature has focused on the direct effects and mediate effects. Chan et al. (2019) analyzed the interaction effect of sustainability orientation and money saliency on crowdfunding success. Previous research tested staff pick and video as explanatory variables, while in this chapter, the authors' approach is very different as as in their study they tested the interaction effect. Although some studies have been conducted on crowdfunding success in Kickstarter, it is unclear whether, because it is not easy to achieve the project success. Therefore, more research is needed in this area.

The model can be considered holistic, across knowledge of multiple disciplines, integrating several theories addressed in the literature and different theoretical models, namely in the context of entrepreneurship, management, finance, business, marketing, and economics. Based on the literature, the authors developed a framework of the success of crowdfunding projects. They defined success as a project that reaches the funding goal, because Kickstarter is an AON platform, and if the goal is not achieved, the proponent does not receive any fund. With a model based on a holistic approach, this study can contribute to research on crowdfunding, because the

*Table 1. Studies which have been carried out on the crowdfunding platform Kickstarter*

| Author | Unit of Analysis (observations) | Dependent Variable |
|---|---|---|
| Mollick (2014) | Project (48 526). | Project was funded (1/0); 1 if the project was funded, 0 if not. |
| Colombo et al. (2015) | Project (669) design, technology, film and video, and video games. | |
| Koch and Siering (2015) | Project (762). | |
| Allison et al. (2017) | • Project (383).<br>• Participants on the Amazon Mechanical Turk (mTurk) crowdsourcing platform (154). | |
| Gafni et al. (2019) | • Art projects.<br>• Artistic/ technological. | • Success in reaching the funding goal (1/0).<br>• Percentage pledged.<br>• Number of backers. |
| Chan et al. (2019) | Games, design, fashion, food, and technology projects (9,120). | • Total amount raised.<br>• Number of backers.<br>• Staff pick.<br>• Funding goal. |
| Kuppuswamy and Bayus (2017) | Project (2017 - 10,000; 2018 -14,704). | Number of daily backers. |
| Kuppuswamy and Bayus (2018a) | | |
| Zheng et al. (2014) | Project (607 Kickstarter; 310 Demohour). | Proportion of goal raised. |
| Mollick and Nanda (2016) | Theater project (120). | • Average score from judges.<br>• Funding share proposed by Judges.<br>• Funding threshold (i.e., 100%, 75% or 50% of the goal).<br>• Characteristics of the projects (i.e., log of goal, average investment size, reward levels, number of updates, number of pictures, number of videos, formal language, log number of Facebook friends, located in NY or CA).<br>• Dimensions (i.e., combined average score, novelty, relevance, quality, feasibility, and commercial viability). |
| Kim and Hann (2019) | Technology and games projects (1,994). | • Change in the number of projects per million people.<br>• Change in total goal amounts of all projects per million people. |
| Lelo de Larrea et al. (2019) | Restaurant projects (1,567). | Success rate. |

authors analyzed empirically the determinants of success using aspects of founders and platform, characteristic projects in several categories, and the interaction effects of staff pick and video.

The authors believe that this chapter adds knowledge for the development of crowdfunding, and contributes about key determinants of crowdfunding for visitors, founders, economists, managers, consultants, and scholars.

## METHODS AND DATA ANALYSIS

Based on the positivist research paradigm, the research approach can be classified into a quantitative and deductive approach.

### Data Collection

In this study, the authors intended to analyze the determinants of crowdfunding success. They chose Kickstarter as the most suitable crowdfunding platform for their propose, in agreement with Nguyen´ (2019) view. In addition, other previous studies used data from Kickstarter (Colombo et al., 2015; Frydrych et al., 2014; Mollick, 2014).

For their analysis, the authors used the database from Harvard Dataverse, Kickstarter Structured Relational Database (Guan-Cheng, 2019). From its creation to January 2019, Kickstarter included 408,637 projects. The authors eliminated 3,163 live projects, 36,659 canceled projects, 1,700 suspended projects, 202 purged projects, and one project with -2 USD pledged and backers. Thus, their sample had 366.912 observations.

### Variables

Table 2 provides the description of the variables the authors included in this study. The dependent variable in their analyses is success. In the authors' understanding, success in a project means achieving the funding goal at the end of the campaign, because the main goal of crowdfunding projects is raising funds. The authors used a dummy variable (i.e., 1: Success, 0: Failed) to measure success. The explanatory variables of this model are presented below: Funding period, funding goal, amount pledged, backers, month launched, country of the proponent, comments, updates, opacity, categories, video, and staff pick. Theses variables consider aspects of the proponent, the platform, and the project.

*Table 2. Description of the variables the authors included in this study*

| Variables of the Crowdfunding Success Model | | | |
|---|---|---|---|
| **Variable** | **Measurement** | **Description** | **Aspects** |
| **Dependent Variable** | | | |
| Sucess | 1: Success, 0: Failled | To achieve the funding goal at the end of the campaign. | |
| **Explanatory Variables** | | | |
| Funding_period | Days | Duration of campaign; funding period. | Project |
| Goal_USD | Funding goal in USD | Funding requested. | Project |
| Pledged_USD | Amount pledged in USD | The money pledged by the backers at the end of the period. | Project |
| Backers | Number of people | Number of people pledging at the end of the funding period. | Project |
| Month_launched | 1 a 12 | Month in which the project was launched. | Project |
| Country | USA: 1 - Yes; 0 - No | The proponent was located in the United States. | Founder |
| Comments | Number of comments | The number of total comments post by backers. | Project |
| Updates | Number of updates | The number of total updates of project descriptions. | Project |
| Opacity | % | the degree of opacity | Project |
| Video | 1- Video; 0 - No | Project that features a video. | Project |
| Staff_pick | 1-Projects We Love; 0 - No | Staff Pick is evolved into “Projects We Love” and represents the best projects. | Platform |
| Category | Art, comics, crafts, dance, design, fashion, film & video, food, games, journalism, music, photography, publishing, technology, and theater. | Set of dummy variables indicating the category, representing 14 of the 15 project categories. | Project |

## RESULTS AND DISCUSSION

In order to achieve the objective of this study, in this section, the authors present descriptive analysis of the crowdfunding and multivariate analysis, and econometric analysis of these data.

### Descriptive Analysis

Table 3 presents summary statistics of the data. In addition, the authors ran correlations between all variables.

*Table 3. Summary statistics*

| Variable | Obs | Mean | Std. Dev. | Min | Max |
|---|---|---|---|---|---|
| Success | 366,912 | .4227989 | .4940047 | 0 | 1 |
| Funding_period | 366,912 | 33.89316 | 12.6524 | 1 | 98 |
| Goal_USD | 366,912 | 40,050.57 | 106,828 | .01 | 1.70e+08 |
| Pledged_USD | 366,912 | 10,701.39 | 97,606 | 0 | 2.03e+07 |
| Backers | 366,912 | 124.3664 | 960.3043 | 0 | 219,382 |
| Month_launched | 366,912 | 6.459982 | 3.305919 | 1 | 12 |
| Country | 366,912 | .7712776 | .4200107 | 0 | 1 |
| Comments | 366,912 | 44.01336 | 1,175.767 | 0 | 393,425 |
| Updates | 366,912 | 5.277696 | 9.914957 | 0 | 412 |
| Opacity | 366,912 | .7997128 | .0387772 | 0 | 1 |
| Video | 366,912 | .7173682 | .4502795 | 0 | 1 |
| Staff_pick | 366,912 | .1027903 | .3036852 | 0 | 1 |
| Art | 366,912 | .0776344 | .2675958 | 0 | 1 |
| Comics | 366,912 | .0322094 | .1765559 | 0 | 1 |
| Crafts | 366,912 | .023616 | .1518498 | 0 | 1 |
| Dance | 366,912 | .010384 | .1013714 | 0 | 1 |
| Design | 366,912 | .0766969 | .2661102 | 0 | 1 |
| Fashion | 366,912 | .0623719 | .2418301 | 0 | 1 |
| Film & vídeo | 366,912 | .1634207 | .3697495 | 0 | 1 |
| Food | 366,912 | .0643778 | .2454251 | 0 | 1 |
| Games | 366,912 | .0908338 | .287373 | 0 | 1 |
| Journalism | 366,912 | .0123981 | .1106544 | 0 | 1 |
| Music | 366,912 | .1409848 | .3480063 | 0 | 1 |
| Photography | 366,912 | .028113 | .1652959 | 0 | 1 |
| Publishing | 366,912 | .1057801 | .3075564 | 0 | 1 |
| Technology | 366,912 | .0815209 | .2736338 | 0 | 1 |
| Theater | 366,912 | .0296583 | .1696432 | 0 | 1 |

## Regression Results

Table 4, Table 5, and Table 6 show the results of multivariate analyses on the determinants of crowdfunding success using STATA. The authors modeled the probability of success using a probit estimates with robust standard errors. Probit regressions have also been used in previous studies (Butticè et al., 2017; Cordova et al., 2015) on success. In order to validate their findings, the authors conducted several estimations.

Table 4 presents two estimations: The first includes all projects, while the second shows the results of the interaction between staff pick and video in all the projects. Nevertheless, statistical significance was not obtained in this interation.

An increase in money pledged, backers, and updates provides the likelihood that the projects will be successful. If the founder is from USA and the project has video, he project can be successful. However, a decrease in the funding goal, comments, and the project being launched in the first months of the year can lead to a successful project as well. The art, comics, crafts, design, fashion, film & video, food, games journalism, music, photography, publishing, and technology categories of the projects have a negative signal.

Therefore, the next step was to test the probability of success by category. The authors ran 15 separate estimations for each category using probit regression models. Table 5 shows the results for art, comics, craft, dance, design, fashion, and film & video variables on models (3) to (9).

Table 6 presents the estimations of the variables of the other categories, namely food, games, journalism, music, photography, publishing, technology, and theater, in models (10) to (17).

Only goal and pledged have significance in all regressions done. The goal has a negative impact on probability of crowdfunding project success, in accordance with prior research (Koch & Siering, 2015; Mollick, 2014). This effect is visible both in estimates with all data and in any category. Kickstarter is an all or nothing and when the goal is high, the visitor must be more afraid to invest, because the project may be more at risk of failing. In line with researcher Koch & Siering (2015), difficult projects or high goals can be more riskier. Higher goal tend to hinder funding and must be compensated with trustworthiness (Koch & Siering, 2015).

Despite the existence of limit for money pledged, for example, for US-based projects there is a maximum limit of 10.000 USD per pledges (Kickstarter, 2019), the money pledged has a positive influence on crowdfunding project success. In several projects, the pledged money not only reach the goal but exceed this amount, this is overfunding.

Previous studies have shown the importance of the staff pick and video to the crowdfunding success, but we test the main effects of Staff_pick and Video and their interation. We created un interaction term "Staff_pick*Video" that explains this joint effect. There is an interaction effect between Staff pick and Video. The effect of Video for Staff pick projects is 1.117 and 1.657 times that for non-Staff pick projects, in art and comic projects respectively. Specifically, art and comic projects are more artistic projects and the backers do not care about the platform´s opinion about the best projects, even having a negative effect. The introduction of video in

*Table 4. Success results from probit regressions*

| | (1) | (2) |
|---|---|---|
| **Success** | **Success** | **Success** |
| Funding_period | -0.000792 | -0.00153** |
| | (0.000586) | (0.000633) |
| Goal_USD | -0.00749*** | -0.00869*** |
| | (0.000216) | (0.000249) |
| Pledged_USD | 0.00742*** | 0.00863*** |
| | (0.000213) | (0.000246) |
| Backers | 0.0373*** | 0.0389*** |
| | (0.00191) | (0.00213) |
| Month_launched | -0.00694*** | -0.00818*** |
| | (0.00246) | (0.00268) |
| Country | 0.0365** | 0.0564*** |
| | (0.0182) | (0.0195) |
| Comments | -0.0154*** | -0.0178*** |
| | (0.000403) | (0.000453) |
| Updates | 0.0996*** | 0.115*** |
| | (0.00989) | (0.0118) |
| Opacity | -0.0237 | 0.311 |
| | (0.237) | (0.247) |
| Video | 0.161*** | 0.196*** |
| | (0.0189) | (0.0199) |
| Staff_pick | 0.0476 | 0.0674 |
| | (0.0942) | (0.115) |
| staff_pickXVideo | | 0.0416 |
| | | (0.186) |
| Category | all | All |
| _cons | 0.888*** | 0.621*** |
| | (0.198) | (0.207) |
| *N* | 366,913 | 366,913 |
| Pseudo $R^2$ | 0.9752 | 0.9781 |
| Wald chi2(25,26) | 4070.81 | 4126.24 |
| Log pseudolikelihood | -6201.2399 | -5466.7087 |

Notes: The numbers in parentheses indicate the standard error. Standard errors in parentheses * p<0.1, ** p<0.05, *** p<0.01

*Table 5. Success by art, comics, craft, dance, design, fashion and film &video categories (results from probit regressions)*

| | (3) | (4) | (5) | (6) | (7) | (8) | (9) |
|---|---|---|---|---|---|---|---|
| **Success** | **Art** | **Comics** | **Craft** | **Dance** | **Design** | **Fashion** | **Film & Video** |
| Funding_period | 0.0000729 | 0.00111 | 0.00638 | 0.00356 | -0.00702 | -0.00951 | -0.00898*** |
| | (0.04) | (0.12) | (0.36) | (0.12) | (-1.58) | (-1.25) | (-4.94) |
| Goal_USD | -0.0229*** | -0.131*** | -0.141*** | -0.0661*** | -0.0160*** | -0.0919*** | -0.0113*** |
| | (-44.78) | (-9.38) | (-11.14) | (-4.77) | (-11.70) | (-15.64) | (-9.92) |
| Pledged_USD | 0.0229*** | 0.133*** | 0.148*** | 0.0693*** | 0.0163*** | 0.0919*** | 0.0114*** |
| | (44.07) | (9.30) | (11.30) | (4.51) | (11.55) | (15.62) | (10.13) |
| Backers | 0.0570*** | -0.0357** | -0.0485 | -0.00408 | -0.00465 | 0.0167 | 0.120*** |
| | (8.49) | (-2.89) | (-1.89) | (-0.07) | (-1.04) | (1.56) | (6.99) |
| Month_launched | -0.0216* | -0.111** | 0.0593 | -0.0656 | -0.00630 | -0.0568* | 0.00494 |
| | (-2.52) | (-2.78) | (0.89) | (-1.37) | (-0.42) | (-1.99) | (0.55) |
| Country | 0.0335 | -0.666 | 0.318 | -0.350 | 0.0303 | 0.507** | 0.0446 |
| | (0.56) | (-1.32) | (0.83) | (-0.45) | (0.31) | (2.67) | (0.79) |
| Comments | 0.0420 | -0.0150 | -0.00259 | 1.432 | -0.0407*** | 0.0735 | -0.111*** |
| | (1.78) | (-1.00) | (-0.02) | (1.17) | (-11.86) | (1.12) | (-11.05) |
| Updates | 0.0583*** | 0.0747 | 0.0387 | 0.402 | 0.203*** | 0.188** | 0.0279 |
| | (3.56) | (1.10) | (0.32) | (1.32) | (6.61) | (2.71) | (0.99) |
| Opacity | -0.0273 | 1.583 | 2.658 | 19.63 | -0.318 | -0.475 | -1.497 |
| | (-0.07) | (1.73) | (0.47) | (1.66) | (-0.47) | (-0.49) | (-1.52) |
| Video | -0.0409 | -0.0320 | -0.0313 | 0.901** | 0.326** | 0.276 | -0.156* |
| | (-0.74) | (-0.11) | (-0.08) | (2.74) | (2.99) | (1.34) | (-2.43) |
| Staff_pick | -0.747** | -3.482*** | 7.291*** | -2.229 | 0.844* | 1.240*** | 0.389 |
| | (-2.86) | (-5.26) | (5.76) | (-1.76) | (2.30) | (3.48) | (1.14) |
| Staff_pickXVideo | 1.117*** | 1.657* | -11.06*** | 2.192 | 0.745 | -1.958*** | -0.0634 |
| | (3.68) | (1.97) | (-6.41) | (.) | (1.79) | (-3.77) | (-0.10) |
| _cons | 0.545 | 1.886 | -1.600 | -14.07 | 0.906 | 2.079* | 1.653* |
| | (1.55) | (1.84) | (-0.39) | (-1.48) | (1.63) | (2.56) | (2.04) |
| *N* | 28485 | 11818 | 8665 | 3810 | 28142 | 22885 | 59961 |
| Pseudo $R^2$ | 0.9820 | 0.9998 | 0.9936 | 0.9995 | 0.9918 | 0.9985 | 0.9869 |
| Wald chi2(12,) | 3708.48 | 353.75 | 2475.80 | . | 383.18 | 390.22 | 256.22 |
| Log pseudolikelihood | -354.49293 | -1,6895691 | -32.888904 | -1.2117023 | -158.05662 | -21.025114 | -535.38947 |

Notes: The numbers in parentheses indicate the standard error. Standard errors in parentheses * p<0.1, ** p<0.05, *** p<0.01

*Table 6. Success by food, games, journalism, music, photography, publishing, technology, and theater categories (results from probit regressions)*

| | (10) | (11) | (12) | (13) | (14) | (15) | (16) | (17) |
|---|---|---|---|---|---|---|---|---|
| **Success** | **Food** | **Games** | **Journalism** | **Music** | **Photography** | **Publishing** | **Technology** | **Theater** |
| Funding_period | 0.00357 | -0.00157 | -0.00589 | -0.00624 | 0.0000688 | -0.00243 | 0.00879 | -0.0237* |
| | (0.86) | (-0.42) | (-0.61) | (-1.93) | (0.01) | (-0.84) | (1.66) | (-2.48) |
| Goal_USD | -0.0549*** | -0.0294*** | -0.0285*** | -0.0433*** | -0.134*** | -0.0233*** | -0.0267*** | -0.0706*** |
| | (-20.41) | (-33.21) | (-13.38) | (-9.38) | (-13.37) | (-6.11) | (-25.70) | (-7.24) |
| Pledged_USD | 0.0547*** | 0.0295*** | 0.0282*** | 0.0432*** | 0.143*** | 0.0233*** | 0.0268*** | 0.0707*** |
| | (20.41) | (33.26) | (13.48) | (9.35) | (12.85) | (6.09) | (25.76) | (7.29) |
| Backers | 0.135*** | -0.00164 | 0.189*** | 0.0198* | 0.239*** | 0.0605*** | 0.00963 | -0.00173 |
| | (6.33) | (-1.32) | (3.54) | (2.23) | (4.46) | (8.24) | (1.47) | (-0.16) |
| Month_launched | 0.0609* | -0.00768 | 0.0146 | -0.0352* | -0.0855 | 0.00458 | -0.0298 | -0.103 |
| | (2.36) | (-0.61) | (0.28) | (-2.23) | (-1.70) | (0.41) | (-1.24) | (-1.62) |
| Country | -0.235* | -0.0738 | -0.413 | 0.241* | 0.145 | 0.0790 | -0.252 | -1.133 |
| | (-1.98) | (-0.87) | (-1.26) | (2.24) | (0.42) | (0.85) | (-1.45) | (-1.41) |
| Comments | 0.170 | -0.00743*** | -0.0647 | 0.00615 | 0.687 | -0.0162*** | 0.0792*** | -0.139*** |
| | (1.94) | (-3.55) | (-0.47) | (0.30) | (1.54) | (-6.98) | (3.69) | (-4.99) |
| Updates | 0.193* | 0.0385** | 0.203 | 0.00924 | -0.167* | 0.0445*** | 0.139*** | 0.0161 |
| | (2.49) | (2.86) | (1.81) | (0.67) | (-2.27) | (3.75) | (3.32) | (0.55) |
| Opacity | 1.796 | 1.464** | -1.166 | 0.199 | -6.357*** | 0.180 | 0.147 | -5.336* |
| | (1.85) | (3.15) | (-0.48) | (0.39) | (-3.60) | (0.29) | (0.15) | (-1.97) |
| Video | -0.544*** | 0.186* | -0.766** | 0.318** | 0.616 | 0.202** | -0.215 | 0.390 |
| | (-3.87) | (2.07) | (-3.14) | (3.01) | (1.64) | (2.65) | (-1.40) | (0.84) |
| Staff_pick | -0.477 | 1.590*** | 1.773** | 0.863*** | 4.505*** | -0.175 | -1.085 | 248.0*** |
| | (-0.72) | (3.41) | (2.86) | (3.40) | (5.31) | (-0.46) | (-1.94) | (289.73) |
| Staff_ pickXVideo | -2.175* | -2.095*** | -2.463 | -1.957*** | -9.612*** | -0.984* | 0.254 | -247.2 |
| | (-2.32) | (-3.99) | (-1.91) | (-5.77) | (-5.21) | (-2.35) | (0.38) | (.) |
| _cons | -1.397 | -0.282 | 2.176 | 1.632** | 5.745*** | 0.411 | 0.991 | 9.291*** |
| | (-1.75) | (-0.67) | (1.09) | (3.23) | (3.96) | (0.78) | (1.20) | (3.32) |
| *N* | 23621 | 33328 | 4549 | 51729 | 10315 | 38812 | 29911 | 10882 |
| Pseudo $R^2$ | 0.9839 | 0.9949 | 0.9917 | 0.9952 | 0.9988 | 0.9929 | 0.9964 | 0.9955 |
| Wald chi2(25) | 971.79 | 2059.14 | 766.86 | 334.10 | 2728.83 | 168.84 | 1206.91 | . |
| Log pseudolikelihood | -228.21525 | -118.14964 | -21.40728 | -171.89357 | -7.6977342 | -180.66235 | -61.218853 | -32.411637 |

Notes: The numbers in parentheses indicate the standard error. Standard errors in parentheses * $p<0.1$, ** $p<0.05$, *** $p<0.01$

Staff pick projects allows greater visibility of these by visitors and consequently greater crowdfunding projects success.

However, the effect of Video for Staff pick projects is 11.06, 1.958, 2.175, 2.095, 1.957, 9.612, 0.984 times less than for non-Staff pick projects, in craft, fashion, food, games, music, photography and publishing models respectively. For other categories models the results show that this interaction is not significant. The interaction indicates how much the effect of Video differs between Staff pick or no Staff pick projects, but in multiplicate terms[1]. In general, the introduction of video on staff pick projects does not drive the crowdfunding projects success.

## LIMITATIONS AND FUTURE RESEARCH DIRECTIONS

This chapter contributes to academic knowledge in crowdfunding. However, its contribution should be understood in the light of the limitations of this work. First, the authors conducted this study based on a crowdfunding platform which is established in the USA, but there are other platforms in the world. Conducting this study in several platforms could lead to different results. Moreover, is the authors also suggest to carry out this study with other indicators of success. It might be interesting to analyze the backer´s perception of crowdfunding success and the backers' behavior. Finally, additional studies should investigate perceived factors that lead to crowdfunding success.

## CONCLUSION

Crowdfunding can be a good alternative to traditional forms for financing projects. Projects can be available 24 hours a day and achieve a high number of views. In this study, the authors analyzed the determinants for the success of crowdfunding projects by categories and the joint effect of staff pick and video. They performed probit regressions to evaluate the probability for a project to be successful. The authors' empirical estimates show that only two variables, namely goal and pledged, have significance in all categories and in all data. While the goal has a negative impact on the probability of success of crowdfunding projects, the pledged has a positive influence. In addition, the launch of the project in the first months of the year can lead to the success of the project, when the authors used all data.

On the one hand, the effect of video for staff pick projects is greater that for nonstaff pick projects, in art and comic projects. On the other hand, the effect of video for staff pick projects is less than for nonstaff pick projects in craft, fashion, food, games, music, photography and publishing models. However, for other categories, this interaction is not significant.

This chapter contributes to the extant knowledge in several aspects. Despite the increasing popularity of crowdfunding, the projects continue to fail. Academic research on crowdfunding needs to be carried out to understand this phenomenon. This study presented determinants for the success of the projects by categories.

Moreover, the authors contributed to the knowledge on crowdfunding platforms by analyzing determinants in several categories and the interaction effects of staff pick and video, and by considering aspects of the founders and platform. Characteristic projects can lead to the success of crowdfunding projects.

Overall, the authors' findings have interesting implications for developer platforms, users, and researchers, as well as scholars. Recommendations for possible solutions are suggested, but it is necessary to understand how crowdfunding works to identify improvements to the tools. These results suggest recommendations that support crowdfunding creators in achieving success with projects, such as providing mechanisms for the most possible interaction between users, because it facilitates transparency and decision making, since the more money is pledged, the easier it is to achieve project success. For the development of crowdfunding, the authors suggest to focus on methods that confirm the identity of the owner of the project in these technological environments. In the face of the greater difficulty of obtaining success from large projects, projects that need a large investment should create a higher degree of trust in the visitors of the crowdfunding platform.

## FUNDING

This work has been funded by national funds through FCT – Fundação para a Ciência e a Tecnologia, I.P., Project UIDB/05037/2020

## REFERENCES

Ahlers, G. K. C., Cumming, D., Günther, C., & Schweizer, D. (2015). Signaling in Equity Crowdfunding. *Entrepreneurship Theory and Practice*, *39*(4), 955–980. doi:10.1111/etap.12157

Allison, T. H., Davis, B. C., Webb, J. W., & Short, J. C. (2017). Persuasion in crowdfunding: An elaboration likelihood model of crowdfunding performance. *Journal of Business Venturing*, *32*(6), 707–725. doi:10.1016/j.jbusvent.2017.09.002

Beaulieu, T., Sarker, S., & Sarker, S. (2015). A Conceptual Framework for Understanding Crowdfunding. *Communications of the Association for Information Systems*, *37*, 1–31. doi:10.17705/1CAIS.03701

Belleflamme, P., Lambert, T., & Schwienbacher, A. (2014). Crowdfunding: Tapping the right crowd. *Journal of Business Venturing*, *29*(5), 585–609. doi:10.1016/j.jbusvent.2013.07.003

Bruton, G., Khavul, S., Siegel, D., & Wright, M. (2015). New financial alternatives in seeding entrepreneurship: Microfinance, crowdfunding, and peer-to-peer innovations. *Entrepreneurship Theory and Practice*, *39*(1), 9–26. doi:10.1111/etap.12143

Burtch, G., Ghose, A., & Wattal, S. (2015). The Hidden Cost of Accommodating Crowdfunder Privacy Preferences: A Randomized Field Experiment. *Management Science*, *61*(5), 949–962. doi:10.1287/mnsc.2014.2069

Butticè, V., Colombo, M. G., & Wright, M. (2017). Serial Crowdfunding, Social Capital, and Project Success. *Entrepreneurship Theory and Practice*, *41*(2), 183–207. doi:10.1111/etap.12271

Cai, Z., Zhang, P., & Han, X. (2020). *The inverted U-shaped relationship between crowdfunding success and reward options and the moderating effect of price differentiation*. China Finance Review International. doi:10.1108/CFRI-11-2019-0152

Cambridge Dictionary. (2019). *Cambridge Dictionary: English Dictionary*. Retrieved 13 07 2019, from Cambridge University Press https://dictionary.cambridge.org/pt/dicionario/ingles/corporate-governance

Chan, H. F., Moy, N., Schaffner, M., & Torgler, B. (2019). The effects of money saliency and sustainability orientation on reward based crowdfunding success. *Journal of Business Research*. Advance online publication. doi:10.1016/j.jbusres.2019.07.037

Cholakova, M., & Clarysse, B. J. E. T. (2015). Does the Possibility to Make Equity Investments in Crowdfunding Projects Crowd Out Reward–Based Investments? *Entrepreneurship Theory and Practice*, *39*(1), 145–172. doi:10.1111/etap.12139

Colombo, M. G., Franzoni, C., & Rossi–Lamastra, C. (2015). Internal social capital and the attraction of early contributions in crowdfunding. *Entrepreneurship Theory and Practice*, *39*(1), 75–100. doi:10.1111/etap.12118

Cordova, A., Dolci, J., & Gianfrate, G. (2015). The Determinants of Crowdfunding Success: Evidence from Technology Projects. *Procedia: Social and Behavioral Sciences*, *181*, 115–124. doi:10.1016/j.sbspro.2015.04.872

Cumming, D. J., Leboeuf, G., & Schwienbacher, A. (2020). Crowdfunding models: Keep-It-All vs. All-Or-Nothing. *Financial Management, 49*(2), 331–360. doi:10.1111/fima.12262

Dushnitsky, G., Guerini, M., Piva, E., & Rossi-Lamastra, C. (2016). Crowdfunding in Europe: Determinants of Platform Creation across Countries. *California Management Review, 58*(2), 44–71. doi:10.1525/cmr.2016.58.2.44

Frydrych, D., Bock, A. J., Kinder, T., & Koeck, B. (2014). Exploring entrepreneurial legitimacy in reward-based crowdfunding. *Venture Capital, 16*(3), 247–269. doi:10.1080/13691066.2014.916512

Gafni, H., Marom, D., & Sade, O. (2019). Are the life and death of an early-stage venture indeed in the power of the tongue? Lessons from online crowdfunding pitches. *Strategic Entrepreneurship Journal, 13*(1), 3–23. doi:10.1002ej.1293

Guan-Cheng, L. (2019). *Kickstarter Structured Relational Database.* Harvard Dataverse., doi:10.7910/DVN/EOYBXM

Kim, K., & Hann, I.-H. (2019). Crowdfunding and the Democratization of Access to Capital—An Illusion? Evidence from Housing Prices. *Information Systems Research, 30*(1), 276–290. doi:10.1287/isre.2018.0802

Koch, J.-A., & Siering, M. (2015). *Crowdfunding success factors: the characteristics of successfully funded projects on crowdfunding platforms.* Paper presented at the Twenty-Third European Conference on Information Systems (ECIS) 2015.

Kuppuswamy, V., & Bayus, B. L. (2017). Does my contribution to your crowdfunding project matter? *Journal of Business Venturing, 32*(1), 72–89. doi:10.1016/j.jbusvent.2016.10.004

Kuppuswamy, V., & Bayus, B. L. (2018a). Crowdfunding Creative Ideas: The Dynamics of Project Backers. In D. Cumming & L. Hornuf (Eds.), *The Economics of Crowdfunding: Startups, Portals and Investor Behavior* (pp. 151–182). Springer International Publishing. doi:10.1007/978-3-319-66119-3_8

Kuppuswamy, V., & Bayus, B. L. (2018b). A review of crowdfunding research and findings. In Handbook of Research on New Product Development (pp. 361-373). Edward Elgar Publishing. doi:10.4337/9781784718152.00028

Lelo de Larrea, G., Altin, M., & Singh, D. (2019). Determinants of success of restaurant crowdfunding. *International Journal of Hospitality Management, 78*, 150–158. doi:10.1016/j.ijhm.2018.10.003

Mamonov, S., & Malaga, R. (2018). Success factors in Title III equity crowdfunding in the United States. *Electronic Commerce Research and Applications*, *27*, 65–73. doi:10.1016/j.elerap.2017.12.001

Mollick, E. (2014). The dynamics of crowdfunding: An exploratory study. *Journal of Business Venturing*, *29*(1), 1–16. doi:10.1016/j.jbusvent.2013.06.005

Mollick, E., & Nanda, R. (2016). Wisdom or madness? Comparing crowds with expert evaluation in funding the arts. *Journal Management Science*, *62*(6), 1533–1553. doi:10.1287/mnsc.2015.2207

Muller, M., Geyer, W., Soule, T., Daniels, S., & Cheng, L.-T. (2013). Crowdfunding inside the enterprise: employee-initiatives for innovation and collaboration. *Proceedings of the SIGCHI conference on human factors in computing systems*. 10.1145/2470654.2470727

Negrão, C. S. V. (2018). Impact of E-Commerce on Agricultural Business Success. In L. dall'Acqua & D. Lukose (Eds.), Improving Business Performance Through Effective Managerial Training Initiatives (pp. 223-253). Hershey, PA: IGI Global.

Negrão, C. S. V. (2020). Impact of Managers on Agricultural Business Success. *Journal of Information Technology Research*, *13*(3), 126–141. doi:10.4018/JITR.2020070108

Nguyen, S. (2019, May 6). *The 8 Best Crowdfunding Sites of 2019*. Retrieved from https://www.thebalancesmb.com/best-crowdfunding-sites-4580494

Ordanini, A., Miceli, L., Pizzetti, M., & Parasuraman, A. J. J. (2011). Crowd-funding: Transforming customers into investors through innovative service platforms. *Journal of Service Management*, *22*(4), 443–470. doi:10.1108/09564231111155079

Shneor, R., & Munim, Z. H. (2019). Reward crowdfunding contribution as planned behaviour: An extended framework. *Journal of Business Research*, *103*, 56–70. doi:10.1016/j.jbusres.2019.06.013

Short, J. C., Ketchen, D. J. Jr, McKenny, A. F., Allison, T. H., & Ireland, R. D. (2017). Research on Crowdfunding: Reviewing the (Very Recent) past and Celebrating the Present. *Entrepreneurship Theory and Practice*, *41*(2), 149–160. doi:10.1111/etap.12270

Simpson, M., Padmore, J., & Newman, N. (2012). Towards a new model of success and performance in SMEs. *International Journal of Entrepreneurial Behaviour & Research*, *18*(3), 264–285. doi:10.1108/13552551211227675

Tomczak, A., & Brem, A. (2013). A conceptualized investment model of crowdfunding. *Venture Capital*, *15*(4), 335–359. doi:10.1080/13691066.2013.847614

Unger, J. M., Rauch, A., Frese, M., & Rosenbusch, N. (2011). Human capital and entrepreneurial success: A meta-analytical review. *Journal of Business Venturing*, *26*(3), 341–358. doi:10.1016/j.jbusvent.2009.09.004

Vismara, S. (2016). Equity retention and social network theory in equity crowdfunding. *Small Business Economics*, *46*(4), 579–590. doi:10.100711187-016-9710-4

Zheng, H., Li, D., Wu, J., & Xu, Y. J. I. (2014). The role of multidimensional social capital in crowdfunding: A comparative study in China and US. *Information & Management*, *51*(4), 488–496. doi:10.1016/j.im.2014.03.003

# Chapter 2
# Investors' Motivations in Different Types of Crowdfunding

**Laurence Attuel-Mendes**
*CEREN EA 7477, Burgundy School of Business, Université Bourgogne Franche-Comté, France*

**Djamchid Assadi**
*CEREN EA 7477, Burgundy School of Business, Université Bourgogne Franche-Comté, France*

**Silsa Raymond**
*CEREN EA 7477, Burgundy School of Business, Université Bourgogne Franche-Comté, France*

## ABSTRACT

*Although the crowdfunding (CF) sector is booming, research focusing on motivation of contributors is mainly exploratory and does not propose an analytical model. This chapter aims to propose a typology of differentiated motivations according to the type of CF. The main results, authentic compared to the existing literature, show that types of motivation are not the same depending on the type of CF considered. These findings provide significant practical guidelines for three major actors of a CF process: CF platforms must communicate according to the segmentation resulting from the respective predominant motivations. Project leaders should go beyond the simple utility and inform contributors according to the life of the project and its segmentation and the required technical tools of contribution. Contributors share personal ties and observe how the projects succeed regarding loan with interest; therefore, certain motivations, found in this research, such as pleasure of contributing, living experiences, and supporting creators should not be put forward in all the CF campaigns.*

DOI: 10.4018/978-1-7998-3226-3.ch002

## INTRODUCTION

Crowdfunding (CF) is protean. Whatever the types, CF platforms have multiplied since 2005 and collected increasingly. As an example, we note the case of CF, which grew by 20% in France between 2017 and 2018 and collected 402 million euros (Financement participatif France (FPF), 2019). This tremendous growth was achieved without the intervention of traditional financial intermediaries. This alternative mode of financing mainly benefits SMEs, which, together with very small enterprises and Mid-Sized-Businesses, represent 65% of project campaigns in 2017 in France (FPF, 2018).

In France since 2008, the number of platforms has increased dramatically with the creation of four new platforms in average per month since the emergence of CF (Ahès Consulting cited by Wardrop et al., 2015, p.26). There are currently more than sixty platforms operating in France, including 22 reward-based, 19 loan-based and 14 equity-based (Ben Slimane and Rousselet, 2016). The French market is now the second largest in Europe in terms of volume after England, ahead of Germany and the Netherlands (Ziegler et al., 2018).

Europe has also witnessed the rise of alternative online finance. 7.671 billion euros were collected in 2016 on CF platforms, representing a growth rate of 41% (Ziegler et al., 2018). Two major factors, combined with the introduction of appropriate and flexible regulations, have created exceptional potential for cooperative initiatives between individuals in general, and for mutual financial assistance.

The first factor is the decrease in support from traditional financial institutions for entrepreneurial projects led by start-ups or young entrepreneurs. Indeed, since the first Basel agreements in 1988, lending conditions have tightened, and liquidity has become a scarce resource. Consequently, the holders of "risky projects" were forced to look for alternative financing channels.

The second factor is the significant decrease in transaction costs due to Web 2.0 and social media technologies. Individuals can now connect to carry out transactions at a lower cost, of which CF is the emblematic example (Assadi, 2016).

However, the emergence of the potential for interpersonal cooperation does not mean that individuals spontaneously exploit the opportunity or contribute to the system. While there are many academic papers on crowdfunding (Mollick, 2014), 7 470 papers bearing the term "crowdfunding" in their titles since 2010 up to 2019, October 12, there is only 35, bearing the words "crowdfunding" and "motivation" in their titles for the same period (no such a paper before) according to an exhaustive search on Google Scholar. For instance, Hossain and Oparaocha (2017), despite their promising article title ("Crowdfunding: Motives, definitions, typology and ethical challenges"), just give a quick overview, not very documented, of the topic. However, motivations are the likely sources of this success. Motivational research is more important when we know that the motivations of contributors are tinged with a strong emotional dimension (Autorité de Contrôle Prudentiel, 2013, p. 1) and have a broader implication than their simple financial contribution (Onnée and Renault, 2014).

The distinctive approach of our research paper resides in studying motivations of contribution not in a single block, but only in a differentiated way through the different forms of CF: a typology of contribution motivations according to the typology of crowdfunding. To our best knowledge, no study provides an analytical comparison of contribution motivations according to the types of CF.

This deficiency is a source of costs and failures for professionals in the sector, particularly in this period of strong growth and increasing competitive pressure. For the entrepreneur to successfully fund their ventures in the period of financial constraints, it is important to understand what motivates the contributors to contribute. By understanding motivations of contribution, the project leaders can adjust their campaigns to increase their chances of getting successfully funded in the type of crowdfunding they choose.

The chapter is organized as follows. First, the literature review, without being exhaustive, will aim to identify the motivations specific to CF. Second, we present the quantitative method which is used to verify the pertinence of the proposed theoretical model of motivations of contributing in CF. Third, the results obtained with the different types of platforms (donation, reward, loan, equity) are discussed. In conclusion, recommendations and avenues for reflection are proposed.

## A LITERATURE REVIEW ON MOTIVATION AND MOTIVATIONAL TYPOLOGIES

In line with the research inquiry, we proceed to a literature review in three successive stages. First, we review the general literature on motivations. Second, we review the motivations of contribution by type of platform as identified in the academic literature. Third, we expose the moderators to motivations of contribution. This three-level literature review provides a conceptual framework of motivations in CF for an extensive quantitative survey.

### General Literature on Motivation

The first layer of this literature review concern the general study of motivation for understanding the factors that drive people to behave and act in a certain way. It is in the 20th century, with the institutionalization of psychology, that the concept of motivation becomes a key. Progressively, its field extends to organization studies. There are now a multitude of theories on motivation.

The term "motivation" is derived from motive, which means an emotion, desire, need, or similar impulse that motivates individuals to act in a way (Payne, 2007, p. 98). There is a certain unanimity among researchers to define motivation: the motivation is above all the activation of one or more needs. The concept aims to describe "the internal and/or external forces that produce the initiation, direction, intensity and persistence of behaviour" (Vallerand and Thill, 1993, p. 18). This is consistent with Russell's (1971) forerunner vision of an internal force that determines the meaning and scope of an action.

We adopt a definition of motivation in line with the previous ones: *motivation derives from the personality and freedom of the individual to choose and adopt actions in order to achieve the objectives pursued (for satisfying needs).*

The concept of motivation is now extensively applied to the different disciplines of management sciences, and mainly in human resources and marketing management. In marketing for example, the postulate is that motivation vehicles a client to act for satisfying an unmet need (Lendrevie and Levy, 2013, p. 126). Consequently, by studying motivations of target customers, a marketing manager can better understand their needs. In perspective of human resources, motivation also means the reason for action individual undertake (Payne, 2007). Consequently, understanding motivations is compulsory for managing people.

To avoid overloading the subject, we propose a synthetic model of the literature dedicated to motivations (Table 1) for focusing about our study, motivation of contribution in CF processes.

Based on the preceding conceptual capsulate, we distinguish between intrinsic and extrinsic motivations which characterize many theoretical references on motivations of contributors in CF campaigns. An intrinsic motivation dwells in the actant's inner self and pushes him towards the accomplishment of an act, while an extrinsic motivation is triggered by circumstances external to the agent.

## Literature on Motivation of Contribution by Type of Crowdfunding

The second layer of our review of literature is on motivations of contribution by type of CF. While there are many academic papers on crowdfunding, there are very few academic papers, as an example, with crowdfunding, motivation and equity in the titles: Pearson et al. (2016) along with Lukkarinen et al. (2019) for instance. Yet, the corpus on crowdfunding motivations we examine is extensive and significantly influenced by the concepts of intrinsic and extrinsic motivations.

*Table 1. Theoretical model of motivational types*

<table>
<tr><th>Maslow pyramid (Maslow, 1954)</th><th>ERG needs (Alderfer, 1969)</th><th>Bifactorial model (Herzberg, 1959)</th><th>Acquired needs theory (McClelland, 1961)</th><th>Self-determination theory (Deci, 1975; Deci & Ryan, 1985; Gagne & Deci, 2005)</th><th></th></tr>
<tr><td>Need for self-accomplishment</td><td>Need for personal development</td><td rowspan="2">Driving factors</td><td>Need for accomplishment</td><td>Need to feel competent</td><td rowspan="2">Intrinsic motivations</td></tr>
<tr><td>Need for esteem</td><td>Need for social relationship</td><td>Need for power</td><td>Need for self-determination</td></tr>
<tr><td>Physiological needs</td><td rowspan="3">Need for existence</td><td rowspan="3">Hygiene factors</td><td rowspan="3">Need to belong</td><td rowspan="3">Need for social relationships</td><td rowspan="3">Extrinsic motivations</td></tr>
<tr><td>Need for security</td></tr>
<tr><td>Need to belong</td></tr>
</table>

Source: (authors, 2019)

## Intrinsic Motivations of Crowdfunding

While the literature observes concretely that contributors' motivations differ according to the platforms on which they contribute, little research clearly dissociates and explores their distinctive features.

Hermer (2011) indicates that the majority of contributors are motivated by intrinsic motivations and intangible rewards and lists eight examples: (1) personal identification with the purpose and goals of the project, (2) contribution to an important societal mission, (3) satisfaction of being part of a community with similar priorities, (4) satisfaction of witnessing the completion and success of the project, (5) satisfaction with being engaged and interacting with project team members, (6) satisfaction with contributing to an innovative project or bringing in pioneers associated with a new technology or company, (7) the chance to expand your network, (8) the hope of attracting contributors in return for your own project. However, these results are to be qualified insofar as the author does not differentiate between contributors by type of platform.

Van Wingerden and Ryan's study (2011) indicate that contributors on donation and reward-based platforms are mostly motivated by intrinsic motivations since just under 76% of respondents report contributing to projects for reasons other than simply obtaining a financial return. 71.3% of respondents are intrinsically motivated by being involved in the creative process, 53.7% by the pleasure of contributing, and 52.2% by helping the creator achieve his or her goal. According to this study, intrinsically motivated contributors participate more frequently than those who contribute with the objective of obtaining a reward.

Different authors assign mainly intrinsic motivations to contribution to philanthropic projects: sympathy and empathy for the cause (Rick et al., 2008), guilt about not giving (Cialdini et al., 1981), hope for strengthening their social identity (Aaker and Akutsu, 2009), and social status (Becker, 1974 ; Glazer and Konrad, 1996). Aitamurto (2011), in her case study about a platform supporting journalism through tipping, exposed that the primary motivation for donating is to contribute to the common good and social change; consequently, donors' motives are essentially more altruistic than instrumental. Under these terms, intrinsic motivations dominate. Gerber et al. (2012) also identify four motivations that characterize contributors to philanthropic projects.

Berglin and Strandberg (2013) highlight three main intrinsic motivations, without expressly naming them as such, knowingly willingness to help, supporting a good cause and being part of a project realization in what they called passive crowdfunding, e.g. donation- and reward-based platforms. They also explore the factors that influenced the size of the investment (Berglin and Strandberg, 2013).

Studies like that of Cecere et al. (2017) focus on backers' motivations in specific types of contribution, that occurring in non-equity crowdfunding, but do not offer any comparative analysis. While the research inquiry of entrepreneurs' motivations of getting funded on equity CF platforms is out of this paper's exploration, we include the paper of Roggan (2015) in this literature review because its findings contribute to better understand contribution motivations: entrepreneurs use equity CF to successfully collect funds from rather emotionally driven investors and to engage them for marketing and feedbacks.

## Extrinsic Motivations of Contribution

Harms' thesis (2007) is one of the first who have identified the extrinsic motivation of contributors in CF. The author developed a theoretical model of the dimensions of value that drive an individual to contribute to a CF project and tested his model by creating a fictitious reward and equity-based CF platform. His model has five dimensions of values subdivided into ten driving values.

The first dimension is the financial value associated with the return on investment. This value is subdivided into three driving values: economic value (the individual's perception of the correlation between what he offers and what he receives), lottery effect (the greater the gain, the more risk behaviours the individual will adopt), and certainty effect (individuals' value projects whose results seem certain). The second dimension is functional and is subdivided into a driving value of personal utility. It is associated with the project's ability to accomplish certain actions. The third dimension is social and related to the perceived operational utility of the project. The two driving values that make up social value are personal expressiveness (human need for expression) and the investor community (being part of a group). The fourth dimension is epistemic which refers to the usefulness of a project associated with its ability to arouse curiosity, provide novelty and satisfy a desire for knowledge. Finally, the fifth dimension of emotional value refers to the utility that arises from the project's ability to generate feelings. This dimension of value is subdivided into three driving values of satisfaction (related to the feeling of joy), involvement (related to the concept of identification) and solidarity (feeling that arises from helping others).

While motivations of contributors on reward and equity-based platforms are mainly extrinsic (Harms, 2007), financial value is the most important. Within which, the economic dimension and the certainty effect favour the motivation of contributors, while the lottery effect seems to be zero. The functional value, associated with the project's ability to carry out certain actions, seems to have an impact on the motivation of contributors as strong as the economic dimension. In terms of social value, only personal expressiveness influences the motivation of contributors. Indeed, the author cannot comment on the motivation of contributors to join an investor community because the proposed fictional project does not include this criterion. The fourth epistemic value does not seem to have any influence on the contributors' intention to participate. Finally, regarding emotional value, only satisfaction has an impact on the intention to contribute. This impact should be put into perspective because it is the lowest of the ten driving values tested.

In line with the results of Harms (2007), Cholakova and Clarysse (2015) also demonstrate that the motivations of contributors on reward and equity-based platforms are mainly extrinsic. As a result, the authors refute the popular belief that contributors on reward-based platforms are dominated by intrinsic motivations while contributors on equity-based platforms are dominated by extrinsic motivations or a combination of both. Indeed, regardless of the type of platform, the motivations of contributors are essentially financial (Cholakova and Clarysse, 2015). The fact that extrinsic motivations have a major impact on contributors' motivation implies that offering an attractive reward is crucial for the success of the campaign.

## Mix of Extrinsic and Intrinsic Motivations of Contribution

Many researchers cross the borders between intrinsic and extrinsic motivations. Hemer (2011) and Wechsler (2013) postulate that, although extrinsic and intrinsic motivations impact contributors, intrinsic motivations have more influence. The results of Hemer (2011) and Van Wingerden and Ryan (2011) in line with Wechsler (2013), confirm the popular belief that contributors on donation and reward-based platforms are dominated by intrinsic motivations.

Analysing the impact of extrinsic motivations on intrinsic motivations, Van Wingerden and Ryan's study (2011) find that while extrinsic motivations reduce the influence of intrinsic motivations, i.e., for contributors mainly motivated by reward, the intrinsic motivations of pleasure, helping someone achieve their goal or feeling involved become secondary, the introduction of extrinsic motivations do not always reduce intrinsic motivations (Van Wingerden and Ryan, 2011).

Cecere et al. (2017) investigate the interactions between intrinsic and extrinsic motivations about non-equity crowdfunding and find that contribution is associated with altruism, thus derived from intrinsic motivation. This positive emotional sensation from giving to and helping others is described as impure altruism. Their findings also suggest that the warm glow effect – satisfaction of helping others – influences the level of contribution when monetary incentives, e.g. extrinsic motives, could crowd out (Frey, 1997) the decisions to contribute of crowdfunders.

Comparing to philanthropic projects, Gerber et al. (2012) investigate whether there are common motivations among these types of contributors. Gerber et al. (2012) and Passebois-Ducros and Puhl (2015) establish a typology of motivations that, without being based on a ranking, indicates that contributors' motivations on donation and reward-based platforms are extrinsic and intrinsic. Following an analysis of the literature and 57 participatory fundraising campaigns in reward and donation-based CF, Passebois-Ducros and Puhl (2015) developed a very similar conceptual model. Indeed, altruistic motivation corresponds to the willingness to help others in Gerber et al.'s model (2012), opportunistic motivation corresponds to the desire to obtain rewards and community motivation to the motivation to support creators/causes in accordance with their identity and linked to their social network and to the willingness to invest in a creative and trusted community. Only the motivation corresponding to the desire to adopt innovative behaviour completes the previous model.

There are four motivations for contributors to finance CF projects in addition to the extrinsic motivations for wanting to consume products and live experiences. First, the search for a reward which translates into a desire to receive a product or service, but also into a desire to receive the product/service in preview or limited edition. A second motivation is related to the willingness to help others and a third to the willingness to support causes. The authors point out that individuals tend to support creators/causes in accordance with their identity and linked to their social network. Finally, there is also the willingness to invest in a creative and trusted community. This motivation has two components: a desire to feel connected to a community that shares the same interests and ideals, and a desire to strengthen connections with its social network.

More recently, Bagheri et al. (2019) explored the motivations of individuals who donate money for funding the projects in charity CF platforms. Their findings revealed a combination of intrinsic and extrinsic individual motivations directed funding behaviour of donors. More specifically, this study suggested a set of intrinsic individual motivations including shared problems, values, thoughts and beliefs, helping a minority, technical knowledge and capacity of the project to learn from and helping to realize ideas and create value that led donations to charity CF. Furthermore, this research explored contribution to fulfilling collective efforts, perceived effectiveness and few risks of CF as the intrinsic social motivations for donations to charity CF projects.

Wechsler (2013) examines the intrinsic and extrinsic motivations of contributors on reward-based platforms and postulates that intrinsic motivations have a greater influence because they are linked to joy, the desire to be part of a community and philanthropic motivations. Extrinsic motivations are related to immediate or deferred rewards and social motivations. Of the five constructs of intrinsic motivation tested in this study, helping others seems to be the most influential construct since the majority of contributors surveyed agree on its importance. This construct is correlated to three other constructs of intrinsic motivation: joy, involvement and identification. The results of the study indicate that rewards do not have a significant impact on the extrinsic motivation of contributors. The author nuances this result by pointing out that the responses of the "friend and family" group influence the analyses. Indeed, the larger this group is, the lower the impact of rewards will be in the results because this group is not motivated by obtaining rewards.

The analysis by Bretschneider et al. (2014) on equity is more nuanced than those of the previous authors. The authors formulate several hypotheses based on both the intrinsic (pleasure, curiosity, altruism, reciprocity, direct identification with the team of the start-up to be financed) and extrinsic motivations (recognition, personal needs, return on investment) and also "situational factors" (characteristics of the team initiating the project and their ideas, herd behaviours) that push contributors to participate in equity crowdfunding. They finally find that investors' motivations are not only extrinsic but also intrinsic in equity crowdfunding (Bretschneider et al., 2014). Pearson et al. (2016) examine motivations in an online survey of 142 investors who contribute with small investments that together fund the venture in equity-based crowdfunding and find that investors are primarily driven by enjoyment, philanthropic but also by financial payoffs in their decision to invest. Mollick (2014) combines these dual considerations (intrinsic and extrinsic) in donation/reward CF campaigns by distinguishing four categories of contributors who value philanthropic actions, the social good, rewards and investments. More recently, Bretschneider and Leimeister (2017) conduct an empirical study on motivations of contribution in incentive-based crowdfunding and reveal that backers are motivated not only by self-interest like prospecting a reward, expecting recognition, hoping fruition and developing image, but also by prosocial motivations such as feelings for a certain venture and/or project team.

Cholakova and Clarysse (2015) investigate whether extrinsic motivations influence the intrinsic motivations of contributors; in other words, if financial rewards as extrinsic motivations risk diminishing the intrinsic motivations to participate in projects that offer no return. They find that contributors who contribute for rewards tend to retain the same expectation when they are offered the opportunity of an equity contribution. Thus, non-financial motivations are not necessarily replaced by financial motivations since, when given the opportunity, contributors do not generally migrate to an equity type contribution. In addition, increasing the material value of the reward increases the influence of the reward as a contribution driver. Finally, the two most important constructed among the extrinsic motivations are page registration and peer pressure (Cholakova and Clarysse, 2015).

The study by Allison et al. (2015) on contributors to interest-free lending platforms shows that contributors' motivations are dual. Contributors combine traditional financial motivations such as return on investment (extrinsic) and philanthropic motivations such as helping others. Despite the presence of both types of motivation, the authors use the theory of self-determination to postulate that, because of this prosocial context[1], the majority of contributors should be motivated in an intrinsic way. To refute this hypothesis, the authors analyse the description of the projects and question the impact of this narrative on the motivation of the contributors. The results indicate that, in the case of crowd-microfinance, the effects of intrinsic signals are stronger than those of extrinsic signals. This result is explained by the fact that contributors are already intrinsically motivated, since they wish to become actors in the microfinance sector. In addition, in accordance with the theory of self-determination, it would appear that extrinsic motivational factors reduce the intrinsic motivational factors among contributors. On the one hand, they promote the need for competence, but on the other hand, they reduce the need for self-determination because they generally involve many constraints. On this point, the results of Allison et al. (2015) are therefore in contradiction with those of Cholakova and Clarysse (2015) and Van Wingerden and Ryan (2011).

Table 2 summarizes the different items composing intrinsic and extrinsic motivations according to literature.

Although we conducted an extensive literature review on motivation and motivational factors, we did not focus on any particular factor or category of factors. Our approach differs from work that focuses on specific factors to explain and explore the motivation for CF contributions.

Kang et al. (2016) adopt the confidence factor of the project leader, project and platform to study the motivation for contribution. Khelladi et al. (2018) apply this approach to the French context. Prpić et al. (2015) study the impact of the cultural

*Table 2. Item composing intrinsic and extrinsic motivations in crowdfunding*

| INTRINSIC MOTIVATIONS | | EXTRINSIC MOTIVATIONS | |
|---|---|---|---|
| **Desire to feel emotions** | Help project to achieve its objective | **Desire to benefit from participation in the project (utility)** | Recognition of personal needs that project addresses |
| | Pleasure of contributing | | Return on investment |
| | Curiosity | | Reward |
| | Desire of knowledge | | Community benefits |
| | Fun | | Opportunist reciprocity |
| | Help others | | Consume products |
| | | | Live experiences |
| **Desire of expressiveness** | Need for self-esteem development | **Desire of association** | Getting involved in a community |
| | Express one's political position | | Getting involved and in interaction with members of the team |
| | Contributing to an innovative project | | Recognition by peers |
| | Need to affirm one's identity | | Support creators with whom I share personal ties |
| | Be involved in the creative process | | Identification with the team |
| | Altruist reciprocity | | Regional identification with the project |
| | Support great causes | | Identify myself personally with the purpose or goal of the project |

Source: (authors, 2019)

space ("Crowd Capital Theory") on the motivation to contribute. We have favoured a neutral and unprejudiced approach; because we have no reason to favour certain specific factors in the analysis of contribution motivations. Based on all the theoretical motivational factors from the literature review, we instead sought to identify those that would apply more specifically to the contribution to the four types of crowdfunding.

## Situational Factors as Moderators to the Motivation to Contribute

Situational factors as moderators to the motivation of contributions constitute the third layer of our literature review. While moderator variables are considerably important in specifying under what conditions and for what subgroups independent variables temper or modulate the impact on dependent ones, surprisingly little attention is devoted to contingent moderators in research on crowdfunding motivations. Pictorially, moderators are at borderline of the relationship between independent variable and dependent variable.

We pay special attention to study whether gender plays in moderating role in the perspective of exploring the possibility of gender discrimination in crowdfunding motivations. Bretschneider and Leimeister (2017) find evidence that herding has a significant moderating effect on backers' reward motivation.Some authors focus on factors that influence the motivations of contribution in CF platforms. We will refer to them as "situational factors" to the extent that they reinforce or temper the contribution. As such, they are considered as moderators that affects the strength of the relationship motivations and contributions of CF.

The study by Lin et al. (2014) on the profile and motivation of contributors in reward-based CF proposes to differentiate between four categories of contributors. Active backers differ from others in that they support a large number of projects, are likely to create projects themselves, generally publish comments on projects, and their interests seem broader. This group generally contributes to projects that they consider to be of high quality and is motivated by the social and reputational benefits they can derive from the project. Trend followers are more risk averse, which translates into a tendency to contribute to projects at the end of the cycle. They seem to be motivated mainly by obtaining rewards. Altruistic support projects that do not offer a reward. They are less risk averse, and contribute mostly for altruistic reasons such as supporting a cause. The fourth group, the crowd, is a group defined as moderate because contributors are relatively risk averse; they generally do not create a project and do not post comments. The motivations of this group are difficult to identify because they are still in the process of exploring the "world" of CF.

In addition, women appear to be less influenced than men by the rewards associated with a project, echoing the findings of Cholakova and Clarysse (2015) that trust is a key element for women. Pearson et al. (2016) find that the moderating factors of age, gender and investor experience have significant impacts on motivations, whilst the location or income do not have any effect on investor motivation.

Ryu et al. (2016) show the influence of time on backers' motivation. They empirically probe the dynamics among reward motivation, e.g. extrinsic motivations, philanthropy motivation, e.g. intrinsic motivations, funding time, and funding amount. The authors find that reward motivation is associated with late funding, whereas prosocial motivation is associated with early funding. Li and Wang (2019) are continuing this study in some way by empirically investigating backers' pledging at different stages of achieving the funding threshold and their associated different motivations. Before the threshold is reached, the desire to help others and support causes plays an important role in backers' decision-making. Besides this prosocial motivation, the economic motivation to collect rewards may also drive backers' funding behaviour (Cholakova and Clarysse, 2015; Gerber et al., 2012). However, at this stage, they face uncertainty about project outcome. After the goal is reached, backers are certain about the success of the project, which is likely to strengthen their economic motivation to collect reward and correspondingly to reduce the prosocial motivation arising from empathy and sense of achievement. These results are reinforced by the fact that two types of threshold effects are shown and that they are more salient in public-good projects.

Another recent study revisits this idea of a predominance of economic considerations, i.e. extrinsic motivations, highlighted by previous research. Dai and Zhang (2019) show that prosocial motivation[2] is an important psychological driver of backers' funding activity. They based their study on data collected on Kickstarter, the world's largest reward-based crowdfunding website, about willingness to fund just before and just after goal attainment. According to their findings, consumers' prosocial motives to help creators reach their funding goals significantly influence funding activities on reward-based platforms and can outweigh the economic considerations emphasized by previous research.

Passebois-Ducros and Puhl (2015) identify three moderating factors that influence the link between motivation and participation. First, trust in the cultural project, which consists of the perceived quality of the project and the reputation of the project holder. The second moderating factor is the attachment to the cultural project. This attachment can be a function of geographical proximity, identity proximity and linked to attitudinal fidelity "reflecting a positive attitude and preference towards the organization" (Passebois-Ducros and Puhl, 2015, p.7). Finally, the last moderating factor is the campaign parameters. It is based on six elements: duration, amount, number of previous requests, support for the campaign (platform), nature of the rewards and the role of the donor. In the same vein, the study by Amara et al. (2014) indicates that the effectiveness and simplicity of the information available on the project have a positive impact on the motivation of contributors. Harrer et al. (2019) explore more in depth the issue of trust in a case of equity CF. This plays an important role throughout the different phases of crowdfunding. But what emerges as new is the importance of institutional (societal level) trust that takes-on a crucial role especially in the early as well as the later stages of a CF campaign as catalyst for other forms of trust.

Agrawal et al. (2015) investigate the impact of geographical distance on the motivation of contributors to lending-based platforms. Although an initial analysis of the results indicates that geographic distance plays a role, further analysis shows that this is not the case. Local contributors invest early because they are usually the creator's family and friends, which we would call the first circle. These investments then send a positive signal to the other investors, the second circle, about the intrinsic qualities of the creator, which encourages them to invest. Investor motivation is therefore subject to a phenomenon described by authors as path dependency to the extent that past investments can increase the propensity to invest. The first circle therefore plays a crucial role in reducing the existing information asymmetry between creators and potential contributors. Indeed, the latter can judge the quality of the project using the tools offered by the platform, but cannot evaluate the project holder's quality. They therefore interpret past contributions as a positive signal about the future success of the project. The size of the first circle and therefore the importance of the network generates, for potential contributors, confidence reinforced by the information available on the project.

The study by Moritz et al. (2014) explores the impact of communication on the decision to invest contributors in equity-based CF. Although the authors do not refer to the motivation of contributors, they explore the driving factors behind investment, which is a relatively similar theme. After postulating that asymmetry of expertise and information were obstacles to the decision to invest, the authors seek to determine the elements that would reduce these asymmetries, and thus promote the act of contributing. Three elements influence the backers' decision to invest. First, as direct communication is difficult, due to the large number of investors and the speed of the campaigns, the overall impression provided by the project team (kindness, authenticity, etc.) is an essential element. Therefore, the indirect means of communication, in particular the video presenting the project, must be convincing and of good quality. Second, there is a "peer influence" to the extent that the fact that other people contribute reduces the perception of information asymmetry that contributors may feel. Two groups of third parties are distinguished in the study: the main peer group (considered by the contributors as their equals), and the higher peer group characterized by third parties whose expertise in the broad sense is recognized, which is reassuring. Finally, external accreditations have an impact on the choice of contributors, such as the opinion of customers, business partners, the platform chosen, etc.

Mollick's exploratory study (2014) on the causes of success and failure of donation and reward-based CF projects indicates that one of the key success factors of a project is the quality that the project reflects to contributors. From this perspective, the quality of a project can motivate the contribution even without a previous intention. In addition, the density of the project holder's social network has a positive impact on the success of the project. It would also appear that the nature of the population to whom the project is communicated influences its success rate. These last two motivations echo the work of Belleflamme et al. (2014), about equity- and reward-based crowdfunding, which indicates that the community benefits generated by contributors are essential to the success of a project. They also echo the work of

Gerber et al. (2012) which highlights the role of the social network and the community as elements of a project's success. Finally, Bretschneider et al. (2014) formulate hypotheses on situational factors that could potentially moderate contributors' motivation. There are three situational factors: the characteristics of the project initiating team, the characteristics of their ideas and the herd behaviours, namely the impact of previous contributions on the motivation of potential contributors.

Ultimately, the information about the project allows the first contributors to get started, usually the family and friendly circle. The network then has a leading role on the second and third circles, the crowd. Finally, as partners, information and the network generate trust for the last circle.

Based on this work, it is possible to develop a conceptual framework of the motivations of contributors in CF (see Figure 1).

*Figure 1. The conceptual framework of CF contributors' motivations*
*Source: (authors, 2019)*

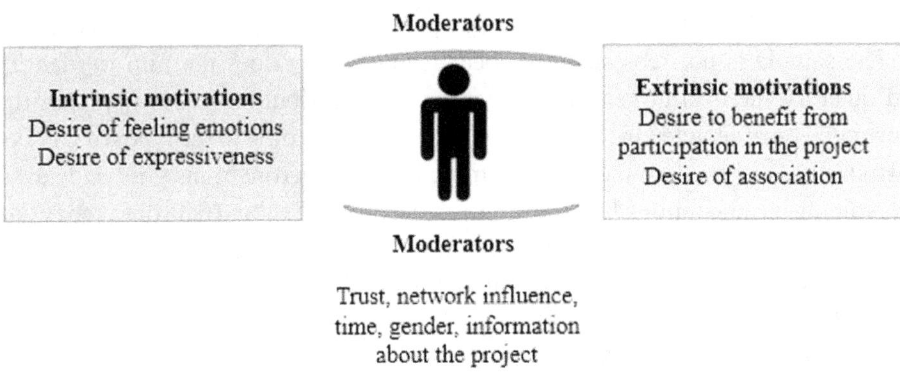


## A QUANTITATIVE METHOD USED IN THE EMPIRICAL STUDY

To verify our conceptual framework, we administer to connoisseurs of the sector an exhaustive questionnaire based on the motivations detected in the literature review. The questionnaire is designed via *Google Forms* and distributed on social networks such as *Facebook, LinkedIn* in 2016, and mainly through the "intermediary" of *Finance Participative France*, an association whose objective is the representation and promotion of crowdfunding with regulatory authorities in France, and through a questionnaire included in the newsletter of March 2016 of a regional platform, "*Graines d'Actions*" operating as a donation/reward. Finally, we administer the questionnaire directly to contributors at an event organized by an interest-free lending and pioneering platform in France, *Babyloan*, which provided valuable feedback and allowed for some control over the front-end responses that respondents would likely make. All these targeting efforts have resulted in a broad coverage covering all types of contributors, from donation to equity via reward and lending.

While the conceptual terms such as intrinsic or extrinsic motivations are not revealed as such to respondents, they were even though coded according to the principle of axiological neutrality in our research design. Respondents are accordingly able to measure 27 types of motivations detected in the literature, whether they are related to the desire to experience emotions (intrinsic motivations) or the desire for external associations (extrinsic motivations). The conceived questionnaire filters out firstly individuals who have already contributed to CF campaigns and those who have not; and secondly distinguishes between respondents by the type of platforms they have contributed on. To do this, one of the first questions was to ask if the respondents had already financed a CF campaign and if so on what type of platform (donation, reward, interest-free or interest lending, equity). The Likert scale was used to allow contributors to express the intensity of their motivations as follows: Strongly agree - Agree - No opinion - Disagree - Strongly disagree. Five tables are reproduced to showcase the results for this purpose in the appendix of this chapter.

The sample is not representative because our study does not aim to identify and quantify the overall generic motivations of contribution but to compare the conceptual ones depicted in the review of literature according to the types of CF. For this purpose, our random indicative sample provides pertinent insights. However, for avoiding basic sampling bias, i.e. non-representativeness and data deficiency due to poor collection, whether due to technological means or respondents' reporting bias, we pay required attention. Several authors in the field of medical studies have used indicative sampling in the early stages of their research projects (Anderson and Vingrys, 2001; Phillips, 2005). Some researchers have even initiated the application of this type of sampling to the social sciences (Al-Fadhli, 2008).

At this stage of our research, factors will be relevant and compatible with the contribution to the different types of CF. They will then allow us to carry out a larger quantitative study with a statistically representative sample to replace this first indicative sample.

## ANALYSIS AND DISCUSSION OF THE RESULTS

124 responded to our questionnaire: 59 men and 65 women, mainly under 35 years of age (65.2%) with a degree equivalent to high school diploma +5 or higher. Table 3 provides extensive flat sorting of collected data.

12% of respondents had contributed on equity-based platforms, which is relatively representative of the CF market in France at the beginning of 2016 (17% of funds

*Table 3. The socio-demographic presentation of the sample according to the types of platform*

| | | Types of platform | | | | | |
|---|---|---|---|---|---|---|---|
| | | **All** | **Credit with interest** | **Credit without interest** | **Donation** | **Equity** | **Reward** |
| **Sex** | Man | 59 | 9 | 6 | 23 | 10 | 11 |
| | Woman | 65 | 5 | 5 | 35 | 5 | 15 |
| **Age** | 18-24 years | 46 | 8 | | 20 | 7 | 11 |
| | 25-34 years | 35 | 2 | 6 | 18 | 1 | 8 |
| | 35-49 years | 19 | 1 | 2 | 6 | 4 | 6 |
| | 50-65+ years | 24 | 3 | 3 | 14 | 3 | 1 |
| **Edu.** | High school and so | 8 | 1 | 2 | 2 | 2 | 1 |
| | High school +2-3 | 28 | 3 | 7 | 18 | 2 | 5 |
| | High school +5-6-8 | 88 | 10 | 2 | 38 | 11 | 20 |
| **Profession** | Craftsmen, traders and entrepreneurs | 5 | | | 3 | | 2 |
| | Persons without professional activity | 36 | 5 | | 20 | 3 | 8 |
| | Senior Managers and Professions | 63 | 6 | 11 | 25 | 11 | 10 |
| | Employees/ Intermediate Professions | 13 | 1 | | 7 | | 5 |
| | Retirees | 7 | 2 | | 3 | 1 | 1 |
| **Tech** | Just interested | 34 | 4 | 3 | 15 | 4 | 8 |
| | Moderately interested | 28 | 1 | 4 | 16 | 7 | |
| | Very/Enthusiast | 62 | 9 | 4 | 27 | 4 | 18 |
| **Mastery** | Master digital technologies | 115 | 13 | 9 | 55 | 12 | 26 |
| | Exceeded by digital technologies | 9 | 1 | 2 | 3 | 3 | |

Source: (authors, 2019)

raised were raised as equity according to FPF, 2016). However, the other sample segments are less in line with the general CF landscape: 67.8% in donation and reward (respectively 46.8 and 21%) for a combined volume of 16.9% in the French market according to the FPF barometer; and 20.2% in lending (11.3% with interest and 8.9% without) in our sample against 66.1% in the total fund raised at a French national level according to FPF.

Intrinsic motivations dominate contributors to donation-based platforms (67%). Intrinsic motivations also dominate on interest-free lending-based platforms by (77%). It is even higher than for the donation. All respondents are executives and

*Figure 2. Intrinsic CF contributors' motivations in donation and interest-free lending*
*Source: (authors, 2019)*

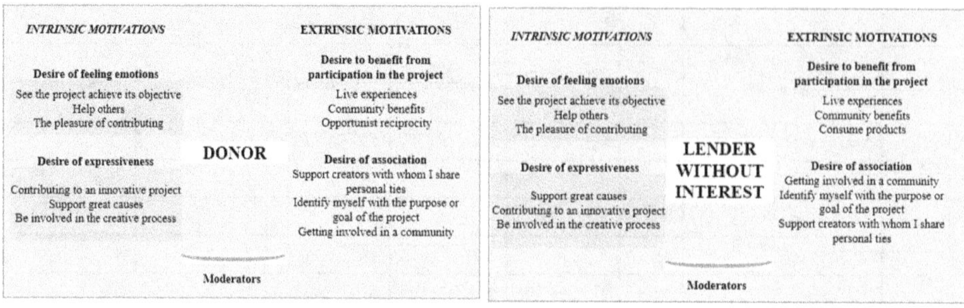


senior professionals. The sample is fairly distributed between men and women with high levels of education.

In application of our conceptual framework, we could summarize and represent the results as follows (see Figure 2).

The analysis of the collected data confirms some of the results already mentioned in the literature, complements some others and proposes new ones. It shows first of all that several types of motivation identified in the literature review do not apply, at least as they are formulated in this research project, to the actual behaviors since the interviewees do not choose them. As evidenced by the table some motivation of contribution are not retained by the interviewees within the intrinsic motivations like "Fun", "Need for self-esteem development", "Express one's political opinion", "Need to affirm one's identity" and "Altruist reciprocity", as well as within extrinsic motivations such as "Getting involved and in interaction with members of the team "and" Recognition by my peers". Extrinsic motivations are retained more than intrinsic ones.

Extrinsic motivations, as our data analysis shows, prevail in reward (55%), equity (55%) and lending with interest (76%), while the literature does not unanimously agree on motivations of contribution for these types of platforms. Results provide new insights on motivations of contribution for lending-based CF with interest, since the latter is never studied as of the date of this study from this angle in the literature. For instance, Herzenstein et al. (2011) explore strategic herding behaviour rather than motivation in peer-to-peer lending in their study about Prosper.com.

In application of our conceptual framework, we could summarize and represent the results as follows (see Figure 3).

We established the top 3 contribution motivations by platform (see Table 5) and observed a surprising result: the top 3 intrinsic motivations of contribution do not correlate to the type of platforms. In other words, out of the thirteen intrinsic motivations tested, the top 3 vary little or not at all in relation to the type of platforms.

*Table 4. Summary of responses by motivation and type of crowdfunding*

| | | | | | | | | |
|---|---|---|---|---|---|---|---|---|
| | | Help project to achieve its objective | 1 | 1 | 1 | - | 1 | **4** |
| | | Pleasure of contributing | 1 | 1 | 1 | - | 1 | **4** |
| | Emotions | Curiosity | - | - | - | 1 | - | **1** |
| | | Desire of knowledge | - | - | - | 1 | - | **1** |
| | | Fun | - | - | - | - | - | **-** |
| | | Help others | 1 | 1 | 1 | 1 | 1 | **5** |
| **INTRINSIC** | | Need for self-esteem development | - | - | - | - | - | **-** |
| | | Express one's political opinion | - | - | - | - | - | **-** |
| | | Contributing to an innovative project | 1 | 1 | 1 | 1 | 1 | **5** |
| | Expressivity | Need to affirm one's identity | - | - | - | - | - | **-** |
| | | Be involved in the creative process | 1 | 1 | 1 | 1 | 1 | **5** |
| | | Altruist reciprocity | - | - | - | - | - | **-** |
| | | Support great causes | 1 | 1 | 1 | 1 | 1 | **5** |
| | | Recognition of personal needs that project addresses | - | 1 | - | - | - | **1** |
| | | Return on investment | - | - | - | 1 | 1 | **2** |
| | | Reward | - | 1 | - | 1 | - | **2** |
| | Utility | Community benefits | 1 | - | 1 | 1 | 1 | **4** |
| | | Opportunist reciprocity | 1 | - | - | - | 1 | **2** |
| | | Consume products | - | - | 1 | - | - | **1** |
| | | Live experiences | 1 | 1 | 1 | - | - | **3** |
| **EXTRINSIC** | | Getting involved in a community | 1 | - | 1 | - | - | **2** |
| | | Getting involved and in interaction with members of the team | - | - | - | - | - | **-** |
| | | Recognition by peers | - | - | - | - | - | **-** |
| | Association | Support creators with whom I share personal ties | 1 | 1 | 1 | - | 1 | **4** |
| | | Identification with the team | - | 1 | - | 1 | - | **2** |
| | | Regional identification with the project | - | - | - | 1 | 1 | **2** |
| | | Identify myself personally with the purpose or goal of the project | 1 | 1 | 1 | 1 | 1 | **5** |

The motivation associated with helping others is found in the top 3 of contributors' motivations on the 5 types of platforms combined. In addition, the motivations associated with seeing the project's objective achieved, and the pleasure of contributing are among the top 3 contributors on 4 of the 5 platforms. Indeed, only contributors on lending-based platforms with interest did not place these two motivations in their top 3.

For the motivational category associated with the desire for personal expressiveness, the top 3 motivations are identical. It consists of the motivations associated with

*Figure 3. Extrinsic CF contributors' motivations in reward, equity and lending with interest*
*Source: (authors, 2019)*

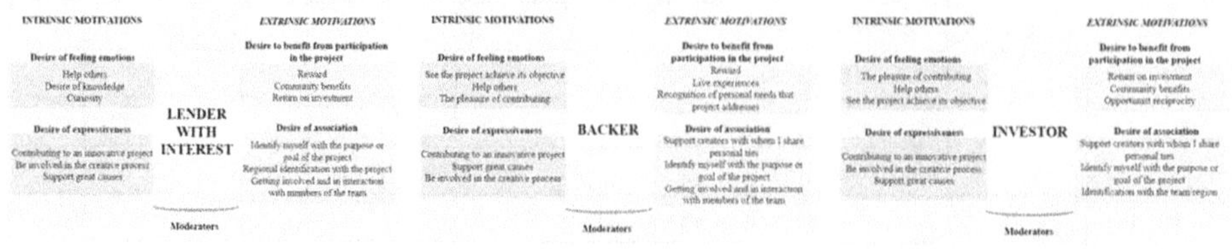


contributing to an innovative project, supporting great causes and being involved in the creative process.

The same approach for the fourteen extrinsic motivations shows (see Table 6) that for the motivational category associated with the desire to get benefits (material or non-material) from participation in the project, the motivation related to community benefits is in the top 3 of contributors in all platforms, except the reward category. Moreover, the fact of living experiences is also in the top 3 motivations of contributors, except for contributors on lending-based platforms with interest and equity.

For the motivational category associated with the desire for association, identifying oneself personally with the object or purpose of the project is among the top 3 of all contributors. Finally, the motivation associated with supporting contributors

*Table 5. Recurrence of intrinsic motivations in the top 3 by platform*

| | Desire of feeling emotions | | | Desire of personal expressiveness | | |
|---|---|---|---|---|---|---|
| | **See the project achieve its objective** | **Help others** | **The pleasure of contributing** | **Contributing to an innovative project** | **Support great causes** | **Be involved in the creative process** |
| Donation | 1 | 1 | 1 | 1 | 1 | 1 |
| Reward | 1 | 1 | 1 | 1 | 1 | 1 |
| Interest-free lending | 1 | 1 | 1 | 1 | 1 | 1 |
| Lending with interest | | 1 | | 1 | 1 | 1 |
| Equity | 1 | 1 | 1 | 1 | 1 | 1 |
| Motivation's recurrence per platform (/5) | 4 | 5 | 4 | 5 | 5 | 5 |

Source: (authors, 2019)

with whom personal links are shared is among the top 3 platforms, except for the lending with interest type.

*Table 6. Recurrence of extrinsic motivations in the top 3 by platform*

| | Desire to benefit (materially or otherwise) from participation in the project | | Desire of association | |
|---|---|---|---|---|
| | **Live experiences** | **Community benefits** | **Support creators with whom I share personal ties** | **Identify myself personally with the purpose or goal of the project** |
| Donation | 1 | 1 | 1 | 1 |
| Reward | 1 | | 1 | 1 |
| Interest-free loan | 1 | 1 | 1 | 1 |
| Loan with interest | | 1 | | 1 |
| Equity | | 1 | 1 | 1 |
| Motivation's recurrence per platform (/5) | 3 | 4 | 4 | 5 |

Source: (authors, 2019)

For discussing the results which might appear paradoxical, we use a theoretical reference (Chen, 2016) we did not integrate into our literature corpus. The reason is that it seemed more relevant to us to mainly focus on the classic literature of motivational studies, even though multidisciplinary, for suggesting a theoretical model to the academic community.

However, the approach of Chen (2016), relying on the critical thinking on Maslow's theory and the discoveries of evolutionary biology, provides insights and we refer to it for discussing the above results. Evolutionary biology studies the evolutionary processes that produced the diversity of life on Earth, starting from a single common ancestor. These processes include common descent, natural selection, and speciation.

Chen (2016) considers the Maslow's model, however, instead of a sequential application of the listed needs. He suggests a three-level triangle of physiology/survival (security), social esteem/standing (association) and self-actualization/fulfillment (aspiration) to explain the investment choice and behavior of humans whose multiple motivations are imbued with affects and emotions such as fear and greed beyond the pure rational mathematical premises. Consequently, they are simultaneously motivated by risk and risk aversion arising from the above three-level Maslow-inspired triangle that Chen (2016) suggests.

The need of security and survival, implying reduction of losses to hostile predators and strangers, gives rise to risk aversion and "risk fearful avoidance" for finally yielding payoffs to an investor. False positive alarms might pay off more than false negative complacency to individuals who remain in danger. When humans feel being threatened, they are less inclined to take risks for venturing in ancient or modern times. At the other end of emotional spectrum, perceptions of power and firmer control encourage risk-seeking behavior. In behavioral terms, investors aspire a premium rate of return in exchange of bearing volatility and the attendant risk of loss. Investors arrange their financial affairs according to emotions and perceptions and link a bottom low aspiration layer of avoiding poverty (risk-free) to a high aspiration layer of maximum payoffs. Among these two highest and lowest levels of needs, Chen (2016) place the associative need of socialization because the need of self-actualization requires socially calibrating to others to fulfill. While the existing studies are largely guided by the idea of egoistically driven backers and not prosaically motivated, Chen (2016) believes that the associative need of socialization clearly explains some charity behavior, such supportive investment and caring contribution, in crowdfunding campaigns.

## RECOMMENDATIONS AND IDEAS FOR CONSIDERATION

This study makes it possible to propose new results compared to the existing literature.

The type of motivation is not the same according to the platform considered. It is therefore appropriate to consider contributors differently according to this same segmentation. Communication on and across platforms must therefore be designed according to the dominant type of motivation. It is necessary to adapt to the motivations of contributors to target a specific market and be consistent with the strategic positioning chosen (Attuel-Mendès, 2017).

However, regardless of the type of platform, certain types of motivations are predominant within the intrinsic and extrinsic motivations. It is therefore necessary to focus on them. As we have seen, four intrinsic motivations are essential to contributors.

As the motivation to help others is shared by all contributors, it is essential that the needs of the project be clearly identified, as well as the solution provided by the fundraising campaign. We could talk about a law of clarity necessary for the success of a project. As such, it becomes essential to answer precisely certain questions when communicating about the project: for whom is the project beneficial? How does the contributor participate to the success ? Etc. Indeed, sending a clear message of the usefulness of the project to its initiator is essential in order to encourage the motivation of contributors. However, it is not enough. It is necessary to go beyond the simple utility for the project holder and also to communicate on the general utility. The latter concerns the community at large insofar as a second key motivation is associated with supporting major causes. These two motivations, far from opposing each other, meet or even complement each other. Contributors thus wish to participate in improving the quality of life of the greatest number of people, which is reflected in terms of motivations in terms of contributing to a great cause. Insisting on participating in the development of SMEs would be part of this approach.

In our opinion, two intrinsic motivations deserve to be treated jointly: being involved in the creative process and seeing the project achieve its objective. The fact that these two motivations are cited by the majority of contributors indicates that the project is perceived dynamically: once contributors have participated, they are interested in the project's life cycle. It is therefore essential to develop an information system to integrate the contributor into the construction/implementation of the project. The latter should not be considered as a shareholder seeking a return on investment, but rather as a stakeholder interested in the overall value creation that the project will generate. This aspect makes sense when it comes to financing an SME with which the contributor can more easily identify. Contributors must therefore be informed throughout the life of the project, i.e. not only before and during money collection but also after its closure. This is all the more important because, as we have seen above, two situational factors related to information moderate the motivation of contributors: (1) the perceived quality of the project, and (2) the simplicity and effectiveness of the information. In response to this observation, it may be considered to determine deliverables to be provided to contributors on the platform at certain key stages of the project life cycle. Ideally, a common breakdown of the deliverables would standardize information, thus facilitating project performance monitoring and comparison. This would enhance the perceived quality of the project, as well as the simplicity of analysis for the backer. As a reminder, six parameters of the campaign influence contributors: its duration, amount, number of previous requests, nature of rewards, role of the donor, and the platform on which the project is launched. These items could lead to future research, particularly on the criteria that should be communicated to contributors in order to reduce information asymmetry and adverse selection problems.

Contributing to an innovative project is an intrinsic motivation widely cited by contributors. It would obviously be unreasonable to support the idea that all projects must be innovative to be successful. Nevertheless, the platform itself can offer an innovative character to all these projects by modernizing its communication mode, for example by developing a more efficient application allowing contributors to access projects from their phones and by using social networks to communicate more about current, favorite, or future projects. Pushing forward the technical tools of contribution also makes it possible to respond to another motivation of contributors: the pleasure of contributing. This motivation can indeed be analysed in two ways. First, the pleasure associated with simply contributing to a project. Secondly, the pleasure associated with the playful nature of contributing. However, anchoring platforms more firmly in the 2.0 era, and offering contributors a real experience are avenues not to be neglected. In the same vein, technical tools could help contributors read the information and develop a sense of personal identification. It would therefore be interesting to consider a segmentation of projects that uses strong identities. This segmentation could be done in two ways. First, it is possible to create tabs on the platform to clearly identify projects that share the same values. This segmentation could usefully be associated with proposals or links such as: "the people who contributed to this project also liked it". Secondly, it may be suggested to segment contributors by introducing a questionnaire to guide their research among the numerous projects.

Extrinsic motivations raise more reflections than recommendations.

First, contributors are motivated by community benefits and experiences. Therefore, the motivation of contributors is broader than the simple contributor/project relationship. Contributing can be seen as a new form of socialization of individuals that would consist in living an experience and sharing it with a community. CF could therefore be considered as a new source of social cohesion. Indeed, being a contributor can emerge from a logic of identity creation linked to lived experiences and the developed network. Internet funders are interested in being able to clearly state that they are contributors and that they belong to a community.

This idea of a dynamic relationship between (1) contributing, and (2) creating an identity, echoes the last two extrinsic motivations: personally identifying with the object or purpose of the project, and supporting creators with whom the contributor shares personal ties. It would seem that the analysis of contributors' motivation is inseparable from the analysis of the creation of the identity they associate with contributing. Contributing is therefore not an insignificant act: it contributes to the creation of an identity. An individual contributes to a project with which he or she identifies; and contributing reinforces that identity. The platforms have understood this well, since they build a discourse in adequacy with their own identity (Attuel-Mendès et al., 2014).

One of the most interesting avenues of research relates to the question of moderators that has not yet been explored. It is linked to the phenomenon of path dependency; in other words, the fact that past investments increase the propensity of potential contributors to invest. The influence of peers in dealing with information asymmetry and the risks of moral hazard to potential contributors seem very important. The success of a campaign is therefore based on a virtuous circle in which past contributions stimulate future contributions.

Also, the project leader must mobilize his network since the members of the first circle (friends and family) are more inclined to contribute, because they share personal links with the project leader (intrinsic motivation in the top 3 of contributors across all platforms). This participation will encourage other contributors to invest, as the participation rate sends a positive signal to other contributors. This effect is referred to as path dependency. This can be explained by the fact that more distant circles are at high risk because of the asymmetry of information between them and the project leader. Therefore, to assess the importance of this risk, contributors refer to past investments as a guarantee of quality. For these herding behaviours to appear, it is essential that information is available to potential contributors. Indeed, the participation rate encourages potential contributors to take an interest in the project. Simple and effective information about the project will more likely turn their will into action.

Finally, it will be necessary to test the moderators from the literature review: trust, network influence, and information about the project. To do this, interviews with project leaders, contributors and administrators should be conducted.

Ultimately, the major contribution of this article lies in the segmentation of platforms, which must adapt their communication on motivations in a relevant way. Our results highlight that intrinsic motivations are predominant for donation and interest-free lending-based platforms, while reward, equity and lending-based platforms with interest are dominated by extrinsic motivations. In concrete terms, the study highlights that the "pleasure of contributing", "living experiences", "supporting creators with whom the contributor shares personal ties" and "seeing the project succeed" are minor elements for lending with interest, whose motivations had never been explored. On this type of platform, these four elements will therefore not need to be highlighted. For equity-based platforms, it is the part of living experiences that should not be valued. Finally, for reward, the community benefits do not require any particular emphasis.

## ACKNOWLEDGMENT

The authors would like to thank the Regional Council of Burgundy Franche-Comté for its financial support.

## REFERENCES

Agrawal, A., Catalani, C., & Goldfarb, A. (2015). Crowdfunding: Geography, social networks, and the timing of investment decisions. *Journal of Economics & Management Strategy*, *24*(2), 253–274.

Aitamurto, T. (2011). The Impact of Crowdfunding on Journalism: Case study of Spot.Us, a platform for community-funded reporting. *Journalism Practice*, *5*(4), 429–445.

Al-Fadhli, S. (2008). Students' perceptions of E-learning in Arab society: Kuwait University as a case study. *E-Learning and Digital Media*, *5*(4), 418–428.

Alderfer, C. P. (1969). An empirical test of a new theory of human needs. *Organizational Behavior and Human Performance*, *4*(2), 142–175.

Amara, M., Ben Cheikh, A., & Abdellati, T. (2014). *Crowdfunding: Determinants and motivations of the contributors to the crowdfunding platforms*. Retrieved from https://papers.ssrn.com/sol3/papers.cfm?abstract_id=2552168

Anderson, A. J., & Vingrys, A. J. (2001). Small samples: Does size matter? *Investigative Ophthalmology & Visual Science*, *42*(7), 1411–1413. PMID:11381039

Ariely, D., Bracha, A., & Meier, S. (2009). Doing good or doing well? Image motivation and monetary incentives in behaving prosocially. *The American Economic Review*, *99*(1), 544–555.

Assadi, D. (2016). In search of crowdfunding business models. In D. Assadi (Ed.), Strategic Approaches to Successful Crowdfunding (pp. 1-33). IGI Global.

Attuel-Mendès, L. (2017). The different ways of collaboration between a retail bank and crowdfunding. *Strategic Change: Briefings in Entrepreneurial Finance*, *26*, 213–225.

Attuel-Mendès, L., Caseau, C., & Bonescu, M. (2014). Brand identity process of financial cooperatives: An Austrian case. *Strategic Change: Briefings in Entrepreneurial Finance*, *23*, 493–506.

Autorité de Contrôle Prudentiel. (2013). *Guide du financement participatif (crowdfunding) à destination du grand public*. Retrieved from https://www.economie.gouv.fr/vous-orienter/entreprise/numerique/crowdfunding-tout-savoir-pour-se-lancer

Bagheri, A., Chitsazan, H., & Ebrahimi, A. (2019). Crowdfunding motivations: A focus on donors' perspectives. *Technological Forecasting and Social Change*, *146*, 218–232.

Batson, C. D. (1987). Prosocial motivation: Is it ever truly altruistic? *Advances in Experimental Social Psychology*, *20*, 65–122.

Belleflamme, P., Lambert, T., & Schwienbacher, A. (2014). Crowdfunding: Tapping the right crowd. *Journal of Business Venturing*, *29*(5), 585–609.

Ben Slimane, F., & Rousselet, E. (2016). Plateformes de financement participatif et acteurs historiques: Pourquoi les partenaires se multiplient-ils? *Revue Banque*, *795*, 62–64.

Berglin, H., & Strandberg, C. (2013). *Leveraging customers as investors: The driving forces behind crowdfunding* (Unpublished bachelor's thesis). Uppsala University.

Bretschneider, U., Knaub, K., & Wieck, E. (2014). Motivations for crowdfunding: what drives the crowd to invest in start-ups? *Twenty Second European Conference on Information Systems, Research in Progress, Tel Aviv 2014*.

Bretschneider, U., & Leimeister, J. M. (2017). Not just an ego-trip: Exploring backers' motivation for funding in incentive-based crowdfunding. *The Journal of Strategic Information Systems*, *26*(4), 246–260.

Cecere, G., Le Guel, F., & Rochelandet, F. (2017). Crowdfunding and social influence: An empirical investigation. *Applied Economics*, *49*(57), 5802–5813.

Chen, J. M. (2016). *Finance and the Behavioral Prospect*. Palgrave Macmillan.

Cholakova, M., & Clarysse, B. (2015). Does the possibility to make equity investments in crowdfunding projects crowd out reward-Based investments? *Entrepreneurship Theory and Practice*, *39*(1), 145–172.

Dai, H., & Zhang, D. J. (2019). Prosocial goal pursuit in crowdfunding: Evidence from Kickstarter. *JMR, Journal of Marketing Research*, *56*(3), 498–517.

Deci, E. L., & Ryan, R. M. (1985). *Intrinsic motivation and self-determination in human behavior*. Plenum.

Financement Participatif France. (2016). *Baromètre du crowdfunding 2015*. Retrieved from http://financeparticipative.org/barometre-du-crowdfunding-2015/

Financement Participatif France. (2018). *Baromètre du crowdfunding 2017, en collaboration avec KPMG*. Retrieved from http://financeparticipative.org/wp-content/uploads/2018/01/Barometre-CrowdFunding-2017_KPMG-FPF_page-%C3%A0-page.pdf

Financement Participatif France. (2019). *Baromètre du crowdfunding en France 2018 réalisé par KPMG pour Financement Participatif France*. Retrieved from https://financeparticipative.org/wp-content/uploads/2019/01/Barom%C3%A8tre-du-crowdfunding-KPMG-et-FPF-%C3%A9dition-2018.pdf

Frey, B. S. (1997). *Not just for money. An economic theory of personal motivation*. Edgar Elgar.

Gagne, M., & Deci, E. L. (2005). Self-determination theory and work motivation. *Journal of Organizational Behavior*, *26*(4), 331–362.

Gerber, E. M., Hui, J. S., & Kuo, P.-Y. (2012). Crowdfunding: Why people are motivated to post and fund projects on crowdfunding platforms. In *Proceedings of the International Workshop on Design, Influence, and Social Technologies: Techniques, Impacts and Ethics* (*vol. 2*). Academic Press.

Grant, A. M. (2008). Does intrinsic motivation fuel the prosocial fire? Motivational synergy in predicting persistence, performance, and productivity. *The Journal of Applied Psychology*, *93*(1), 48–58. PMID:18211134

HarmsM. (2007). *What drives motivation to participate financially in a crowdfunding community?* (Unpublished master's thesis). Vrije Universiteit Amsterdam. Retrieved from http://ssrn.com/abstract=2269242

Harrer, T., Lehner, O. M., & Weber, C. (2019). Do(n't) Trust This! –A Longitudinal Exploration of Institutional Trust in Crowdfunding. *BAM2019 Conference Proceedings*. Retrieved from https://www.bam.ac.uk/sites/bam.ac.uk/files/contribution212.pdf

Hemer, J. (2011). A snapshot on crowdfunding. Working papers firms and region, No. R2/2011. *Site Econstor*.Retrieved from http://hdl.handle.net/10419/52302

Herzberg, F., Mausner, B., & Bloch Snyderman, B. (1959). *The motivation to work*. John Wiley & Sons, Inc.

Herzenstein, M., Dholakia, U. M., & Andrews, R. L. (2011). Strategic herding behaviour in peer-to-peer loan auctions. *Journal of Interactive Marketing*, *25*(1), 27–36. doi:10.1016/j.intmar.2010.07.001

Hossain, M., & Oparaocha, G. O. (2017). Crowdfunding: Motives, definitions, typology and ethical challenges. *Entrepreneurship Research Journal*, *7*(2), 1–14. doi:10.1515/erj-2015-0045

Howe, J. (2006). *Crowdsourcing: A Definition*. Retrieved from https://crowdsourcing.typepad.com/cs/2006/06/crowdsourcing_a.html

Kang, M., Gao, Y., Wang, T., & Zheng, H. (2016). Understanding the determinants of funders' investment intentions on crowdfunding platforms: A trust-based perspective. *Industrial Management & Data Systems*, *116*(8), 1800–1819. doi:10.1108/IMDS-07-2015-0312

Khelladi, I., Castellano, S., & Bertaud, A. (2018). Les déterminants de la confiance de l'internaute dans le contexte d'une collecte de crowdfunding. *Innovations*, *2*(56), 117–140. doi:10.3917/inno.pr1.0040

Kuti, M., & Madarasz, G. (2014). Crowdfunding. *Public Finance Quarterly*, *59*(3), 355–366.

Lederer, E. (2015). *La finance participative accélère son incroyable expansion*. Retrieved from https://www.lesechos.fr/31/03/2015/LesEchos/21909-119-ECH_la-finance-participative-accelere-son-incroyable-expansion.htm

Li, G., & Wang, J. (2019). Threshold effects on backer motivations in reward-based crowdfunding. *Journal of Management Information Systems*, *36*(2), 546–573. doi:10.1080/07421222.2019.1599499

Lin, Y., Boh, W. F., & Goh, K. H. (2014). *How different are crowdfunders? Examining archetypes of crowdfunders and their choice of projects*. Retrieved from https://papers.ssrn.com/sol3/papers.cfm?abstract_id=2397571

Lukkarinen, A., Wallenius, J., & Seppälä, T. (2019). *Investor motivations and decision criteria in equity crowdfunding*. Retrieved from https://papers.ssrn.com/sol3/papers.cfm?abstract_id=3263434

Mcclelland, D. C. (1961). *The achieving society*. doi:10.1037/14359-000

Mollick, E. (2014). The dynamics of crowdfunding: An exploratory study. *Journal of Business Venturing*, *29*(1), 1–16. doi:10.1016/j.jbusvent.2013.06.005

Moritz, A., Block, J. H., & Lutz, E. (2014). *Investor communication in crowdfunding: A qualitative-empirical study*. Retrieved from https://papers.ssrn.com/sol3/papers.cfm?abstract_id=2462282

Onnee, S., & Renault, S. (2014). Crowdfunding: Vers une compréhension du rôle joué par la foule. *Revue Management & Avenir*, *74*(8), 117–133. doi:10.3917/mav.074.0117

Passebois-Ducros, J., & Pulh, M. (2015). *Vers un modèle conceptuel des facteurs explicatifs de la participation et de la réussite d'une opération de crowdfunding dans le secteur culturel non marchand*. Retrieved from https://www.researchgate.net/profile/Mathilde_Pulh/publication/281554469_Vers_un_modle_conceptuel_des_facteurs_explicatifs_de_la_participation_et_de_la_russite_d%27une_opration_de_crowdfunding_dans_le_secteur_culturel_non_marchand/links/55ed869108ae21d099c75cbb.pdf

Pearson, A., Johdet, J., & Näselius, M. (2016). *Understanding the crowd: A quantitative study on investor motivation in equity crowdfunding*. Retrieved October 2, 2019 on http://www.diva-portal.org/smash/record.jsf?pid=diva2%3A932955&dswid=6652

Phillips, J. R. (2005). Monovision slows juvenile myopia progression unilaterally. *The British Journal of Ophthalmology*, *89*(9), 1196–1200. doi:10.1136/bjo.2004.064212 PMID:16113381

Prpić, J., Shukla, P., Roth, Y., & Lemoine, J. F. (2015). *A geography of participation in IT-mediated crowds*. Retrieved from https://papers.ssrn.com/sol3/papers.cfm?abstract_id=2494537

Roggan, J. (2015). *Motivation of German entrepreneurs to seek equity via crowdfunding: An exploratory study* (Doctoral dissertation). Retrieved October 2, 2019 on https://bibliotecadigital.fgv.br/dspace/bitstream/handle/10438/13623/John%20Roggan_Master%20Thesis_EAESP_2015_Final.pdf

Ryu, S., Kim, K. & Kim, Y. (2016). Reward versus philanthropy motivation in crowdfunding behaviour. *PACIS 2016 Proceedings, 87.*

Van Wingerden, R., & Ryan, R. (2011). *Fighting for funds: An exploratory study into the field of crowdfunding*. Degree Project in International Marketing and Brand Management, Lund University School of Economics and Management. Retrieved from http://lup.lub.lu.se/luur/download?func=downloadFile&recordOId=1982630&fileOId=2436193

Wardrop, R., Zhang, B., Rau, R., & Gray, M. (2015). *Moving Mainstream. The European alternative finance benchmarking report*. University of Cambridge.

Wechsler, J. (2013). *Know your crowd: The drivers of success in reward based crowdfunding* (Unpublished master's thesis). University of Fribourg Department of Mass Media and Communication Research Master of Arts in Business Communication. Retrieved from https://crwdfnd.files.wordpress.com/2013/07/know-your-crowd-jonaswechsler.pdf

Ziegler, T., Shneor, R., Garvey, K., Wenzlaff, K., Yecolemou, N., Hao, R., & Zhang, B. (2018). *Expanding horizons, The 3rd European alternative finance industry benchmarking report.* University of Cambridge. Retrieved from https://www.jbs.cam.ac.uk/fileadmin/user_upload/research/centres/alternative-finance/downloads/2018-02-ccaf-exp-horizons.pdf

## ENDNOTES

1. This is defined as a context where individuals have a voluntary iteration to help others.
2. The prosocial motivation is defined as "the desire to expend effort to benefit other people" (Batson, 1987; Grant, 2008), which encompasses with the intrinsic and image motivations presented in Arieli et al. (2009).

# APPENDIX

*Table 7. Intrinsic and extrinsic motivations for credit with interest crowdfunding*

| | | Totally agree | Agree | Without opinion | Disagree | Totally disagree |
|---|---|---|---|---|---|---|
| INTRINSIC | Desire of feeling emotions | 19 | 19 | 9 | 3 | 34 |
| | Desire of personal expressiveness | 16 | 31 | 27 | 17 | 7 |
| EXTRINSIC | Desire to benefit (materially or otherwise) from participation in the project | 24 | 38 | 18 | 12 | 6 |
| | Desire of association | 21 | 32 | 24 | 18 | 3 |

*Table 8. Intrinsic and extrinsic motivations for credit without interest crowdfunding*

| | | Totally agree | Agree | Without opinion | Disagree | Totally disagree |
|---|---|---|---|---|---|---|
| INTRINSIC | Desire of feeling emotions | 28 | 14 | 8 | 10 | 6 |
| | Desire of personal expressiveness | 14 | 28 | 15 | 12 | 8 |
| EXTRINSIC | Desire to benefit (materially or otherwise) from participation in the project | 3 | 17 | 25 | 15 | 17 |
| | Desire of association | 15 | 31 | 11 | 12 | 8 |

*Table 9. Intrinsic and extrinsic motivations for donation crowdfunding*

| | | Totally agree | Agree | Without opinion | Disagree | Totally disagree |
|---|---|---|---|---|---|---|
| INTRINSIC | Desire of feeling emotions | 127 | 96 | 55 | 32 | 38 |
| | Desire of personal expressiveness | 77 | 125 | 92 | 69 | 43 |
| EXTRINSIC | Desire to benefit (materially or otherwise) from participation in the project | 35 | 112 | 109 | 92 | 58 |
| | Desire of association | 50 | 155 | 120 | 61 | 20 |

*Table 10. Intrinsic and extrinsic motivations for equity crowdfunding*

| | | Totally agree | Agree | Without opinion | Disagree | Totally disagree |
|---|---|---|---|---|---|---|
| INTRINSIC | Desire of feeling emotions | 25 | 36 | 12 | 6 | 11 |
| | Desire of personal expressiveness | 18 | 46 | 26 | 9 | 6 |
| EXTRINSIC | Desire to benefit (materially or otherwise) from participation in the project | 13 | 57 | 24 | 11 | 0 |
| | Desire of association | 16 | 50 | 27 | 9 | 3 |

*Table 11. Intrinsic and extrinsic motivations for rewards crowdfunding*

| | | Totally agree | Agree | Without opinion | Disagree | Totally disagree |
|---|---|---|---|---|---|---|
| INTRINSIC | Desire of feeling emotions | 54 | 49 | 25 | 14 | 14 |
| | Desire of personal expressiveness | 39 | 55 | 47 | 22 | 19 |
| EXTRINSIC | Desire to benefit (materially or otherwise) from participation in the project | 34 | 70 | 46 | 21 | 11 |
| | Desire of association | 39 | 75 | 38 | 24 | 6 |

# Chapter 3
# Lending Crowdfunding and Regional Development:
## An Empirical Study

**Susana Bernardino**
https://orcid.org/0000-0002-1639-3553
*CEOS, ISCAP, Polytechnic of Porto, Portugal*

**J. Freitas Santos**
https://orcid.org/0000-0001-8233-5039
*CEOS, ISCAP, Polytechnic of Porto, Portugal*

## ABSTRACT

*By analysing the operations of a lending crowdfunding platform in Portugal, the investigation aims to study the potential contribution of CF for entrepreneurship and regional development. The results reveal that small organisations are especially prone to use CF as a financing strategy, regardless of their seniority, as well as ventures that have a moderated risk profile. However, coastal regions have been more dynamic on CF use than interior located ventures, since most of the operations were realized on the littoral of the country. The results suggest that interior organisations that use CF could have more financing difficulties that led them to look for new fundraising solutions, since they typically have higher size than coastal located organisations, although the risk rating is quite similar. The CF loans period is also shorter. The average interest rate charged is quite similar between both type of locations, although a higher variability exists in the funding conditions of interior organisations. The average offer per investor is also higher in the interior case.*

DOI: 10.4018/978-1-7998-3226-3.ch003

## INTRODUCTION

The term crowdfunding (hereafter CF) derives from the concept of crowdsourcing and could be characterized as the collective cooperation of people who pool their money together to support efforts initiated by others. In the digital world, CF can be defined as an open call for raising funds, essentially through the internet, in the form of exchange for some sort of reward to support private initiatives.

CF has grown very quickly (Yu *et al.*, 2017). According to the World Internet Development Report 2017 "CF was started in 2001 and then began to grow explosively. Database of Forward Information Co., Ltd. shows that from 2010 to 2016, the CF saw the annual compound growth rate of over 80%. Its scale reached US$198.96 billion in 2016, and it is anticipated to reach US$300 billion by 2025, with US$96 billion in developing countries" (Chinese Academy of Cyberspace Studies, 2019, p. 145).

Researchers have highlighted the importance of CF as an emerging topic from different perspectives (Butticè, Colombo, & Wright, 2017; Harrison, 2013; Hu, Li, & Shi, 2015; Kitch, 2013). However, the role of CF platforms on regional development has received little attention from scholars, regardless the increasing number of entrepreneurs that use these platforms to different purposes (Cho & Kim, 2017; Brown, Boon & Pitt, 2017).

The ability of digital technologies to provide almost instantaneous data gathering and feedback, computationally validate contributions and the ability to reach both broad and niche groups through loose networks have all been particularly important for entrepreneurship. This type of platforms has been growing rapidly and changing the dynamics of entrepreneurship as they attract attention and create opportunities for raising capital from individuals and investors across the world (Mollick, 2014).

The study of this type of financial instrument in the context of the regional development is important as investment and financing are two relevant topics for the initial stages of the new venture and the robustness of the less developed regions. To our best knowledge, the literature on CF suffers from a lack of contributions on the benefits of these new platforms for entrepreneurship that are at the core of the regional dynamism. The objective of the paper is to address this gap by examining the potential contributions of CF for the development of entrepreneurship and the dynamism of the regions.

The chapter is organized into six parts. First, we present the concepts of CF, the main types of CF and advantages that provide this innovative external financing mechanism. Specifically, we emphasize how CF might attract investors for different projects from different geographical origins inside and outside the country. After that, in line with the research inquiry, we cover two sets of literature. one focuses on the disparity of economic development among different regions; the other assesses the impact of entrepreneurship on regional development. The next section explains the methodology used in the investigation. In the following section, the results attained are presented and discussed. Then, based on the findings attained, some solutions and recommendations are presented. Thereafter, some future research directions are outlined. The paper ends with the main conclusions.

## CROWDFUNDING

CF is a concept that encompasses the outsourcing of an organizational function (capital formation) to a defined network of actors (the crowd) in the form of an open call (the campaign) via dedicated CF platforms (Paschen, 2017; André *et al.*, 2017; Belleflamme, Lambert, & Schwienbacher, 2014). In this context, a website acts as an intermediary (online platform) through which promoters of start-ups, projects or ventures advertise their business ideas and seek small amounts of money from a huge number of prospective investors (Joshi, 2018). The platform establishes the connection between entrepreneurs, who aim to raise capital, and novel investors, who form an emerging source of capital and are willing to invest through internet-based intermediaries (Valanena & Jegeleviciute, 2014).

A common process of crowdfunding is summarized in Figure 1. The process begins with an entrepreneur using the crowdfunding platform to communicate the business idea that call for funding. Then: (a) the investment opportunity is posted through the platform to potential investors; (b) the prospect investors analyze the different business proposals and invest their money in the projects they prefer to fund, in accordance with their profile of risk; (c) in addition to funding, investors typically also provide other kind of intangible assets, such as feedback or advice; (d) the process ends when the investor received some kind of reward, that could be monetary or no, and the crowdfunding platform administrator charge some fee for the intermediation role (Valanaene & Jegeleviciute, 2014).

To the European Commission (2014, p. 2), "there is great potential in CF to complement traditional sources of finance and contribute to the financing of the real economy". The traditional financing options include conventional debt (loans), equity or hybrid instruments that combine debt and equity. On the contrary, CF offers entrepreneurs and the small and medium enterprises (SMEs) a more flexible way to raise funds, where communication between funders and fundees plays a special role. With CF, in response to an open call, members of a large audience voluntarily decide to finance directly some kind of a goal. Each individual usually provides only a small sum of contribution in exchange for money, a product or a service or even when they are not promised anything in return (Belleflamme, Lambert, Schwienbacher, 2013; 2014). CF platforms are websites that enable managers, entrepreneurs and the initiators of other projects to solicit funding through an open

*Figure 1. The general process of crowdfunding (Valanaene & Jegeleviciute, 2014)*
*Source: Valanaene and Jegeleviciute, 2014*

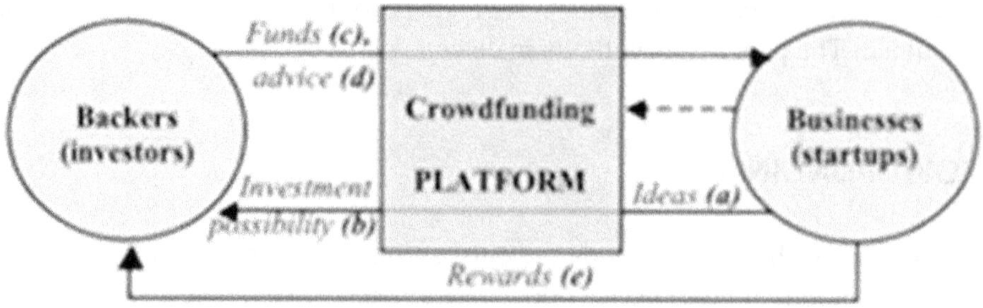


call and post details about the projects. Potential backers may browse through the projects and support the ones they find attractive by providing funds. Through the use of the current digital technology, countless users, initiators and potential donors can sign on these sites easily and inexpensively. Through CF, entrepreneurs and businesses can more easily use the crowd to obtain ideas, collect money, and solicit input on the product – fostering an environment of collective decision-making and allowing businesses to connect with potential customers (Kuti & Madarász, 2014).

There are two groups of CF that traditionally have been divided into four basic types: the models based on investment more oriented to commercial entrepreneurship, include the equity-based and the lending-based models; the models based on donation more oriented to social entrepreneurship, include the pure donation based and the reward-based model (World Bank, 2013; Kuti & Madarász, 2014), as follows:

- Lending-based CF - funds contributed by individual creditors are disbursed as personal loans to requestors through internet platforms without financial intermediation and collateral, with high risks involved. In this case, small sums of contributions are made by supporters which can be considered as an attempt to minimize losses and diversify risks. Certain sites offer access to the funds of private backers to pre-screened enterprises (peer-to-business lending, P2B lending). It has become a trend that institutional investors take recourse to peer-to-peer (P2P) lending, which shifts certain platforms to an institution-to-peer type of lending (Schwienbacher & Larralde, 2012; World Bank, 2013; Belleflamme *et al.*, 2014).
- Equity-based CF - involves the cheap issuance of shares through the internet, where investors can acquire stock in corporations for a small amount of money, with a claim over the company's future cash-flow. It has proved to be a viable form of financing corporate growth and innovation and access funding, which have failed to get funds from angel investors, government

programs, friends or family alike (Belleflamme, Lambert & Schwienbacher, 2014; Schwienbacher & Larralde, 2012; World Bank, 2013).

- Donation-based CF - This type of CF is aimed at supporting charitable, research, creative and personal projects, where contributors do not expect any financial or non-financial returns. The reward is more of an emotional nature and beneficiaries have no obligations whatsoever toward their backers (World Bank, 2013; Gajda & Walton, 2013; Mollick, 2014; Lehner & Nicholls, 2014).
- Reward-based CF - This type of CF can be used to provide funding to startups, expand existing companies or finance personal creative projects. In this case, funders receive either real products or services in exchange. The process of reward-based CF started with the project initiators posting all relevant information on the website and is continued by offering sales incentives through digital marketing strategies. The precise goal of the project, the investment needs and the deadline are posted on the project website. If the project fails to receive the solicited amount, depending on the platform, supporters may be refunded. The different reward categories established by the initiators depend on the amount of support. Supporters offering more money are classified in a higher category and can expect a proportionately higher reward. Sometimes expanded objectives are set up, which can be implemented in case the project receives a significant amount of overfunding (World Bank, 2013; Kuti & Madarász, 2014).

Paschen (2017) argues that each venture should select the type of crowdfunding that best fits their features and needs, especially regarding the life cycle where they are located, as summarized in figure 2.

In the last few years, different types of crowdfunding emerge. For instance, civic crowdfunding is a sub-type of crowdfunding through which citizens, in collaboration with government, voluntary participate in projects providing ideas, funds or another kind of community services (Bernardino & Freitas Santos, 2018). A similar concept is social crowdfunding that can be defined as an open call for raising funds, essentially through the internet, in the form of donation or in exchange for some sort of reward in order to support initiatives for social goals (Bernardino, Freitas Santos & Cadima Ribeiro, 2016).

The main advantage of CF is that the funders are also potential customers and ambassadors of the project or business model they support, and they help to promote it through their own networks. Crowdfunding could be especially beneficial for new ventures and small companies, as crowdfunding allows to bridge the existing gap of financing options that organizations with no track record typically have (Cruz, 2018; Valanaene & Jegeleviciute, 2014).

*Figure 2. A comparison of the different types of crowdfunding*
*Source: Paschen, 2017*

| Startup Stage | Pre-startup | Startup | Growth |
|---|---|---|---|
| Resources needed to achieve... | Problem/Solution Fit | Product Validation; Market Validation | Market Penetration; Market Expansion |
| Verifiability of Information | Yes No | Yes No | Yes No |
| Optimal Type of Crowdfunding | Donation | Lending | Equity |
| Reward Offered | No (tangible) return | Interest ($), Product | Securities, Profit Sharing |
| Best Practices | 1. Choose a specialized platform and all-or-nothing payout model<br>2. Be transparent and accountable<br>3. Publicize backer information | 1. Offer tangible rewards<br>2. Detail the startup founder's credentials<br>3. Frequently update a funding crowd | 1. Provide third-party verifiable reports<br>2. Attract reputable early investors<br>3. Target a crowd that can empathize |

The funder usually identifies with the project, has a mind for change and is happy to help provide the social proof of concept. The risk of failure does not necessarily translate into a risk of loss of capital, because success for the funder is usually not defined through financial return alone. While multiple funders share the financial risk and therefore limit the extent of a potential financial loss to individuals, the actual perceived loss is not necessarily financial but linked to funders' expectations and thus correlated to their motivations. In case of failure, the perceived loss of the funder may, therefore, be the disappointment regarding non-financial rewards, including intrinsic rewards (Gajda & Walton, 2013; Kuti & Madarász, 2014).

The evolution of CF is influenced by different contextual factors. According to Best *et al.* (2013), CF depends on a supportive ecosystem and enabling factors, including forward-thinking regulations, effective technological solutions, and cultures that can adapt to the new investment vehicle. However, the most important factor found in the study developed by Best *et al.* (2013) was social media penetration, particularly the use of Facebook. Also, cultural factors seemed to be significant predictors of CF. The more a culture stresses performance, the more likely CF platforms will succeed in that environment. In contrast, aversion to uncertainty, face-saving orientation, and in-group collectivism are strong negative predictors of CF success (Best *et al.*, 2013). CF platform creation varies across countries according to the size of the national population, national entrepreneurial rates, and the presence of platforms operated by incumbent financial organizations (e.g., large banks, cooperative banks, and angel networks) (Dushnitsky *et al.*, 2016).

## CROWDFUNDING, ENTREPRENEURSHIP AND REGIONAL DEVELOPMENT

The crowdfunding phenomenon is intrinsically linked to entrepreneurship and the financing of entrepreneurial activities. A comprehensive definition of entrepreneurship states that "is the manifest ability and willingness of individuals, on their own, in teams, within and outside existing organizations to perceive and create new economic opportunities (new products, new production methods, new organizational schemes and new product-market combinations), and to introduce their ideas in the market, in the face of uncertainty and other obstacles, by making decisions on location, form and the use of resources and institutions" (Wennekers & Thurik, 1999, p. 46). Regional development is seen by regional scientists as a dynamic process concerning the provision and assurance of equal opportunities as well as the sustainable economic and social well-being of individuals in areas that typically are less developed (Fischer & Nijkamp, 2009).

The socioeconomic imbalances among regions appear in all countries. The origins for the disparities are, among others, industrial structure, peripherality, regional environment and innovation (OECD, 1986). Every region has a typical economic structure as far as the sectoral composition of its economy is concerned. The industrial structure concentrated on declining industries and a failure to attract new ones leads to grave employment problems and could be a cause for the regional disparity. The geographic isolation of certain regions in respect of the economic center of the country (peripherality of a region) can handicap development prospects as above-average transport costs, capacity to gain economies of scale, obtain on-time market information and regular customer contact may be limited. The regional environment is very important for companies, managers and entrepreneurs, as a poor socioeconomic structure (transport system, education and other facilities) could be inhibiting factors. Innovation is frequently a source of formation of new ventures. Any of these factors addressed could be instrumental for the economic development of a region. However, most base their prosperity or find their disadvantage in a combination of causes.

In this light, the political concern must be to assure equality of income among individuals, as spatial disparities may indicate a misallocation of resources which reduces output for the economy as a whole. The asymmetry of income could be due to low wage levels that indicate inferior skills, education, organization or management. Also, unemployment may arise due to the deficiency in aggregate demand for goods and services or to a mismatch between the demand for and supply of labor. The environmental argument is related to the economic congestion in urban centers and the desertification of the underprivileged regions that calls for assistance. In this context, the role of entrepreneurship on regional development is to optimize the utilization of all factors of production through the creation of new firms, increasing employment and income in less developed regions. Therefore, attenuating the disparities among regions.

Previous entrepreneurship and regional development research focus on two fundamental issues. The first one investigates how regional structures or conditions influence entrepreneurship. Specifically, it focuses on whether entrepreneurship activity could be influenced by different regional/spatial contexts. The second issue focuses on how entrepreneurship contributes to regional development. Specifically, it focuses on whether entrepreneurship activity can contribute to regional well-being and development beyond the traditional measures of growth and job creation.

Past entrepreneurship studies suggest that regional social and economic conditions tend to influence new firm formation rates (Fischer & Nijkamp, 2009; Müller, 2013; 2016). For instance, a study by the OECD (1998) shows that entrepreneurial activity varies across regions within a country. Country studies by different authors found important spatial differences in economic activity in Swedish, Irish, UK and German regions, and Italian macro-regions (Müller, 2013). Malecki (1997) stresses the crucial role of social, economic, market, political and infrastructure dimensions of the entrepreneurial environment for the entrepreneurial activity. Roberts (1991) emphasizes aspects of local culture and attributes as critical to building a local environment that fosters entrepreneurship. Fischer & Nijkamp (2009) reinforces the role of culture stating that an environment in which entrepreneurship is esteemed and in which stigma does not attach to legitimate business failure will almost certainly be conducive to entrepreneurship.

In an extensive review of literature of the impact of structural conditions on entrepreneurial activity, Müller (2013; 2016) identifies four major positive structural factors: i) systemic/institutional; ii) economic; iii) social; iv) spatial/geographical. The first includes the formal role of governmental initiatives to encourage entrepreneurial activity, such as foster technical knowledge base, eliminate legal and administrative obstacles, implementation of support services. This factor also includes an informal systemic structure that endorses entrepreneurship in the local community that is characterized by a favorable public attitude towards entrepreneurship, an entrepreneurial culture that promotes risk-taking, creativity, innovation, entrepreneurial attitude and ability and dynamism, and the presence of many entrepreneurs, and new and young firms. The positive effects of economic factor include availability or presence of human capital, highly skilled/educated labor, high level of knowledge and education, access to financial capital (local banks, angel investors, seed capital) and venture capital, high household incomes, knowledge-intensive industries and a large number of small and medium-sized firms. The third factor is social structures, specifically social capital and networks. Finally, the spatial/geographical factor encompasses availability of hard and soft infrastructure, existence of regional assets/resources, attractive living conditions and natural amenities, proximity to urban centers, universities and research institutions, regional entrepreneurial dynamism and capacity/capital, role models, and a favorable environment that promotes diversity and creativity (Müller, 2013; 2016). Figure 3 summarizes the main contributions of entrepreneurship to regional development.

*Figure 3. main contributions of entrepreneurship to regional development (Author's own elaboration)*
*Source: Authors own elaboration*

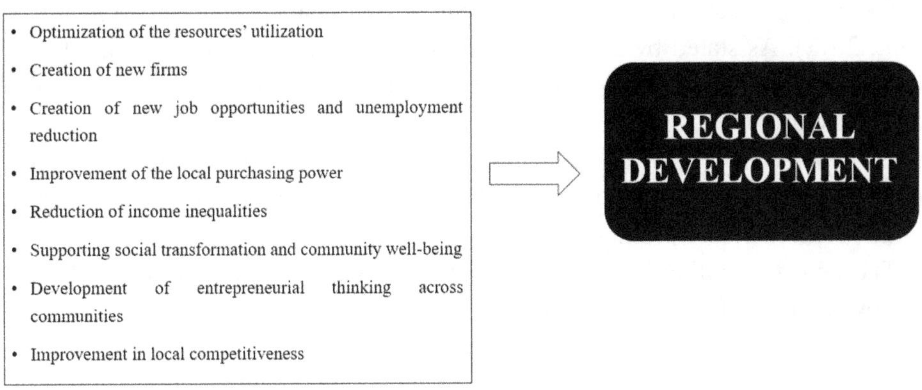


Another issue concerns the relation between entrepreneurship and regional development. There is a general consensus in the literature that entrepreneurship does have a positive impact on regional development (Fischer & Nijkamp, 2009; Dejardin & Fritsch, 2011; Müller, 2013; 2016). Audretsch and Fritsch (2002) state that small businesses are a locomotive of regional growth and employment creation. Birch (1987) reinforces this idea stressing that new and small businesses are a crucial driver for regional development and growth. As argued by Bellavitis *et al.* (2017, p.1) "entrepreneurial firms are the backbone of economies and the drivers of both economic development and employment". In the authors own words (Bellavitis *et al.*, 2017, p. 13) "entrepreneurial ventures represent important "engines" for future economic growth. However, for these ventures to form and subsequently grow, financial resources are critical".

In a synthesis of the empirical literature on the relationship between entrepreneurship and regional/economic development Müller (2013; 2016) found direct and indirect effects. The first ones relate to new job creation, employment growth and gross domestic product growth, whereas indirect effects relate, for instance, to the negative crowding-out of existing firms and competitors, resulting in closures and job losses (Müller, 2013, p. 66). The author adds some social impacts, such as social transformation, community well-being and entrepreneurial thinking (Müller, 2013; 2016).

The conjoint analysis of the CF literature and the regional conditions for entrepreneurship suggest that among many other structural factors, the availability of CF platforms, risk capital and generally well-functioning market mechanisms for allocating capital efficiently across a wide range of size, risk and return configurations is an important condition to attract entrepreneurial ventures to certain regions within a country (OECD, 1998). Recent research has also highlighted the positive role that crowdfunding might play on energizing the financial ecosystem, by fostering innovation and efficiency within the financial sector (Baumgardner *et al.*, 2017). As stated by Bellavitis *et al.* (2017, p.1), "the proliferation of new sources of entrepreneurial finance potentially makes it easier for ventures to raise capital and grow".

Further, the analysis of CF mechanisms and regional development research also supports the assertion that CF might facilitate the investment in new entrepreneurial ventures and therefore promote the growth of a region.

The study that will follow is an attempt to demonstrate the importance of CF for the development of the regions within a country, in this case, Portugal.

## METHODOLOGY

The chapter aims to study the potential of lending crowdfunding for regional development and for increasing the investment in less developed regions. Thus, the research question that emerges is to understand if lending CF supports entrepreneurship and economic development in less developed regions.

Taking into account this purpose, we have considered the following specific objectives: (i) to identify the characteristics of the organizations that have resorted to lending crowdfunding; (ii) to analyze the features of the crowdfunding operations that have been carried out in the platform; (iii) to evaluate to what extent the nature of the regions are capable of influencing the use of CF. For this purpose, we have classified the ventures in accordance with its geographical location, specifically if they are located in the littoral or interior part of the country.

Given the exploratory nature of the research, the projects posted on a specific crowdfunding platform were analyzed according to the seniority of the organization, the annual revenues, the total assets, the loan amount and period, the risk rating, the average interest rate, the number of offers per loan, the average amount per offer, the lending status and the geographical location of the project.

In our study, we have focused on lending crowdfunding, since lending-based models are more oriented to support commercial entrepreneurship. Further, lending crowdfunding is the crowdfunding type that involves a higher amount of funds, is in the stage of maturity and is part of the emerging FinTech sector (Dushnitsky *et al.*, 2016; Yu et al., 2017).

For the empirical investigation, as units of analysis we have considered the companies that have collected funds through the CF Platform Raize. Raize is the first lending crowdfunding platform in Portugal. According to its website information, through its intermediation, Raize made possible more than 800 financing operations since its creation, that provided more than 16.524.226 € to finance enterprises and involved more than 33.718 investors.

Raize works on a peer-to-peer lending system, in which an enterprise asks for a loan of a given amount. The lending offers will be made for several small investors that lend the amount they are willing to invest in the company, that could range between a minimum amount of 20€ and a maximum of 2.495€ for each company.

Raize is just an intermediary in the lending operations that transmits information between lenders and borrowers. The platform also registers the terms of execution of the loan agreement between both parts- borrowers (crowdfundees) and lenders (crowdfunders), which are freely agreed between them. Some previous analysis is made by the CF platform to ensure that the applications that go to the market comply with the eligibility conditions defined by Raize, such as not being in default in other operations in the CF platform. Based on the financial information that Raize experts have access, the crowdfundees (borrowers) are classified by its risk profile. Raize uses a 6-risk scale for classifying the companies, A, B+, B, B-, C+ and C, where the "A" grade is used to characterize companies with potentially greater financial stability. Also, the classification "SME" will be used to characterize companies of lower risk and with more than 1,5 million euros of annual revenues, and "S" (start) for companies with less than two years of activity. Notwithstanding, this rating scheme has just an informational purpose, that should be complemented by the analysis of each individual investor, in which he/she should assess the financial solvability of each enterprise he/she intend to invest.

Companies interested in getting funding could apply to the CF platform. Each application (lending operation) could range between 2.500 euros and 150.000 euros.

The period loan could vary between 6 and 60 months (more specifically, 6, 12, 18, 24, 36, 48 or 60 months). A fixed-rate loan with fixed monthly instalments is used.

When an investor decides to proceed with an offer for a given lending loan application, he/she must decide the amount he/she is willing to lend, as well as the interest rate that he/she will require to provide the funds. Then, if the enterprise accepts the investors offer, the investor will receive by e-mail the loan agreement and the amortization schedule. Notwithstanding, the loan effective implementation will be conditioned by the company's ability to complete the totality of the financing asked among other investors. Moreover, the companies that borrow the funds only will receive the financing after successfully completing its fundraising request, in an all or nothing scheme. The effective financing rate will depend exclusively on the interaction between the various investors and the company, during the financing request period.

To perform the investigation, secondary data was used, namely, a database provided by Raize, were all the lending CF operations were registered (https://www.raize.pt/). The database was accessed in September 2018 and the data were then codified in accordance with the investigation purposes (Table 1).

The investigation uses a quantitative method that is characterized by its objectivity, prediction and control, and enable the comparison and generalization of the results obtained (Eisenhardt, 1989; Vissak, 2010). Data analysis were then performed in the software IBM SPSS, version 24. Given, the exploratory nature of the research, descriptive statistics analysis techniques were used. Also, we have used correlation analysis and inferential statistical tests, specifically the Mann-Whitney test.

## RESULTS, ANALYSIS AND DISCUSSION

### Descriptive Analysis

Since the lending CF platform was launched, 812 operations were funded. From these loans, the clear majority of the operations (N=701, 86.3%) were made to projects located in the coastal regions of the country. Only a small percentage of the operations were realized in projects located in interior regions of the country (N=111, 13,7%).

The results show that organizations using lending CF differs significantly in accordance with its seniority, since about a third of these entities (34,4%) are aged less than 5 years old and about a quarter (25,2%) works for over than 15 years (Table 2). The organizations' average seniority is around 12 years old (11,8 years). We observe that the use of lending CF for very recent ventures is slightly more common in the littoral case (35,5%) than for interior regions (27.0%). The percentage of

*Table 1. Categorization of the variables*

| Variable | Code |
|---|---|
| Organization Seniority | 1. <= 5 years<br>2. <= 10 years<br>3. <= 15 years<br>4. > 15 years |
| Annual revenues | 1. < 100.000 euros<br>2. 100.000 - 350.000 euros<br>3. 350.000 – 500.000 euros<br>4. 500.000 – 1.500.000 euros<br>5. >= 1.500.0000 euros |
| Total assets | 1. < 100.000 euros<br>2. 100.000 - 350.000 euros<br>3. 350.000 – 500.000 euros<br>4. 500.000 – 1.500.000 euros<br>5. >= 1.500.0000 euros |
| Loan amount | 1. <= 10.000 euros<br>2. <= 15.000 euros<br>3. <= 25.000 euros<br>4. <= 50.000 euros<br>5. > 50.000 euros |
| Loan period | 1. <= 1 year<br>2. <= 2 years<br>3. <= 3 years<br>4. <= 4 years<br>5. > 4 years |
| Risk rating | 1. SME<br>2. A<br>3. B+<br>4. B<br>5. B-<br>6. C+<br>7. C<br>8. S<br>9. R |
| Average interest rate | 1. <= 5%<br>2. <= 7%<br>3. <= 8,5%<br>4. 4>8,5% |
| Number of offers per loan | 1. <=100<br>2. <=200<br>3. <=400<br>4. <=600<br>5. <=1.000<br>6. > 1.000 |
| Average amount per offer | 1. <= 25<br>2. <= 50<br>3. <= 100<br>4. <= 150<br>5. > 150 |
| Lending status | 1. Paid out<br>2. In regular payment<br>3. In recovery<br>4. Irrecoverable loan |

Source: Author's own elaboration

*Table 2. General characterization of the crowdfundees*

| | Total | | Littoral | | Interior | |
|---|---|---|---|---|---|---|
| | N | (%) | N | (%) | N | (%) |
| Organisations seniority | | | | | | |
| <= 5 years | 279 | 34,4% | 249 | 35,5% | 30 | 27,0% |
| <= 10 years | 206 | 25,4% | 175 | 25,0% | 31 | 27,9% |
| <= 15 years | 122 | 15,0% | 106 | 15,1% | 16 | 14,4% |
| > 15 years | 205 | 25,2% | 171 | 24,4% | 34 | 30,6% |
| Annual revenues | | | | | | |
| <100.000 | 146 | 18,0% | 124 | 17,7% | 22 | 19,8% |
| 100.000-350.000 | 370 | 45,6% | 323 | 46,1% | 47 | 42,3% |
| 350.000-500.000 | 111 | 13,7% | 93 | 13,3% | 18 | 16,2% |
| 500.000-1.500.000 | 146 | 18,0% | 130 | 18,5% | 16 | 14,4% |
| >=1.500.000 | 39 | 4,8% | 31 | 4,4% | 8 | 7,2% |
| Total Assets | | | | | | |
| <100.000 | 186 | 22,9% | 170 | 24,3% | 16 | 14,4% |
| 100.000-350.000 | 334 | 41,1% | 295 | 42,1% | 39 | 35,1% |
| 350.000-500.000 | 95 | 11,7% | 79 | 11,3% | 16 | 14,4% |
| 500.000-1.500.000 | 154 | 19,0% | 130 | 18,5% | 24 | 21,6% |
| >=1.500.000 | 43 | 5,3% | 27 | 3,9% | 16 | 14,4% |

Source: Author's own elaboration

organizations over 15 years old using lending CF as a fundraising strategy is more frequent in inner located projects (30,6%) than in the coastal ones (24.4%).

The data analysis also reveals that the organizations have a very small size, almost all of them could be considered microenterprise. In fact, as shown in Table 2, the annual revenues generated are lower than 100.000 euros (18.0%) or 350.000 euros (45.6%) for most of them. The number of organizations having annual revenues of 1.500.000 euros or more is only about 4.8%. Notwithstanding, this percentage is higher in organizations located in interior regions (7.2%) than in coastal regions (4.4%).

Likewise, the total assets of the organizations are very low. The majority have assets valued less than 100.000 euros (22.9%) or 350.000 euros (41.1%). We also observe that organizations located in the inner regions of the country tend to have a larger size (14.4% of them have total assets valued at 1.500.000 euros or more). Thus, firms located in inner regions could face more difficulties in accessing financing, although some of them have a higher size, which leads them to look for a lending CF platform.

Concerning the CF characteristics, we observe that the lending amount asked by the organizations ranged between 2.500 euros and 400.000 euros (the last one was observed in a single organization located in an interior region). Overall, the average loan amount collected through the CF platform is low, since about a quarter of the organizations have borrowed 10.000 euros or less (22.8%) and another quarter of the entities have asked less than 15.000 euros (26.1%). Only a small percentage has borrowed between 25.000 euros and 50.000 euros and a very small proportion (1.5%) have obtained a loan higher than 50.000 euros. On average, the loan period is about 2,5 years (30 months). In fact, the most common loan maturity ranged between 2 and 3 years (39.7%), followed by loans between 1 and 2 years (38.7%). The cases of low maturity loans are less frequent (loans during less than 12 months represents only 11.2% of the operations). Loans that last more than 3 years are also quite uncommon (only 2.3%). The result attained could reflect the organizations' funding needs. Another point of view might suggest some risk aversion from investors to lend for more extended periods, which leads organizations to refrain from apply funds for very long periods of time. Further, credits with a maturity of less than one year could not justify the effort required to mobilize resources through the CF platform, as the cost advantages of financing (interest rate charged) could not justify the use of CF compared to traditional funding sources.

Although the average maturity of loans is quite similar between organizations (about 30 and 26 months, respectively in coastal and inner regions), we observe that the proportion of organization that applies to short-term credits (equal or less than equal to one year) is higher in organizations located at the interior (26.1%, compared with 8.8% observed in organizations located at the littoral areas). Also, the percentage of organizations located in peripheral regions that have collected loans between 2 and 3 years is lower (29.7%) than the observed in organizations located in littoral areas (41.2%). Once again, the results suggest that firms located in the interior areas could face more significant difficulties in fundraising.

Concerning the risk ranking, we observe that the most common situation between the borrowers is rating B- (29.1%) or B (20.6%), suggesting a moderated risk profile. After that, we observe the relevance of organizations rated wit C+ (16.4%) or C (14.1%). The percentage of more secure organizations (Rating A, 2.7%), very risky organizations (R= 1.7%) or even start-ups is less frequent (S, 2.1%). Curiously, the risk profile observed in littoral and interior located organizations is not very different.

This pattern concerning the risk profile of the investors might anticipate two scenarios: the first one, where ventures with better creditworthiness could have not too much incentive to use CF, as they are able to access other more traditional financial sources, with more suitable credit conditions; the second, where more risky ventures could not be sufficiently appealing to investors, especially because they are risky and have no guarantee of return for their savings.

The average loan interest rate observed is 7,3%, which is very similar between the two types of organizations. Notwithstanding the average interest rate applied in each operation ranged between 3% and 11,2%. The percentile analysis reveals that a quarter of the borrowers were charged 6,4% or less and another quarter of the organizations was charged on average an interest rate of 8,7% or more. Although the average interest rate is quite similar in interior and littoral organizations, the frequency analysis (table 3) indicates that inner organizations benefit from lower (below 5%) and also higher interest rates (between 7% and 8.5%) than organizations that belong to coastal areas. Thus, we observe that the variability of the financing conditions that the organizations are capable of obtaining is worse in the case of organizations located in peripheral regions.

With respect to the number of offers per loan, the analysis indicates that it is quite frequent that each loan operation encompasses between 100 and 200 offers (37.1%), followed by the categories between 200 and 400 offers (24,3%) and less than 100 offers (11.2%). The percentage of loans that have received 1.000 or more offers to be completed was 10.3%. Thus, we observed that as suggested by the CF principles, the fundraising is generally gathered through many small contributions. In fact, most of the lenders (62.2%) have offered 100 euros or less, where the most common situation is the offers ranged between 50 and 100 euros (37.1%). The percentage of crowdfunders who lent more than 150 euros in each fundraising operation was just about 6.0%. The median value is about 91,40, which reinforces the low amount committed by each investor to CF. In addition, we observe that the number of offers per loan is slightly lower on interior located organizations (310, compared with 467 loan offers in coastal regions), as well as the average amount per offer. In fact, we observe that in inner regions it is more frequent to found offers higher than 100 euros, rather than in coastal located regions.

Finally, concerning the lending status, we observe that most of the CF operations was already paid out (26.1%) or are in a regular payment in accordance with the proposed payment schedule (72,5%). The percentage of lending operations already fully amortized is higher in interior located regions (42.3%), where only 63 loans are currently active, and where the borrower organizations regularly pay the debt service. By contrast, in coastal located organizations, the number of current regular paid loans is of 526. This result might suggest a higher dynamism of CF in some regions of the country than in others, specifically in peripheral regions where it is more difficult to attract new financing operations. Nevertheless, the percentage of entirely unrecoverable loans and loans that have already defaulted (and are in recovery programs) is higher in coastal regions (1.1% and 0.3%). Even so, it should be noted that the loan default rates are considerably low.

## Correlation Analysis

In order to have a deeper understanding of the relationship between the lending crowdfunding operations and the territory characteristics, a bivariate analysis is performed. To assess the association between both pairs of variables, we used the correlation analyses, namely the non-parametric Spearman's correlation (Table 4).

As previously suggested by descriptive analysis, we observe that there is some association between the characteristics of the territory and the use of CF as a financing mechanism. Indeed, we observe a statistically significant correlation between the location of the project and the variables organization seniority (ρ= 0,061, α=0,10), total assets (ρ=0,137, α=0,01), loan amount (ρ=-0,085, α=0,05), loan maturity (ρ= -0,118, α= 0,01), number of offers per loan (ρ= -0,119, α=0,01), average amount of each loan (ρ= 0,087, α= 0,05) and the status of the lending operation (ρ= -0,145, α= 0,01). Moreover, we observe that the location of the project is able to shape either the ventures that are more likely to access CF, as well as the characteristics of the lending operation.

Finally, the analysis shows that there is no significant association between the territory characteristics and the venture's annual revenues, risk rating and the average interest rate charged.

## Inferential Statistical Tests

The inferential statistical tests confirm that the location of the project is able to influence the type of organization that use CF to raise funds as well as the financial conditions of the completed operations. These results could be statistically generalized to all the projects displayed in the platform (Maroco, 2007).

The Mann-Whitney test (Table 5) indicate that organizations located in the interior areas have higher seniority (Mean rank=440,91) than ventures located in coastal regions (Mean rank= 401,05; Mann-Whitney U= 35.085,50, p=0,083).

Concerning the organization's size, no significant differences are found in the annual volume of revenues, whose average values are very similar, regardless of the venture location. On the contrary, the median total assets differ significantly between the two groups under analysis (Mann-Whitney U= 30.380,50, p<0,000).

Regarding the lending crowdfunding conditions, we observe that the loan amount and maturity also differ according to the location of the crowdfundee. Indeed, as correlation analysis also had suggested, we observe that ventures from littoral areas use CF to access slightly larger amounts of credit and also for longer periods of time (Mann-Whitney U= 33.546,50, p=0,015, and Mann-Whitney U= 31.706,00, p=0,001, respectively). In other words, the results indicate that organizations located in inner regions are willing to make the efforts to launch a CF campaign even for

*Table 3. General characterization of the CF operations*

| | Total | | Littoral | | Interior | |
|---|---|---|---|---|---|---|
| | N | (%) | N | (%) | N | (%) |
| **Loan amount** | | | | | | |
| <= 10.000 | 185 | 22,8% | 151 | 21,5% | 34 | 30,6% |
| <=15.000 | 212 | 26,1% | 181 | 25,8% | 31 | 27,9% |
| <= 25.000 | 293 | 36,1% | 259 | 36,9% | 34 | 30,6% |
| <= 50.000 | 110 | 13,5% | 100 | 14,3% | 10 | 9,0% |
| > 50.000 | 12 | 1,5% | 10 | 1,4% | 2 | 1,8% |
| Loan period | | | | | | |
| <= 1 year (12 months) | 91 | 11,2% | 62 | 8,8% | 29 | 26,1% |
| <= 2 year (24 months) | 314 | 38,7% | 276 | 39,4% | 38 | 34,2% |
| <= 3 year (36 months) | 322 | 39,7% | 289 | 41,2% | 33 | 29,7% |
| <= 4 year (48 months) | 66 | 8,1% | 57 | 8,1% | 9 | 8,1% |
| > 4 years (> 48 months) | 19 | 2,3% | 17 | 2,4% | 2 | 1,8% |
| Risk rating | | | | | | |
| SME | 2 | 0,2% | 2 | 0,3% | 0 | 0,0% |
| A | 22 | 2,7% | 20 | 2,9% | 2 | 1,8% |
| B+ | 106 | 13,1% | 90 | 12,9% | 16 | 14,4% |
| B | 167 | 20,6% | 155 | 22,1% | 12 | 10,8% |
| B- | 236 | 29,1% | 192 | 27,4% | 44 | 39,6% |
| C+ | 133 | 16,4% | 120 | 17,1% | 13 | 11,7% |
| C | 114 | 14,1% | 94 | 13,4% | 20 | 18,0% |
| S | 17 | 2,1% | 15 | 2,1% | 2 | 1,8% |
| R | 14 | 1,7% | 12 | 1,7% | 2 | 1,8% |
| Average interest rate | | | | | | |
| <= 5% | 51 | 6,3% | 46 | 6,6% | 5 | 4,5% |
| <= 7% | 265 | 32,6% | 229 | 32,7% | 36 | 32,4% |
| <= 8.5% | 273 | 33,6% | 232 | 33,1% | 41 | 36,9% |
| > 8.5% | 223 | 27,5% | 194 | 27,7% | 29 | 26,1% |
| Number of offers per loan | | | | | | |
| <=100 | 91 | 11,2% | 70 | 10,0% | 21 | 18,9% |
| <=200 | 301 | 37,1% | 253 | 36,1% | 48 | 43,2% |
| <=400 | 197 | 24,3% | 178 | 25,4% | 19 | 17,1% |
| <=600 | 61 | 7,5% | 52 | 7,4% | 9 | 8,1% |
| <=1.000 | 78 | 9,6% | 70 | 10,0% | 8 | 7,2% |
| >1.000 | 84 | 10,3% | 78 | 11,1% | 6 | 5,4% |
| The average amount of each loan offer | | | | | | |
| <=25 euros | 119 | 14,7% | 110 | 15,7% | 9 | 8,1% |
| <= 50 euros | 85 | 10,5% | 75 | 10,7% | 10 | 9,0% |
| <= 100 euros | 301 | 37,1% | 260 | 37,1% | 41 | 36,9% |
| <= 150 euros | 258 | 31,8% | 216 | 30,8% | 42 | 37,8% |
| > 150 euros | 49 | 6,0% | 40 | 5,7% | 9 | 8,1% |
| Lending status | | | | | | |
| Paid out | 212 | 26,1% | 165 | 23,5% | 47 | 42,3% |
| In regular payment | 589 | 72,5% | 526 | 75,0% | 63 | 56,8% |
| In recovery | 3 | 0,4% | 2 | 0,3% | 1 | 0,9% |
| Irrecoverable loan | 8 | 1,0% | 8 | 1,1% | 0 | 0,0% |

Source: Author's own elaboration

*Table 4. Correlations analysis*

| Variable | Coefficient correlation | Sig. |
|---|---|---|
| Organization seniority | 0,061* | 0,083 |
| Annual revenues | -0,001 | 0,972 |
| Total assets | 0,137*** | 0,000 |
| Loan amount | -0,085** | 0,015 |
| Loan period | -0,118*** | 0,001 |
| Risk rating | 0,039 | 0,264 |
| Average interest rate | 0,010 | 0,783 |
| Number of offers per loan | -0,119*** | 0,001 |
| Average amount per offer | 0,087** | 0,013 |
| Lending status | -0,145*** | 0,000 |

*. The result is statistically significant, for α=0.10;
**. The result is statistically significant, for α=0.05;
***. The result is statistically significant, for α=0.01;
Source: Author's own elaboration

relatively low amounts and maturities, possibly due to their greater difficulties in accessing other funding sources. Notwithstanding, the analysis indicates that the organizations did not differ significantly with respect to the risk rating (Mann-Whitney U= 36.342,00, p=0,264) and the average interest rate charged (Mann-Whitney U= 38.304,00, p=0,783).

The results show that there are some significant differences in the crowdfunders' behavior regarding the organization's location. We observe that organizations located in the interior of the country, compared to organizations located on the coast, are able to complete the fundraising campaign with a fewer number of crowdfunders involved, who offer higher amounts for each loan operation. Indeed, we observe that the number of offers per loan differs significantly (Mean rank littoral= 417,19, Mean rank interior=339,01, Mann-Whitney U= 31.414,00, p=0,001), as well as the average amount per offer (Mean rank littoral= 398,71, Mean rank interior=455,71, Mann-Whitney U= 33.443,00, p=0,013).

As the descriptive and bivariate analysis also has suggested, there are significant differences in the lending status regarding the organizations' location (Mann-Whitney U=31.533,50, p<0,000), as the percentage of paid out loans is higher in inner regions than in the littoral ones.

*Table 5. Inferential statistic tests for comparison between projects located in the coastal and interior regions*

| Variable | U de Mann-Whitney | Wilcoxon W | Z | Sig. | Groups | Mean rank | Sum of ranks |
|---|---|---|---|---|---|---|---|
| Organization seniority | 35 085,50 | 281 136,50 | -1,731 | 0,083 * | Littoral | 401,05 | 281 136,50 |
| | | | | | Interior | 440,91 | 48 941,50 |
| Annual revenues | 38 829,50 | 45 045,50 | -0,035 | 0,972 | Littoral | 406,61 | 285 032,50 |
| | | | | | Interior | 405,82 | 45 045,50 |
| Total assets | 30 380,50 | 276 431,50 | -3,893 | 0,000 *** | Littoral | 394,34 | 276 431,50 |
| | | | | | Interior | 483,30 | 53 646,50 |
| Loan amount | 33 546,50 | 39 762,50 | -2,432 | 0,015 ** | Littoral | 414,14 | 290 315,50 |
| | | | | | Interior | 358,22 | 39 762,50 |
| Loan period | 31 706,00 | 37 922,00 | -3,347 | 0,001 *** | Littoral | 416,77 | 292 156,00 |
| | | | | | Interior | 341,64 | 37 922,00 |
| Risk rating | 36 342,00 | 281 692,00 | -1,118 | 0,264 | Littoral | 402,42 | 281 692,00 |
| | | | | | Interior | 428,59 | 47 574,00 |
| Average interest rate | 38 304,00 | 284 355,00 | -0,275 | 0,783 | Littoral | 405,64 | 284 355,00 |
| | | | | | Interior | 411,92 | 45 723,00 |
| Number of offers per loan | 31 414,00 | 37 630,00 | -3,382 | 0,001 *** | Littoral | 417,19 | 292 448,00 |
| | | | | | Interior | 339,01 | 37 630,00 |
| Average amount per offer | 33 443,00 | 279 494,00 | -2,490 | 0,013 ** | Littoral | 398,71 | 279 494,00 |
| | | | | | Interior | 455,71 | 50 584,00 |
| Lending status | 31 533,50 | 37 749,50 | -4,143 | 0,000 *** | Littoral | 417,02 | 292 328,50 |
| | | | | | Interior | 340,09 | 37 749,50 |

Source: Author's own elaboration

## SOLUTIONS AND RECOMMENDATIONS

The results of the study show that lending CF might be a good option to financing Portuguese organizations located in different regions of the country. Since the launching of the platform, several organizations have used lending CF to channel financial resources for new projects, regardless of the dynamics of local investors.

The organizations that have applied to CF show different characteristics, for example, related to its location, seniority (experience) or risk profile. Even so, some patterns could be identified. Specifically, CF is more frequently used by small organizations and for ventures located in the coastal areas of the country. Organizations that have been in the market for a longer period of time and have the largest size use CF as a financial mechanism mainly if they are located in the interior regions. The impact of size is observed essentially in relation to the variable total assets.

Concerning the organization's risk profile, the study suggests that CF could be especially suitable for companies having an intermediate risk level, regardless of their location. Less risky organizations could have no interest in using CF, as they could have access to other financing sources, with more favorable financial conditions. Differently, organizations having a higher risk profile might not be sufficiently attractive for investors that participate in a CF campaign.

CF allowed the organizations to obtain financial resources of small amount of money, as underlined by the concept of CF. It should be emphasized that the vast majority of the operations involved less than 25.000 euros. Further, the results show that the loan amount is even smaller in the case of organizations located in the interior. Once again, this pattern could suggest the greater financing difficulties to which the organizations located in the interior of the country are exposed.

The investigations show that lending CF is especially suitable for intermediate maturities. Indeed, we observe that CF is used as a short-term strategy for a small percentage of organizations, and just for those ventures located in the interior regions of the country. It is also not very common to use the CF for very long periods, which may be due to investors' reluctance to allocate funds in the longer term for no collateral loans. Thus, the investigations seem to suggest that the decision to use CF as a fundraising strategy derives from an analysis of the firm financial needs, that could be shaped by the firms' location, and the efforts required to obtain funds through a CF campaign.

Also as suggested by the CF idea, the loans are achieved through the offers made by a high number of crowdfundees, that offer small amounts of money to each campaign. Here again, some regional differences are observed, as typically people who invest in companies located in inner regions commit a higher amount of money to each project and a smaller number of investors are engaged in each financing operation. The result could still be interpreted by the motivations for investment in operations and the (emotional) linkage that the investors may have with the organizations to be financed. It also might suggest that people who invest in organizations located at the interior of the country are particularly committed with the projects that they have decided to support, while in the other operations there is no such engagement.

In this case, the lending process is performed at an almost experimental basis and potentially with a high diversification of the investment portfolio. However, future investigations should investigate in more detail this result, as well as any potential herd behavior. Notwithstanding, the investigation seems to suggest that the crowd effect may be slightly more diffused in the inner regions compared with the littoral ones.

It is also worthy to mention, that although the investors' behavior could vary according to the organizations' location, the average interest rate achieved is quite similar, even though a higher variability is observed in the inner areas.

CF is a new financing instrument that could provide advantages either to crowdfundees and crowdfunders. For crowfdunders CF could be beneficial since it provides an additional funding source, that could be more flexible and cost less than traditional sources. For crowdfundees, CF could also be interesting since it could allow potential investors to have access to new opportunities for investment, to select the investment according to their risk profile and provide return on investment above the market average interest rates, at very low credit default rates.

Further, CF could positively impact the economic structural conditions for entrepreneurship, as pointed out by Müller (2013, 2016), due to the improvement of access to financial capital. CF could also have a possible impact on social structures, by facilitating the relationships between investor and entrepreneurs, and fostering networks and social capital.

Notwithstanding, the investigation shows that CF has gained a different vitality within different areas of the country and growth at different speeds, in accordance with the territory characteristics (littoral versus interior). Thus, despite the benefits that CF could have to attenuate some regional imbalances, if nothing is done by public institutions CF could even contribute to increasing the gap between regions, since the regional impacts are different in the littoral and inner territories. The geographical isolation of inner regions could even be intensified if this alternative funding mechanism is not properly communicated to future investors. In this context, it is important to raise awareness of the advantages of CF, mainly among entrepreneurs with a higher profile of risk and more willing to invest in the inner regions of the country.

## FUTURE RESEARCH DIRECTIONS

Despite the broad potential that CF represents for regional development, this new raising tool is still a largely unexplored area. This investigation allowed to make significant advances in the existing knowledge on this topic. Nevertheless, the investigation suffers from some limitations. Specifically, it is based on secondary data, has a descriptive and exploratory nature and is restricted to the Portuguese context. Moreover, the research was based only on completed CF applications.

The research deserves to be complemented by future work. Specifically, it would be worthy of study, through in-depth research, the reasons for the uneven attraction of the lending CF platform between the different regions of the country. Also, it would be interesting to study the main motivations, concerns and barriers faced by the entrepreneurs that have applied to lend platforms, as well as the profile and motivations of crowdfunding supporters (lenders).

Thus, in the future it would be important to study the extent to which the expectations of either crowdfunders or crowdfundees are equally balanced. Also, it would be interesting to assess if they intend to use CF in future campaigns and ascertain if CF is a short-term strategy that derives from an experimentation attempt, or, otherwise, if it is a financing mechanism that fulfils all the actors' needs. Also, it would be worthy to understand how the preparation of a CF campaign have been developed from the start and if the organizations with small size, that typically apply to CF, have the required abilities to perform it.

The comprehension of the role of entrepreneurs' social network in the success of a CF campaign deserves to be studied in the future. Herein, it would be interesting to study if entrepreneurs having larger social networks rely more on other fundraising sources. Further, it will be interesting to study if CF is seen by entrepreneurs as an important funding strategy, or a second-best financing option, after all the other funding applications had been refused. In the future, it would also be either worthy to study in-depth the role played by the public sector to support crowdfunding and the extent to which existing legislation is favorable to the development of the field.

## CONCLUSION

Entrepreneurship is seen as an important driver for economic development. Raising capital has also been recognized as one of the barriers to entrepreneurship, especially in less developed regions. Through the analysis of the ventures characteristics and lending operations, we aimed to assess the extent to which the existing lending CF platform in Portugal was able to contribute to regional development.

Lending CF has had significant growth in Portugal over the last few years. Since the first lending CF platform was launched in Portugal, several hundreds of financing operations and new ventures took place. The digital platform had promoted the matching between ventures that needed capital and entrepreneurs that were looking for potential investors. These investors could select the projects they are willing to invest, in accordance with its risk profile, loan maturity and the interest rate offered, as well as the amount they are ready to lend to each entrepreneur. As suggested by the crowdfunding principles, for each funding request typically were involved a large number of investors (the crowd) that commits a small number of resources to each venture.

The research showed that lending CF is used mainly by organizations of small size, with different seniority (experience) levels. CF platforms are also able to attract organization with a slightly larger size, located at inner regions due to its difficulties in obtaining funding. The financial needs of the organizations shape the CF operations characteristics, namely its maturity. The investigation also reveals that although the average costing of using CF is very similar between different regions, the variability of the rate required by crowdfunders to support the ventures is higher in more isolated regions. Moreover, the research reveals that investors could have a slightly different risk profile, in accordance with the characteristics of the territory, where supporters of inner organizations are able to provide a larger amount per loan.

The investigation suggests that the CF platform had allowed fundraising both in littoral and inner located organizations. Based on financial disintermediation, the CF platform has helped to improve the funds available to support new ventures, as well as contributing to reinforcing the institutional and economic conditions to entrepreneurship. Notwithstanding, the majority of the operations have been realized in organizations located in the coastal areas of the country which suggest that CF has achieved a different dynamism in distinct regions of the country. Thus, although CF could contribute to promoting regional development, some paradox exists since the regions where CF could have a higher impact are also those regions where CF is in a more embryonic stage. Therefore, in a worst-case scenario, if nothing has changed in the future by the public authorities in the promotion of CF these new platforms could reinforce the asymmetries in economic activity in the country.

## FUNDING INFORMATION

This research received no specific grant from any funding agency in the public, commercial, or not-for-profit sectors.

## REFERENCES

André, K., Bureau, S., Gautier, A., & Rubel, O. (2017). Beyond the Opposition Between Altruism and Self-interest: Reciprocal Giving in Reward-Based Crowdfunding. *Journal of Business Ethics, 146*(2), 313–332. doi:10.100710551-017-3652-x

Audretsch, D. B., & Fritsch, M. (1994). The geography of firm births in Germany. *Regional Studies, 28*(4), 359–359. doi:10.1080/00343409412331348326

Baumgardner, T., Neufeld, C., Huang, P., Sondhi, T., Mursalin, F., & Talha, A. (2017). Crowdfunding as a Fast-Expanding Market for the Creation of Capital and Shared Value. *Thunderbird International Business Review, 59*(1), 115–126. doi:10.1002/tie.21766

Bellavitisa, C., Filatotchev, I., Kamuriwob, D., & Vanackerd, T. (2017). Entrepreneurial finance: New frontiers of research and practice. *Venture Capital, 19*(1-2), 1–16. doi :10.1080/13691066.2016.1259733

Belleflamme, P., Lambert, T., & Schwienbacher, A. (2013). Individual crowdfunding practices. *Venture Capital, 15*(4), 313–333. doi:10.1080/13691066.2013.785151

Belleflamme, P., Lambert, T., & Schwienbacher, A. (2014). Crowdfunding: Tapping the right crowd. *Journal of Business Venturing, 29*(5), 585–609. doi:10.1016/j.jbusvent.2013.07.003

Bernardino, S., & Freitas Santos, J. (2018). Unleashing the Intelligence of Cities by Social Innovation and Civic Crowdfunding: An Exploratory Study. *International Journal of Technology and Human Interaction, 14*(2), 54–68. doi:10.4018/IJTHI.2018040104

Bernardino, S., Freitas Santos, J., & Cadima Ribeiro, J. (2016). Social Crowdfunding: A New Model for Financing Regional Development? *Journal of Urban and Regional Analysis, 8*(2), 97–115.

Best, J., Neiss, S., & Swart, R. (2013). *Scaling innovation: Crowdfunding's potential for the developing world.* Information for Development Program, The World Bank.

Birch, D. L. (1987). *Job creation in America: How our smallest companies put the most people to work.* The Free Press.

Brown, T. E., Boon, E., & Pitt, L. F. (2017). Seeking funding in order to sell: Crowdfunding as a marketing tool. *Business Horizons, 60*(2), 189–195. doi:10.1016/j.bushor.2016.11.004

Butticè, V., Colombo, M. G., & Wright, M. (2017). Serial crowdfunding, social capital, and project success. *Entrepreneurship Theory and Practice*, *41*(2), 183–207. doi:10.1111/etap.12271

Chinese Academy of Cyberspace Studies. (Ed.). (2019). *World Internet Development Report 2017*. Springer.

Cho, M., & Kim, G. (2017). A cross-cultural comparative analysis of crowdfunding projects in the United States and South Korea. *Computers in Human Behavior*, *72*, 312–320. doi:10.1016/j.chb.2017.03.013

Cruz, J. (2018). Beyond financing: Crowdfunding as an informational mechanism. *Journal of Business Venturing*, *33*(3), 371–393. doi:10.1016/j.jbusvent.2018.02.001

Dejardin, M., & Fritsch, M. (2011). Entrepreneurial dynamics and regional growth. *Small Business Economics*, *36*(4), 377–382. doi:10.100711187-009-9258-7

Dushnitsky, G., Guerini, M., Piva, E., & Rossi-Lamastra, C. (2016). Crowdfunding in Europe: Determinants of platform creation across countries. *California Management Review*, *58*(2), 44–71. doi:10.1525/cmr.2016.58.2.44

Eisenhardt, K. (1989). Building theories from case study research. *Academy of Management Review*, *14*(4), 532–550. doi:10.5465/amr.1989.4308385

European Commission. (2014). *Unleashing the potential of Crowdfunding in the European Union*. Communication from the Commission to the Parliament, the Council, the European Economic and Social Committee and the Committee of the Regions. Brussels, 27.3.2014 COM(2014) 172 final.

Fischer, M. M., & Nijkamp, P. (2009). *Entrepreneurship and regional development*. Working Paper: Serie Research Memoranda 0035. VU University Amsterdam, Faculty of Economics, Business Administration and Econometrics. Amsterdam.

Gadja, O., & Walton, J. (2013). *Review of crowdfunding for development initiatives. IMC Worldwide for Evidence on Demand*. UK Department for International Development. doi:10.12774/eod_hd061.jul2013.gadja;walton

Harrison, R. (2013). Crowdfunding and the revitalisation of the early stage risk capital market: Catalyst or chimera? *Venture Capital*, *15*(4), 283–287. doi:10.1080/13691066.2013.852331

Hu, M., Li, X., & Shi, M. (2015). Product and pricing decisions in crowdfunding. *Marketing Science*, *34*(3), 331–345. doi:10.1287/mksc.2014.0900

Joshi, M. (2018). Crowdfunding for Startups in India. *WEshkar*, *24*(1), 37–48.

Kitch, E. W. (2013). Crowdfunding and an Innovator's Access to Capital. *Geo. Mason L. Rev.*, *21*, 887.

Kuti, M., & Madarász, G. (2014). Crowdfunding. *Public Finance Quarterly*, *3*, 333–366.

Lehner, O. M., & Nicholls, A. (2014). Social finance and crowdfunding for social enterprises: A public-private case study providing legitimacy and leverage. *Venture Capital*, *16*(3), 271–286. doi:10.1080/13691066.2014.925305

Malecki, E. J. (1997). Entrepreneurs, networks, and economic development. *Advances in Entrepreneurship, Firm, Emergence, and Growth*, *3*, 57–118.

Maroco, J. (2007). Análise estatística com utilização do SPSS (3rd ed.). Lisboa: Edições Sílabo.

Mollick, E. (2014). The dynamics of crowdfunding: An exploratory study. *Journal of Business Venturing*, *29*(1), 1–16. doi:10.1016/j.jbusvent.2013.06.005

Müller, S. (2013). *Entrepreneurship and regional development: on the interplay between agency and context* (Unpublished PhD Thesis). Business and Social Sciences of Aarhus University.

Müller, S. (2016). A progress review of entrepreneurship and regional development: What are the remaining gaps? *European Planning Studies*, *24*(6), 1133–1158. doi:10.1080/09654313.2016.1154506

OECD. (1998). *Fostering entrepreneurship - the OECD jobs strategy*. OECD.

OECD. (2006). *Reestructuring the regions: analysis, policy model and prognosis*. OECD.

Paschen. (2017). Choose wisely: Crowdfunding through the stages of the startup life cycle. *Business Horizons*, *60*, 179-188.

Roberts, E. B. (1991). *Entrepreneurs in High Technology*. Oxford University Press. doi:10.1093/acprof:oso/9780195067040.001.0001

Schwienbacher, A., & Larralde, B. (2012). Crowdfunding of small entrepreneurial ventures. In D. Cumming (Ed.), *The Oxford Handbook of Entrepreneurial Finance* (pp. 369–392). Oxford University Press.

Valanciene, L., & Jegeleviciute, V. (2014). Crowdfunding for creating value: Stakeholder approach. *Procedia: Social and Behavioral Sciences*, *156*, 599–604. doi:10.1016/j.sbspro.2014.11.248

Vissak, T. (2010). Recommendations for using the case study method in international business research. *Qualitative Report, 15*(2), 370–388.

Wennekers, S., & Thurik, R. A. (1999). Linking Entrepreneurship and Economic Growth. *Small Business Economics, 13*(1), 27–55. doi:10.1023/A:1008063200484

World Bank. (2013). *Crowdfunding's Potential for the Developing World.* Finance and Private Sector Development Department.

Yu, S., Johnson, S., Lai, C., Cricelli, A., & Fleming, L. (2017). Crowdfunding and regional entrepreneurial investment: An application of the CrowdBerkeley database. *Research Policy, 46*(10), 1723–1737. doi:10.1016/j.respol.2017.07.008

## ADDITIONAL READING

Giudici, G., Guerini, M., & Rossi-Lamastra, C. (2018). Reward-based crowdfunding of entrepreneurial projects: The effect of local altruism and localized social capital on proponents' success. *Small Business Economics, 50*(2), 307–324. doi:10.100711187-016-9830-x

Lenz, R. (2016). Peer-to-Peer Lending: Opportunities and Risks. *European Journal of Risk Regulation, 7*(4), 688–700. doi:10.1017/S1867299X00010126

Vassalo, W. (2016). *Crowdfunding for Sustainable Entrepreneurship and Innovation.* IGI Global.

Wang, J. G., & Yang, J. (2016). Born to Serve the Small": Crowdfunding for SMEs. In *Financing without Bank Loans.* Springer. doi:10.1007/978-981-10-0901-3_12

Willfort, R., Weber, C., & Gajda, O. (2016). The Crowdfunding Ecosystem: Benefits and Examples of Crowdfunding Initiatives. In R. Egger, I. Gula, & D. Walcher (Eds.), *Open Tourism. Tourism on the Verge.* Springer. doi:10.1007/978-3-642-54089-9_32

## KEY TERMS AND DEFINITIONS

**Crowdfundee:** Company or venture that use crowdfunding platforms for attracting funds.

**Crowdfunder:** People that offer funds to support a crowdfunding campaign, that could or not be repaid and rewarded.

**Crowdfunding:** Fundraising operation through which an organization asks funds through an open call directly to a large number of people (the crowd), who typically contribute with small amounts.

**Crowdfunding Platforms:** Digital platforms that disseminate on their website the projects that are asking funding (crowdfundees), and collect the offers made by crowdfunders. Crowdfunding platforms also defines the rules to be used in the CF operations.

**Entrepreneurship:** Process that involves the identification and exploration of opportunities. Involves innovative models, proactiveness and risk-taking.

**Lending Crowdfunding:** Subtype of crowdfunding that encompasses small loans made by a large number of people (the crowd) directly to the company that asked fund through a call. The operation has a given maturity, to which the capital loan will be repaid, and involves a reward (interest rate) agreed between the crowdfunders and the crowdfundee in a peer-to-peer basis.

**Regional Development:** Set of activities carried out in order to reduce social and economic inequalities between developed and less developed regions.

# Chapter 4
# Crowdfunding:
## A New Type of Solidarity for the Digital Era

**Francesca Moretti**
*La Sapienza, Italy*

## ABSTRACT

*Thanks to the spread of internet technologies, there has recently been a significant upsurge of innovative forms of human cooperation. In an ecosystem characterized by unsteadiness and parceled relations, crowdfunding has quickly become one of the most popular expression of the new wave of the sharing economy philosophies. Although it is undeniable that the success of crowdfunding has increased during a dramatic financial period, characterized by a wide-ranging credit crunch, we can't interpret this phenomenon just as a fade or as a side effect of the economic crisis. However, through a multidisciplinary approach of analysis and through a qualitative explorative research it will be possible to observe what type of solidarity this system is currently promoting.*

## INTRODUCTION

Thanks to the spread of Internet technologies, there has recently been a significant upsurge of innovative forms of human cooperation. In an ecosystem characterized by unsteadiness and parceled relations, crowdfunding has quickly become one of the most popular expressions of the new wave of the sharing economy philosophies. Essentially, this alternative financing model allows people with a creative idea to pitch their project on some specific web platforms, launch an internet campaign

DOI: 10.4018/978-1-7998-3226-3.ch004

and potentially receive a large number of micro donations without the mediation of traditional credit institutions (Schwienbacher, Larralde, 2010). From 2008, platforms like Kickstarter and Indiegogo - two of the most famous web sites for *reward based crowdfunding* – have promoted a grant model that permits to a person or group in need of money to speed up the funding process by cutting a whole string of intermediaries. These platforms have popularized a model focalized on the backers, who can decide freely how much capital they want to invest, without the promise of any actual profits.

*The basic idea is always the same: instead of raising the money from a very small group of sophisticated investors, entrepreneurs try to obtain it from a large audience, where each individual will provide a very small amount.*

*(Belleflamme; Lambert; Schwienbacher, 2010, p.1)*

Like several internet services launched with the advent of the Web 2.0, even crowdfunding plays with the idea that consumers ought not to be considered as passive, instead they should be perceived as *inter-actors* (Epifani, 2007). This change of paradigm was a central turning point that has inspired the growth of multiples ventures founded on ideals of shared knowledge and collective participation (Cometto; Piol, 2013). As Francesca Comunello (2010) asserts: from the blog to the advent of the Social Network Sites, the most popular applications are the one that as a central element have the users, who can now unceasingly appropriate and influence the symbolic material provided by the media system. Thus, digital media, compared to their predecessors, appear to be more horizontal, and potentially seem to have all the features able to trigger users' participation. While observing these phenomena, the scholar Henry Jenkins (2006) has introduced the concept of *participatory culture*, in which he proposes to overcome the dualism between producers and consumers, Nowadays, these two worlds collide in an incessant collective creative process.

Consequently, the first analysts of crowdfunding were very keen on decant the disruptive potential of this system because of its ability of connecting creatives with their audience well before the project is realized.

By observing the evolution of crowdfunding, it is undeniable that this financing model has founded his initial success on the perception that it could give an actual and concrete alternative to the general credit crunch that has invested the global economy in the years after crisis of 2008. Though, it's fallacious to interpret this phenomenon just as a side effect of the crisis, in fact, crowdfunding has now become mature enough to play an increasingly important role in the capital market (Gerber; Hui; Kuo 2012; Marakkath; Attuel-Mendes, 2015).

However, what is important to underline is that crowdfunding it's not a volatile fade, instead its configuration has roots in numerous and previous experiences all of which promoted a more inclusive outlook on the credit system. Indeed, it is possible to trace a certain historical proximity between crowdfunding and microfinance (Morduch, 1999) that can be detected through some ancestors of microfinance like ROSCAs (Ardener, 1964) the *rotating savings and credit associations, and credit cooperatives*. As Attuel-Mendes underline:

*Their common trait is that the money lent comes from the crowd. Nevertheless, the main difference is that the crowd and the borrower necessarily know each other in the archaic mode. This is not the case for crowdfunding if the first circle of investors, family and friends, is overrun.*

*(Attuel-Mendes, 2016, p.4)*

Additionally, in analyzing the structuration of crowdfunding we should also refer to the Irish Loan Fund, designed by Jonathan Swift, as one of the first foundational experience. The Irish writer, during the early 1700s, planned a system which purpose was to provide small sums of money to the poor of Dublin (Hollis; Sweetman, 2004). Due to the great success of the Loan Fund, during the following years, there was an explosion of independent charitably organizations aimed at lending capital to the poor.

Another central experience that has concurred in shaping crowdfunding is the Grameen Bank conceived by the Nobel Peace Prize winner Muhammad Yunus in 1976. The main purpose of the bank was to help the local population - mainly feminine (Attuel-Mendes, 2016) - of Bangladesh and India by pledging them money without any type of collateral. Fundamentally, the system is based on the idea that it is vital to give to underprivileged people faith because they have innate entrepreneurial skills (Yunus, 1999).

Granted that the Grameen Bank and the Irish Loan Fund have similarities with crowdfunding because they seem to promote a broader conceptualization of the financing system - a conceptualization that is strongly tied to ideals of solidarity - yet, it's important to remember that in the early 2000s it was already possible to observe the harbinger of what was then established with the advent of Kickstarter and Indiegogo. The British fundraising platform JustGiving, for example, was one of the first web platforms who allowed individuals to give money to aid organization and to charitable causes (Abigail; Scharf; Smith, 2014).

Currently, the upsurge of a new wave of microcredit experiences linked with a more participative notion of the Web (Jenkins; boyd; Ito, 2015) has also led economists to actuate a more anti-utilitarian approach to finance. During the last twenty years, in fact, even economic studies are slowly shifting away from the paradigm of the *homo oeconomicus*, led solely by a rational mindset, preferring, instead, the architype of the *homo reciprocans*, more connected with his instinct and emotions.

This outlook will be beneficial to understand the more anthropological and sociological aspects of the crowdfunding system, especially in regard of the reward based model where the donation act is reciprocated exclusively through a symbolic prize.

The great popularization of reward based crowdfunding has led many to believe that we are witnessing the growth of a digitalized and postmodern gift culture and that crowdfunding is the emblem of this movement. In the next pages, it will be possible to address if those assumptions are substantiated by the experience of the people involved in the management of crowdfunding campaigns. This trajectory of analysis was chosen indeed, because crowdfunding studies have too often neglected the more relational traits of this phenomenon by centering the research almost exclusively on the financial and normative aspects.

## Solidarity in Complex Societies

Whereas the advent of postmodernity has unquestionably driven individuals towards some unceasing processes of differentiation and individualism, coincidentally we are now developing a different form of sociability centered on the individual, or more specifically, on the roles that he has to play from time to time (Castells; 2006). Yet, in almost paradoxical way, these tendencies have produced an environment directed by partial systems. To refer to this reality, sociologists affirm that we live in a *complex society*, highly differentiated and led by principles of autonomy, freedom and pluralism. If those ideals represent the main focus of the contemporary conscience, complex societies have ended up to satisfy the instances of partial systems, neglecting the human ones. Essentially people are not the *raison d'être* of society itself (Luhmann; 1986).

Even though, the postmodern individual is celebrated for its independence, essentially, he is at the margins of society, immerged constantly in the environment of social systems - like the media, the market and the politic - all of which have their specific codes and regulations that function in an autopoietic way. However, the more these partial systems are developed according to their functional imperatives, the clearer are the dysfunctions produced by their application. Subsequently, the more functionalistic the society become, the more pressing become the need to return to actions that connect and engage people with ideas like commonweal and more civil society (Belardinelli; 1999).

So, it is not a coincidence that with the advent of phenomenon like crowdfunding the academic debate is returned at questioning the value of solidarity. Solidarity, as recalled by Massimo Rosati (2001), has always been one of the cornerstones of classical sociology, as it is closely connected to questions concerning the social order.

This concept can be defined as a *form of social intelligence* (Rosati, 2001), a resource capable of smoothing out problems related to human coexistence. Though, once overcame the more voluntarist view - very close to the Weberian idea of brotherhood ethics (Weber, 2006) - today we prefer to bring solidarity back to the idea of *unconditional conditional*, an act that is at the junction of something charitable and obliged at the same time.

Following this logic, the rediscovery by the social sciences of the theoretical contribution provided by Marcell Mauss (1925) must be observed and connected with the growth of some new phenomena of cooperation. The French scholar had examined how in archaic societies, where the Potlach ritual was practiced, the exchange of goods could be identified as a *total social fact*, an event able to influence and determine most of the dynamics of the community. Nevertheless, this exchange, marked by the threefold obligation to give, accept and give back, had as its ultimate goal the need to create and nurture the bond between people, thus confirming the hypothesis - already expressed by Georg Simmel (1950) - that societies are form primarily by association. Indeed, according to Mauss, through a single total social fact is it possible to explain the complex of social relationships that act inside a community.

Consequently, this three-phase exchange ritual should be used as a useful hermeneutical tool to explain the emergence of social ties (Prandelli, 1998); the gift, however, it can no longer be classified as a Christian àgâpe nor can it be defined solely by logics of interest. It is, by its nature, paradoxical as it is obliged and free, interested and disinterested (Caillé, 2008). It is obligatory because the act of receiving necessarily requires a restitution, but it is good to remember that in the act of giving, there is a real risk of not being reciprocated. The exchange necessarily requires a gesture of trust and is based on the unsecured expectation of a return. Without the primitive assumption of a risk the social bond cannot be established. Hence, «the logic of giving-receiving-reciprocating is the social performer par excellence» (Rosati, 2001 p.74) on which the societies are based. To describe this form of exchange it seems central to recover the concept of *munus*, that is, of a gift that is also and above all a duty, inextricably linked to the idea of gratitude, which represents the moral memory of humanity (Simmel, 1907), whose extinction would generate the total disintegration of society.

The practical impact of the gift paradigm, in economic and political terms, has led many observers to invoke the advent of an «associative socialism, a proponent of a solidarity economy» (Rosati, 2001 p.76). Thus, starting from the theories linked to the Easterlin paradox, even economists have shown themselves to be more open to considering human behavior, no longer only according to an exclusively individualistic criterion, but characterizing it with a greater degree of complexity, capable also of take into account the aspects related to the relational sphere (Boltanski; Chiapello, 2000). Therefore, if in the classical economy goods and services had a value determined by the needs that they were able to satisfy, the introduction of paradigm of the gift necessarily implies a general rethinking of this system (Caillé, 2008). In this context, in fact, the importance of the so-called "bond value" (Aime; Cossetta, 2010) must also be contemplated: goods and services are in fact able to generate social capital. Taking into account these factors, and the paradoxical nature of the gift, influential studies have abandoned thesis like *The theory of games* (von Neumann; Morgenstern, 1944), highlighting that in moving subjects there are not, exclusively rational calculations linked to the profit and the advantages of the instrumental exchange, but also reasons connected with the pleasure of performing a service for the positive consequences that this could give to individuals. Furthermore, these motivations appear to be stronger, especially if related to activities that require particularly intense or extensive involvement. In congruence with this stance, Yochai Benkler (2011) has outlined that some phenomena of collaboration produced on-line are the signal that we ought to change the way we perceive individual behavior. From the Leviathan (Hobbes) criterion, where men are led by their egoistical nature and controlled by the invisible hand of the free market and the iron fist of the State, it is now possible to switch to the Penguin paradigm (called in this way after the logo of the crowdsourced operative system Linux), a more liberating system. This approach seems useful to explain the upsurge of grassroots cooperation experiences displayed on the Web, especially if we consider that several studies seem to emphasize the assumption that people, who are occupied in activities that require an emotional involvement, are more determined. As Pierluigi Grasselli (2008) notes, whereas happiness is conceived as *eudaimonía* - namely as the purpose of life and as the foundation of ethics - obtaining it requires a diffuse and intense structure of interpersonal relationships: it is not enough to accumulate material goods, individuals needs to take care of their spiritual needs through the use of relational goods.

It is clear, however, that in order to not fall in a fallacious discussion, academics and analysts should not promote generosity as a constitutive element of the gift culture to be contrasted with the coldness of market exchanges. As Marci (2012) points out, underestimating the paradoxical component of the gift is a risk because it may lead to an immanent and programmatic idea of the act of donation, something that can be seen as the only remedy against social disintegration. Indeed, anti-utilitarianism does not pay enough attention to the hidden side of the gift, which can be recognized by accepting that «there is never an immanent gift to oneself» (Marci, 2012). Actually, the act of gift is both internal and external to the social context: on the one hand it exceeds the social, as an event that escapes the immanence of the fact and its obligatory nature; on the other hand, however, due to its paradoxical nature, it is above the social bond. Following this perspective, Marci suggests a re-reading of Marcell Mauss's essay that goes beyond the holistic or utilitarian perspective and, at the same time, does not fall into the anti-utilitarian rhetoric. The gift, in fact, precisely because it is a total social fact, finds its foundation «in an oblige that has the same conditions of generosity and in an obligation that exist in its gratuitousness» (Marci, 2012, p.122).

In the light of these considerations, it is possible to find a frame of reference for the analysis of the numerous experiences of civil economy - characterized by a high degree of trust and reciprocity between the subjects involved - that thanks to the advent of network technologies are finding new lymph. These experiences have had the merit of bringing to light a new type of mass collaborative economy, inspired by four key principles: openness, peering, sharing and global action (Tapscott; Williams, 2007). Furthermore, the ongoing global economic, social and ecological crisis it is requiring to reconsider the existing criteria for the allocation of capital in order to drive toward a paradigmatic diversification in finance, and to create new paths for financial research (Lagoarde-Segot; Paranque, 2017).

In this sense, relatively recent experiences such as crowdfunding can be studied from a perspective that considers them as a digitalized form of *survivances* of the archaic gift paradigm enunciated by Mauss. In doing this, however, it is necessary to take into account the fact that the postmodern gift, unlike the archaic one, almost exclusively involves a type of secondary sociality, where relationships develop according to the function and abilities of individuals rather than personalization of connections. As noted by Aime and Cossetta (2010, p.29): «Technologies have broadened the potential field of relationships and community limits, therefore more and more in our society the gift is presented as a gift to strangers.» Godbout (1998) goes even further, stating that the gift among strangers - increasingly popular in digitalized societies - does not serve much to cement pre-existing bonds, but rather serves to open new networks; it goes beyond the mere concrete reciprocity (Rosati, 2001). Hence, what is realized on the Internet can be defined as an impersonal and generalized gift, a "gift without relationships" (Aime; Cossetta, 2010), as the exchange takes place between strangers united only by the common purpose of achieving a goal. This is the case, for example, of crowdsourcing or file sharing communities where connections are established between two points that do not share any kind of personal involvement. The network seems, almost in an incongruous way, to promote the diffusion and necessity of a new gift culture, without however making the act of gift as a total social fact. Not surprisingly, for Bauman (2001) those that are created online are *aesthetic communities* of short duration that revolve exclusively around a common interest or goal.

These are bonds without any type of consequences. As Marco Aime and Anna Cossetta note, the online one is, in many cases, a gift that retains its primary value but that due to the liquidity of the context in which it develops, reduces its social function, as it no longer gives itself for giving time and space to a relationship (Montesi; Grasselli, 2008).

In this framework, even though, crowdfunding is celebrated for his power to connect people on a global scale, these new forms of gift seem unable to generate social capital spendable beyond the contingent backing act. Nevertheless, people who are active on crowdfunding platforms donate without any interest in giving time and space to build a relationship (Aime; Cossetta; 2010). The act of giving money is basically framed as just another escapist and luddites action (Bogost; 2012).

## The Investors' Motivations

At this point it is necessary to focus on users' motivations in order to give a more in-depth look on the type of solidarity activate through crowdfunding. Nonetheless, it appears central to recuperate the distinction made by Ryan and Deci (1985) between actions whose motivation is intrinsic and those for which it is extrinsic. In the first case the subject evaluates an activity for its substantial value, while, instead, in the second it is taken into consideration exclusively based on the possibility of receiving something in return. When people decide to collaborate on creative projects – like in the case of crowdsourcing for the creation of artworks - it seems clear that their action seems to fall into the intrinsic motivation model of action, and more specifically this seems to be enjoyment-based (Lakhani, 2003).

The ludic aspect connected to online operations should not be underestimated (Mollick, 2013). In the early 2000s, Linus Torvalds had predicted what is now visible to everyone: what drives users to participate is the pleasure they find in combining their hobbies with an expansion of their knowledge. In this sense, the web represents for individuals a place of experimentation where practices of appropriation can be put in place. Consequently, what is it possible to observe is a general *gamification* of the participation where the purpose of collective actions is an end in itself. Csikszentmihalyi (2000) was one of the first psychologists to examine this behavior from a perspective that focused on the need of entertainment as the main motivation. The scholar came to propose the definition of a *state of flow* that occur when a person's skill matches the challenge of a task (Csikszentmihalyi, 2000). According to Lakhani, it has been possible to attest the achievement of this "state of grace" in the experience of people involved in software writing experiences. However, in more recent research a substantial overcoming of this dichotomous vision has emerged. This dualistic vision between extrinsic and intrinsic motivations, in fact, does not go beyond what are situational and environmental factors, and does not even take into account of the personal dispositions of individuals. Furthermore, he traditional theory does not have the ability to explain a wide range of behaviors implemented especially in some online contexts. Consider, for example, those who decide to share knowledge only with some specific communities and not with others, even in cases where the expectations in terms of intrinsic / extrinsic motivations are similar.

In the light of these considerations, Leonard (1999) conceives a more complex and multi-faceted picture, introducing a Self-Concept-Based perspective according to which each individual has a set of perceptions about the skills and knowledge he possesses and those he would like to have. Therefore, individuals act so as to make their ideal ego congruent with their real one. Based on this perspective of analysis, Leonard (1999) identifies the *External-Self-Concept-Motivation*, to be understood as the primary motivations that push people to undertake an activity that is congruent with the expectations of a specific group and when the success of the group is celebrated as a success of their individual skills. With regard to this type of motivation, it is important to emphasize that the individual identification in the values of a group influences the decision to share competences. Chiu, Hsu and Wang (2006) also highlight how this positive association between identification and activity of knowledge sharing, is strongly present in virtual communities. Yet Leonard (1999) also identifies an *Internal-Self-Concept-Motivation* to be understood as a force that guides the subjects to undertake an action that reflects their personal standards. In this case, when you receive a positive feedback, you will likely repeat that action. This type of motivation is essential to induce individuals to participate in virtual communities based on shared knowledge (Yang; Lai, 2010).

What is important to clarify are the motivations that push users to donate their money to projects launched on crowdfunding platforms. The extrinsic and social aspects of crowdfunding actions have been explored in the literature (Allison et al., 2015; Bretschneider, Leimeister, 2017; Choy and Schlagwein, 2016; Gleasure and Feller, 2016). The framework to which reference is the one that involve solidarity actions, however, if we look more in-depth is it clear that the backing act perpetrated trough crowdfunding platforms should not be solely observed through the solidarity lens of analysis. As Mollick (2013) and Belleflamme (2012) underline: crowdfunding differs from other methods of funding because the relationship between backers and fundraisers varies by context and the nature of the funding effort. However, it is important to remind that many times, these contexts intersect as crowdfunding campaigns may allow funders to achieve several different goals simultaneously (Mollick, 2013).

Whilst regular investors are mostly motivated by a combination of intrinsic, social and monetary motives (Collins; Pierrakis, 2012), it's interesting to notice that especially in the case of reward based crowdfunding, backers are driven by non-financial intrinsic and individual motives (Bagheri; Chitsazan; Ebrahimi, 2019).

*Table 1 The goals of funders according to Mollick (2013)*

| | |
|---|---|
| HUMANITARIAN/ART PROJECT | In this context, funders can be identified as philanthropists, who expect no direct return for their donations |
| **LENDING MODEL** | With this model, funds are offered as a loan, with the expectation of some rate of return on the capital invested |
| **MICROFINANCED LOANS** | Like in the case of reward based crowdfunding, the giver may be more interested in the social good promoted by the venture than any return generated by the loan, thus including patronage model elements as well. |
| **EQUITY CROWDFUNDING** | Shares of future profits or royalties; a portion of returns for a future planned public offering or acquisition; or a share of a real estate investment, among other options |

Gerber, Hui and Kuo (2012) link the conduct of the backers of rewards base crowdfunding to three different motivations: the first concerns the possibility of receiving a reward, like a product or a service offered in exchange for the donation. In this case, investors behave just like consumers, with very specific expectations about the products they will receive. The second, instead, concerns the possibility of supporting projects that reflect one's own value system or, alternatively, creators who belong to our smallest circle and who share with us the same outlook of the world. Individuals, therefore, seem motivated to support projects in which they recognize themselves, creating a *long tail* (Anderson, 2006) effect on the market.

The last reason that seems to push people to donate money for crowdfunding projects seems to be the possibility of joining a community and collaborating with it openly, giving life to an «uplifting force» (Gerber, et al., 2012).

In conclusion, we can affirm that programming, uniting one's knowledge with those possessed by others and donating money for crowdfunding campaigns are then revealed to be activities that once again focus on the human's need for connection with others.

## The Research Question About Crowdfunding

In order to explore the social qualities of crowdfunding it is central to bring out the experiences of those who have decided to use reward based crowdfunding to finance their project. Therefore, the research will be primarily focused on comprehend if crowdfunding can be considered a form of solidarity typical of complex societies and what kind of relations it is possible to form through this financial instrument.

Is it possible to hypnotize that, beyond the financial goal, crowdfunding is able to produce social capital?

In the next pages, in order to address these pending questions, the research will bring to the light the experience of twelve selected individuals who, in the latest two years, have launched a campaign on one of the following crowdfunding platforms: Cinecrowd; CroFun; Indiegogo; Kickstarter; Produzioni dal Basso; Ulule.). However, the aim of this research it is not to take in account all of the features of the projects, instead, it will be central to produce some consideration on how the crowdfunding system is structured in regard of the gift culture and if the current configuration can be sustainable in the years to come.

## The Methodology

After several considerations, it was decided that qualitative methodology was the most suitable for the developments of the study. In fact, the main purpose of the whole research is to bring out interviewees' ways to define the world through their perceptions, opinions and motivations (Gianturco, 2004). Qualitative methodology appears to be very effective because it makes possible for the researcher to read reality through the eyes of the subjects of the study. Hence, the use of this methodology involves: qualitative information gathering procedures, the absence of purely statistics data, a narrow number of interviewees and the use of informal practices of analysis. Among the many techniques, the most suitable appeared to be the semi-structured interview. Indeed, the aim of the study is to stimulate the productions of a chronicle by the respondents, a narrative able to highlight their view on the whole crowdfunding phenomenon.

Nevertheless, the researcher has a key responsibility: he/she ought to absolve almost a maieutic role; in fact, not only does he/she has to understand the background environment but he/she also needs to display empathy and capitalize on the tacit knowledge.

Therefore, the subjects of the interviews were a selected number of individuals that, in the last two years, had launched a crowdfunding project on the platforms available in their region.

For the selection of the subjects to be involved during the research it was initially decided to proceed with a platforms analysis. After an in-depth study phase the choice was narrowed on the following platforms: Kickstarter (USA) and Indigogo (USA), CroFun (Belgium), Hello Crowd! (Belgium), Cinecrowd (Netherlands) and Produzioni dal Basso (Italy). This preference was primarily dictated by the desire to select a heterogeneous sample of platforms that not only differed in terms of regulation and business model, but also operated in European and non-European contexts, in order to map the crowdfunding phenomenon without necessarily refer to a single specific reality. During the first phase, therefore, an analysis was conducted to evaluate both the structuring of the sites and the type of campaigns present on the platforms. Although some of these platforms allow the selection among various crowdfunding models, it was decided in advance to consider only reward based campaigns aimed at the production of a cultural asset. The choice was made because these category of projects is the only available in all of the platforms selected and it is very popular both in the European and American context.

For the project selection, the strategy was not designed at examining the type of fundraiser (age; sex; profession; level of education) but rather it was aimed at assessing the intrinsic properties of the campaign. So firstly, it was decided to involve in the research only reward based project active for maximum a week from the start of the monitoring[1]. Additionally, in order to have a heterogeneous sample it was decided to include both *You'll get all* and *All or nothing* campaign.

Between September 2017 and May 2018, almost sixty fundraisers were consulted but, unfortunately, it was immediately necessary to deal with obvious difficulties: most of the fundraisers interviewed have refused to participate in the study, citing the lack of free time due to the stressful campaign management. It is worth noting, however, that some creatives would have accepted to participate only in the face of a monetary donation by the researcher or in exchange for available contacts to support the campaign. Obviously, this solution was not considered neither ethical nor opportune.

Between October 2017 and July 2018, the semi-structured interviews[2] were administered to twelve fundraisers; these were made either face to face and through video calls, using Microsoft's Skype. After a careful transcription of the interviews, in order to proceed with the hermeneutical analysis, all the texts have been analyzed and categorized. Following a careful re-reading of the transcripts, the most significant excerpts were selected and commented, highlighting some considerations in regard of the current crowdfunding configuration and the type of solidarity produced by this system.

As it will come out from the analysis, the fundraisers selected have proved to be authentic key informant because, in the course of the interviews, they were able to provide a great number of insight about the crowdfunding mechanisms.

## The Platforms

The platforms taken in account for the research are Cinecrowd (Netherlands); CroFun (Belgium); Hello Crowd! (Belgium); Indiegogo (Usa); Kickstarter (Usa); Produzioni dal Basso (Italy). From the analysis produced it emerged that the *all or nothing model*[3] is - despite the obvious difficulties that entails this choice - still very popular. However, it is worth highlighting that, with the exception of Cinecrowd,

*Table 2. Comparison between crowdfuniding platforms*

| | Country | All or nothing | You'll get all | Donation | Generalist platform | Specialized platform | Success fee | Languages available on the platform |
|---|---|---|---|---|---|---|---|---|
| **Cinecrowd** | Netherlands | • | | | | • | 10% | EN/NDR/FR |
| **Crofun** | Belgium | • | • | | • | | 4% | EN/NDR/FR |
| **Hello Crowd!** | Belgium | • | | | • | | 8.07% | EN/NDR/FR |
| **Indiegogo** | USA | • | • | • | • | | 4% | EN |
| **Kickstarter** | USA | • | | | • | | 5% | EN |
| **Produzioni dal basso** | Italia | • | • | • | • | | 5% | IT/EN |

European platforms seem to prefer a hybrid configuration which, just like in the case of Indiegogo, delegates completely the choice of the model at the will of the fundraiser. Furthermore, it is interesting to note that most of the platforms analyzed can be classified as generalist, because they accept various categories of projects.

Though, Cinecrowd stands out from the others: the Dutch site, in fact, it is not only the only one among Europeans to apply the model proposed by Kickstarter, but it is also the only platform specialized exclusively in financing audiovisual projects. If on the one hand Cinecrowd can ensure an expertise and a network of contacts active in the Dutch entertainment industry, on the other hand it is evident that the high taxation applied in case of success - equal to 10% on the total collected - represents a clear disadvantage for fundraisers. In general, the success fee applied by the platforms is between 5% and 4% and this variable can strongly affect the choice made by the creators.

In conclusion, it seems necessary to underline that exclusively Kickstarter and Indiegogo are platforms with an international vocation; European competitors are actually more designed according to a distinctly local logic, even though they accept international donations. Fundraisers, for example, in the case of Produzioni dal Basso or Hello Crowd!, must prove that they have a bank account open in Italy or in Belgium in order to launch their campaigns on the websites. Additionally, is it possible to hypothesize that for European creators is easier to rely on national options rather than foreign ones mostly because of a simple reason: language. It is clear that for a fundraiser, Italian or Belgian, it is very important to facilitate the actions of their givers, making them operate on a site written in their mother tongue. Therefore, although we are not in possession of data that confirm this hypothesis, we can still infer from this analysis that true competition between platforms is played almost entirely on the national territory rather than on the international one.

## The Analysis of the Interviews

In order to put the interviewees at ease, it was decided in a preliminary way to start the conversation by stimulating the subjects to disclose the theme of their project. Most of them responded by showing strong enthusiasm and pride in their work. Since the first interview the researcher has decided to not intervene in this initial phase, in order to give to the interviewees the opportunity to express themselves freely, without the anxiety of having to give a "right" answer. It is, in fact, necessary to point out that during the initial phase of contact with the researcher, it was evident that some of the fundraisers had the distinct fear of being misjudged. This attitude occurred especially in cases where the campaign failed[4].

Also during this preliminary phase, it was decided to drive the respondents to talk about their role both in the realization of their project and for the crowdfunding campaign. This approach has allowed the emersion of a thought-provoking point: the majority of the interviewees had to cover more than one role - both during the campaign and in the actual creation of the artistic product. This datum should not be surprising and it is strictly connected with the fact that respondents use a vocabulary that denote a state of stress:

*«I really felt I was going constantly, like, on some kind of stress because I felt it is a part time job if you want to do it. »*

Although with varying degrees, all respondents have revealed a certain level of fatigue related to the management of their campaign. It is therefore possible to deduce that for fundraisers the choice of crowdfunding cannot be interpreted as a playful act. However, the motivation of the fundraisers - despite the obvious need of capital – seems to be justified by the strong conviction that they are putting out a work of collective interest with an *inspirational* value. In these cases, the act of asking for money takes on a strong ideological features typical of civic engagement projects.

*«Themes like: persistence, performance and purpose in order to achieve your dreams. And I think it's about inspiration and I think that this is one of the greatest things that we can do to other people, to make their life meaningful.»*

At a general level and despite these first complexities emerged, it is possible to point out that the interviewees have expressed towards crowdfunding positive opinions. Their vision, sometimes utopist, seems to follow the rhetoric that defined the debate around this alternative financing system. Several times it was mentioned that crowdfunding gives a lot of freedom to creatives, thus making possible greater artistic experimentation.

It is worth noting, though, that some of the interviewees do not seem to have developed an overall vision consistent with their personal experience; an interviewee, for example, quite paradoxically with respect to the progress of his campaign, has stated that he felt the supported of a "crowd" of people.

*«You basically, literarily have a crowd behind you! We felt like we didn't do it this alone, there were people looking forward to see the results and that was nice. »*

The data provided by the same interviewee regarding his unsuccessful campaign, however, highlights a completely different reality, so these statements on crowdfunding seem quite surprising and totally detached from the experience lived by the subject. This, in fact, in addition to having covered only 22% of the monetary target, was able to receive the support of only thirty-five people who, by the same admission of the interviewee, were almost exclusively friends and relatives. Consequently, it is legitimate to hypothesize that the support received was not originated from intrinsic qualities of the project, but rather from the personal network of the fundraiser. Therefore, crowdfunding was, in this context, only a tool that facilitated the launch of supporting actions that probably would have been activated anyway in other and more direct forms.

More realistic, instead, seem to be the evaluations offered by another interviewee who interprets the grassroot financing model in a perspective that we could define as *marketing based.* In this case crowdfunding is interpreted as a means able not only to generate money, but also as a tool capable of generate awareness and connections with the audience.

*«There are always two goals in a crowdfunding campaign: getting the funding is one but really generating buzz and press and audience and conversation about your project is another»*

Through an analysis of the experiences told by the respondents, it was also possible to provide a detailed picture about the emotions and moods experienced by the fundraisers during the campaign management. The most recurrent feeling among the interviewees is a sense of shame connected to having to request money; for some this gesture was an (almost) insurmountable obstacle which on many occasions caused embarrassment and states of psychological malaise:

*«I'm a very independent person and it was very difficult for me to ask for help, especially like money, it's a very challenging thing to do, personally! [...]Because it just hard to put herself out there and ask for help, it was very hard for her to watch*

*me do that, asking family members, you know. It just raised a lot of emotional issues for various members of my family* »

Some studies of social psychology have identified the possession of money in an ambivalent way, highlighting how money makes individuals feel self-sufficient but at the same time acts on their behavior exactly like a drug (Lea; Webley, 2006). As demonstrated by the research conducted by Vohs, Mead and Goode (2006) when people are stimulated with a memory that involves money, on the one hand they claim the need to affirm and emancipate themselves, on the other hand they do not want others depend on them[5]. It is clear, however, that all of this has a certain effect also on the sense of solidarity that individuals are able to develop towards others. If receiving a request for money can create a certain level of uneasiness associated with a feeling of deprivation of the personal freedom, it is good to remember that, at the same time, the act of requesting money implies a certain degree of submission (and therefore humiliation) and when this request is not accepted this can, in some cases, generate a certain degree of disappointment and resentment.

«*You kind of start feeling like a beggar because you're like, calling people and asking them for money and it's not the nicest feeling. [...] it doesn't feel nice to have to go the people and you notice that some people might just say no, which is fine but you also notice a lot of people ignoring you. And that is a horrible feeling because it feels like you are asking for money they are like: "no, who are you? Go away!"* »

In this sense, it is illustrative that in the vocabulary used by the interviewees to describe the work of the fundraiser there were plenty of expressions that denoted a state of anxiety and fear - «super scary»; «freaked out» - as well as idiomatic words or phrases that prompt feelings connected to a state of mortification like: «beggar» and «swollen some dignity». However, it is good to remember that the funding through reward / donation based crowdfunding is actually a form of gift, as it does not imply an actual return of the invested money. The act of reciprocity, typical of gift systems, is accomplished through the creation and subsequent fruition of the cultural good, beyond the symbolic rewards paid to investors. This, on closer inspection, makes the request for a donation even more problematic because what is required is a totally altruistic act, free from of any rational logic.

Nevertheless, asking money seem, for Western cultures, still a taboo, furthermore, this negative emotion seems to be amplified when money is asked for creative projects that do not have a real impact on people's lives, as in the case of philanthropic projects. In the *mare magnum* of charitable projects, why people should take an interest - and therefore donate their money - to a project that seems only the caprice of an unknown artist?

Nonetheless, whilst the feeling of shame was transversally experienced by the interviewees, it is necessary to stress on the fact that many have expressed a strong sense of gratitude towards investors. In this context, crowdfunding is defined in terms of humbling/growth experience, capable of making the artist more responsible: «Crowdfunding makes you get over with yourself».

It is interesting to note, however, that if the feeling of gratitude is expressed in terms of inner improvement, in other cases it is expressed in the explicit intention of not to take advantage of the backers' generosity. Crowdfunding is a one-time thing that if repeated might have repercussions on interpersonal relationships.

Another of the main issues that emerged during the interviews, concerns investors' motivations; as it was assumed in the previous pages, investors' motivation is a central issue in crowdfunding studies and more researches and efforts should be made in this direction. From the narrations provided by the interviewees, though, it has emerged that one of the reasons that inspired the donors is - as already underlined - the existence of a direct relationship with the fundraiser lived outside the online environment. Basically, people support a project to honor a preexistent bond. The act is not done in the name of a rational calculation, in these cases it's the sentimental sphere that comes into play:

*«Most of the donations came from people who knew me and just wanted to help and they didn't have to go like: "oh why we should give it to you while there is somebody else who is doing it"»*

Very often, according to the interviewees, friends and relatives are those who have followed the evolution of the project from the get go, they know and believe in the artistic talents of the fundraiser, they know how much passion was put into the project.

*«First of all, people I knew and they know I am busy on this project and I'm really like passionate about this project since a long time and they know I really want to make this film»*

According to the interviewees another reason that has stimulated people to donate is the topic on which the work is focused. This was generally considered as key element that has allowed the achievement of the monetary goal. Some of the fundraisers put the *emotional engagement* as the primary reason for donation. According to them, the specific topic of an artwork can actually succeed in animating and motivating people to donate precisely because it can make appeals to personal experiences of the audience.

However, it's important to underline how some of the fundraisers have decided to do a partnership with some aid organization. Essentially, all the money collected that exceeded the goal has be given to charity. The explicit intent seems to be to ennoble the act of donation through crowdfunding, charging it with a greater meaning. In this case, the financing deed had less to do with prosaic values and more with the charitable morals.

In conclusion, what is clear is that there is never a single motivation to inspire the financiers' action. What we can only infer from the words of the interviewees - in the absence of other data - is that the theme of the project has a certain weight in the backers' decision process, however, unexpectedly face to face bonds seem to have the lion's share regarding the motivations.

However, it seems quite interesting - and worthy of further studies - that influence of the parental and friendly network was influential for the European context and particularly when the campaigns had very modest monetary goal. The belief here is that there is a certain degree of correlation between the dimension of a crowdfunding campaign and the motivations that investors can adduce in supporting a project; the smaller the campaign and the greater the possibility that the donors support it by virtue of a pre-existing bond. In this case, therefore, we would like to say that backers donate in order *to maintain a relationship*.

## CONCLUSIONS

At the end of this chapter, it is essential to reflect on some points that have been focalized: first of all, it is necessary, if still needed, to emphasize that crowdfunding is a form of solidarity typical of complex societies because of its volatile and networked configuration. However, if at the beginning of this analysis the conviction was that the grassroot financing model was able to activate a type of sociality that involves individuals solely on the basis of their interests, rather than on the personalization of relationships, currently this conviction seems to lose strength. Whilst, Aime and Cossetta (2010), referring to the current online context, talk about a «gift without relationships» as the exchange takes place between strangers united only by the common purpose of achieving a goal; after have taken in account the opinion of those who have actually used crowdfunding, it is evident that the point of view of the two Italian scholars seems to be myopic and too intent on comparing this type of grassroot financing model with other forms of on-line cooperation.

Moreover, while on the one hand it is undeniable that some projects have the innate ability to take hold of a wide audience, on the other hand, instead, it is evident that in many cases the donors act because stimulated by the presence of a face to face relationship with the fundraiser. This seem to be even more central when the creative doesn't have a track record of success (Agrawal; Catalini; Goldfarb, 2011). In this case, the information asymmetries faced by family and friends are lower than those faced by other sources of capital (Hampton; Wellman, 2002). Hence, what kind of social capital is it possible to generate through crowdfunding?

Give a univocal answer to this question is quite difficult and probably the narrow dimensions of this study do not allow us to make extensive generalizations. What needs to be clearly expressed, however, is that crowdfunding in some cases seem to be more useful in order to cement a pre-existent relationship and to enlarge the network of contacts.

Furthermore, it's interesting to notice that differently from the American counterpart, in Europe crowdfunding seem to have develop a much more local vocation - also due to the absence of a single directive - and in general the platforms seem to be populated by nano-projects with much smaller monetary goal. The thesis that we want to support here is that crowdfunding in the European context, rather than activating the interest of individuals outside the fundraiser network, actually is turning out to be a valuable tool in facilitating the support from the fundraisers' closest contacts. Not surprisingly, most Italian and Belgian respondents claimed to know almost all of their financiers personally.

Therefore, in these cases, the donation through crowdfunding ought to be considered as of a *total social fact*, precisely because it can be used to consolidate interpersonal bonds (Gerber et al., 2012) built before the launch of the campaign. In this particular contingency, then, crowdfunding is, for all intents and purposes, a *survivance* of Mauss's *paradigm du don* and the act of reciprocity is expressed in the fundraiser's desire to commit himself totally to the realization of his own project.

However, as in the interpretation of Aime and Cossetta (2010), while it's true that crowdfunding is a tool capable of involving people exclusively on the basis of their own interests, what it is more problematic is the idea that in order to understand the mechanisms of this model it is essential to refer to the so-called *aesthetics communities* (Bauman, 2001). The very idea of a *bond without consequences* (Bauman; 2001) seems to be far from the actual relationship between fundraiser and financier even in the US. With crowdfunding is it possible to build relationships based on a *weak tie* (Rainie; Wellman, 2012) but the lifespan of this connection - if the campaign is wisely managed – can survive well beyond the act of donation.

At this point it is necessary to answer another key question: what is the reason that pushes people to donate? Even in this case the answer cannot be unambiguous. First of all, although the parallelism conceived by Ian Bogost (2012) between reality shows and crowdfunding is suggestive, this vision appears too critical and incapable of catching certain nuances typical of the phenomenon. Although, we do not want to negate the hypothesis that there is an aspect of gamification of the donation act, however, in the light of the interviews carried out, this seems to be an almost irrelevant component in driving the backers. This analytical approach, more suitable if used to describe crowdsourcing actions, seems to lose pace in favor of a study perspective aimed at interpreting the financiers' behavior as form of vicar support.

In light of these considerations, it is essential to say that the current configuration of crowdfunding does not seem to be actually meritocratic and not even as disruptive as it is narrated; moreover, the judgment on the actual potential of this system must deal with an apparatus not yet able to provide real guarantees for investors. These, in fact, are not protected either by the platforms - which do not undertake to check that the projects are actually put into practice, limiting their action to a rigorous phase of selection - nor to the legislator (American or European) which does not provide for any effective form of surveillance, despite the fact that crowdfunding is considered a high-risk type of investment.

In conclusion, it is clear that the original configuration of crowdfunding seems to be dead and perhaps - as we have shown in these pages - it never existed. More than ten years after the advent of Web 2.0, many of the phenomena that were born with it are experiencing a phase of downsizing and hybridization. The disenchantment that emerged regarding the potential of this financial model, however, must stimulate scholars to investigate this system in more depth, implementing a multidisciplinary analysis modality designed to question all the actors that play a central role in this system: fundraisers, backers and platforms. All this is necessary both to make this system safer and more transparent - thus facilitating the work of the legislator - and to provide a more complete picture regarding the form of relationality produced. The open questions are various and the studies on this subject seem not to have reached an effective maturity.

This research work must therefore be considered as an exploratory study and certainly the contribution provided by the interviewees, was also central in order to bring out a certain difference between the European and American contexts, which must certainly be inspected with greater care, expanding the studies' perspective also to the crowdfunding' market present in developing countries. The hope is that this type of financing - so complex and multifaceted - can in the coming years resolve all its multiple problems in order to become a more efficient solidarity system.

## REFERENCES

Abigail, Scharf, & Smith. (2014). *Online Fundraising-The Perfect Ask?* Competitive Advantage In the Global Economy (CAGE).

Afsaneh, B., Hasti, C., & Ashkan, E. (2019). Crowdfunding motivations: A focus on donors' perspectives. *Technological Forecasting and Social Change*, *146*, 218–232. doi:10.1016/j.techfore.2019.05.002

Agrawal, Christian, & Avi. (2011). *The geography of crowdfunding*. National Bureau of Economic Research.

Aidan, H., & Sweetman, A. (2004). Microfinance and famine: The Irish loan funds during the great famine. *World Development*, *32*(9), 1509–1523. doi:10.1016/j.worlddev.2004.04.002

Alain, C. (2008). *Il Terzo Paradigma: Antropologia Filosofica Del Dono*. Bollati Boringhieri.

Allison, T. H., Davis, B. C., Short, J. C., & Webb, J. W. (2015). Crowdfunding in a prosocial microlending environment: Examining the role of intrinsic versus extrinsic cues. *Entrepreneurship Theory and Practice*, *39*(1), 53–73. doi:10.1111/etap.12108

Armand, M. (2002). *Storia Della Società Dell'informazione*. Einaudi.

Armin, S., & Larralde, B. (2010). Crowdfunding of small entrepreneurial ventures. In *Handbook of entrepreneurial finance*. Oxford University Press.

Belleflamme, Lambert, & Schwienbacher. (2012). Crowdfunding: Tapping the Right Crowd. Academic Press.

Bogost, I. (2012). *Kickstarter, Crowdfunding Platform Or Reality Show?* Fast Company. Www.Fastcompany.Com/1843007/Kickstarter-Crowdfunding-Platform-Or-Reality-Show

Chiu, C.-M., Hsu, M.-H., & Wang Eric, T. G. (2006). Understanding Knowledge Sharing In Virtual Communities: An Integration Of Social Capital And Social Cognitive Theories. *Decision Support Systems*, *42*(3), 1872–1888. doi:10.1016/j.dss.2006.04.001

Chris, A. (2006). The Long Tail. *Wired*. https://Archive.Wired.Com/Wired/Archive/12.10/Tail_Pr.Html

Deci Edward, L., & Ryan Richard, M. (1985). The General Causality Orientations Scale: Self-Determination In Personality. *Journal of Research in Personality*, *19*(2), 109–134. doi:10.1016/0092-6566(85)90023-6

Deci Edward, L., & Ryan Richard, M. (2000). Self-determination theory and the facilitation of intrinsic motivation, social development, and well-being. *The American Psychologist*, *55*(1), 68–78. doi:10.1037/0003-066X.55.1.68 PMID:11392867

Don, T., & Williams, A. D. (2007). Innovation In The Age Of Mass Collaboration. *Business Week*, 1.

Ethan, M. (2013). The dynamics of crowdfunding: An exploratory study. *Journal of Business Venturing*, *29*(1), 1–16.

Francesca, C. (2010). *Networked Sociability*. Academic Press.

Geert, L. (2016). *Social Media Abyss. Critical Internet Cultures And The Force Of Negation*. Polity Press.

Georg, S. (1903), *Die Großstädte Und Das Geistesleben*. Dresden: Petermann.

George, S. (1950). *The Sociology Of Georg Simmel* (Vol. 92892). Simon and Shuster.

Gerber Elizabeth, M., & Hui, J., S., & Kuo, P.-Y. (2012). Crowdfunding: Why People Are Motivated To Post And Fund Projects On Crowdfunding Platforms. *ACM Conference On Computer Supported Cooperative Work*.

Gianturco. (2004). *L'intervista Qualitativa*. Guerini Studio.

Godbout, J. T., & Alain, C. (1998). *Il Linguaggio Del Dono*. Bollati Boringhieri.

Hampton, K., & Wellman, B. (2002). Neighboring in Netville: How the Internet supports community and social capital in a wired suburb. *City & Community*, *2*(3), 277–311.

Henry, J. (2006). *Cultura Convergente*. Apogeo.

Henry, J., Ito, M., & Boyd, D. (2015). Participatory Culture In A Networked Era: A Conversation On Youth, Learning, Commerce, And Politics. John Wiley & Sons.

Jonathan, M. (1999). The microfinance promise. *Journal of Economic Literature*, *37*(4), 1569–1614. doi:10.1257/jel.37.4.1569

Kathrine, C., & Daniel, S. (2016). Crowdsourcing for a better world. *Information Technology & People*, *29*(1), 221–247. doi:10.1108/ITP-09-2014-0215

Lakhani KarimR. (2003), *Why Hackers Do What They Do: Understanding Motivation and Effort in Free/Open Source Software Projects*. doi:10.2139srn.443040

Laurence. (2016). Crowdfunding and Crowdmicrofinance, an Evolution of Models for Entrepreneurship of the Poor. *Open Access Library Journal, 3*(12), 1.

Lea Stephen, E. G. (2006). Money As Tool, Money As Drug: The Biological Psychology Of A Strong Incentive. *Behavioral and Brain Sciences*, *29*(2), 161–209. doi:10.1017/S0140525X06009046

Lee, R., & Barry, W. (2012). *Networked: The New Social Operating System*. MIT Press.

Leonard, H., Beauvais, L., & Scholl, W. (1999). Work Motivation: The Incorporation of Self-Concept-Based Process. *Human Relations, 52*(8), 969-998.

Liam, C., & Yannis, P. (2012). *The venture crowd: crowdfunding equity investment into business*. NESTA.

Luke, B., & Eve, C. (2000). *Le Nouvel Esprit Du Capitalisme*. Gallimard.

Manuel, C. (2002). La Nascita Della Società. In *Rete*. Università Bocconi.

Marcell, M. (1925). Essai Sur Le Don. Forme Et Raison De L'échange. In *Les Sociétés*. Ristampato Da Einaudi.

Marco, A., & Anna, C. (2010). *Il Dono Al Tempo Di Internet*. Einaudi.

Massimo, R. (2001). La Solidarietà Nelle Società Complesse. In Solidarietà In Questione. Contributi Teorici E Analisi Empiriche. Meltemi.

Mihaly. (1975). *Beyond Boredom And Anxiety: Experiencing Flow In Work And Play*. San Francisco: Jossey-Bass.

Muhammad. (1999). *Banker To The Poor: Micro-Lending And The Battle Against World Poverty*. New York: Public Affairs.

Nadiya, M., & Laurence, A.-M. (2015). Can Microfinance Crowdfunding Reduce Financial Exclusion? Regulatory Issue. *International Journal of Bank Marketing*, *33*(5), 624–636. doi:10.1108/IJBM-06-2014-0080

Niklas, L. (1986). The Autopoiesis Of Social Systems. Sociocybernetic Paradoxes, 6(2), 172-192.

Pierluigi, G., & Cristina, M. (2008). *L'interpretazione Dello Spirito Del Dono*. Francoangeli.

Riccardo, P. (1998). *Le Radici Fiduciarie Del Legame Sociale*. Franco Angeli.

Rob, G., & Joseph, F. (2016). Does heart or head rule donor behaviors in charitable crowdfunding markets? *International Journal of Electronic Commerce*, *20*(4), 499–524. doi:10.1080/10864415.2016.1171975

SchwienbacherA.LarraldeB. (2010). Crowdfunding of small entrepreneurial ventures. doi:10.2139srn.1699183

Sergio, B. (1999). Individuo E Bene Comune Nella Società Complessa. *Acta Philosophica*, *8*, 7–22.

Shirley, A. (1964). The comparative study of rotating credit associations. *The Journal of the Royal Anthropological Institute of Great Britain and Ireland*, *94*(2), 201–229. doi:10.2307/2844382

Sørensen Inge, E. (2015). Go Crowdfund Yourself: Some Unintended Consequences Of Crowdfunding For Documentary Film And Industry In The UK. In Moneylab Reader, An Intervention In Digital Economy. Institute Of Network Cultures.

Stefano, E. (2007). *Appunti Sul Rapporto Tra Media E Reti*. Http://Blogstefanoepifani. It

Teresa, C. M., & Piol, A. (2013). Tech and the city Startup a New York un modello per l'Italia. Guerini e associate.

Thomas & Bernard. (2017). *Sustainability and the reconstruction of academic finance*. Academic Press.

Tito, M. (2012). *Il Circolo Della Gratuità – Il Paradosso Del Dono E La Reciprocità Sociale*. Tangram Edizioni Scientifiche.

Kitchens & Torrence. (2012). The JOBS Act-crowdfunding and beyond. *Economic Development Journal, 11*(4), 42.

Ulrich, B., & Leimeister, J. M. (2017). Not just an ego-trip: Exploring backers' motivation for funding in incentive-based crowdfunding. *The Journal of Strategic Information Systems*, *26*(4), 246–260. doi:10.1016/j.jsis.2017.02.002

Vohs Kathleen, D., Mead Nicole, L., & Goode Miranda, R. (2006). *The Psychological Consequences Of Money. Science*, *314*(5802), 1154–1156. PMID:17110581

von Neumann & Oskar. (1944). *Theory Of Games And Economic Behavior*. Princeton University Press.

Weber, M. (2006). *Considerazioni Intermedie. Il Destino Dell'occidente*. Armando Editore.

Yang & Lai. (2010). Motivations Of Wikipedia Content Contributors. *Computers in Human Behavior*, *26*(6), 1377–1383.

Yochai, B. (2007). *La Ricchezza Della Rete: La Produzione Sociale Trasforma Il Mercato E Aumenta Le Libertà*. Egea.

Yochai, B. (2011). *The Penguin And The Leviathan: How Cooperation Triumphs Over Self-Interest*. Crown Business.

Zygmunt, B. (2000). *Liquid Modernity*. Polity Press.

Zygmunt, B. (2001). Community. Seeking Safety. In *An Insecure World*. Polity Press.

## ENDNOTES

1. 10 september 2017
2. An interview outline was formulated and was tested in the spring of 2017 with a pilot interview.
3. Reward based crowdfunding follow two different models: *All or nothing*, where the fundraiser sets a monetary goal and keeps nothing unless the goal is achieved and the *You'll get all*, where the fundraiser keeps the entire amount raised regardless of whether or not they meet their initial goal.
4. Of all the ten campaigns, only six of them has reached the monetary goal.
5. Cfr. Vohs Kathleen D., Mead Nicole L., Goode Miranda R. (2006), *The psychological consequences of money*, in science 314.5802: 1154-1156.

# Chapter 5
# Crowdfunding Platforms Dynamics:
## When Local Connections Matter

**Amaya Erro-Garcés**
https://orcid.org/0000-0002-1858-1363
*Public University of Navarra, Spain*

**Begoña Urien**
*Universidad de Navarra, Spain*

## ABSTRACT

*This chapter compares two national crowdfunding markets based on their platforms and regulatory legislation on crowdfunding. Spain and France were selected though a cluster analysis since both differ on those characteristics. Mean comparison tests were carried out to estimate differences. Data were based on a survey specifically designed and conducted for this research. While crowdfunding is an internet-powered activity with global accessibility, national boundaries and geographic proximity play a significant role in shaping the performance of crowdfunding platforms. Regarding practical implications, as each country developed its specific legislation, it is concluded that this legislation may boost or hinder the growth of crowdfunding. On the other hand, the different way platforms managed their business does not affect their outcomes in terms of number of projects and funds raised. As a result, although platforms are indispensable as an intermediate agent between funders and investors, they determine neither the number of projects hosted nor the funds raised.*

DOI: 10.4018/978-1-7998-3226-3.ch005

## INTRODUCTION

Over the last decade, the situation of companies to obtain capital for new projects has changed drastically due to the crisis. The lack of access to financing through banks or subsidies, the uncertainty of the return on investment, and the need for funding from the public sector reduced the possibilities of obtaining financial resources. Additionally, new firms face difficulties to access to external finance during their first years of activity, and some of them remain permanently unfunded (Chen et al. 2009; Cosh et al. 2009). According to Beck, and Demirguc-Kunt (2006), SMEs found major barriers to obtain financing through traditional channels, such as bank loans, due to a lack of solvency, and their own working background. Private capital and venture capital companies mainly finance large companies, and a very short selection of SMEs. So paradoxically, the companies that most need funding are the ones experiencing severe limitations to gain resources. In addition, financing interest rates usually are too high for them to be easily repaid.

This background drives to the increase of alternative financing methods, such as crowdfunding (Prpić 2014; Paschen 2017). Even more, according to Bellihi, and Berachid (2018), crowdfunding permit to fill the funding gap that most new ventures suffer from especially in the early stages of their lifecycle. Relatedly, two more trends are worth mentioning to better explain crowdfunding growth. Firstly, the expansion of social networks that collaborate with each other be it for profit or non-profit reasons expect to have a boom in crowdfunding in the coming years. Secondly, another important factor for entrepreneurs and SMEs to opt for this formula is the raising of capital flows without financial intermediaries.

With regard to crowdfunding management, platforms seem to play a key role and its operational understanding will be essential in the future. However, only a limited number of papers have dealt with the importance of platforms and how they work. In this context, since crowdfunding mostly happens in crowdfunding platforms (Belleflamme et al. 2015), the main contribution of this chapter is to analyze the role that crowdfunding platforms play from a comparative perspective. In so doing, this chapter focuses on crowdfunding platforms, complementing extant studies, which have mostly focused on project success on a single platform. Another contribution is that this present study analyses European platforms whereas most studies to date reported data from U. S. platforms. Finally, this chapter analyses crowdfunding platforms and the factors that drive their creation.

After designing and conducting a specific survey, this chapter presents a comparative research between Spanish and French platforms. In so doing, it enlarges the research carried out by Belleflamme et al. (2015), and Greenberg et al. (2013), offering a wider explanation of how crowdfunding platforms work by specifically analyzing number of projects, success or time. In fact, the present research compares the situation of crowdfunding in Spain and France, and suggests some recommendations in order to strengthen this financial alternative model. Previous research was mainly focused on the number of platforms, whereas this research explores additional variables such as their success and costs. Additionally, the regulation of crowdfunding in France and Spain is also compared presenting crowdfunding policies and the importance of platforms as intermediates between entrepreneurs and investors. As a result, platforms analysis could be essential in improving the situation of crowdfunding as an actual financing alternative.

The present chapter is organized as follows. In the second Section, an evolution of crowdfunding is described to show the growth of this financing tool. Several extant literature on crowdfunding is identified, and the present chapter contribution is also specified. Next section explains data and the method of research applied as well as the conducted survey. Results are shown in the fourth section and finally, conclusions and implications are also outlined.

## Theoretical Background

There are multiple definitions of crowdfunding, which textually translated means ‘mass financing’, ‘collective financing’, ‘micro collective financing’ or ‘micro-financing’ (Oxford Dictionary). As stated by the Department of Studies at the University of California (Wheat et al. 2013), crowdfunding is defined as a collective cooperation to obtain money or other resources. The Internet is usually the platform used to finance initiatives of individuals or private organizations, public or non-profit making. Along the same lines, Belleflamme, Lambert, and Schwienbacher (2013) posited that ‘crowdfunding involves an open call, mostly through the Internet, for the provision of financial resources either in the form of donation or in exchange for the future product or some form of reward to support initiatives for specific purposes’ (p. 585). In a broader sense, crowdfunding was described as pooling money from a group of people to support another´s effort to accomplish a specific goal (Bannerman 2012; Griffin 2012). To sum up, crowdfunding means mobilizing people to finance projects posted by proponents, mostly on specific websites known as crowdfunding platforms. Extant literature (Baumgarder, Neufeld, Chien-Tarng Huang, Sondhi, Carlos, and Ahmad 2015) divides crowdfunding’ business models into four: donation (funders do not receive anything in return); reward (funders receive a non-financial reward, that is, a first edition release); lending (funders receive fixed periodic income and expect repayment of the investment); and equity (funders receive compensation based on fundraiser’s revenue or profit-share). This research is based on reward crowdfunding. In fact, the reward model (both material and immaterial rewarding) is applied to differentiate types of crowdfunding.

The reward model can be divided into direct and indirect crowdfunding. In direct crowdfunding, funds move from investors to funders whereas in the indirect an intermediary is involved (Bouncket et al. 2015). Indirect crowdfunding is more common as it is difficult for funders to contact to investors without the support from an intermediary. In this context, platforms acquire a relevant role in crowdfunding markets as they connect funders and investors.

From a sociological perspective, crowdfunding contributes to spreading entrepreneurship (Aldrich 2014) and community efforts to support crowdfunding have also been analyzed (e.g., Hui et al. 2014) as crowdfunding is open to everyone (Blohm et al. 2013; Bouncket et al. 2015).

Over the last decade, many publications have addressed crowdfunding. Although it is a relatively new phenomenon, it has attracted a lot of attention. This fact has been confirmed by the large number of published papers over the last few years (Dushnitsky, Guerini, Piva, and Rossi-Lamastra 2016). Just a Google Scholar search of the term 'crowdfunding' yields to an incredible return (76,600 items). Crowdfunding started in 2008, as something small and quickly grew to an explosion of queries from 2009 to 2013, and especially in Spain since 2011 (Lehner 2014). In fact, crowdfunding has experienced an impressive growth worldwide (Belleflamme et al. 2014; Bruton et al. 2014; Short et al. 2017).

Rubinton (2011), and Mollick (2013) proposed a more academic approach in order to understand the dynamics of successful crowdfunding, and the use of crowdfunding mechanisms (Agrawal et al. 2010; Burtch et al. 2011). In order to fill in this gap, research studies on crowdfunding cover several areas such as: 1) comparison between crowdfunding models (Belleflamme et al. 2014; Dushnitsky, et al. 2016); 2) geographic origin of investors and entrepreneurs (Agrawal et al. 2011; Mollick 2014); 3) factors explaining the success of a project in a platform (Cholakova, et al. 2014; Koch et al. 2015; Ahlers et al. 2015; Vismara 2016; Steigenberger 2016; Brown et al. 2017; Josefy et al. 2017; Zhao et al. 2017; Wuillaume et al. 2018; Xu 2018); 4) moral hazards and the role played by social information as well as the length and transparency of the campaign (Ahlers et al. 2012; Chemla et al. 2016; Kuppuswamy, and Bayus 2013; Colombo et al. 2015; Courtney et al. 2016); 5) barriers to use crowdfunding platforms for certain professionals and projects (Davidson et al. 2015; Niemand et al. 2018); and 6) the use of crowdfunding in social, cultural and civic projects (Solesvik 2016; Caré et al. 2018).

With regard to the 'state of the art' of crowdfunding in Spain and France, Moreau and Nicolas (2018) described participative financing in France between 2013 and 2017, while Matthews and Vachet (2014) addressed the situation of platforms, projects, and crowdfunding environment in France. In the case of Spanish crowdfunding, Barral, and Barral (2014) studied the motivations of citizens to invest in crowdfunding projects, and Sastre-Canelas (2016) analyzed the projects promoted on Spain's leading reward crowdfunding platform called Verkami.

## The Exponential Growth of Crowdfunding

Since 2011, the number of crowdfunding platforms, the number of projects posted on these platforms, and the total capital raised through crowdfunding have grown exponentially (TheCrowdDataCenter 2018). For example, according to a study by the Indiana University Kelley School of Business (2013), since its inception Kickstarter has raised more than 370 million dollars for 72,317 projects.

According to data extracted from the Platform Crowdfunding Universe (2012), it is estimated that about 536 platforms worldwide had come into existence at the end of that year, and by the end of 2013, this figure was already approaching 600 so the progression is evident. As Massolution (2015) affirms, the total funding volume worldwide has gradually been increasing from 0.8 billion US$ in 2010, to 1.4 billion US$ in 2011, 2.5 billion US$ in 2012, and 6.1 billion US$ in 2013, and in 2014 were around 16.2 billion US$. Along the same lines, 1,470 millions of dollars in the world was collected through crowdfunding, while in 2012 that amount almost doubled to $ 2.806 billion (Universe Crowdfunding 2011). The increase continued during 2013, as the percentage doubled again, encouraged by the multiple legislations that were passed in several countries. On the other hand, the estimates of the consultant Gartner Group (2013) show that by 2020 between 30 and 35 percent of the funds invested in companies will come from individual crowdfunding investments. More recent data shows that the amount of funds raised by crowdfunding worldwide from 2014 to 2016 was $ million 2,098.56 (Statista, 2018). According to Bouncken et al. (2015), digitalization is one of the reasons that explain the development of crowdfunding, as it is mainly a web based service.

Nevertheless, the crowdfunding growth differs between countries. France has been considered the most active country in crowdfunding development (Dushnitsky et al. 2016), whereas several countries, such as Spain, follow behind these financial alternative models.

## Crowdfunding Platforms

A crowdfunding process involves three main actors: entrepreneurs who look for financing to start their businesses, investors that offer those funds and platforms, which intermediates between investors and entrepreneurs. Each entrepreneur presents projects and offers shares in the company, looks for donation or offers any other outcome. Investors select projects according to their profitability or play a donor role, helping social projects. Finally, crowdfunding platforms are motivated to generate income by connecting projects with funders. Their role in crowdfunding is essential; without their intermediation, entrepreneurs simply would not be able to contact with investors, so they would not get the financing they need. In fact, without platforms, no crowdfunding would be possible.

According to a survey conducted by Iizuka (2014), 60 percent of the crowdfunding platforms have been created in Europe. In Europe, the United Kingdom is leading the platforms market, with 2.3 billion euros collected in 2014, which represent 79 percent of the total amount collected in Europe. France, Germany, and Sweden come next with, respectively 154, 140 and 107 million euros (Wardrop et al. 2015). In 2017, these same countries were still leading the European crowdfunding market (Statista, 2017). According to this data, France raised 661 million euros whereas Spain, 160 million.

As was mentioned, only a limited number of publications have dealt with the importance of platforms and how they work. This is the case of some research published on particular platforms such as Verliyantina (2012), and Ibrahim (2012) in Indonesian platforms, or Agrawal, Catalini, and Goldfarb (2015) in the Netherlands. Additionally, other extant studies analyzed what motivates entrepreneurs to use platforms, and the behavior of founders (Davidson et al., 2015; Gerber et al. 2012). In a more specific way, Belleflamme et al. (2015) conducted a research on crowdfunding platforms, analyzing asymmetric information and external effects of crowdfunding platforms. Similarly, Lehner (2014) wrote about the types of webs 2.0 used by crowdfunding platforms and Greenberg et al. (2013) examined the exchange of resources and social interactions processes within platforms. Finally, Dushnitsky, et al. (2016), reported the role of the country as a determinant of platforms development.

In this context, this chapter enlarges the research carried out by Belleflamme et al. (2015), and Greenberg et al. (2013), offering a wider explanation of how crowdfunding platforms work by specifically analyzing number of projects, success or time. While exploring in more detail Spanish and French platform, we also complete the study of Dushnitsky et al. (2016). Lehner (2014) analyzed technological characteristics of the platforms, whereas in this case, several ways of functioning are included (e.g., commissions charged by the platform, time that the project is active in the platform). Finally, Greenberg et al. (2013) collected data from the platforms, but this chapter is based on contacting with those platforms as they filled out a survey specifically designed for this research. In completing the mentioned studies, this research contributes to a better understanding on the role that platforms play in crowdfunding markets.

Related to the supported initiatives, the classification of crowdfunding platforms (CFPs) could be categorized into three classes (Massolution 2015). The first category includes specialized platforms focused on crowdfunding services for specific industries such as video games, music recording, or independent television (Ries

2014). The second category consists of specific platforms sorted out by projects rather than the type of industry (for example, hardware development, technology, or creative projects), and general platforms. General platforms raise funding for any type of project ranging from individuals soliciting funding for a medical procedure to technology start-ups trying to develop new innovative products.

According to the European Crowdfunding Network, platforms can also be classified by the type of industry or theme they consider: cultural sector, SMEs or themes like sustainability or social entrepreneurship. Nevertheless, there are platforms that act across a wide variety of themes and industries.

The allocation of funding can also be a way to differentiate platforms. Most representative criteria in applying the classification of crowdfunding platforms are based on how funds are allocated and the type of initiatives being supported. With regard to how funds are allocated, Cumming, Leboeuf, and Schwienbacher (2014) divided crowdfunding platforms into two categories. 'All-or-Nothing' (AON) type, disburses funding only if the funding threshold set in advance is either met or surpassed within the funding period. Eventually, if the project does not meet its threshold, investors are reimbursed and the project ended. In contrast, the "Keep it all" type (KIA) transfers all the raised funds to the project regardless of whether the capital-raising goal is met. In general, this kind of projects are less successful since they could start even though they are underfunded.

Finally, costs charged can also be a criteria for classifying platforms, depending on when, how much and who will have to pay. According to Belleflamme et al. (2015), platforms charge fees corresponding to mission cost, bank fees, communication fees, etc.

Crowdfunding success cannot be understood without the Internet and its impact on the drastic reduction in transaction costs contributing to directly connecting funders with founders without any intermediary (Wilson, and Testoni 2014). Although platforms are available to the global market, some scholars insist on the importance of the geographical proximity between the project and the investors (Agrawal et al. 2011; Mollick 2014). Nevertheless, as platforms are on the Internet, and so open to a global market, French and Spanish platforms could theoretically compete for projects. Competition among platforms and the market of crowdfunding are studied by Rochet and Tirole (2016) or Reisinger (2014). In fact, fees can be determined by the competition among platforms and the Internet facilitates this competition.

Keeping these statements in mind, no significant differences between French and Spanish prices in crowdfunding platforms should be expected. Along the same lines, there should not be significant differences with regard to the commissions those platforms charge.

H1. There are no differences with regard to commission fees in both French and Spanish platforms, beyond the ones related to the general standard of living.

Assuming that success in search for funding depends on several variables such as project quality, return on investment, or particular preferences of the investor (Ross 1978), no significant differences in success could be expected. Even more, in line with the previous hypothesis, competition among platforms forces the existence of no difference among platforms success; otherwise, most funders would participate in the most successful platform. Along this line, Reisinger (2014) affirmed that funders have no information on the success probability of their campaigns.

Lastly, as it was previously mentioned, several scholars analysed the factors that explain the success of a project in a platform. They assumed this success depends on projects´ characteristics, rather than in the performance of the platform (Cholakova, et al. 2014; Koch et al. 2015; Ahlers et al. 2015; Vismara 2016; Steigenberger 2016; Brown et al. 2017; Josefy et al. 2017; Zhao et al. 2017; Wuillaume et al. 2018; Xu 2018).

Because of these reasons, we assume there are not differences in success between both countries, as platforms compete in an international framework.

H2. There should not be any significant differences with regard to success between French and Spanish platforms.

According to Li, and Duan (2014), most funds are collected in a funding in a given time period. For that reason, crowdfunding platforms limit the days a campaign is active in their webs. Once again, as platforms competition is international, there should be no differences among platforms in the duration of the campaign. In addition, there is no reason to assume that country's location could be related to the time a project is on one particular platform. Consequently, no differences in campaigning days are expected between Spanish and French platforms.

H3. Campaigning days should be similar in both countries since this variable is important to raise funds within a time framework.

In the same line, the maximum time a project is maintained in a platform is expected to be similar in France and Spain. Therefore, the days a campaign is active on the platforms should be similar in both countries. Relatedly, platforms management could be similar in both countries since projects deadlines could help to get the necessary amount of money within a reasonable period of time. It is assumed that the longer the period the project is available on the platform, the higher the funds it would be able to obtain, up to one point in which no further funds are going to be raised. As was mentioned, platforms should be similar, as they act on the Internet.

H4. Limited time should be similar in both countries since this variable is important to raise funds within a time framework.

## Regulation Differences

Within the European Union, there is no common regulation on this subject[1]. Consequently, each European country has developed its own regulations. Nevertheless, in recent years there have been legal developments at European level too[2]. Different rules that are already in force in each country do not facilitate a specific and unique legislation. This fact generates a legal uncertainty that could be an added difficulty for the growth and development of this sector.

Although figures of crowdfunding financing are already relevant, there is no coherent legislative framework related to all types of crowdfunding in Spain. In 2015 a new law on the promotion of business financing was released, regulating the operation of participatory financing platforms in Spain (Law 5/2015, April 27th on promoting business financing). However, not all types of crowdfunding were included in this new law. This regulation established a specific legal framework for crowdfunding related to loans, bonds or equity financing. As was mentioned, these platforms are now under the authorization, supervision, inspection, and sanction of the National Securities Market Commission (CNMV), and have to comply with certain administrative and financial requirements to be allowed to operate as participatory financing platforms. Among these requirements, several measures could be mentioned, such as the obligation to have a minimum paid-in capital of 60,000 €, or to have civil liability insurance with a minimum coverage of 300,000 € for damages and 400,000 € in total. When the financing sum obtained by the platform over a 12 month period exceeds two million euros, the minimum own resources required will become 120,000 €. If the total collected over the last year exceeds five million euros, the required own resources will increase by 0.2 percent of that amount. If the total revenue exceeds 50 million euros, the required amount of own resources will increase 0.1 percent. In any case, the total quantity required may be greater than two million euros (Law 5/2015, April 27th on promoting business financing).

Additionally, crowdfunding platforms must include mandatory information on their websites. This information should include basic requirements, such as the risks involved in participating in loans or underwriting shares, the risk of partial or total loss of the invested capital, or the risks of not obtaining the expected returns, as well as other information on procedures, rates and other aspects. All this information is set forth in article 61 of title V of the above-mentioned law. Moreover, and according to this law, such platforms must only participate in projects published on their platform without exceeding 10 percent of the funding objective of each project, while they are not allowed to participate in projects uploaded on other platforms. Finally, these platforms have to set a funding objective and a deadline for participation in each project, which can be exceeded by 25 percent.

With regard to individuals or companies submitting their projects to the platforms, there are some limitations established by the law. The promoters will be responsible for the information they provide to the investors through the platform. On the other hand, the law also establishes limitations for investors. Firstly, the law establishes two types of investors: accredited and non-accredited[3].

In fact, after the analysis of the above-mentioned law, it seems that Spanish government adopted an over-protectionist stance, establishing excessively low investment limits that could be detrimental to experienced investors, for fear that small investors could lose their money.

In 2014, French government approved the regulation number 2014-559. In this law, different measures are included depending on the platforms offering crowdfunding operations of loan or equity. In the first case, an official registration is created for those platforms that are not managed by banks or investment companies. The registration should be in written form and this contract imposes limits for both the applicant and the investor. More specifically, the issuer may not raise more than one million euros per project and the investor acquires the obligation of not contributing with an amount higher than 1,000 euros per project, expandable to 4,000 in the case of loans without interest.

As a result, the established limits are inferior if they are compared with the Spanish case, which, as we have mentioned, established a maximum funding per project of two million euros (expandable to five million for exclusively accredited investors), and a limit for investors of 3,000 euros per project. Similarly, an official register was also created for those participative crowdfunding platforms that are not managed by banks or investment companies, In addition, some limits were imposed on the issuer of one million euros each 12 months. However, no limits were set for the investor. Another important aspect is that the platforms do not require a minimum capital for their constitution as they do in Spain.

In fact, France has developed crowdfunding since 2004. First French regulation on crowdfunding was published in 2014, whereas Spanish regulations were released in 2015. In the case of Spain, regulation placed different restrictions to invest in crowdfunding, creating legal limitations to crowdfunding projects (for example, an authorization is required for equity-based and lending-based models; European Crowdfunding Network AISB, and Clarke 2017). There are less restrictions in France and other European countries, although most countries limit crowdfunding through regulation. As a result, it could be assumed that French projects collect more funds due to an earlier regulation and less legal restrictions.

H5. Funds obtained by French platforms are higher than funds raised by Spanish platforms.

Related to hypothesis 5, since in France platforms have been in use for a longer period compared to Spain, they would have also had more time to manage projects than the Spanish counterparts. So, based on both time of development and legislation, French entrepreneurs could be more used to search for funds through crowdfunding platforms than their Spanish counterparts.

H6. French platforms manage more crowdfunding projects than their Spanish counterparts.

## Data and Analysis

The present research is based on a survey conducted on Spanish and French platforms that operate with reward crowdfunding. Data was collected from the researchers between 2015 and 2016. Firstly, a survey was specifically designed for this study. Meanwhile, databases from platforms were gathered. To have a direct access to platforms, a member of the research team was located in Paris and another in Spain. The survey was creating using Google tools and was sent by email to all the platforms in each country. This method simplifies the empirical data gathering, although phone contacts were also required in most cases as was stated earlier. Even more, in so doing, legitimacy of data is covered and sample biases are omitted as the research team did not choose a sample of platforms; all platforms received the described survey.

Secondly, platforms were contacted by phone. From these locations, the French researcher phoned to the French platforms whereas the Spanish researcher did it for the platforms from Spain. Both Spanish and French surveys included the same items in order to allow further comparisons between these countries.

The mentioned survey included several items related to the operations of the platforms. The quantity of funds received by the project refers to the funds each platform collects ("*What is the average of funds obtained for a project?*"). The days of campaign indicate the time the project is on the platform ("*What is the average length of a crowdfunding campaign on your platform?*") whereas the limited time shows if there is a maximum time allowed in days to obtain the financing ("*Is there a limit of time for getting the money?*") and time shows this length ("*If there is a limit of time, what is that time limit?*"). Commissions reflect the cost of financing

(*"What is the percentage of the average commission compared to the total funds collected?"*). Finally, the survey ask for the number of projects received per platform (*"How many project applications do you receive each month?"*) and its success (*"What level of acceptance of projects do you have on your platform?"*).

## Description of the Data Used

According to the Crowdacy platform´s census, from the 95 Spanish platforms, only 62 of them are currently active. After sending the survey to these 62 platforms, 32 replies were obtained. As, initially, the process of collecting these replies was complicated, this process was completed by telephone contacts. Finally, a higher participation was achieved, with a response rate of 51.6 percent from the Spanish platforms. Table 1 depicts the descriptive statistics from Spanish data.

*Table 1.* **Descriptive Statistics. Spanish Platforms.**

| | Number | *Min.* | *Max.* | *Mean* | *S.D.* | *Variance* | *Asymmetry* | | *Kurtosis* | |
|---|---|---|---|---|---|---|---|---|---|---|
| | | | | | | | *Statistic* | *Standard error* | *Statistic* | *Standard error* |
| Quantity of funds received by the project | 30 | 1 | 5 | 2.13 | 1.04 | 1.08 | 1.09 | .42 | .94 | .83 |
| Days_campaigne | 2 | 1 | 1 | 1 | .00 | .00 | . | . | . | . |
| Commission | 31 | 1 | 4 | 1.87 | .85 | .71 | .61 | .42 | -.37 | .82 |
| Limited_time | 32 | 1 | 2 | 1.03 | .17 | .03 | 5.65 | .41 | 32 | .80 |
| Time | 16 | 45 | 90 | 67.50 | 16.43 | 27 | .52 | .56 | -1.21 | 1.09 |
| Number_of_ projects | 24 | 2 | 300 | 68 | 74.81 | 5596.87 | 1.95 | .47 | 3.28 | .91 |
| Types of crowdfunding | 31 | 1 | 4 | 2.06 | 1.06 | 1.13 | nd | nd | nd | nd |
| Success | 27 | .20 | 1 | .76 | .21 | .04 | -1.77 | .44 | 2.72 | .87 |

With regard to France, 54 out of 125 platforms participated in the empirical data collection. Similarly, Table 2 shows the descriptive statistics from French data. In order to compare these data, T-test for independent samples (i.e., analysis of variance differences) were estimated to compare variables under study in both French and Spanish platforms. However, before these tests were carried out, funds collected were divided into five intervals: from 0 to 5,000, from 5,000 to 20,000 euros, from 20,000 to 50,000 euros, from 50,000 euros to 200,000, and more than 200,000 euros

In addition, it is necessary to underline that each platform includes data from several projects, so each figure represents the average of multiple projects.

*Table 2. Descriptive Statistics. French Platforms.*

| | Number | Min. | Max. | Mean | S.D. | Variance | Asymmetry | | Kurtosis | |
|---|---|---|---|---|---|---|---|---|---|---|
| | | | | | | | Statistic | Standard error | Statistic | Standard error |
| Quantity of funds received by the project | 42 | 1 | 5 | 2.17 | 1.41 | 1.99 | .99 | .36 | -.36 | .72 |
| Days_campaigne | 35 | 1 | 4 | 2.22 | .84 | .711 | .46 | .40 | -.08 | .78 |
| Commission | 43 | 1 | 4 | 2.93 | 1.14 | 1.30 | -.46 | .36 | -1.32 | .71 |
| Limited_time | 45 | 1 | 2 | 1.24 | .43 | .18 | 1.23 | .35 | -.51 | .69 |
| Time | 30 | 10 | 1800 | 275.67 | 530.56 | 281502.98 | 2.60 | .42 | 5.37 | .83 |
| Number_of_ projects | 28 | 2 | 7302 | 400.07 | 1418.09 | 2010995.47 | 4.67 | .44 | 22.73 | .86 |
| Types of crowdfunding | 44 | 1 | 4 | 2.47 | 1.13 | 1.276 | nd | nd | nd | nd |
| Success | 33 | .01 | 1 | .44 | .35 | .13 | .10 | .41 | -1.69 | .80 |

Based on data from the European Crowdfunding Association (2017)

Figure 1 presents the value of funds raised through crowdfunding in France and Spain in 2015 and 2016. In both countries, the activity of crowdfunding has risen over these years. Nevertheless, France shows much higher an activity than Spain,

*Figure 1.* **Value of Funds Raised through Crowdfunding in France and Spain**

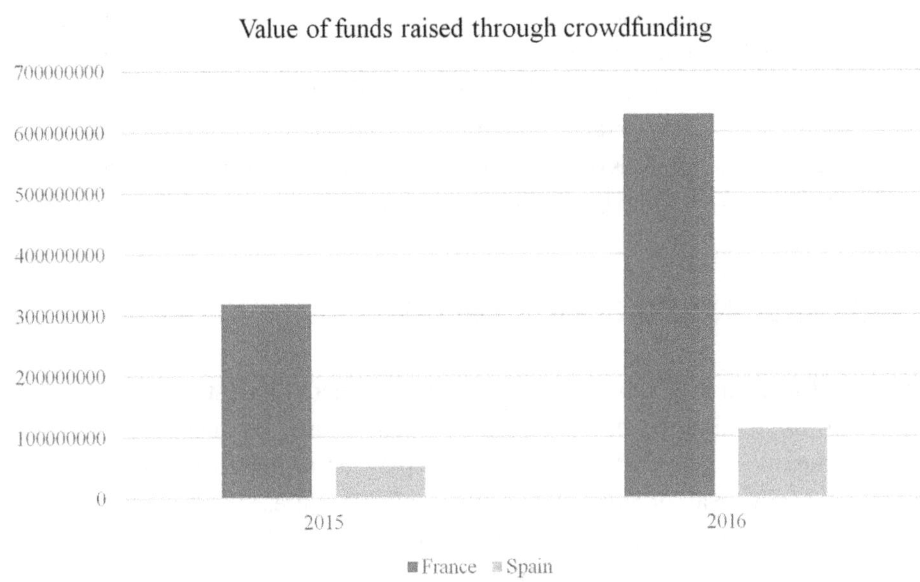

which confirms the differences between countries according to their performance in crowdfunding.

## Results

After conducting a t-test analysis to measure differences between countries, main results are presented (table 3). This analysis allows to observe if there are significant differences in means in the two countries considered.

From these results, it could be concluded that there is no significant difference in the number of projects and funds collected by platforms from the two countries. Thus, the average for projects and funds is a little higher in France than in Spain (2.17 versus 2.13 €). Although data shows differences between the averages 'funds collected' and the 'number of projects' on the platform, these differences are not statistically significant. From these results hypothesis 5 and 2 are rejected.

However, there is a significant difference between 'commissions' charged by platforms from both countries ($F$=8.38, $p \leq 0.001$). French platforms charge higher fees to the uploaded projects compared to Spain. Thus, from these results, hypothesis 5, that considers commission fees charged by crowdfunding platforms similar in both countries, has to be also rejected.

Success is measured as the percentage of projects accepted by the platform compared to the number of projects received. Results are significantly different ($F$=23.68, $p \leq 0.001$), favorable to Spanish platforms, meaning that Spanish platforms are more eager to accept projects. Consequently, hypothesis 6 is accepted.

With regard to the campaigning days, there is no significant difference in the days a campaign is active in France and Spain ($F$=3.14, $Sig \leq 0.09$). Thus, hypothesis 3 has to be rejected, although this result is close to being significant. As for the 'limit of time' a project is published on a platform, a significant difference can be reported (F=42.40, $p \leq 0.001$) with France's platforms being the ones in which projects are maintained for longer periods of time. Therefore, Hypothesis 4 cannot be confirmed.

Finally, Table 4 summarizes the hypothesis and main results.

# 5. DISCUSSION AND CONCLUSIONS

Since the financial crisis, both SMEs and entrepreneurs have faced problems in the search for funding to start or maintain their businesses. This chapter, then, analyzed the role that crowdfunding platforms play in the growth and consolidation of this alternative way of financing. Additionally, this present research also dealt with the study of crowdfunding regulations in France and Spain. So this chapter is well aligned with recent literature on the subject that points to the need for further

*Table 3.* **Crowdfunding Platforms**

| Independent samples | | | | | | | | | | |
|---|---|---|---|---|---|---|---|---|---|---|
| | | *Levene test* | | *T-test (means)* | | | | | | |
| | | *F* | *Sig.* | *t* | *gl* | *Sig. (bilateral)* | *Dif means* | *error estandar differences* | *95%* Lower | *95%* Upper |
| NType | Equal variances assumed | 1.95 | 0.17 | 1.60 | 73.00 | 0.12 | 0.41 | 0.26 | -0.10 | 0.93 |
| | Equal variances not assumed | | | 1.61 | 67.15 | 0.11 | 0.41 | 0.26 | -0.10 | 0.92 |
| Quantity of funds received by the project | Equal variances assumed | 4.77 | 0.03 | 0.11 | 70.00 | 0.91 | 0.03 | 0.30 | -0.57 | 0.64 |
| | Equal variances not assumed | | | 0.12 | 69.91 | 0.91 | 0.03 | 0.29 | -0.54 | 0.61 |
| Days_campaigne | Equal variances assumed | 3.14 | 0.09 | 2.03 | 35.00 | 0.05 | 1.23 | 0.60 | 0.00 | 2.46 |
| | Equal variances not assumed | | | 8.62 | 34.00 | 0.00 | 1.23 | 0.14 | 0.94 | 1.52 |
| Commission | Equal variances assumed | 8.38 | 0.01 | 4.37 | 72.00 | 0.00 | 1.06 | 0.24 | 0.58 | 1.54 |
| | Equal variances not assumed | | | 4.58 | 71.93 | 0.00 | 1.06 | 0.23 | 0.60 | 1.52 |
| Limited_time | Equal variances assumed | 42.40 | 0.00 | 2.57 | 74.00 | 0.01 | 0.21 | 0.08 | 0.05 | 0.38 |
| | Equal variances not assumed | | | 2.93 | 62.85 | 0.01 | 0.21 | 0.07 | 0.07 | 0.36 |
| Time | Equal variances assumed | 9.87 | 0.00 | 1.56 | 44.00 | 0.13 | 208.17 | 133.38 | -60.64 | 476.97 |
| | Equal variances not assumed | | | 2.15 | 29.10 | 0.04 | 208.17 | 96.96 | 9.90 | 406.43 |
| Number_of_ projects | Equal variances assumed | 5.11 | 0.03 | 1.14 | 50.00 | 0.26 | 332.07 | 290.22 | -250.86 | 915.00 |
| | Equal variances not assumed | | | 1.24 | 27.18 | 0.23 | 332.07 | 268.43 | -218.53 | 882.68 |
| Success | Equal variances assumed | 23.68 | 0.00 | -4.15 | 58.00 | 0.00 | -0.32 | 0.08 | -0.48 | -0.17 |
| | Equal variances not assumed | | | -4.35 | 53.58 | 0.00 | -0.32 | 0.07 | -0.47 | -0.17 |
| Funds | Equal variances assumed | 4.77 | 0.03 | 0.11 | 70.00 | 0.91 | 0.03 | 0.30 | -0.57 | 0.64 |
| | Equal variances not assumed | | | 0.12 | 69.91 | 0.91 | 0.03 | 0.29 | -0.54 | 0.61 |

analyzes (1) legislation and its variations by country (Cumming and Zhang 2016), and (2) crowdfunding functioning and crowdfunding contexts (McKenny et al. 2017). Since most of the crowdfunding activity is concentrated on crowdfunding platforms as they help funders to find investors (indirect crowdfunding), this study compared platforms from France and Spain.

Findings pointed to four main implications related to crowdfunding platforms functioning and the impact of legislation in French and Spanish markets. Firstly, while crowdfunding is an Internet-powered activity with a potential for global accessibility and democratized access to capital, national boundaries play a significant role in shaping the performance of crowdfunding platforms. The evolution of digital skills in both countries may affect the situation of crowdfunding as it is a web based

*Table 4. Summary of hypothesis and results*

| Hypotheses | Measure | Support |
|---|---|---|
| *H1*. There are no differences with regard to commission fees in both French and Spanish platforms, beyond the ones related to the general standard of living. | Commissions | No |
| *H2*. There should not be any significant differences with regard to success between French and Spanish platforms. | Number of projects | No |
| *H3*. Campaigning days should be similar in both countries since this variable is important to raise funds within a time framework. | Days of campaign | No |
| *H4*. Limited time should be similar in both countries since this variable is important to raise funds within a time framework. | Time | No |
| *H5*. Funds obtained by French platforms are higher than funds raised by Spanish platforms. | Quantity of funds received by the project | No |

activity. Secondly, countries developed their particular regulations in order to control this new financing tool. These regulations may boost or hinder the growth of this alternative financing tool. The fact that some countries imposed crowdfunding specific regulation before could also exert some effect on the state of crowdfunding. Thirdly, although significant differences in commissions were found, no significant differences on the number of projects and funds were reported. Derived from these results, it can be assumed that the different way platforms managed their activity does not affect their outcomes in terms of number of projects and funds raised. In fact, although platforms are indispensable as an intermediate agent between funders and investors, they do not play an essential role in terms of outcomes (number of projects and funds) of crowdfunding.

From a more in-detail perspective, results pointed to a significant difference between commissions charged by platforms from both countries. In a global market, commissions would be a key decision-making factor for entrepreneurs to host their projects in Spanish or French platforms in order to minimize the cost of intermediation. As this is not the case, this result could be explained based on the geographical closeness between investors and funders, as proposed by Agrawal et al. (2011) and Mollick (2014). Along this line, Lin, and Viswanathan (2013) highlighted the relevance of friendship networks for the success of projects. These friendship networks are usually developed locally.

Another relevant result to be mentioned was the success of projects hosted in each platform. Success was also different in both countries, where Spanish platforms were less restrictive accepting projects.

A significant difference in the limit of time a project is hosted in the platform was also found as French projects are available on the platform for longer periods of time compared to Spanish ones. Similarly, there was a significant difference in the maximum time a project is published in each platform. Extant research concluded that there is a relationship between the time that a project is hosted and the funds collected so that the shorter the period, the higher the funds (Lehner 2013). Although the time hosted is different, no significant differences in funds collected were revealed, and this finding could imply that there is no direct relation between the time a project is hosted with the funds it raises.

As with every research study, this chapter presents some limitations. To comply with the regulations on data protection, crowdfunding platforms interviewed were not identified. Identification of the platforms would have allowed us to classify platforms by the type of projects managed by each of them (for example, social initiatives, cultural projects, health proposals), and, as a result, conclusions might have been more precise. In addition, methodology could have also been improved by including personal interviews to confirm the results of the questionnaires. Another line for future studies could be on the role that legislation could play in boosting or hindering crowdfunding. Legislation differences have an impact on our hypothesis and, consequently, on the results of the empirical research. Conducting a study in two countries with similar legislation would help to understand the role of regulatory schemes in this field. Further research could also be extended to other countries in order to not only study their legislation but also the role that cultural differences might play. Since crowdfunding has been associated with economic and entrepreneurial activity, the existence of supportive environments and certain cultural traits could also have exerted some influence (De Falco, Vargas-Sánchez, and Cucarini 2015). This kind of approach would demand a holistic understanding of the crowdfunding phenomenon.

Crowdfunding reveals itself as a useful mechanism to raise funds particularly for SMEs and entrepreneurs. However, and even though crowdfunding platforms are essential to link founders with funders, the way platforms function does not seem to play any particular key role in this process. Conversely, national legislations and proximity between the entrepreneur, the founder and the platform are more important for the success of a project.

## REFERENCES

Agrawal, A., Catalini, C., & Goldfarb, A. (2015). Crowdfunding: Geography, Social Networks, and the Timing of Investment Decisions. *Journal of Economics & Management Strategy*, *24*(2), 253–274. doi:10.1111/jems.12093

Ahlers, G. K., Cumming, D., Günther, C., & Schweizer, D. (2015). Signaling in Equity Crowdfunding. *Entrepreneurship Theory and Practice*, *39*(4), 955–980. doi:10.1111/etap.12157

Aldrich, H. E. (2014). The democratization of entrepreneurship? Hackers, makerspaces, and crowdfunding. *Annual Meeting of the Academy of Management*. 10.5465/ambpp.2014.10622symposium

Bannerman, S. (2013). Crowdfunding Culture. *Journal of Mobile Media*, *7*(1).

Barral, L. M., & Barral, L. M. (2014). ¿Por qué la Gente Financia Proyectos Vía Crowdfunding? Investigación realizada entre la Comunidad de Mecenas de Lánzanos. Ed. Two much Research studio, Madrid.

Baumgardner, T., Neufeld, C., Huang, P. C. T., Sondhi, T., Carlos, F., & Talha, M. A. (2015). Crowdfunding as a Fast-Expanding Market for the Creation of Capital and Shared Value. *Thunderbird International Business Review*, *59*(1), 115–126. doi:10.1002/tie.21766

Beck, T., & Demirguc-Kunt, A. (2006). Small and Medium-size Enterprises: Access to Finance as a Ggrowth Constraint. *Journal of Banking & Finance*, *30*(11), 2931–2943. doi:10.1016/j.jbankfin.2006.05.009

Belleflamme, P., Omrani, N., & Peitz, M. (2015). The economics of crowdfunding platforms. *Information Economics and Policy*, *33*, 11–28. doi:10.1016/j.infoecopol.2015.08.003

Belleframme, P., Lambert, T., & Schwienbacher, A. (2014). Crowdfunding: Tapping the Right Crowd. *Journal of Business Venturing*, *29*(5), 585–609. doi:10.1016/j.jbusvent.2013.07.003

Bellihi & Berachid. (2018). Perceiving Success among Shariah Compliant Crowdfunding Social Entrepreneurs. *Revue de Gestion et d"Économie*, *6*(3), 264-293.

Berger, A., & Udell, G. (1995). Relationships Lending and Lines of Credit in Small Firm finance. *The Journal of Business*, *68*(3), 351–381. doi:10.1086/296668

Bessiere, V., & Stephany, E. (2014). *Le Crowdfunding: Fondements et Pratiques*. Deboeck.

Blohm, I., Leimeister, J.-M., Wenzlaff, K. & Gebert, M. (2013). *Crowdfunding Studie 2013/2014*. Berlin: epubli.

Bradford, C. S. (2012). *Crowdfunding and the Federal Securities Laws*. Working paper.

Brown, T. E., Boon, E., & Pitt, L. F. (2017). Seeking Funding in Order to Sell: Crowdfunding as a Marketing Tool. *Business Horizons*, *60*(2), 189–195. doi:10.1016/j.bushor.2016.11.004

Bruton, G., Khavul, S., Siegel, D., & Wright, M. (2015). New Financial Alternatives in Seeding Entrepreneurship: Microfinance, Crowdfunding, and peer-to-peer Innovations. *Entrepreneurship Theory and Practice*, *39*(1), 9–26. doi:10.1111/etap.12143

Burtch, G., Ghose, A., & Wattal, S. (2013). An Empirical Examination of the Antecedents and Consequences of Contribution Patterns in Crowd-funded Markets. *Information Systems Research*, *24*(3), 499–519. doi:10.1287/isre.1120.0468

Carè, S., Trotta, A., Carè, R., & Rizzello, A. (2018). Crowdfunding for the Development of Smart Cities. *Business Horizons*, *61*(4), 501–509. doi:10.1016/j.bushor.2017.12.001

Cassar, G. (2004). The Financing of Business Start-ups. *Journal of Business Venturing*, *19*(2), 261–283. doi:10.1016/S0883-9026(03)00029-6

Chemla, G., & Tinn, K. (2016). *Learning through Crowdfunding*. Working paper.

Chen, A., Cumming, D., & Hughes, A. (2009). Outside Entrepreneurial Capital. *Economic Journal (London)*, *119*(540), 1494–1533. doi:10.1111/j.1468-0297.2009.02270.x

Cholakova, M., & Clarysse, B. (2015). Does the Possibility to Make Equity Investments in Crowdfunding Projects Crowd out Reward-based Investments? *Entrepreneurship Theory and Practice*, *39*(1), 145–172. doi:10.1111/etap.12139

Colombo, M. G., Franzoni, C., & Rossi-Lamastra, C. (2015). Internal Social Capital and the Attraction of Early Contributions in Crowdfunding. *Entrepreneurship Theory and Practice*, *39*(1), 75–100. doi:10.1111/etap.12118

Comisión Europea. (2016). *Una Agenda Europea para la Economía Colaborativa*. Author.

Courtney, C., Dutta, S., & Li, Y. (2017). Resolving Information Asymmetry: Signaling, Endorsement, and Crowdfunding Success. *Entrepreneurship Theory and Practice*, *41*(2), 265–290. doi:10.1111/etap.12267

Cumming, D., Leboeuf, G., & Schwienbacher, A. (2014). *Crowdfunding Models: Keep-it-all vs. All-or-nothing* (Vol. 10). Paris Finance Meeting EUROFIDAI-AFFI Paper.

Cumming, D., & Zhang, Y. (2016). Alternative Investments in Emerging Markets: A Review and New Trends. *Emerging Markets Review*, *29*, 1–23. doi:10.1016/j.ememar.2016.08.022

Danmayr, F. (2013). Archetypes of Crowdfunding Platforms: A Multidimensional Comparison. Springer Science & Business Media.

Davidson, R., & Poor, N. (2014). "The Barriers Facing Artists" use of Crowdfunding Platforms: Personality, Emotional Labor, and Going to the Well One too many Times. *New Media & Society*, *17*(2), 289–307. doi:10.1177/1461444814558916

De Falco, S. E., Vargas-Sánchez, A., & Cucarini, N. (2015). *Social Innovation Practices: Focus on Success Factors for Crowdfunding*. Available at: www.naplesforumonservice.it/uploads/files/EspositoDeFalco

Dushnitsky, G., Guerini, M., Piva, E., & Rossi-Lamastra, C. (2016). Crowdfunding in Europe: Determinants of Platform Creation Across Countries. *California Management Review*, *58*(2), 44–71. doi:10.1525/cmr.2016.58.2.44

European Commission's Capital Market Union. (2016). *Report on Crowdfunding in the EU Capital Markets Union*. Brussels: Author.

European Crowdfunding Network AISB. (2017). *Identifying Market and Regulatory Obstacles to Cross-border Development of Crowdfunding in the EU*. Brussels: European Commission.

Financement Participatif France. (2014). *Observatoire du Crowdfunding chez les Français*. Available at: https://financeparticipative.org/

Financement Participatif France. (2015). *Baromètre du Crowdfunding*. Available at: https://www.gartner.com/en

Gartner Group. (2013). Available at: https://www.gartner.com/en

Gerber, E. M., Hui, J. S., & Kuo, P. Y. (2012). Crowdfunding: Why People are Motivated to Post and Fund Projects on Crowdfunding Platforms. *Proceedings of the International Workshop on Design, Influence, and Social Technologies: Techniques, Impacts and Ethics, 2*, 11-21.

Greenberg, M. D., Hui, J., & Gerber, E. (2013). *Crowdfunding: A Resource Exchange Perspective. In CHI"13 Extended Abstracts on Human Factors in Computing Systems*. ACM. doi:10.1145/2468356.2468514

Griffin, Z. J. (2012). Crowdfunding: Fleecing the American Masses. *Case W. Res. JL Tech. & Internet, 4*, 375.

Hellmann, T. (2007). Entrepreneurs and the Process of Obtaining Resources. *Journal of Economics & Management Strategy, 16*(1), 81–109. doi:10.1111/j.1530-9134.2007.00133.x

Hossain, M. (2015). A Review of Literature on Open Innovation in Small and Medium-sized Enterprises. *Journal of Global Entrepreneurship Research, 5*(1), 1–12. doi:10.118640497-015-0022-y

Hui, J. S., Greenberg, M. D., & Gerber, E. M. (2014). Understanding the role of community in crowdfunding work. In *Proceedings of the 17th ACM conference on Computer supported cooperative work & social computing* (pp. 62-74). ACM. 10.1145/2531602.2531715

Ibrahim, N., & Verliyantina. (2012). The Model of Crowdfunding to Support Small and Micro Businesses in Indonesia through a Web-based Platform. *Procedia Economics and Finance, 4*, 390–397. doi:10.1016/S2212-5671(12)00353-X

Iikuza, M. (2014). *Le Crowdfunding: Les Rouages du Financement Participatif-édition 2015*. E. Editions, Ed..

Josefy, M., Dean, T. J., Albert, L. S., & Fitza, M. A. (2017). The Role of Community in Crowdfunding Success: Evidence on Cultural Attributes in Funding Campaigns to "Save the Local Theater". *Entrepreneurship Theory and Practice, 41*(2), 161–182. doi:10.1111/etap.12263

Kim, K., & Hann, I. H. (2014). *Crowdfunding and the Democratization of Access to Capital: a Geographical Analysis*. Robert H. Smith School Research Paper.

Koch & Siering. (2015). *Crowdfunding Success Factors: The Characteristics of Successfully Funded Projects on Crowdfunding Platforms*. Academic Press.

Kuppuswamy & Bayus. (2015). *Crowdfunding Creative Ideas: The Dynamics of Project Backers in Kickstarter*. Academic Press.

Lehner, O. M. (2013). Crowdfunding Social Ventures: A Model and Research Agenda. *Venture Capital, 15*(4), 289–311. doi:10.1080/13691066.2013.782624

Li & Duan. (2014). *Dynamic Strategies for Successful Online Crowdfunding*. Academic Press.

Lin, M., & Viswanathan, S. (2014). *Home Bias in Online Investments: an Empirical Study of an Online Crowd Funding Market*. Mimeo.

Massolution. (2013). *The Crowdfunding Industry Report, 2013CF.* Academic Press.

Massolution. (2015). *The Crowdfunding Industry Report, 2015CF.* Academic Press.

Matthews, J., & Vachet, J. (2014). Le Crowdsourcing et le Crowdfunding Culturels dans le Web Collaborative. La Culture par les Foules, 28-39.

McKenny, A. F., Allison, T. H., Ketchen, D. J. Jr, Short, J. C., & Ireland, R. D. (2017). How Should Crowdfunding Research Evolve? A Survey of the Entrepreneurship Theory and Practice Editorial Board. *Entrepreneurship Theory and Practice*, *41*(2), 291–304. doi:10.1111/etap.12269

Mollick, E. (2014). The Dynamics of Crowdfunding: An Exploratory Study. *Journal of Business Venturing*, *29*(1), 1–16. doi:10.1016/j.jbusvent.2013.06.005

Moreau, F., & Nicolas, Y. (2018). *Financement Participatif: une Voie d"avenir pour la Culture? Lectures, Publications Reçues*. M. de la Culture, Ed.

Niemand, T., Angerer, M., Thies, F., Kraus, S., & Hebenstreit, R. (2018). Equity Crowdfunding across Borders: A Conjoint Experiment. *International Journal of Entrepreneurial Behaviour & Research*, *24*(4), 911–932. doi:10.1108/IJEBR-07-2017-0256

OECD, European Commission. (2014). *Pallier la Pénurie d"entrepreneurs: Politiques d"entrepreneuriat Inclusif en Europe*. OECD Publishing. . doi:10.1787/9789264188211-fr

Palacios, M., Martinez-Corral, A., Nisar, A., & Grijalvo, M. (2015). Crowdsourcing and Organizational Forms: Emerging Trends and Research Implications. *Journal of Business Research*, *69*(5), 1834–1839. doi:10.1016/j.jbusres.2015.10.065

Paschen, J. (2017). Choose Wisely: Crowdfunding through the Stages of the Startup Life Cycle. *Business Horizons*, *60*(2), 179–188. doi:10.1016/j.bushor.2016.11.003

Prpić, J., Shukla, P. P., Kietzmann, J. H., & McCarthy, I. P. (2015). How to Work a Crowd: Developing Crowd Capital through Crowdsourcing. *Business Horizons*, *58*(1), 77–85. doi:10.1016/j.bushor.2014.09.005

Reisinger, M. (2014). Two-part Tariff Competition between Two-sided Platforms. *European Economic Review*, *68*, 168–180. doi:10.1016/j.euroecorev.2014.03.005

Ries, J. (2014). *A Few Concerns with Crowdfunding*. Retrieved from http://blog.hbs.edu/dighbs/a-few-concerns-with-crowdfunding/

Rochet, J. C., & Tirole, J. (2006). Two-sided Markets: A Progress Report. *The RAND Journal of Economics*, *37*(3), 645–667. doi:10.1111/j.1756-2171.2006.tb00036.x

Ross, S. A. (1978). Some Notes on Financial Incentive-signalling Models, Activity Choice and Risk Preferences. *The Journal of Finance*, *33*(3), 777–792. doi:10.1111/j.1540-6261.1978.tb02018.x

Rubinton, B. J. (2011). *Crowdfunding: Disintermediated Investment Banking*. Academic Press.

Sartre-Canelas, E. (2016). Reward Based Cultural Crowdfunding in Spain: Opinions of Project Promoters. Lillehammer: Knowledge Works National Centre for Cultural industries.

Schwienbacher, A., & Larralde, B. (2010). *Crowdfunding of Small Entrepreneurial Ventures. Handbook of Entrepreneurial Finance. Academic Press.*

Short, J. C., Ketchen, D. J. Jr, McKenny, A. F., Allison, T. H., & Ireland, R. D. (2017). Research on Crowdfunding: Reviewing the (Very Recent) Past and Celebrating the Present. *Entrepreneurship Theory and Practice*, *41*(2), 149–160. doi:10.1111/etap.12270

Solesvik, M. (2016). Crowdfunding and Entrepreneurial Finance. *International Journal of Entrepreneurial Behaviour & Research*, *22*(1), 175–177. doi:10.1108/IJEBR-09-2015-0206

Spain Parliament. (2015). *Ley del Fomento de la Financiación Empresarial* (Ley 5/2015). Madrid: BOE.

Statista. (2018). *Value of funds raised through Crowdfounding worldwide from 2014-2016*. Retrieved from: https://www.statista.com/statistics/360512/funds-raised-via-crowdfunding-globally/

Statista. (2019). *Amount of funding delivered via alternative finance platforms in selected European countries as of 2017*. Retrieved from https://www.statista.com/statistics/412372/europe-alternative-finance-funding-amounts-country/

Steigenberger, N. (2017). Why Supporters Contribute to Reward-based Crowdfunding. *International Journal of Entrepreneurial Behaviour & Research*, *23*(2), 336–353. doi:10.1108/IJEBR-04-2016-0117

Stemler, A. R. (2013). The JOBS Act and Crowdfunding: Harnessing the Power- and Money- of the Masses. *Business Horizons*, *56*(3), 271–275. doi:10.1016/j.bushor.2013.01.007

The Crowd Funding Center. (2018). *The Crowd Data Center*. Retrieved from https://www.thecrowdfundingcenter.com/data

Verliyantina, N. I. (2012). The Model of Crowdfunding to Support Small and Micro Businesses in Indonesia through a Web-based Platform. *Procedia Economics and Finance*, *4*, 390–397. doi:10.1016/S2212-5671(12)00353-X

Vismara, S. (2016). Information Cascades among Investors in Equity Crowdfunding. *Entrepreneurship Theory and Practice*.

Wardrop, R., Zhang, B., Rau, R., & Gray, M. (2015). Moving Mainstream, The European Alternative Finance Benchmarking Report. Cambridge Centre for Alternative Finance.

Wheat, R. E., Wang, Y., Byrnes, J. E., & Ranganathan, J. (2013). Raising Money for Scientific Research through Crowdfunding. *Trends in Ecology & Evolution*, *28*(2), 71–72. doi:10.1016/j.tree.2012.11.001 PMID:23219380

Wilson & Testoni. (2014). *Improving the Role of Equity Crowdfunding in Europe's Capital Markets* (No. 2014/09). Bruegel Policy Contribution.

Wuillaume, A., Jacquemin, A., & Janssen, F. (2018). The Right Word for the Right Crowd: An Attempt to Recognize the Influence of Emotions. *International Journal of Entrepreneurial Behaviour & Research*. Advance online publication. doi:10.1108/IJEBR-10-2017-0412

Xu, L. Z. (2018). Will a Digital Camera Cure your Sick Puppy? Modality and Category Effects in Donation-based Crowdfunding. *Telematics and Informatics*, *35*(7), 1914–1924. doi:10.1016/j.tele.2018.06.004

Zhao, Q., Chen, C. D., Wangand, J. L., & Chen, P. C. (2017). "Determinants of Backers" Funding Intention in Crowdfunding: Social Exchange Theory and Regulatory Focus. *Telematics and Informatics*, *34*(1), 370–384. doi:10.1016/j.tele.2016.06.006

## ENDNOTES

1 Similarly, the United States published the JOBS law –which includes a section about crowdfunding- in 2012 (Stemler 2013). In this context, some authors defend an exemption that would free crowdfunding from the registration requirements (Bradford 2011).

2 This fact can be supported by the document published by the General Internal Market Department of the European Commission in October 2013 on techniques to boost crowdfunding in Europe and the report published by the European Commission on regulation barriers (European Crowdfunding Network AISB, and Clarke 2017).

3 There are two options to be qualified as an accredited investor. Such consideration will be given to those entrepreneurs who individually meet at least two of the following conditions: (1) the total of assets should be equal to or greater than 1 million euros; (2) the amount of its annual turnover should be equal to or greater than 2 million euros; or (3) its own resources should be equal to or exceed 300,000 euros.

Another way to be considered an accredited investor will be for those individuals who meet the following conditions: (1) accredit an annual income of more than 50,000 euros or a financial capital of more than 100,000; (2) request to be considered as previously accredited investors, and expressly waive their treatment as an unaccredited client.

# Chapter 6
# Is an Offline Sharing Economy Innovation Transmissible Online?
## Exploring the Role of Conformity in Group Lending

**Djamchid Assadi**
*CEREN, EA 7477, Burgundy School of Business, Université Bourgogne Franche Comté, France*

**Arvind Ashta**
https://orcid.org/0000-0002-6160-5375
*CEREN, EA 7477, Burgundy School of Business, Université Bourgogne Franche Comté, France*

**Nathalie Duran**
*Université de la Réunion, Réunion*

## ABSTRACT

*Group lending is a social innovation because the substitution of the guarantee on assets by the collective guarantee of the group of belonging leads to the financial inclusion of the excluded. In a lending group, members who know each other mutually control each other to guarantee repayment of the loan and its circulation among the members. Is the social collateral that supported the development of the offline microcredit to the world level transposable to social lending on the internet? To answer this question, this chapter aims at determining the factors of mutual supervision and control of the members within the affiliation group and examine the potential of their transposition on the internet. Understanding the conditions for transposing social security is not only a solution to the problem of the unbanked; it is also a source of inspiration for peer-to-peer activities which develop considerably on the internet.*

DOI: 10.4018/978-1-7998-3226-3.ch006

## INTRODUCTION

There is a significant difference between the financial and the bank excluded. The latter are rejected because they are offenders of banks. The former are excluded because they are commercially unfit to banks (Tasque, 2011).

The exclusion from the banking services is explained by the supply-sided reasons like small loans valuation, risk and costs of transaction with the poor and fragile individuals (Akula 2010), along with the demand-sided reasons such as the lack of financial education and the inability to provide guarantees to reduce risk (Armendariz and Morduch 2005).

Adult bank excluded count for 2.5 billion in the world at the beginning of the 2010s (Global Findex, Demirguc-Kunt et al., 2015) and around 1.7 billion around the end of the same decade (Global Findex, Demirguc-Kunt et al., 2018). The improvement is evident; however, there is still a huge population to financially integrate.

Technological and social innovations can overcome the problem of non-banking. The technology of mobile money now accounts for 12% of adults (64 million) in sub-Saharan Africa, compared to only 2% in the rest of the world (Global Findex, Demirguc-Kunt et al., 2015). Social innovation contributes no less to financial inclusion. The best known or at least the most high-profile example is the group loan whose originality lies in the substitution of the asset-based guarantee by the guarantee of belonging to a group.

The research inquiry of this contribution bridges the two types of innovation and addresses the transposition of social innovation: *Can the social innovation of social collateral (guarantee) in offline group lending be transposed to cyberspace?*

Transposition means adapting knowledge of solving an acute problem from one area to another. This contribution addresses the transposition of the knowledge of social guarantee to the problem of the unbanked from offline to online. While the transposition of a social innovation from one country to another is already studied (Boxenbaum and Battilana 2005), the transposition of a social innovation such as social collateral from offline microfinance to online crowdfunding is to the best of our knowledge is the first of its kind.

This transposition is legitimate because its two ends aim to leverage sharing within groups to address individual problems. In France, the *"Association for Development and Economic Initiative" ("Adie")* refinances since 2011 a part of the microcredits granted via the online crowdfunding platform *Babyloan*. Inversely, crowdfunding platforms like *Kiva* and *Babyloan* support microfinance among modest populations in both developing and developed countries.

The results of this research provide useful academic and managerial insights. Transposing the dynamics of social collateral from offline to online is important not only because it is a decisive solution to the problem of non-banking that often leads to poverty, marginalization and deviation, but also because it is a source of inspiration for the spontaneous activities that are created between individuals in the cyberspace.

This paper is structured as follows: first, we proceed to a review of multidisciplinary literature to propose a theoretical framework. Second, we discuss the methodology of research. The third part is devoted to the presentation of the results and our analysis by comparing the cases of our samples out of and online between them and the conceptual model. The fourth part rises the discussion of our results and the refinement of the conceptual model that outlines the conditions of conformity of the individual to groups outside and online.

## Review of Literature

In line with the essence of our research inquiry, we review three sets of literature relative to different aspects of our research inquiry. First, we study the founding concept of conformity in groups which institutes trustworthy behaviors of members and consequently social collateral. Second, we present group lending and substitution of assets-based collateral by social collateral. Three, we explore cyber-communities as online extension of conventional communities along with the P2P social lending platforms. Four, we define the concept of social innovation in line with the research inquiry which addresses the transmissibility of social collateral as an innovation from off to online communities. Five, we suggest a conceptual framework of individual conformity according the preceding literature reviews.

## Individual Conformity in Groups

Individual conformity in groups underlines the social guarantee. By compliance, we mean the modification of perceptions, opinions and behaviors in response to the real or imaginary pressure of others.

Sociology, the discipline of functioning of groups, distinguishes primary reference groups, intimate with face-to-face interaction (Witt and Bruce 1972), from secondary groups, created intentionally by peers (War and Reingen 1990). Groups are formal by specific rules, or informal, by less structured rules of friendship and customs.

In the marketing literature, the role of consumer compliance is a key factor in brand-user relationships (Escalas and Bettman 2005; Muniz Jr and O' Guinn 2001; Xia et al., 2012). Some authors, however, contrast the attitude of escapism with compliance to suggest that some consumers may become loyal to a brand because of their desire to evade (leak), unlike others who do so because of their desire to comply (compliance) (Labrecque et al. 2011).

Why should individuals accept compliance for cognitive (informational), emotional (value-expression) and conative reasons at the expense of their freedom? They do so because they have difficulty assessing objects and events. Ideas and comments from the group members give them cognitive benefits (Calder and Burnkrant, 1977) and evidence of reality (Burnkrant and Alain, 1975). Individuals also conform because they desire to associate with admired and respected peers and accept to comply to collective norms to avoid rejection (Asch, 1951; Ross and al., 1976; Venkatesan, 1966).

In the compliance process, the collective or influential agent monitors, rewards and punishes for respect or disrespect for collective rules.

Group lending bypasses the risk of lending to peers with inadequate assets and the conventional financial system's preference for client creditworthy by group member trustworthy due to the warranty of group pressure and individual conformity within the group (Ashta and al., 2013).

## Group Lending and Social Collateral

The idea of lending through non-conventional financial channels has long existed between family and friends in almost every culture of the world. The "Rotating Savings and Credit Association, ROSCA", (Bouman, 1983, Schmidt et al. 2016) and "Cooperative and mutual banks" (Pytkowska, 2006, Ashta and al. 2016, Schmidt and al, 2016) are two of the many forms of formally meeting among peers to save and lend each other. Muhammed Yunus, the Nobel Peace Prize winner in 2006, standardizes and markets the model worldwide (Yunus, 1994, 1999, 2010).

Mutual process of acceptance, control and barring characterize the dynamism of group lending and social collateral (Homans, 1961). The basic idea of the social collateral with group lending is encouraging members to closely monitor and put pressure on each other for appropriate behavior with the objective of avoiding the blockage of the turning access to credit. Members jointly exercise the governance by compliance for ensuring the extension and perhaps expansion of the credit. They even deposit a small amount of money into a reserve fund in anticipation of default.

Individuals preferably form (secondary) loan groups with reliable peers (Ghatak, 1999), mostly from common primary groups, generally living in close neighborhoods and acquainted in kinship (Lawont and N'Guessan, 2000). Group peers initially set formal qualification criteria such as the amount of money contribute, the frequency of contributions and the amount of the loan.

An experimental study in South Africa and Armenia finds that social homogeneity and prior links between individuals have a positive effect on group performance (Cassar and al., 2007). However, Etang and al. (2011) illustrate that members of a type of *ROSCA* in a village in Cameroon do not necessarily have prior kinship or friendship. Yet, inhabitants of a small village have most likely strong or weak social ties and know each other. In Bolivia, each lending group has 20 to 40 self-select members (Vik, 2010). In India, each of the 7.9 million self-help groups has an average of 13 members (Sa-Dhan, 2016).

The four different levels of governance that Williamson (2000) distinguishes provide insights for the analysis of control instruments among individuals: customs and manners, formal laws and rules, direct arrangements and organization. Each level mutually imposes constraints at and undergoes feedbacks from the next level. Accordingly, control instruments within the group lending seem relying on customary standards in ROSCA, customary standards and formal rules in group loans, and formal rules in cooperatives.

In all these groups, members align with the rules for accessing loans. Compliance also results from mutual surveillances (group pressure), search for adequate solutions, fears of financial deterioration, credit refusal and community exclusion and the reward of the renewal of larger appropriations.

In ROSCAs, individuals adopt new behaviors of savings and borrowing. In some group loans, a member's ability to save becomes a condition of entering a group. In cooperative associations, peers learn values of solidarity and entrepreneurship.

Each member is simultaneously monitor and monitored within the society of peers. Reputation among acquaintances safeguards suitable conducts and cheating avoidance even in absence of formal enforcement (Klein Daniel, 1997). The sense of shame in (rural) community is a strong deterrent of defaulting behaviors. Borrowing peers for fear of losing face in their community conduct properly and even sometimes turn to loan sharks for being able to cope with repayments (Armendáriz de Aghion and Morduch, 2005). Group members conform more when they serve a common goal rather than individual goals, probably because they believe that deviance on their part would be punished more severely.

Regular meetings allow monitoring of each other's projects and behaviors (Armendáriz de Aghion and Morduch, 2005). Improper manners are subject to penalties (Etang and al, 2011). In Ghana and Cameroon, cooperatives that dependent on members' savings rather than on public or commercial funds survive better (Marx and Seibel, 2012) most likely due to more involvement in the process of mutual monitoring.

Group loan cases confirm and reproduce elements of group pressure and individual conformity and reveal the presence of officers who organize the entire process of circulating loan and strengthen the mutual supervision of peers. In general, there is always an official or de facto organizer who monitors peer commitments and possible breaches. We call this actor "compliance officer" in our conceptual model.

This role is played by an informal leader in a ROSCA, a credit officer in a loan group or cooperative, and, as we later see, a community manager on social websites.

*Table 1. Source of collective pressure in different offline microfinance groups*

| | | ROSCA | Group lending | Cooperatives |
|---|---|---|---|---|
| **Admission requirement** | Characteristics | ▪ String social ties | ▪ Strong and weak tiess<br>▪ Ability to save | ▪ Weak links<br>▪ Local affiliation |
| **Membership motivations** | Cognitive | ▪ Understand the conditions for accessing loans<br>▪ Getting to grips with finances<br>▪ Faster access to the loan<br>▪ Getting to grips with finances | | ▪ Terms of access<br>▪ Networking to optimize costs and sales |
| | Affective | ▪ Social affiliation,<br>▪ Assistance | | ▪ Financial assistance<br>▪ Promotion locale |
| | Conative | ▪ Getting funds | | ▪ Getting funds<br>▪ Networking |
| **Group types** | Primary, secondary; formal, informal | ▪ Secondary formal | | ▪ Formal, secondary for the most part, |
| **Instruments of influence & control** | Reward/ Punishments Surveillance/ Control | ▪ Social exclusion,<br>▪ Possible penalty<br>▪ Control by norms | ▪ New credits/ Refusal of loans in default<br>▪ Group exclusion<br>▪ Control by norms | ▪ High penalty<br>▪ New credits<br>▪ Physical guarantee requirement<br>▪ Control by rules |
| **Nature of compliance** | Acceptance, submission | Acceptance of standards and rules for accessing loans | | |
| **Forms of influence** | Normative | ▪ Save and then borrow | ▪ Save and then borrow | ▪ Saving<br>▪ Optional borrowing |
| | Value-expression (shared value) | ▪ Solidarity<br>▪ Democracy | ▪ Solidarity<br>▪ Autonomy | ▪ Solidarity<br>▪ Democracy |
| | Informational | ▪ Know the inner working rules of alternative finance and the networking benefits | | |

This role of external supervisor complements the conceptual model we suggest later and also verifies through the observation of off and online cases.

In many types of group lending, a credit officer manages the group and sometimes even the order of the beneficiaries of the loans. Most of the time, the managers or collectors are men, while the beneficiaries are women.

The default rate is generally low in loan groups most likely because of the effectiveness of social collateral and accessorily the credit officer's monitoring. The recovery rate is over 95% in the "Self-Employed Women's Association" (SEWA) (Kapoor, 2007).

This low rate of default incites some cooperative banks to secure funds at low interest rates and then lend it locally at reasonable interest rates to microfinance institutions (Schmidt and al, 2016).

## Cyber-communities and Peer-to-peer Social Lending Platforms

Cyber-communities extend group spirit online. They are born with the Web for supporting affiliation, social and professional networking on the Internet (Burt 2010, CBNews): "Classmates" (founded in 1995), "Six Degrees" (1996-2000), "Livejournal" (1997, blogging), "Ryze" (2001), "Friendster" (2002), "LinkedIn" (2003), "hi5 (2003), MySpace (2003), Orkut (2004), and Facebook (2004). Of this list of ten, "Six Degrees" does not exist anymore.

Broadband moves online communities from an alphanumeric experience to an audiovisual experience (Watkins, 2009). The online community finally becomes to be among the 25 major management tools of our time (Bain and Company 2009).

Relations among peers differ in off and online communities. They are actual, geographically close and usually relying on shared cultural codes in offline groups, while virtual, distancing and not necessarily based on common rules online (Okleshen and Grossbart 1988).

Added to this is that members in face-to-face gatherings are more inhibited and impressed than peers in cyber-communities who feel more comfortable (Fischer and al. 1996; Kuan 1996). As identities are not verified in online meetings, peers can claim to be who they please and reach more communities than they would have joined in the offline world (Angwin, 2009).

However, these relations of different kind do not radically alter the communication habits among individuals of similar interests and concerns (Comley, 2008). Watkins (2009) disagrees with the assumption that intensive use of the Internet further isolates people and finds that MySpace bloggers feel less isolated and see themselves as more part of a community. Ryan (2012) finds peer-to-peer (P2P) exchanges on "Tribe", an early social network launched in 2003, as normal. The quality of contact might fall; however, the peers can improve it thanks to the power of excommunicating members who unfit to the sustainability of online communities (Ryan, 2012).

The supervisory role can be played by individuals officially assigned to this task or by individuals often spontaneously (self)referred to as cyber communities.

On the business front, Brown and al. (2002) find that online communities like chatrooms, product evaluation pages and others of the same ilk, increase the attractiveness of commercial websites and client value. They study 40,000 visits on commercial websites and find that online community peers generate two-thirds of sales, even though they account for only one-third of visits. Community peers are loyal and buyer as almost twice (Brown et al., 2002).

The emergence and rise of Web 2.0 technologies demonopolize the power of networking and communication and enable individuals to form communities of complicity without needing the allowance of conventional media hubs.

The resulting P2P platforms bridge direct contacts between sets of peers, for (narrow/broad) casting, networking, sharing, and transacting. eBay creates in 1995 one of the first community platforms to link individuals for direct transactions. Ten years later, around 2005, P2P lending platforms, later dubbed crowdfunding, begin to compete seriously traditional financial institutions by delivering an alternative mode of financing which directly links providers and recipients of funds (Hulme and Wright, 2006).

Many research endeavors reveal that social affiliations like being member of high rated groups, recommended by friends on crowdfunding platforms and affiliation to communities on social media increase the likelihood of obtaining loans at reasonable rates even by the unbanked because, for the lenders, the subjective information of social affiliation alludes to the creditworthiness of prospective borrowers in the absence of objective credit records and even minimize adverse impacts of demerits of debt or low credit ratings (Ryan et al. 2007, Freedman and Jin 2008; Herzenstein and al. 2008, Berger and Gleisner, 2009; Herrero-Lopez, 2009; Iyer and al. 2009).

Ashta and Assadi (2009) underline that these online social lending platforms, not only establish direct relationships but also considerably reduce information asymmetry, transaction costs and consequently risks between partners.

We postulate that the model of two-sided market (Rochet and Tirole 2006) is the pertinent conceptual foundation for P2P platforms (Eloranta and Turunen 2016). On a two-sided market, the attraction of each set of clients requires that of the other market. The two markets organically depend and appeal each other (Rochet and Tirole 2006). P2P platforms also depend on two sets of clients. In crowdfunding, recipients come only if there are enough contributors; and contributors come only if there are an enough recipient with projects. As a result, the value of a P2P platform depends on the quantity and quality of clients of two sets of markets and the intermediation ability of the platforms to reduce information asymmetry and transaction costs between them. The existence and development of online lending platforms, particularly with increased competition, requires the simultaneous presence of large number of contributors and recipients.

The business model behind this type of P2P platforms that neither provide nor request, but simplify, accelerate and facilitate supply and demand among peers is studied at length. Tapscott and al. (2000) identify the digital collaboration matrix. Mahadevan (2000) distinguishes three types of online business models of which that of market-makers for linking buyers and sellers. Assadi (2004) singles out "exchange facilitators" as accelerators, simplifiers and facilitators of P2P exchanges in a typology of seven online business models.

Studies on online groups abound to explore the characteristics of the crowd (Belleflamme and al., 2014; Bouaiss and al., 2015; Onnée and Renault, 2014), the social capital of the loan network (Marconatto and al. 2016), the influence of the group's peers in the decision-making of contributors (Colombo and al. 2015) and the geographical distribution of support for project owners (Agrawal and al. 2015).

Our research pursues a different theme and aims at exploring the possibilities of transposing the conformity of the individual to the behavioral rules in group lending (social guarantee) from offline to online crowdfunding. This transposition in case of feasibility is a social innovation.

## What is Social Innovation?

Innovations originated in product, organization, marketing, business model, technology, and social. The two formers are particularly studied in this paper.

There is currently a near-unanimity to define social innovation. It consists of developing innovative, transformative and sustainable responses to new or ill-met social needs in current market and social policy conditions, involving the participation and cooperation of using actors (Auerswald, 2009; CSESS 2011; The ESS Act 2014; Phills and al., 2008). This definition a social innovation brings together three major elements:

- New, underserved or unmet social needs in areas of aging, early childhood, housing, health, poverty, exclusion and discrimination that are not addressed by state policies and/or the market mechanism (IDEO.org 2015).
- Social entrepreneurs (Bornstein, 2007; Martin and Osberg, 2007; Phills and al, 2008) and volunteering citizens (Ellerman 2005) take initiative and develop solution to the above needs.
- Social innovations quite often cross traditional boundaries between non-profit, public and lucrative sectors (Phills and al., 2008).

Researchers increasingly measure the impact of social innovations (Auerswald 2009; Bugg-Levine and Emerson 2011; Turan 2008).

Under the above, it is appropriate to consider as social innovation the transmission of individual conformity (social collateral) from off (group lending) to online (crowdfunding) because it allows the social entrepreneurs and volunteers to provide solutions to financial exclusion, poverty, and discrimination unsatisfied by conventional state and market solutions.

## A Conceptual Framework of Individual Conformity in Group

Referring to the preceding review and new references, we design a conceptual framework, Figure 1, to explain the individual conformity within a group, the resulting predictable good behavior and, *in fine*, the social collateral (guarantee) in offline groups.

The model begins with the conditions of admission and social links for membership as the study of offline cases of group lending reveal earlier in this section.

The model contains the instruments of control. They rely on rewards and punishments relative to reception or rejection of recycling loans. They also refer to the mutual surveillance and control the group members undertake toward each other. Added to this is the authority that the control officers who are not part of the peers but part of the group exercises. This is an external factor which enhances the intrinsic process of group pressure.

Individuals comply and admit group pressure by acceptation (conviction) or submission (obligation) because they receive in return cognitive, affective and conative rewards.

The cognitive rewards mainly consist of financial education (Baltaca and Mavrenko 2009) and familiarity with the access to loans.

The affective recompenses include cooperation, assistance, control autonomy from government and support for local income-generating businesses (Baltaca and Mavrenko 2009),

The conative gains involve pooling of resources, flexible and reliable reimbursement, (Baltaca and Mavrenko, 2009), (collective) ownership promotion, pre-purchase of production and profit sharing, (Datta and Gailey, 2012). For the group loan and crowdfunding platforms, we study the mainly peers agree to comply to have access to loans (conative motivation) that conventional lenders rarely grant fearing adverse selection and moral risk.

This model nullifies, improves and replaces the linears model of Assadi and Ashta (2014) and that of Alijani and al. (2016) with notions of strong and weak social ties (Granovetter, 2005, 1973).

## RESEARCH METHODOLOGY

We adopt a netnographic approach in accordance with the research inquiry which investigates the transmission of individual conformity from off to online groups. We actually participate into the selected communities for meeting individuals in situ and observing whether they effectively comply to some rule and their compliance behaviors resemble to the offline ones.

This netnographic research on transposition still subject to hazard because members of an offline group generally know each other, while those in online groups do not always know each other at first or know each other only through their avatars.

*Figure 1. The conceptual framework for the individual's conformity to the group*

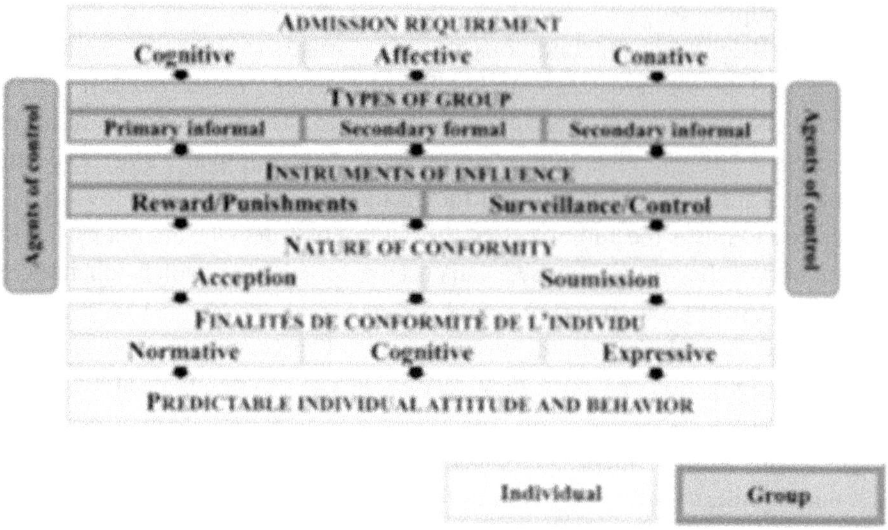


It is necessary to distinguish between ex-ante communities, in which individuals spontaneously juxtapose and often know each other, and ex-post communities, most of which, here on the Internet, are intentionally created by individuals who are foreign to one another.

We have defined a netnograhic protocol containing the building blocks of field observation (Arborio and al., 2015; Emerson and al., 2011 ; Peneff, 2009):

1) Problematic: are the items of the individual's compliance with the offline group also found in online groupings around the crowdlending theme?

Our netnography does not seek to discover whether the social guarantee is practiced online, but whether all constituent elements of individual compliance are present on the Internet.

2) Observer status: Total assignment of attending online lending activities to one of the coauthors who is specialist and proceeds since 2014 to almost daily netnographic observation on many French crowdlending platforms and subscribes to their mailing lists to explore new campaigns successful projects and interactions between them.

For the research project on hands, the coauthor-observer visits the communities incognito as a peer among others, financially participates in crowdlending projects with interest and no interest and shares opinions.

3) Observation field: in situ crowdlending platforms, lending communities, interest groups, and blogs to witness actions and reactions of peers.

We consider the variety of the field: platforms' non-for-profit (Kiva, Babyloan) or lucrative (Lendopolis, October) legal status, business or personal (HelloMerci, without, Younited Credit with interest) loans, loans without (solidarity loan at 0%, on Babyloan) or with interest (between 3 and 10.5% on Lendopolis, voted of the most transparent French crowdlending by lenders, in 2017 for publicly divulgating successful, unfinished, fraudulent, defect projects and payment delays,), interest rates based on credit history or loan partners, dis or re-intermediated channel between contributing and receiving individuals and platforms' strategic positioning like Lendopolis specialized in renewable energy and real estate since 2019.

The coauthor-observer also becomes member of the "crowdlending.fr" forum, a well-attended blog in France, where individual lenders, project managers and platform managers extensively interact.

Secondary data such as press articles, chats, and information available online prepare the above netnographic visits.

4) Observation grid (see table 2): Derived from the conceptual framework suggested earlier.

It consequently contains admission requirements, membership motivations, group types, control instruments, nature of compliance and forms of influence.

5) Relationships on the ground: Spontaneous contacts are privileged.

In line with the ethnographic foundations of our approach, the coauthor-observer does not select informants. Insights and information are spontaneously obtained out of expressions and often chats to deepen data. Exchanges are informal and intuitive with the aim of discovering the proper attitudes and behaviors of contributing and requesting peers.

Often, initial observations stimulate focusing on specific lending and borrowing behaviors and lead to specific chatting with peers (Chabaud and Germain 2006; Renault, 2017).

When data are inaccessible by netnographic observation, supplementary data are obtained through open conversations the coauthor-observer proceeds to with crowdlending regional lending and borrowing individuals. With confidence set in, the actors voluntarily share feelings on specific issues of crowdlending loan groups.

6) The field diary: taking notes instantly during online explorations, then revising to prepare final diaries.

The coauthor-observer carefully respects the chronology of the notes for comparing different observation sequences and distinguishes the personal points of view and objective data corresponding to the grid. In addition to reporting observation data and report, methodological reflections, theoretical reminders and idiosyncratic reflections are added.

7) The timing of observations: the observation sessions are regular and continuous.

The coauthor-observer systemically resumes exploring crowdfunding communities from October and December 2019 at varying times during the day or evening depending on personal availability, publication of information and topics and mainly new projects.

8) The indigenous lexicon: based on the typical expressions identified on the online crowdfunding community by specifying their meaning,

In this perspective, the barometer conducted by Mr. George and his team first monthly and now quarterly to rank lending platforms has been continuously analyzed. A robot scans the platforms daily to carry out the barometer.

9) Restitution: The account of observations. Encountered difficulties are also reported.
10) Description and analysis: Elements are described and discussed in the following section.

## MAIN RESULTS AND ANALYSIS

In this section, we present the results of our netnographic explorations through online platforms of which has encountered difficulties and holds no campaigns. The following are the discussion of data obtained according to the items of the conceptual framework.

*Table 2. Netnographic Observation Grid*

| | |
|---|---|
| Admission requirements | ▪ Who can enter the community?<br>▪ Should he have strong ties with former members?<br>▪ What are the membership criteria? |
| **Membership motivations** | ▪ Why do individuals join this community?<br>▪ Cognitive motivation?<br>▪ Which one, which ones?<br>▪ Emotional motivation? Which ones?<br>▪ Conative motivation? Which ones? |
| **Group types** | ▪ What kind of group is this community formed?<br>▪ Primary, secondary?<br>▪ Shape, informal?<br>▪ Is the band ex-ante or ex-post? |
| **Instruments of influence & control** | ▪ By what type of surveillance, are members' behaviours controlled?<br>▪ Are good behaviours rewarded?<br>▪ Are bad behaviours punished? |
| **Nature of compliance** | ▪ Do members comply with group standards and rules by acceptance or submission |
| **Forms of influence** | ▪ Is the group's form of influence on the individual:<br>▪ Prescriptive,<br>▪ Expressive (value-expression, shared value)<br>▪ Informational |

## Requirements Admission to the Crowdfunding Platforms

On the borrower's side, the conditions are explicit and public. The platform clearly indicates status, characteristics of accepted projects and types of financing.

For the lender, terms and conditions are also clear and detailed. A lender member just needs to provide some personal information. Individual lender can only lend up to 2000 euros per project. Geographical distance is irrelevant.

The social ties between lenders and borrowers essentially emerge after the loans. Previously, they only know each other by their pseudonyms.

Although some events allow some to meet. They might announce on forums messages such as: *"I will be at the live evening of February 9, 2017. So, I'll have the chance to see some of you in REAL. Who's going to be there?*

Often, some lenders group on forums to strengthen the links and exchange on the projects presented on all platforms. Together, they create management tools to limit risk and help each other in their choices: *"what do you think of Company X?* I'll *bet 100 euros, my minimum bet* to see". They look for the validation of the other members before investing: *"What do you think of the last 4 projects put online by Lendopolis and especially the last 2?"*

Lenders might also take initiative of meeting borrowers, and, project leaders who campaign for a business close to them. A borrower witnesses: *"One day a lender came to greet me and told me to have participated in the campaign"* or came to see if the money was used. *"I have passed and still no new restaurant"*.

## Membership Motivations

The motivations for membership are varied and varied.

The project owner is often motivated by access to the loan, either because he is excluded from the traditional banking system or because of simplicity and speed of access to funds.

Another motivation is sometimes that of testing the project's popularity with individuals who are potential consumers: *"A way to see if our project pleases and if the French want to see it succeed, if they believe it"*.

Online, borrowers expose their history, needs and ability to repay.

Lenders who have available money and are looking for either higher profits than conventional investments or to " make sense of their savings."

Some lenders want to discover and learn about this alternative finance: *"There is a rewarding side to both the investor and the entrepreneur. Knowing that there are people behind you, whether they are 10, 20, 100 or 10,000, gives you a dynamic, pushes you. People they don't necessarily know but who believe in their project, company and activity. That's really the spirit"*.

## Group Types

Online lending in France is highly regulated, users must accept the terms and conditions of use and comply with the entry rules.

Crowdfunding platforms have the status of intermediary which allows the link between lenders and borrowers. The platform differs from a traditional financing intermediary in the sense that it does not hold the money deposits on its own account and therefore does not bear the financial risk. It allows the exposure on the canvas of projects, and visibility that increases the opportunities to obtain the loan for the borrower. Here is an excerpt from an answer to a lender's question: *"Beyond the functionality of the tools, it is particularly important to our teams to comply very precisely with the legislation applicable to crowdfunding. Indeed, we would like to contribute to the support of as many people as possible in the highest quality crowdfunding"*.

Platforms are generally paid in levying a commission on the borrower if the loan is successful (except Younited credit, the only platform in Europe approved by the ACPR).

For the two sets of clients, lenders and borrowers, some data are only available to registered members who complete the required applications and accept the terms of use.

Loan groups, whether with or without interest, among individuals or companies, are formal.

## Instruments of Control and Influence

Despite differences in the statutes, social lending platforms have a common denominator that is the trust factor between individuals who meet only on the Internet (Galloway, 2009): borrowers share personal and financial information and lenders decide whether to trust the information provided and whether or not to contribute to loan applications.

The platforms amplify their *ex-ante* controls, in order to strengthen their credibility with lenders, for whom transparency is essential, analysts also communicate on forums: *"We take advantage of this forum to offer you suggestions for improvements on our site* http://www.lendopolis.com.*"*

Following the general dissatisfaction with default rates, Lendopolis, revises the risk analysis policy and forms control teams. The platform analysts are the first control agents: *"I'm waiting for a history to get an idea of the profitability or not of an investment on your platform."* Their role is crucial to the reputation of the platform and the general confidence in crowdlending. They do audits both upstream and downstream of financing to improve this loan model.

*Lendopolis* has also partnerships with the "Order of Accounting Experts", "Gan Insurance", and the "Postal Bank," which can also increase confidence. A digital portal developed by the "Senior Council, the Accountant" fulfils the function of a trusted third party by authenticating requests for financing and transmitting a certificate of financial information which is systematically required by Lendopolis. The accountant's involvement in crowdfunding is praised by both entrepreneurs and financiers.

After auditing of some fraudulent requests*: "Lendopolis initiates legal proceedings against the company and its executives and files a criminal complaint, in addition to a civil liability. Action will be brought in the Commercial Court against the social agents and their accomplices"* ... "We can only applaud this energetic action, which may make other potential fraudsters think. Even if the outcome is more than uncertain".

Besides the platforms, the fund-raisers, micro-lenders, become the second supervisor. The final decision is theirs, so their role is of major importance to the sustainability of the model.

Many active lenders monitor the information provided or even do additional research before trusting to invest. Lenders immediately alert the community on the forums when they have doubts about the feasibility of the project: *"The same project is presented on 2 platforms a few weeks apart"*.

We identify in our netnographic exploration some leading lenders with low default stake in their loan portfolio. *"I became even more selective. I have invested in 261 projects and 64 are completed, 3 of them in losses. On my current investments (197) I have provided 7 loans. All this (including premiums) makes me a net annual return of 4.21%."* These lenders become leaders and their opinions and decisions are strongly followed, they influence other lenders to diversify their investments *"I signed up on the platform out of curiosity and also because Mathieu advertised it"* but they also influence lending decisions. *"Thanks to the forum and the aggregator: I am much more selective"*.

Lenders also state uncertainties about competence: *"On closer inspection, Mr. Boubeker Aissaoui has already liquidated two companies in the past where he was manager and closed a third"*.

They clearly benefiting from their experience *"For the record, I have invested in more than 200 loans in 3 years (investor since 10/2015) but I have learned to manage risk as I go along. I remain profitable at my level with an average profitability of 2% net"*.

Moreover, ignoring the applicants credit records and history is seen as a factor amplifying the risk of non-repayment: *"Certainly, I see around me that local banks are starting to make credit without a deposit ... but they know much better their clients, their personality, their mentality, their personal property, their investments, their family, their environment, etc. etc. what a crowdlending platform whose files are studied superficially, without knowledge of the terrain"*, but solidarity and mutual aid remains common strengths of the two models: *"On this subject, I saw that some boxes are really helped by the crowd and I am ... Uh... Happy? Proud? ... Short... I think some of them would not have been able to grow or survive without us. »*

We note, however, that the lack of projects sometimes leads to a lack of rationality among lenders: "*A number of projects put online that progress little from year to year*" because their loan deeds sometimes had to be rushed due to the lack of accessible projects. "*I get email alerts when I issue projects. I click and often it's already too late*".

Most lenders are aware of the risk and the necessity of control. However, they do not always do so: *"We lenders are also responsible for not finding the "flaws" of the file before lending. It's always easier to find when the file fell into RJ. »* Some are more skeptical *"The default rate on companies is abominable. And they often intervene very early ... the model is not viable"*.

SME/SMEs took advantage of the starting system's flaws in its early days to obtain loans that they were unable to repay.

Projects proposed during the launch phase of on Lendopolis show a high default rate of 20% in 2014. Lendopolis performs well since mid-2016, however, early defects cause trouble among lenders: *"Does anyone on this forum have any news of this company in default since 16/05/18? (...) Two new unpaid monthly payments have therefore been added since those of 16/11 and that of 16/12.I fear the worst".*

On the forums, it is the administrator who acts as a supervisor the benevolence of exchanges and regularly creates new topics of discussion or risk analysis tools to drive the craze around crowdlending. A community administrator might censor or even exclude a member with inappropriate comments: *"I don't block anyone on this forum because it gives facts, reports these bad results, criticizes platforms, ... I block people because they lack courtesy, always repeat the same things, leave no room for dialogue and exchange, even though I understand that we can be exaggerated now."*

The lenders of this forum are rather asking for a period during which they can study the project. *"Just look at the interesting discussions about our aggregator."*

Discussions on the forums show that lenders, project owners and platform administrators communicate very regularly to improve the online lending model: *"Thank you for bringing back this little detail that will be corrected during the day."*

The loan group is also influenced by the information provided, either by the project owner or by the lenders on the blogs: *"What do you think of the paper company project? I think it's a good deal, I intend to put a small ticket in it."* .... *"Congratulations to the authors of this barometer for the quality of their work. Anything that goes in the direction of information to lenders, transparency must be supported."*

## Nature of Conformity

Crowdlending platforms of which many operate in "all or nothing" mode proceed to double selections of projects of recipients and crowd-contributors. We have already discussed the compliance to the requirements of admission for joining the crowdfunding platforms.

However, we mention the important conformity of maximum amount of 2000 euros per project.

## Instruments of Control and Influence and Forms of Influence

The first influence for both lenders and borrowers is normative due to the loan. For example, the interest rate is based on the estimated level of risk.

There is also a form of influence through values. Many lenders claim to be acting to help small off and online projects to emerge. *"It's really a state of mind. Certainly, there is a financial aspect. You invest and you get paid because there is a risk — which is still acceptable compared to other investments or financial products. But for me, crowdfunding is part of a collective effort. Helping people who are either starting out or wanting to develop or have real ideas, real projects"*. However, the online lending suffers more from unreasonable cares. Individuals desire to break with traditional models of financing and savings to tie with extra-financial values of solidarity, pride, availability: *"I really do by conviction; I don't have any particular filters. Indeed, I have a sensitivity for all that is sustainable development, but I can finance franchise, development projects, business creation, real estate ... My goal is really to help as much as possible entrepreneurs who are sources of activities and jobs... »*. As behavioral finance describes, it appears that lenders also test and often act by mimicry. *"These experiences experienced by each other prompted me to turn quickly to the EnR (out of sympathy at first, then out of confidence), real estate, a little in agriculture (to see) and in solidarity projects via Solylend"*.

In this perspective, we sometimes observe similarities with behavioral finance which witnesses with the presence of biases of cognitive selections such as affect heuristics, psychological anchoring or overconfidence (Kahneman and Tversky, 1979).

The online model which benefits from an initial collective enthusiasm, sometimes suffers from unreasonable supports: *"For my part, average return over 4 years with a rate that must be close to booklet ... I participated in a lot of loans (about 300) based on both the opinions and advice of the aggregator members and my feelings of the project (I mean a project that corresponds to my beliefs)"*.

On the forums since the beginning of 2019, there is a growing interest in renewable energy and real estate. "*We must not forget that crowdlending starts and as with all new activities there is a time to set up and trial and error. What is important is that we and the platforms learn from our mistakes to advance this great activity.*"

## DISCUSSION: PERSPECTIVES OF TRANSMITTING INDIVIDUAL CONFORMITY FROM OFFLINE TO ONLINE GROUPS

After applying finds to our conceptual framework, we propose to discuss the limitations and perspectives of the model of social guarantee. We find all elements of the model in the mechanism of social guarantee of loans foo or online. However, these elements seem to function with less vigor online than offline, most likely because they rely on ex-post relationships rather than not ex-ante, relations which exist between peers in offline communities. We discuss below some differences and similarities between these elements off and online.

## Admission Requirements

Social connections generally precede offline loan groups and succeed online ones. Therefore, there are stronger social lies between project leaders and backers offline, often friends and family relatives, than online, often the unknown. We observe a peculiarity on the Hellomerci platform which is specialized on loans backed by friends where social bonds are necessarily strong.

## Membership Motivations

Individuals join to offline group loans mainly for learning about financial services and conditions of loan access (cognitive motivations), feeling supported (affective motivations) and to have effective access to funds (conative motivations).

Individuals participate in online communities for the same reasons with this difference that peers might meet each other not only on the crowdfunding platforms (Babyloan, Lendopolis) but also on social media (Facebook Younited Credit, crowdlending.fr) for broader discussions. In this perspective, backers can also virtually meet borrowing entrepreneurs they support, however, this remains a secondary motivation.

## Group Types

The significant difference we find between offline group lending and online platforms, as illustrated in table 3 is that the former generally represent a one-sided market while the latter express the two-sided market which rapidly evolve online (Muzellec and al., 2015) with multi-homing pricing policies effects (Rochet and Tirole, 2003, 2006).

All types of offline group loans are formal secondary organizations. Informal primary groups are originators of offline group loans, however, they with operational formalities like the amount of contribution, the lifespan, the meeting frequency, the reimbursement amount, etc. Online lending groups are mostly secondary, except on platforms like *HelloMerci,* where the borrower can activate his/her social ties. Applicants who prompt their relatives to raise initial funds on crowdfunding platforms generally attract more strangers to back them up. In this case, the platform is simply a trusted amplifier because it allows the loan to be formalized through a contract and automatic repayments. In the credit market, the dominant logic is that of sharing financial resources.

## Instruments of Control and Influence

All detected factors that contribute to the individual's compliance with the rules of good behavior in offline lending groups are reproducible online. However, as social ties are rather ex ante in offline groups and ex post in online groups, the collective pressure as a mode of governance is naturally stronger offline than online. The default rate for borrowers exceeds 17% at the end of 2018 for Lendopolis.

## Nature of Conformity

Membership is voluntary in off and online groups and individuals corollary comply to the expectations. Members align themselves with group standards not only to gain access to credits, but also to ensure social integration.

## Forms of Influence

The common criterion for offline or offline loans seems to be solidarity.

The major difference is that roles are rarely exchanged in online groups. Individual lenders never borrow in turn and in the same way project leaders rarely register as lenders. Some project leaders sometimes repeat their loan requests by emigrating or not around the platforms. Online peers seem to remain in a single role unlike offline group lending where role reversal is more frequent.

Some of the online lenders believe the model improves if the platform also invests in the projects presented. Some already do, and risk sharing is appreciated: *"A platform that takes the same risks that you do when you diversify your investments!"*

# CONCLUSION AND RESEARCH IN PERSPECTIVE

This contribution explores whether the social innovation of social collateral relying on individual conformity in offline group lending is transposable online. The objective is not to know how individual conformity in group and social collateral are effectively deployed online, but whether the constituent elements of individual conformity and the social guarantee exist in cyber-communities and crowdfunding.

We find the constituent elements of individual conformity are reproducible online, with some adaptations close. Therefore, the social innovation of collective collateral is transposable from offline to online.

We finally propose a theoretical model of individual compliance with the expectation of good behavior within groups and believe this is a spontaneous popular mode of governance. This model can be used not only to analyze group loans offline and online, but also to analyze all activities from individual to individual (P2P) that is developing on the Internet.

The interest of this mode of governance extends beyond the financial sector and includes a growing number of sectors that operate in the “Sharing economy”.

The netnographic approach of this research project provides other academic and practical findings.

Once the euphoria of the novelty passed, the default rates panic the actors. Crowdlending platforms are heavily impacted by surveillance deficiencies. Controls carried out by artificial intelligence and analysts are progressively added to the platforms to anticipate the manipulation of ill-intentioned borrowers.

The results of this research relate to the compliance factors of individuals within a single group of belonging. However, individuals often belong to multiple reference groups simultaneously. The elements of the individual’s conformity to one group may converge or diverge with those in other groups of belonging. In other words, memberships in various groups may be in conflict or at peace. This question, however crucial, was outside the scope of this article’s study. It can give a major research axis in the future.

## REFERENCES


Agrawal, A., Catalini, C., & Goldfarb, A. (2015). Crowdfunding: Geography, Social Networks, and the Timing of Investment Decisions. *Journal of Economics & Management Strategy*, *24*, 253–274.

Akula, V. (2010). *A Fistful of Rice: My Unexpected Quest to End Poverty Through Profitability*. Harvard Business Press.

Alijani, S., Assadi, D., & Ashta, A. (2016). Can Social Dynamics Be Channeled from Offline to Online Communities? Commitment, Compliance and Cooperation from Microfinance to Crowdfunding. In D. Assadi (Ed.), *Strategic Approaches to Successful Crowdfunding* (pp. 210–227). IGI Global.

Angwin J. (2009), *Stealing MySpace: The Battle to Control the Most Popular Website in America*. Random House.

Arborio, A. M., Fournier, P., de Singly, F., & Fournier, P. (2015). l’observation directe. Armand Colin.

Armendáriz de Aghion, B., & Morduch, J. (2005). *The Economics of Microfinance*. The MIT Press.

Asch, S. E. (1951). Effects of Group Pressure on the Modification and Distortion of Judgments. In H. Guestzkow (Ed.), *Groups, Leadership, and Men*. Carnegie Press.

Ashta, A., & Assadi, D. (2009). Do Social Cause and Social Technology Meet? Impact of Web 2.0 Technologies on peer-to-peer lending transactions in general and microfinance in particular. *Proceedings of the The First European Research Conference on Microfinance*.

Ashta, A., & Dayson, K. (2013). Microcredit as a Social Innovation. In The International Handbook on Social Innovation. Edward Elgar.

Ashta, A., Demay, I., & Couchoro, M. (2016). The Role of Stakeholders in the Historical Evolution of Microfinance in Togo. *Economic History of Developing Regions*, *31*, 303–344.

Assadi, D. (2004). *Les 7 modèles économiques d'Internet: pour vendre sur Internet en gagnant de l'argent*. Gualino éd.

Assadi, D. (2004). *Les 7 modèles économiques sur Internet*. Gualino Editions.

Assadi, D., & Ashta, A. (2014). Innovative Transposition of Trust Mechanisms in Social Lending Groups from Offline to Online Strategic Change. *Briefings in Entrepreneurial Finance*, *23*, 461–480.

Auerswald, P. E. (2009). Creating social value. *Stanford Social Innovation Review*, 51–55.

Bain and Company. (2009). *Management tools and Trends*. http://www.bain.com/management_tools/home.asp

Baltača, B., & Mavrenko, T. (2009). Financial Cooperation As A Low-Cost Tool For Effective Microfinancing. *Journal of Business and Management*, 56–64.

Belleflamme, P., & Lambert, T., & Schwienbacher, A. (2014). Crowdfunding: Tapping the right crowd. *Journal of Business Venturing*, *29*, 585–609.

Berger, S., & Gleisner, F. (2009). *Emergence of Financial Intermediaries on Electronic Markets: The Case of Online P2P Lending*. http://www.business-research.org/early_view/berger_gleisner_preview.pdf

Bornstein, D. (2007). *How to change the world: Social entrepreneurs and the power of new ideas*. Oxford University Press.

Bouaiss, K., Maque, I., & Méric, J. (2015). More than Three's a Crowd… in the Best Interest of Companies! Crowdfunding as Zeitgeist or Ideology? *Society and Business Review*, *10*, 23–39.

Bouman, F. J. A. (1983). Indigenous savings & credit societies in the developing world. In A. D. Von Pischke (Ed.), *Rural Financial Markets in the Developing World*. World Bank.

Boxenbaum, E., & Battilana, J. (2005). Importation as innovation: Transposing managerial practices across fields. *Strategic Organization*, *3*, 355–383.

Brown S., Tilton A., Woodside D. (2002). *The case for on-line communities*. McKinsey Quarterly.

Bugg-Levine, A., & Emerson, J. (2011). Impact investing: Transforming how we make money while making a difference. *Innovations*, *6*, 9–18.

Burnkrant, R., & Alain, C. (1975). Informational and Normative Social Influence in Buyer Behavior. *The Journal of Consumer Research*, 206–215.

Burt S. (2010). Always On. *London Review of Books*.

Calder, B., & Burnkrant, R. (1977). Interpersonal Influence on Buyer Behavior: An Attribution Theory Approach. *The Journal of Consumer Research*, 29–38.

Cassar, A., Crowley, L., & Wydick, B. (2007). The Effect Of Social Capital On Group Loan Repayment: Evidence From Field Experiments. *Economic Journal (London)*, *117*, F85–F106.

Chabaud, D., & Germain, O. (2006). La réutilisation de données qualitatives en sciences de gestion: un second choix? *M@ n@ gement*, *9*(3), 199-221.

Chiteji, N. S. (2002). Promises kept: Enforcement and the role of rotating savings and credit associations in an economy. *Journal of International Development*, *14*, 393–411.

Colombo, M.G., Franzoni, C., & Rossi-Lamastra, C. (2015). Internal social capital and the attraction of early contributions in crowdfunding. *Entrepreneurship Theory and Practice*, *39*, 75–100.

Comley, P. (2008). Online research communities. *International Journal of Market Research*, *50*, 679–694.

CSESS. (2011). *Rapport de synthèse du Groupe de travail Innovation Sociale*. Conseil supérieur de l'économie sociale et solidaire, Téléchargé le 25 octobre 2017 sur http://www.avise.org/sites/default/files/atoms/files/20140204/201112_CSESS_GTIS_Synthese.pdf

Datta, P.B., & Gailey, R. (2012). Empowering Women Through Social Entrepreneurship: Case Study of a Women's Cooperative in India. *Entrepreneurship Theory and Practice*, *36*, 569–587.

Demirguc-Kunt, A., Klapper, L., Singer, D., Ansar, S., & Hess, J. (2018). *The Global Findex Database 2017: Measuring financial inclusion and the fintech revolution.* The World Bank. Retrieved May 5, 2020 on https://globalfindex.worldbank.org/

Demirguc-Kunt, A., Klapper, L., Singer, D., & Oudheusden, P. V. (2015). *The Global Findex Database 2014: Measuring Financial Inclusion around the World.* Policy Research Working Paper 7255. World Bank.

Ellerman, D. (2005). *Helping people help themselves.* University of Michigan Press.

Eloranta, V., & Turunen, T. (2016). Platforms in service-driven manufacturing: Leveraging complexity by connecting, sharing, and integrating. *Industrial Marketing Management*, *55*, 178–186.

Emerson, R. M., Fretz, R. I., & Shaw, L. L. (2011). Writing Ethnographic Fieldnotes. University of Chicago Press.

Escalas, J.E., & Bettman, J.R. (2005). Self-construal, reference groups, and brand meaning. *The Journal of Consumer Research*, *32*, 378–389.

Etang, A., Fielding, D., & Knowles, S. (2011). Trust and ROSCA membership in rural Cameroon. *Journal of International Development*, *23*, 461–475.

Fischer, E., Bristor, J., & Gainer, B. (1996). Creating or Escaping Community? An Exploratory Study of Internet Consumers' Behaviors. *Advances in Consumer Research. Association for Consumer Research (U. S.)*, *23*, 178–182.

Flamant, N. (2005). Observer, analyser, restituer. Conditions et contradictions de l'enquête ethnologique en entreprise. *Terrain, Anthropologies & Sciences Humaines, 44*, 137-152. https://journals.openedition.org/terrain/2505

Freedman, S., & Jin, G.Z. (2008). *Do Social Networks Solve Information Problems for Peer to-Peer Lending? Evidence from Prosper.* Retrieved at: http://www.fas.nus.edu.sg/ecs/events/seminar-papers/12Mar09.pdf

Galloway. I. (2009). *Peer-toPeer Lending and Community Development Finance.* Working Paper, Community Development Center, Federal Reserve of San Francisco. Retrieved on frbsf.org/cdinvestments

Ghatak, M. (1999). *Group lending, local information and peer selection.* Academic Press.

Granovetter, M. (2005). The Impact of Social Structure on Economic Outcomes. *The Journal of Economic Perspectives*, *19*, 33–50.

Granovetter, M. S. (1973). *The Strength of Weak Ties. American Journal of Sociology*, *78*, 1360–1380.

Herrero-Lopez, S. (2009). Social Interactions in P2P Lending. *Proceedings of the 3rd workshop on Social Network Mining and Analysis (SNA), International Conference on Knowledge Discovery and Data Mining*. Retrieved at: http://www.snakdd.com/AcceptedPapers/snakdd2009_submission_5.pdf

Herzenstein, M., Andrews, R., Dholakia, U., & Lyandres, E. (2008). *The Democratization of Personal Consumer Loans? Determinants of Success in Online Peer-to-Peer Lending Communities*. Retrieved at: http://www.rice.edu/nationalmedia/multimedia/online

Homans, G. (1961). *Social Behavior: Its Elementary Forms*. Harcourt.

Hulme, M., & Wright, C. (2006). *Internet Based Social Lending: Past, Present and Future*. Social Futures Observatory.

IDEO.ORG. (2015). *The Field Guide to Human-Centered Design*. Téléchargé le 25 octobre 2017 sur http://www.designkit.org//resources/1

Iyer, R. I., K.A., Luttmer, E.F.P., & Shue, K. (2009). *Screening in New Credit Markets: Can Individual Lenders Infer Borrower Creditworthiness in Peer-to-Peer Lending?* NBER Working Paper No. 15242. Retrieved at: http://www.nber.org/papers/w15242

Kahneman, D., & Tversky, A. (1979). Prospect theory: An analysis of decision under risk. *Econometrica*, 263–291.

Kapoor, A. (2007). The SEWA way: Shaping another future for informal labour. *Futures*, *39*, 554–568.

Klein, D. B. (1997). *Reputation: Studies in the Voluntary Elicitation of Good Conduct*. University of Michigan Press.

Kozinets, R. V. (2002). The field behind the screen: Using netnography for marketing research in online communities. *JMR, Journal of Marketing Research*, *39*, 61–72.

Kuan, T. S. (1996). Life on the Net: The Reconstruction of Self and Community. Advances in Consumer Research 23 Association of Consumer Research.

La Loi, E. S. S. (2014). *LOI n° 2014-856 du 31 juillet 2014 relative à l'économie sociale et solidaire*. In NOR: ERNX1315311L, Téléchargé le 25 octobre 2017 sur https://www.legifrance.gouv.fr/affichTexte.do?cidTexte=JORFTEXT000029313296&categorieLien=id

Labrecque, L., Krishen, A., & Grzeskowiak, S. (2011). Exploring social motivations for brand loyalty: Conformity versus escapism. *Journal of Brand Management, 18*, 457–472.

Lawont, J.J., & N'Guessan, T. (2000). *Group lending with adverse selection*. Academic Press.

Mahadevan, B. (2000). Business models for Internet-based e-commerce: An anatomy. *California Management Review*, *42*, 55–69.

Marconatto, D. A. B., Barin-Cruz, L., & Pedrozo, E. (2016). Lending groups and different social capitals in developed and developing countries. *Revista de Administração Contemporânea*, *20*, 651–672.

Martin, R. L., & Osberg, S. (2007). Social entrepreneurship: The case for definition. *Stanford Social Innovation Review*, 5.

Marx, M. T., & Seibel, H. D. (2012). The Evolution Of Financial Cooperatives In Nigeria:Do They Have A Place In Financial Intermediation? In Cooperative Finance in Developing Economies. Soma Prints Limited.

Meyer, T. (n.d.). *Financial services 2.0: How social computing and P2P activity are changing financial research and lending*. Deutsche Bank Research. Retrieved on www.dbresearch.com

Muniz, A.M., & O'Guinn, T.C. (2001). Brand community. *The Journal of Consumer Research*, *27*, 412–432.

Muzellec, L., Ronteau, S., & Lambkin, M. (2015). Two-sided Internet platforms: A business model lifecycle perspective. *Industrial Marketing Management*, *45*, 139–150.

Okleshen, C., & Grossbart, S. (1988). Unset Groups, Virtual Community and Consumer Behavior. In J. W. Alba & J. W. Hutchinson (Eds.), *Advances in Consumer Research 25* (pp. 276–282). Association of Consumer Research.

Onnée, S., & Renault, S. (2014). Crowdfunding: Vers une compréhension du rôle joué par la foule. *Management et Avenir*, *8*, 117–133.

Peneff, J. (2009). *Le goût de l'observation. Comprendre et pratiquer l'observation participante en sciences sociales*. Paris: La Découverte/Grands repères.

Phills, J. A., Deiglmeier, K., & Miller, D. T. (2008). Rediscovering social innovation. *Stanford Social Innovation Review*, *6*, 34–43.

Pytkowska, J. (2006). Is Commercial Financing a Growth Engine for Microfinance Institutions? *Finance & the Common Good/Bien Commun*, 101-104.

Rayskin, V. (2016). Dynamics of Two-Sided Markets. *Review of Marketing Science*, *14*, 1–19.

Renault, S. (2014). Crowdsourcing: La nébuleuse des frontières de l'organisation et du travail. *RIMHE: Revue Interdisciplinaire Management, Homme & Entreprise*, 23-40.

Rochet, J. C., & Tirole, J. (2003). Platform competition in two-sided markets. *Journal of the European Economic Association*, *1*(4), 990–1029.

Rochet, J. C., & Tirole, J. (2006). Two-sided markets: A progress report. *The RAND Journal of Economics*, *37*, 645–667.

Ross, L., & Bierbrauer, G. S. H. (1976). The Role of Attribution Processes in Conformity and Dissent. *The American Psychologist*, 148–157.

Ryan, J. (2012). The Digital Graveyard. In Human no more: Digital subjectivities, unhuman subjects, and the end of anthropology. University Press of Colorado.

Ryan, J., Reuk, K., & Wang, C. (2007). *To Fund or Not To Fund: Determinants Of Loan Fundability in the Prosper.com Marketplace*. Stanford Graduate School of Business. Retrieved at: http://www.prosper.com/about/academics.aspx

Sa-Dhan. (2016). The Bharat Microfinance Report 2016. Sa-Dhan.

Schmidt, R. H., Seibel, H. D., & Thomes, P. (2016). From Microfinance to Inclusive Finance: Why Local Banking Works. Wiley-VCH Verlag.

Stake, R. (1995). *The art of case research*. Sage Publications.

Tapscott, D., Lowy, A., & Ticoll, D. (2000). *Digital capital: Harnessing the power of business webs*. Harvard Business Press.

Tasque, S. (2011). La lutte contre l'exclusion bancaire des particuliers. Une perspective franco-américaine. *La Revue de l'Ires*, (3), 61-88. Retrieved May 5, 2020 on https://www.cairn.info/revue-de-l-ires-2011-3-page-61.htm#

Turan, M. T. (2008). *Measuring and/or estimating social value creation: Insights into eight integrated cost approaches: The Gats Foundation Website*. Téléchargé le 25 octobre 2017 sur https://docs.gatesfoundation.org/documents/wwl-report-measuring-estimating-social-value-creation.pdf

Venkatesan, M. (1966). Experimental Study of Consumer Behavior Conformity and Independence. *JMR, Journal of Marketing Research, 3*, 384–387.

Vik, E. (2010). In Numbers We Trust: Measuring Impact or Institutional Performance? *Perspectives on Global Development and Technology, 9*, 292–326.

War, J.C., & Reingen, P.H. (1990). Socioconitive Analysis of Group Decision Making among Consumers. *The Journal of Consumer Research, 17*, 245–261.

Watkins, C. (2009). *The Young and the Digital: What the Migration to Social Network Sites, Games and Anytime, Anywhere Media Means for Our Future*. Beacon Press.

Williamson, O. E. (2000). The New Institutional Economics: Taking Stock, Looking Ahead. *Journal of Economic Literature, 38*, 595–613.

Witt, R. E., & Bruce, G. D. (1972). Group Influence and Brand Choice. *JMR, Journal of Marketing Research, 9*, 440–443.

Xia, W., Chunling, Y., & Yujie, W. (2012). Social Media Peer Communication and Impacts on Purchase Intentions: A Consumer Socialization Framework. *Journal of Interactive Marketing, 26*, 198–208.

Yin, R. (1994). *Case study research: Design and methods*. Sage Publishing.

Yunus, M. (1994). *Grameen Bank, as I See it*. Grameen Bank.

Yunus, M. (1999). *Banker to the Poor: Micro-Lending and the Battle Against World Poverty*. PublicAffairs.

Yunus, M. (2007). *Creating A World without Poverty: Social Business and The Future Of Capitalism*. Public Affairs.

Yunus, M. (2010). *Building Social Business: The New Kind of Capitalism that Serves Humanity's Most Pressing Needs*. Public Affairs.

# Chapter 7
# Characteristics of Successful Securities Crowdfunding Campaigns in the United States

**William Frank Wright**
https://orcid.org/0000-0002-1307-1532
*University of Illinois at Urbana-Champaign, USA*

**Margaret MacFarlane Wright**
*University of Illinois at Urbana-Champaign, USA*

## ABSTRACT

*Title III of the Jumpstart Our Business Startups Act (JOBS Act) enacted by the U.S. Congress enables a new crowdfunding source of investment capital for entrepreneurs and a new opportunity for all investors (Regulation CF). Given the information asymmetry, the SEC requires that managers provide information to investors (Form C). Using this information, this research tests whether business attributes, financial risks, and offering characteristics are associated with successful crowdfunding efforts for 277 offerings originating during 2016-2017 and closed as of May 2018. The following attributes are positively correlated with funding success: product idea; prior managerial experience with startups; financial risks reported by management; availability of an independent CPA review; and, especially for companies reporting revenue, accounting risk measurements. Finally, the funding intermediary chosen is important and some were more successful than others. Overall, the results provide new insights concerning characteristics of successful security-based crowdfunding offerings.*

DOI: 10.4018/978-1-7998-3226-3.ch007

## INTRODUCTION

The United States Congress has created an easily accessible, online opportunity for all investors to provide capital to startup and early-stage companies. Title III of the Jumpstart Our Business Start-Ups Act (JOBS Act), implemented by the Securities and Exchange Commission (SEC), enables securities crowdfunding. All potential investors are now able to invest in startup and early-stage companies that may turn out to be successful. Title III provides for fewer restrictions on solicitation of investors[1] and reduced SEC reporting requirements, while making capital acquisition less costly for issuers (SEC, 2015a)[2]. The rules became effective as of May 16, 2016 and are known as Regulation Crowdfunding (Reg. CF) (SEC, 2015a).

While new investment opportunities are now available, significant information asymmetry exists for potential investors in private companies (Hoegen, Steininger & Veit, 2018). To reduce the information asymmetry, the SEC requires information on an issuer's business plans, business and financial risks, and accounting information which are filed as Form C. Form C includes product and business model information, income and balance sheet data for risk assessment, and offering details presented in a standardized format. One aspect of Reg. CF is that companies must use an intermediary, i.e., a "funding portal" or a broker/dealer platform, which will present characteristics of an offering, accept investments and function as the required portal for issuer management to communicate with existing and potential investors during the offering.

The objectives of this study are to test for whether the three major dimensions of a crowdfunding offering are relevant for investor decisions and, therefore, funding success: (1) attributes of the business proposed by management, especially the type of product or service offered, (2) aspects of a company's financial structure and (3) offering characteristics, especially the portal/platform selected by management given portal curation. The hypotheses indicate research questions within the three dimensions. The time period is the first year of Reg. CF. Two measures of funding success are used: meeting a threshold of requested funding and, if the funding threshold is met, the total amount funded.

Study of funding success (and a lack thereof) is important as it reveals the "wisdom of the crowd" regarding salient characteristics of companies and offerings (e.g., Mollick & Nanda, 2016). In addition, previous research has not concentrated on whether different product types have different levels of appeal to investors—and the possibility of different funding levels (Lukkarinen, Teich, Wallenius and Wallenius, 2016). For example, Ahlers, Cumming, Gunther and Schweizer (2015) and Mollick (2014), and for Reg. CF campaigns, Knyazeva and Ivanov (2017), treat "industries" as control variables without any substantive analysis of the products offered and customers served. Therefore, additional insights remain to be gained by further study. In order to develop hypotheses regarding the information in Form C and from funding intermediaries, strategic management theory (Casadesus-Masanell & Ricart, 2010; Teece, 2010) and financial risk analysis concepts (Palepu & Healy, 2013) are employed.

This research uses hand collected data from SEC Form C filings and from funding intermediaries for 277 offerings originating during 2016-2017 and closed for further investment as of May 2018. The final data include 277 of 296 offerings (see below), including 155 that achieved funding success. Given the necessity of establishing a value chain to serve customers, generation of revenue is a challenging milestone for startup companies (Halt, Donch, Stiles & Fesnak, 2017; Leach & Melicher, 2018; Younkin & Kashkooli, 2016). Based on this milestone, this study partitions the 277 companies into 146 "startup" companies that do not report revenue and 131 "early stage" companies that do report revenue.

The results permit understanding of the characteristics of offerings that are associated with success of a Reg. CF offering. One result is the substantial relevance of the type of product chosen by management. Also relevant is previous experience managing a new and evolving business (Ahlers, et al., 2015; Piva & Rossi-Lamastra, 2017). Financial risks reported by management are associated with the likelihood of successful funding. Especially for the 131 companies that report revenue, accounting risk measurements of liquidity and profitability, and availability of an independent accountant's report, are associated with funding success. As the SEC intended, funding intermediaries perform an important function with some funding intermediaries being more effective than others at supporting successful campaigns. Finally, demand is indicated for several types of securities including a new and controversial form of possible future equity, the Simple Agreement for Future Equity or SAFE security.

## SECURITIES CROWDFUNDING: BACKGROUND AND PRIOR RESEARCH

### World-Wide Equity Crowdfunding

While implementation of equity crowdfunding has been ongoing in Australia (Ahlers, et al., 2015), Canada (Cumming, Johan & Zhang, 2019), Germany (Hornuf & Schwienbacher, 2018), Italy (Piva & Rossi-Lamastra, 2017) and the UK (Vulkan, Astebro & Sierra, 2016), each country specifies its own required information, market rules, regulatory structure and taxation incentives (Agrawal, Catalini & Goldfarb, 2014). For example, in Germany issuance of equity shares is costly given transfer fees and a required prospectus (Schmitt, 2017). In contrast, U.K crowdfunding investors receive very favorable income tax incentives to own equity shares, and the government imposes minimal regulation (Estrin, Gozman & Khavul, 2018). Also, total funding limits for crowdfunding are much higher, and are being increased, in Europe (Torris, 2018) with ongoing discussions to do so in the U.S. (Alois, 2018a,b).

## Regulation Crowdfunding in the United States

The U.S. has its own set of unique crowdfunding rules and government regulations, e.g., flexible duration periods to raise funds and the pivotal role of funding intermediaries (Knyazeva & Ivanov, 2017). Further, pursuant to Title III, the SEC requires that the issuer must select a "targeted" minimum amount of funding that it hopes to raise for a specific phase of the business. The issuer also indicates a maximum amount of funding that will be acceptable with a limit of $1,070,000 over a rolling twelve-month period. (The limit was increased from $1,000,000 as of April 5, 2017.) Reg. CF offerings are an "all or nothing" situation, i.e., the amount raised must at least equal the minimum amount or no funding will be received by the company. Investment from non-accredited investors is limited by a person's net worth and income[3]. No investor can invest more than $107,000 in an Reg. CF offering.

All investments must be made online using a funding portal or a broker/dealer platform that is registered with the SEC and is a member of the Financial Industry Regulatory Authority ("FINRA"). FINRA maintains oversight of funding portals. The intermediary serves as a continuing source of information and communication between investors and issuer management. Portal management is responsible for investigating that founders are not fraudulent and have provided the information required by the SEC ("due diligence"). Portal management also oversees whether investors are compliant with the monetary limitations placed on their investment. While portals do curate offerings, they may not promote an offering based on expected investment returns (SEC, 2016b).

## Previous Research on Characteristics of Funding Success

There are four general types of crowdfunding: donation, reward (pre-selling of a product), lending and securities-based (equity) crowdfunding (Vulkan et al., 2016). While the Reg. CF context is distinct given its investment focus (Mollick, 2014; Vismara, 2018a), potentially relevant literature exists on characteristics of successful rewards-based crowdfunding campaigns (Belleflamme, Lambert, & Schwienbacher, 2014; Short, Ketchen, Jr., McKenny, Allison & Ireland, 2017; Madsen & McMullin, in press). Rewards-based crowdfunding, e.g., Kickstarter.com, emphasizes projects where a product is pre-sold, or a token of appreciation is provided, instead of an investment opportunity, thereby creating a group of customers versus investors (Mollick, 2014). Regarding aspects of the business and offering characteristics,

Mollick (2014) reports increased odds of success given smaller minimum amounts, availability of a video, shorter funding periods, more project updates, and whether a project is featured on the Kickstarter initial web page. Cordova, Dolci and Gianfrate (2015) report similar results except that the presence of a video is not related to funding success. Focusing on project risks, Madsen and McMullin (in press) report that emphasis on more risks conveyed using voluntary disclosures is associated with lower funding results for risky Kickstarter projects.

Results from research on securities-based crowdfunding in other countries are more relevant, even though different national rules and regulations cause results to be country-specific (Hornuf and Schwienbacher, 2018). Ahlers, et al. (2015) use 104 offerings during 2006-2011 from the AASOB portal in Australia to test for the impact of three forms of capital on crowdfunding success. Their findings indicate the importance of management capital signaled by a graduate business degree, however, neither social capital nor intellectual capital are associated with the likelihood of funding success. Results reported by Piva and Rossi-Lamastra (2017) also emphasize the potential importance of startup experience and business education.

Vulkan, et al. (2016) test for factors that are associated with success for 636 securities crowdfunding campaigns on the SEEDRS platform in the U.K. They report that, relative to rewards-based campaigns, securities crowdfunding campaigns involve higher minimum amounts, higher average amounts invested, and the expectation of a positive return on investment, confirming the investment focus of security-based versus rewards-based crowdfunding. Higher minimum amounts are associated with less likely success; early substantial investments are associated with more likely funding (also see Abrams, 2017).

Two studies have been completed that evaluate Reg. CF offerings. Abrams (2017) provides results for Reg. CF offerings during 2016, including 50 closed offerings. The results document differences in the distributions of accounting metrics for successful versus unsuccessful offerings. Companies with stronger balance sheets, i.e., more assets and less long-term debt, tend to raise larger amounts. The results also emphasize the importance of funding during the first week of the offering and, subsequently, the economic potential of the company (also see Hornuf and Schwienbacher, 2018; Vulkan et al., 2016).

Knyazeva and Ivanov (2017) report findings on the characteristics of both offering success and the magnitude of total funding achieved for 173 closed offerings during the first year of Reg. CF. The authors concentrate on "hard" versus "soft" information regarding issuer quality and certification of issuer information. Hard information is more objective, e.g., financial accounting information, and soft information is more subjective, e.g., social media postings. Forms of certification include an independent accountant's report and due diligence performed by an intermediary, which includes searching for fraudulent behavior by founders and making sure that the necessary background documents and filings have been submitted (SEC, 2016b). The results indicate that accounting data on assets and profitability are not correlated with funding success. Funding success is more likely by having an accountant's review report and positive social media data. The market position and reputation of an intermediary is associated with total funding of an offering but not the likelihood of funding success. Offering perks and investment funding minimums are not significant characteristics at conventional levels of Type I error.

In summary, findings reported to date suggest that increasing magnitudes of the minimum amount are likely to be negatively correlated with the probability of funding success. While availability of an independent accounting (review) report is associated with funding success, financial accounting risk measures have not been shown to be relevant. Funding intermediaries do impact the magnitude of successful total funding (Knyazeva and Ivanov, 2017). However, the impact of different types of products on investor decision making has not been addressed directly. While industry classifications are used as control variables (Ahlers et al., 2015; Knyazeva and Ivanov, 2017; Mollick, 2014), there has not been analysis of how different products and services affect investor Reg CF funding decisions.

## HYPOTHESES REGARDING THE LIKELIHOOD OF FUNDING SUCCESS

### Investments in Private Companies and Information Asymmetry

Information asymmetry inhibits investor analysis of investment quality and uncertainty creating the possibility of moral hazard conditions for investors and markets (Ahlers et al., 2015; Vismara, 2018b). The SEC requires filing of Form C to diminish the asymmetry. Information is also conveyed when managers signal their beliefs and expectations via their decisions and behaviors. Signals (Spence, 1973; Connelly, Certo, Ireland and Reutzel, 2011) in a Reg. CF context are management's observable actions intended to inform investors of the impact of unobservable aspects of investment quality (Vismara, 2018b). Management's signals include the confidence implied by advocating a product idea (and a product market), previous experience with startup companies and a higher minimum funding threshold. Different signals can be complementary or dilutive regarding their joint impact on the perceived quality of an offering (Bapna, 2019; Courtney, Dutta and Li, 2017).

## Business Risks: Product Ideas and Management Competence

Perhaps the most informative signal from management is confidence in, and advocacy of, a product idea (Courtney et al., 2017). Management's commitment to a product idea is an important determinant of Angel and VC investment decisions (Warnick, Murnicks, McMullen and Brooks, 2018) and it may also result in significant investor interest in a Reg. CF offering (Hoegen et al., 2018; Li, Chen, Kotha & Fisher, 2017).

Management chooses a product idea, strategy and business model to create value for targeted customers (Huelsbeck, Marchant & Sandino, 2011; Teece, 2010; Vera-Muñoz, Shackell & Buehner, 2007). Startup business models emphasize product innovation and differentiation (Porter, 1980) given the need to generate initial, and continuing, customer demand (Bentley, Omar & Sharp, 2013; Davila, Foster & Li, 2009; Davis, Hmieleski, Webb, & Coombs, 2017; Hervé & Schwienbacher, 2018; Osiyevskyy, Chernenko, & Biloshapka, 2018). The market appeal of a product will affect the level of revenue and net cash flow from operations.

Certain product types and targeted customers may present more appealing investment opportunities to Reg. CF investors because of their perceived economic potential, and investor beliefs and preferences (Lukkarinen et al., 2016). If so, offerings of different types of products may have different rates of funding success (Cordova et al., 2015). Four product types with targeted customers are predicted to be funded more frequently. First, local investors respond favorably to the availability of new sites for consumption and entertainment that they may patronize and communicate their pride of ownership: funding for new or expanded breweries and/or bars/restaurants may be more likely (Hornuf & Schmitt, 2017). Second, results from rewards-based crowdfunding studies suggest that distinctive entertainment and media products and services may generate significant customer interest and funding from Reg. CF investors (Mollick, 2014). Third, Agrawal et al., (2014) propose that consumer products may be a more fundable product type because of highly differentiated products and the ease of communicating a value proposition to targeted customers (also Ibrahim, 2017a). Fourth, medical devices and services provide opportunities to serve the needs of patients given increasing demand from both doctors and patients (Hage, 2018). The following hypothesis (stated in alternative form) is implied:

Hypothesis One: The type of product or service offered will affect the likelihood of funding success.

A major business risk is the level of entrepreneurial competence of management. The activities involved in creating and operating a startup are demanding, and many are different from the demands of operating an established company. For example, management must hire people with an entrepreneurial perspective, put new business processes in place such as product development and marketing, establish a supply chain, and provide a level of leadership for the company's evolving business model (Osiyevskyy et al., 2018).

Previous startup experience and business school education of directors and senior management provide a basis for investor assessment of entrepreneurial competence (Ahlers et al., 2015; Piva & Rossi-Lamastra, 2017). Agrawal et al. (2014) point out that VCs often emphasize the startup experience of the founders and senior management (however see Baum and Silverman (2004) for evidence of over-emphasis). Business school education, especially MBA programs, provides an overall awareness of business strategy and processes, and how they contribute to a successful business. The company's presentation on Form C and at the funding intermediary introduce members of the management team and their pertinent experiences and accomplishments. Startup experience and MBA education are relevant signals for Reg. CF investors, and they are likely to be associated with funding success:

Hypothesis Two(a): Startup experience will be positively associated with the likelihood of funding success.

Hypothesis Two(b): MBA education will be positively associated with the likelihood of funding success.

## Financial Risks and Accountant's Report

For a new company's business model to be feasible and effective, a suitable financial structure must be in place (Osiyevskyy et al., 2018). Startup and early-stage firms have a continuing need for capital and may be reporting losses. Liquidity and profitability risks are especially relevant given the high risk of insolvency and the uncertainty of product revenue (Hoegen et al., 2018). The SEC recognized this by specifying disclosure requirements for available balance sheet and income statement data on Form C (SEC, 2015b).

A major financial risk is the risk of insufficient liquidity, which would cause a startup to be unable to take advantage of opportunities or meet short-term obligations. Cash is necessary to implement a product idea and a business model: this need for cash is a major reason for a security offering (Halt et al., 2017). A high level of solvency risk ("running out of cash") results in additional uncertainty for future cash flows. The research question is whether a company's current level of liquidity is associated with funding success.

Hypothesis Three(a): Increasing liquidity will be positively associated with the likelihood of funding success

A second financial risk is insufficient profitability and cash flow from operations. There are different implications of two relevant profitability measures: reported revenue and net income. The magnitude of revenue measures the results of operating a value chain of processes and satisfying targeted customers. Generation of significant revenue is a major milestone for a startup (Leach and Melicher, 2018). While revenue is a component, net income adds expenses incurred, providing a measure of net operating performance.

Financial risk analysis of Reg. CF companies requires consideration of where the company is in its funding life cycle (Halt et al., 2017). Companies in the startup phase have an idea for a product, a tentative business model, and no revenue. In this study, "startup" companies are those that do not report any revenue. In contrast, "early-stage" companies have operating business models and do report revenue. Companies in the early-stage phase also have more financial data available for financial risk analysis. The following financial risk hypothesis is implied:

Hypothesis Three(b): Increasing profitability will be positively associated with the likelihood of funding success

Next, investors may conclude that the presence of an independent CPA's report on a company's financial statements indicates higher credibility of the statements—providing a form of third-party certification (Knyazeva and Ivanov, 2017). SEC rules state that an independent accountant's review (or audit) of financial statements will be provided with a Form C filing during the first year for offerings greater than $100K ($107K as of April 5, 2017); otherwise executive management certification of financial statements is required (SEC, 2015a). Compared with a financial audit, a review is more limited in scope and, therefore, its assurance. A review involves application of analytical procedures to assess the reasonableness of statement balances and judgments of whether the applied accounting principles are appropriate. However, Reg. CF firms have limited financial information relative to public companies. Therefore, the presence of an accountant's review opinion may have little effect on investor funding decisions.

Alternatively, management's provision of an independent CPA review provides assurance that applicable accounting principles are applied, and statement relationships are reasonable. In addition, management's provision of a review is a positive signal of confidence in the accounting and its depiction of the business, while also implying transparency regarding prevailing information asymmetry. Therefore, will availability of an independent accountant's review (or audit) report on the financial statements be associated with funding success?

Hypothesis Four: Availability of an independent accountant's review (or audit) of a Reg. CF company's financial statements will be positively associated with the likelihood of funding success.

## Important Role of a Funding Intermediary

A funding intermediary provides company and offering information to investors and facilitates investments. A portal or broker/dealer platform provides "the legal groundwork, pre-selection, the ability to process financial transactions, etc." (Cordova et al., 2015, 116). The intermediary also provides a marketing opportunity for the offering company to emphasize attributes of a product and its business model (Ibrahim, 2017a). In order to provide these services a Reg. CF funding portal must register with the SEC and become a member of FINRA. Jegeleviciute and Valanciene (2015) note that FINRA performs an important regulatory function because it "establishes a rule set specifically designed for funding portals." (p. 269).

Portal managements curate offerings and compete to obtain high-quality crowdfunding offerings (Cumming et al., 2019). In addition to furnishing marketing advice, portal managements contribute to funding success by performing due diligence services (Cumming et al., 2019; Hornuf & Schwienbacher, 2018). They reduce an investor's information asymmetry and potential moral hazard. Ibrahim (2017b) argues that expert portal services are essential for Reg. CF crowdfunding to succeed as a source of startup financing. Knyazeva and Ivanov (2017) suggest that reputed portals provide third-party certification of offerings. Evidence of a successful portal would be a large market share, a high percentage of funded campaigns and a high level of average total funding. In summary, the quality of services offered, and the reputation maintained by an intermediary, may affect the likelihood of funding success (Hornuf & Schwienbacker, 2018).

Hypothesis Five: Funding intermediaries will be differentially associated with the likelihood of funding success.

# METHOD AND DATA

## Data

The data include 296 offerings listed over the period May 16, 2016 to May 15, 2017 with all offerings closed as of May 31, 2018. The data were hand-collected from the SEC website as Form C (both HTML and textual content) and funding intermediaries. Excluded are 16 offerings listed by UFP, LLC dba uFundingPortal because of alleged rule violations (Drinker Biddle, 2017). Also, three offerings were excluded because they are for solar energy construction projects with large funding minimums ($100-350K). All three had raised negligible amounts and were closed as of February 2018. The net number of offerings is 277, of which 155 are successful. The 277 offerings include a wide range of types of products (Table 1) and represent companies at the two different phases of funding, i.e., 146 startup and 131 early-stage offerings.

SEC Form C provides balance sheet and income statement information. There is a wide range of accounting numbers, especially for the early-stage companies (see Table 2). Some distributions of data have large observations relative to a symmetric, unimodal distribution. Transformations and robust standard errors are used for model estimation.

## Product Types, Business and Financial Risks, and Intermediaries

In order to understand a company's product (or product idea) and business, several sources were examined. Primary sources are the narrative section of a company's Form C, a company's presentation on the web pages of the funding intermediary, and the web pages maintained by each of the companies. Form C instructions entitled "Business and Anticipated Business Plan" (questions 7-8) indicate a strategic management perspective for description of a business. A large variety of products are offered by the 277 companies compared with, for example, rewards-based sites such as Kickstarter.com (Mollick, 2014). The product types range from bars/breweries/restaurants to entertainment and media, health products and services, and transportation vehicles (see Table 1). So that investor funding preferences can be captured across products, the companies are classified based on the type of product offered and customer served, instead of partitioning based on the process used to produce the product, e.g., processes such as an artistic endeavor, an information technology application (unless the application is the product), or a construction or manufacturing/assembly process.

To develop the product type classification, the authors studied classifications used by funding intermediaries and crowdfunding industry publications. After refining a classification, the authors independently applied it to the 277 companies (Table 1). The interrater agreement is 88.4%. Cohen's kappa is .863, $p<.0001$. The disagreements were then reconciled, which mostly involved the services.

Form C includes information on the relevant experiences of directors and members of senior management. The authors tabulated whether each individual has 1) startup experience, and/or

*Table 1. Product types offered by regulation crowdfunding companies*

| Product Type | Description |
|---|---|
| Consumer Products and Services | Companies that engage in the process of making products and services available to consumers. |
| Education | Firms that provide services and information for learning to people of any age. This category does not include entertainment or professional services. |
| Energy | Sources of energy, principally oil and gas properties, etc. |
| Entertainment and Media | Focus on movies, theater productions, sports, etc., including ownership interests, videos, documents, newsletters, etc. Internet-based computer games are included. |
| Food and Drink: | Bars, breweries and restaurants, and their suppliers. |
| Health Products and Services | Includes both "*Fitness and Wellness,*" i.e., personal fitness monitoring devices and services, and "*Medical Devices and Services,*" i.e., products and services for patients or would be patients. The two categories are combined to have a larger sample size |
| Information Technology | Software applications for networking/Internet. |
| Professional Services | Legal, income tax, recruiting, job search, mentoring, etc. |
| Real Estate Services | Services for real estate professionals and land ownership. |
| Transportation | Vehicles and devices for movement of people and things. |

Notes: The authors developed the 10 product classifications by studying classifications used by funding portals and crowdfunding industry publications. After a few rounds of refining a classification and applying it to a sample of companies, we independently applied the final classification of 10 product categories to each of the 277 companies. The type of product or product design for each company was coded by each of the authors based on Form C materials, the portal presentation of a company's offering, a company's web pages, etc. Interrater agreement is 88.45% before reconciliation of the disagreements. Cohen's kappa is .863, $p<.0001$.

2) an MBA degree (Ahlers, et al., 2015; Piva & Rossi-Lamastra, 2017). It was then determined whether each management team has at least one such individual in each of the two categories.

Management is required by the SEC to report on Form C a list of specific business and financial risks "... that make an investment in the issuer speculative or risky." (SEC, 2015b, 8). A profile of ten business risks was developed that management of any company in the data could report (Casadesus-Masanell and Ricart, 2010; Teece, 2010). In addition, a profile of four financial risks was developed. The frequency of occurrence of each of the 14 risks was tabulated and 14 corresponding binary variables were created. When the frequencies of the 10 business risks in the profile were related to the likelihood of funding success, the result was an inconclusive pattern of insignificant associations. Therefore, this analysis was excluded. Results for the four financial risks are reported below.

*Table 2a. Descriptive company and funding statistics for offerings. Panel A: Unsuccessful (122) and successful (155) offerings*

| | Unsuccessful | | | | Successful* | | | |
|---|---|---|---|---|---|---|---|---|
| Variable | Mean | .25 | .50 | .75 | Mean | .25 | .50 | .75 |
| Minimum Funding | $122,010 | $25,000 | $100,000 | $100,000 | $83,503 | $40,000 | $50,000 | $100,000 |
| Maximum Funding | $582,878 | $100,000 | $612,500 | $1,000,000 | $666,967 | $300,000 | $999,950 | $1,000,000 |
| Total Funding | NA | NA | NA | NA | $289,760 | $89,772 | $189,229 | $347,113 |
| Years in Business | 3.46 | 2.00 | 2.00 | 4.00 | 4.29 | 2.00 | 3.00 | 5.00 |
| Number of employees | 3.15 | 0 | 2.00 | 4.00 | 6.77 | 2.00 | 4.00 | 6.00 |
| Revenue* | $132,323 | 0 | 0 | $21,681 | $465,641 | 0 | $194 | $282,981 |
| Cash+A/R | $43,172 | 0 | $2,430 | $30,269 | $142,958 | $400 | $22,199 | $135,765 |
| Short-Term Debt | $71,190 | 0 | 0 | $46,210 | $224,917 | 0 | $6,168 | $120,000 |
| Long-Term Debt | $179,304 | 0 | 0 | $12,250 | $313,857 | 0 | 0 | $230,909 |
| Net Income (Loss) | ($164,610) | ($135,511) | ($2,930) | 0 | ($252,480) | ($233,552) | ($45,992) | 0 |

* Of the 155 successful offerings, 79 reported revenue and 76 did not.

The analysis focuses on whether characteristics of companies and campaigns will affect the likelihood of offering success using four logistic regressions for the odds (logits) of funding success and four regressions for the log of total funding, both using robust standard errors. Two control variables are included: the minimum funding amount, a likely determinant of funding success (Cordova et al., 2015; Vulkan et al., 2016), and "number of employees" from Form C as a measure of company size. We use a log transformation to obtain a symmetric, unimodal distribution for each control variable.

## RESULTS

### Overall Results for Regulation Crowdfunding Offerings

The minimum funding amount is the funding needed to accomplish a major phase of a business (SEC, 2015a). The mean (median) minimum funding amount for all 277 companies is $100,463 ($50,000) with a standard deviation of $122,627 (also see Table 2). The percent of successful offerings is 56%, i.e., 155 of 277. The success rate is approximately the same for increasingly demanding funding minimums. For example, it is 55.0% for 211 offerings having a minimum funding threshold of

*Table 2b. Panel B. "Startup" companies (146 without revenue) and "early-stage" companies (131 with revenue)*

| | Startup Companies | | | | Early-Stage Companies | | | |
|---|---|---|---|---|---|---|---|---|
| Variable | Mean | .25 | .50 | .75 | Mean | .25 | .50 | .75 |
| Minimum Funding | $111,400 | $40,000 | $50,000 | $100,000 | $88,270 | $50,000 | $60,000 | 100,000 |
| Maximum Funding | $599,424 | $150,000 | $500,000 | $1.000,000 | $663,932 | $200,000 | $1,000,000 | $1,000,000 |
| Total Funding* | $260,163 | $85,008 | $174,679 | $294,215 | $318,234 | $100,000 | $197,000 | $424,067 |
| Years in Business | 2.80 | 2.00 | 2.00 | 3.00 | 5.18 | 3.00 | 4.00 | 6.00 |
| Number of employees | 2.97 | 1.00 | 2.00 | 4.00 | 7.63 | 3.00 | 5.00 | 8.00 |
| Revenue | NA | NA | NA | NA | $674,183 | $12,792 | $116,730 | $670,261 |
| Cash+A/R | $33,754 | 0 | $100 | $14,426 | $171,736 | $9,126 | $39,687 | $189,887 |
| Short-Term Debt | $48,493 | 0 | 0 | $11,793 | $278,377 | $966 | $25,516 | $200,713 |
| Long-Term Debt | $59,123 | 0 | 0 | 0 | $472,449 | 0 | $47,954 | $450,442 |
| Net Income (Loss) | ($89,388) | ($45,992) | 0 | 0 | ($352,414) | ($330,953) | ($91,338) | ($11,521) |

*Notes:* The number of successful campaigns is 76 for the startup companies and 79 for the early-stage companies. *Minimum Funding* is the minimum level of investor funding commitments necessary for a campaign to result in any funding for the issuing company. *Maximum Funding* is the maximum amount of funding that issuer management will accept. Minimum and maximum funding levels are specified by issuer management in Form C. *Total funding* is the total funding commitment of investors at the end of a campaign. *Years in Business* and *Number of Employees* are specified in Form C. *Revenue* is reported revenue for the most recent fiscal year. Cash+A/R is the sum of reported cash and equivalents plus accounts receivable.

$50K or more and 48.7% for 123 offerings that have a minimum of $100K or more. For the 155 successful offerings, the mean (median) minimum funding amount is $83,503 ($50,000) versus $122,010 ($100,000) for the 122 unsuccessful offerings, a difference that is significant, $F(1,275) = 6.88$, $p = .009$.

## Characteristics of Successful Offerings

### Impact of Issuer's Business: Product Types and Management Business Risk

For the ten product types, Table 3, Panel A indicates the mean minimum funding amounts, Panel B summarizes the frequency of funding success and Panel C indicates the frequency of product type choices for startup versus early-stage companies. Prior research suggests that the product types "Food and Drink," "Entertainment and Media," "Consumer Products and Services," and "Health Products and Services" could result in more successful crowdfunding campaigns. These four plus "Professional Services" are the product types chosen most frequently by company managements. Professional Services is included for the same reasons as Consumer

*Table 3a. Results for product types (277 offerings) Panel A. Product types and targeted (minimum) requested funding*

| Product Type | Mean | Std. Deviation | N |
|---|---|---|---|
| Consumer Products and Services | $91,146 | $92,157 | 70 |
| Education | $62,500 | $36,075 | 10 |
| Energy | $203,000 | $46,573 | 3 |
| Entertainment and Media | $130,570 | $173,129 | 44 |
| Food and Drink | $100,802 | $101,108 | 50 |
| Health Products and Services | $103,421 | $113,088 | 19 |
| Professional Services | $85,617 | $90,722 | 34 |
| Real Estate Services | $210,714 | $354,982 | 7 |
| Information Technology | $73,333 | $95,354 | 27 |
| Transportation | $84,453 | $68,520 | 13 |
| Total | $100,463 | $122,627 | 277 |

Products and Services, i.e., highly differentiated products and services, and ease of communicating a value proposition to targeted customers. We also include the "Transportation" product type given that it has the largest mean number of investors per offering (see below). These six product types are included in the first logistic regression (Model 1, Table 4).

*Table 3b. Panel B: Product types and frequency of unsuccessful and successful campaigns*

| Product Type | Unsuccessful | Success | Total (%Success) |
|---|---|---|---|
| Consumer Products and Services | 32 | 38 | 70 (54.3%) |
| Education | 5 | 5 | 10 (50.0%) |
| Energy | 1 | 2 | 3 (66.7%) |
| Entertainment and Media | 22 | 22 | 44 (50.0%) |
| Food and Drink | 12 | 38 | 50 (76.0%) |
| Health Products and Services | 2 | 17 | 19 (89.4%) |
| Professional Services | 20 | 14 | 34 (41.1%) |
| Real Estate Services | 5 | 2 | 7 (28.6%) |
| Information Technology | 18 | 9 | 27 (33.3%) |
| Transportation | 5 | 8 | 13 (61.5%) |
| Total | 122 | 155 | 277 (56.0%) |

*Table 3c. Panel C: Product types and two phases of company capital acquisition*

| Product Type | Startup | Early-Stage | Total |
|---|---|---|---|
| Consumer Products and Services | 34 | 36 | 70 |
| Education | 4 | 6 | 10 |
| Energy | 2 | 1 | 3 |
| Entertainment and Media | 26 | 18 | 44 |
| Food and Drink | 26 | 24 | 50 |
| Health Products and Services | 8 | 11 | 19 |
| Professional Services | 18 | 16 | 34 |
| Real Estate Services | 4 | 3 | 7 |
| Information Technology | 15 | 12 | 27 |
| Transportation | 9 | 4 | 13 |
| Total | 146 | 131 | 277 |

*Notes:* Product types are binary variables. They are defined in Table 1. Success is defined as an offering meeting the targeted minimum amount of funding (Panels A and B). Companies in the "startup" phase of funding do not report any revenue; "early-stage" companies do report revenue (Panel C).

Two product types are significant in Model 1: "Food and Drink" and "Health Products and Services" (both p<.005), consistent with H1. The exponentiated coefficients are positive and large, i.e., 4.209 and 12.477, respectively, indicating major increases in the odds of successful funding. It is noteworthy that these two product types are significant even though their minimum funding thresholds are large and challenging to achieve, i.e., means of $100,802 for Food and Drink) and $103,421 for Health Products and Services) (Table 3, Panel A). The frequencies of product types are not significantly different between the 146 startup companies without revenue and the 131 early-stage companies (Table 3, Panel C).

The startup experience of company management poses a business risk (H2a). When at least one member of the team has startup experience, the result is positive and significant, p=.045, consistent with H2a (Model 1, Table 4). Separately, having at least one person with an MBA degree is not significant (p=.522) and this variable is excluded from the analysis (H2b).

## Impact of Reported Financial Risks, Liquidity and Profitability

### Financial Risks Reported by Management

The authors applied the profile of four financial risks to the risks reported by issuer managements. The risks and report frequencies are "Unaudited financial

*Table 4. Logistic regression models of achieving the minimum funding (277 offerings)*

| Variable | Model 1: Business Attributes | Model 2: +Financial Risks | Model 3 +Intermediaries | Model 4 Final Model |
|---|---|---|---|---|
| Intercept | *2.700 | ***6.556 | ***6.683 | ***6.410 |
| Food and Drink | ***1.437(4.209) | **1.153(3.168) | *1.139(3.123) | **.912(2.489) |
| Entertainment/Media | .481(1.618) | .248(1.281) | .448(1.566) | |
| Consumer Prod./Serv. | .631(1.879) | *.674(1.962) | *.832(2.297) | *.572(1.771) |
| Professional Services | -.010(.990) | .040(1.041) | .043(1.044) | |
| Health Prod./Services | ***2.524(12.477) | ***2.652(14.18) | ***2.836(17.05) | ***2.583(13.24) |
| Transportation | .859(2.362) | .557(1.746) | .928(2.529) | |
| Startup Experience | **.543(1.721) | *.567(1.762) | *.535(1.707) | *.522(1.685) |
| No Revenue/Profit | | **-.636(.530) | **-.642(.526) | **-.664(.515) |
| Need More Capital | | ***-.895(.408) | **-.739(.478) | **-.704(.495) |
| Accountant's Report | | ***1.447(4.249) | ***1.466(4.333) | ***1.499(4.479) |
| StartEngine.com | | | -.314(.731) | |
| Wefunder.com | | | **.763(2.145) | **.756(2.129) |
| SeedInvest.com | | | .049(1.050) | |
| Log (Target Amount) | **-.366(.694) | ***-.727(.483) | ***-.766(.465) | ***-.726(484) |
| Log (# of Employees) | ***.569(1.766) | ***.609(1.838) | ***.580(1.786) | ***.585(1.795) |
| Pseudo-R2 | .245 | .362 | .384 | .377 |
| -2 log likelihood | 324.034 | 292.896 | 286.560 | 288.630 |
| Percentage correct | 69.3% | 73.3% | 75.1% | 74.4% |

*Notes:* Logistic regression models are applied using robust standard errors. Cell entries are coefficient and exponentiated coefficient. ***p<.01, **p<.05 and *p<.10. The product types are binary variables and are defined in Table 1. Startup Experience measures whether one or more members of senior management indicate experience with a startup company on SEC Form C. No Revenue/Profit and Need More Capital are financial risks reported by management on Form C. Accountant's Report indicates availability of an independent review (or audit). StartEngine.com, Wefunder.com and SeedInvest.com are funding intermediaries. The control variables are (1) (log of) the targeted level of necessary minimum funding and (2) (log of) Number of Employees as a measure of company size. Model 1 focuses on product types and management business risk. Model 2 adds reported financial risks and availability of an independent CPA's review (or audit) report. Model 3 adds the three funding intermediaries with large market shares (see Table 6). Model 4 is the final model.

statements" (60 of 277), "No revenue" (127), "Will need more capital" (129) and "No public resale market for security" (157). The reported risks reveal a consistent and significant pattern. In an untabulated logistic regression the first three risks are significant (p<.051 or lower) with expected negative signs and exponentiated coefficients of .479 to .596. Because the exponentiated coefficients are less than 1.0, each risk indicates significantly decreased odds of offering success. When included in Model 2 (Table 4), two risks are significant, and each has the predicted negative sign: "Will need more capital" (p=.005) (reference H3a) and "No revenue" (p= .020) (consistent with H3b). The exponentiated coefficients are, respectively, .436 and .511.

Each of the four financial risks are reported less frequently, on a percentage basis, for the 155 companies that achieved funding success. The frequency percentages for the 155 successful [122 unsuccessful] offerings are: "Unaudited financial statements" 14.8% [30.3%], "No revenue" 38.0% [55.7%], "Will need more capital" 36.7% [59.0%], and "No public resale market for security" 52.2% [62.3%]. The frequency percentages for the 146 startup and 131 early-phase companies are more evenly dispersed. For the startup [early-stage] companies, the percentages are "Unaudited financial statements" 22.6% [20.6%], "No revenue" 53.4% [37.4%], "Will need more capital" 46.6% [46.6%], and "No public resale market for security" 54.8% [58.8%].

## Liquidity (Solvency) Risk and Accounting Data

One reason for a Reg. CF offering is to fund a major phase of a business (SEC, 2015a). A second reason is to enhance the company's liquidity and diminish solvency risk. A customary liquidity measurement is the current ratio, defined as the magnitude of cash and equivalents, accounts receivable (A/R) and short-term securities divided by short-term debt (Palepu & Healy, 2013). But only 201 of 277 companies have cash and equivalents plus accounts receivable, i.e., "Cash+A/R", and 149 of 277 have short-term debt. A measure suitable for all 277 companies is whether a firm reports any Cash+A/R, resulting in a binary "cash available" variable. When this variable is included in Model 2 (Table 4) it is not significant.

Considering whether the firm is in the startup versus early stage of funding highlights the relevance of current liquidity for funding success. The 146 startup companies report much lower levels of liquidity (Panel B, Table 2), including 71 that do not report any Cash+A/R, and Cash+A/R is not correlated with funding success (.093, p=.206). In contrast, for the 131 early-stage companies, the magnitude of Cash+A/R is significantly higher for the 79 successful versus 52 unsuccessful offerings, \$233,574 versus \$77,790, F(1,128) = 5.142, p =.025 with "years in business" from Form C included as a proxy for the scale of the business. Moreover, the magnitude of Cash+A/R is significantly associated with funding success for the 131 companies, r= .270, p<.001. In summary, higher current liquidity, and lower solvency risk, are associated with a higher likelihood of funding success for the 131 early-stage companies (H3a).

## Profitability (Cash Flow) Risk and Accounting Data

Regarding levels of profitability and cash flow from operations, an absence of current revenue is an indicator that a product may not be successful. Similar to the binary "cash available" measure, when we compute a binary "revenue reported" measure for all 277 firms and add it to Model 2 (Table 4), the measure is not significant.

The 146 startup companies do not report any revenue (by definition). Alternatively, for the 131 early-stage firms that do report revenue, levels of revenue are significantly associated with funding success, r= .252, p <.001. Mean revenue is significantly higher for the 79 successful versus the 52 unsuccessful offerings, $913,601 versus $310,452, F(1,129) = 6.719, p =.011. A similar result occurs for prior-year revenue, i.e., $605,489 versus $210,073, F(1,129) = 4.066, p=.046.

Net income adds expenses to revenue and provides a current measure of operating performance. However, for many of the companies, expenses exceed revenue, in many situations by a wide margin (Panel A, Table 2). Focusing on the 146 startup companies, 70 report a net loss with a mean (median) loss of $186,438 ($50,133) and 76 report zero net income. The correlation between funding success and the magnitude of a net loss is not significant. In contrast, for the 131 early-stage firms that report revenue and income (loss) data, the mean (median) net loss is $352,414 ($91,338) (Panel B, Table 2): 110 companies report a net loss, four firms report zero and seventeen report net income. Also for the 131 firms, levels of net loss are not associated with funding success, r = -.076, p= .388.

In summary, for the 131 early-stage companies, revenue is significantly higher for the successful companies and revenue is correlated with funding success (H3b). For both the 146 startup and 131 early stage companies, levels of a net operating loss are not correlated with funding success.

## Impact of Independent Accountant's Report.

Availability of an independent accountant's report on a company's financial statements is predicted to be associated with more frequent funding success (H4). The first test addresses the overall impact of a review or audit opinion. One hundred-seventy-two of 277 offerings include an audit report, i.e., 164 reviews and eight audit opinions. Availability of a report is significantly associated with funding success (H4), chi-square= 7.198, p=.007. Availability of a report is included in Model 2 (Table 4) and the result is significant (p=.0001); the exponentiated coefficient is a relatively large 4.249. Sixty-nine percent (107) of the successful offerings included an accountant's report while 53.3% (65) of the failed offerings did so.

The SEC rules do not require that firms making an offering of less than, or equal to $100K/$107K include a review of their financial statements (four chose to do so); instead, executive certification of financial statements is required. Offerings greater than $500K/$535K require an audit but, for a company's first Reg. C offering, the report can be a review (SEC 2015a). Therefore, offerings greater than $100K/$107K are expected to include a review (or audit). Of the 210 of 277 companies expected to file a review/audit, 42 are coded as having not done so[4]. As a result of these omissions, the likelihood of successful funding is significantly reduced. In an untabulated logistic regression for funding success including availability of a review (or audit) and the log of the minimum amount, report availability is significant (p=.018) with a large exponentiated coefficient of 2.721 (consistent with H4).

## Impact of the Intermediary

While intermediaries curate offerings, an intermediary's reputation for funding success and quality of services offered may cause some intermediaries to be chosen more frequently by issuer managements. Table 6 provides information on the performance of the portals/platforms including the number of listings, the funding success percentage, the average minimum funding required, and total funding achieved.

*Table 5a. Results for product types (155 successful offerings) Panel A: Product types and magnitude of targeted minimum funding levels*

| *Product Type* | *Mean* | *Median* | *N* | *Standard Deviation* |
|---|---|---|---|---|
| *Consumer Products and Services* | *$68,215* | *$50,000* | *38* | *$57,223* |
| *Education* | *$33,000* | *$25,000* | *5* | *$20,797* |
| *Energy* | *$225,500* | *$225,500* | *2* | *$36,062* |
| *Entertainment and Media* | *$106,136* | *$75,000* | *22* | *$105,874* |
| *Food and Drink* | *$99,476* | *$87,500* | *38* | *$88,009* |
| *Health Products and Services* | *$97,941* | *$50,004* | *17* | *$117,354* |
| *Professional Services* | *$65,357* | *$50,000* | *14* | *$47,331* |
| *Real Estate* | *$87,500* | *$87,500* | *2* | *$88,388* |
| *Information Technology* | *$47,778* | *$50,000* | *8* | *$34,920* |
| *Transportation* | *$54,353* | *$50,000* | *8* | *$33,552* |
| *Total* | *$83,504* | *$50,000* | *155* | *$81,802* |

Mean minimum funding amounts are significantly different (using the log transformation), $F(9, 145) = 2.010, p=.042$.

*Table 5b. Panel B. Product types and magnitude of total funding*

| Product Type | Mean | Median | N | Standard Deviation |
|---|---|---|---|---|
| Consumer Products and Services | $233,779 | $131,091 | 38 | $296,508 |
| Education | $51,153 | $54,620 | 5 | $26,590 |
| Energy | $240,225 | $240,226 | 2 | $15,633 |
| Entertainment and Media | $331,994 | $206,785 | 22 | $269,286 |
| Food and Drink | $320,906 | $270,115 | 38 | $262,651 |
| Health Products and Services | $336,303 | $140,530 | 17 | $360,415 |
| Professional Services | $356,534 | $219,454 | 14 | $341,161 |
| Real Estate | $209,865 | $209,865 | 2 | $29,183 |
| Information Technology | $120,846 | $106,366 | 9 | $102,280 |
| Transportation | $447,345 | $246,066 | 8 | $400,988 |
| Total | $289,760 | $189,229 | 155 | $292,604 |

Mean total funding mounts are significantly different using the log transformation), F9, 145) = 3.137, p=.002.

## Additional Results

### Number of Investors

For 135 (155-20) successful offerings, the mean (median) number of investors for each product type is indicated in Table 5, Panel C. (Two portals did not report the number of investors for every campaign, resulting in the smaller sample size of 135.) The overall mean (median) number of investors is 358 (236) with a standard deviation of 415.60, and a range of 22 to 3143 investors. The differences in the number of investors for the 10 product types are not significant. The correlation for number of investors and the magnitude of the total (minimum threshold) amount is .754 (.321), both p<.0001. Given that the number of investors is a determinant of the total funded amount, the impact of the company and offering characteristics on the number of investors is very similar to the regression results reported below using negative binomial regressions for this count data.

### Types of Securities

Reg. CF investors may find certain types of securities to be more desirable investments. We combined the eight types of securities offered into three categories: equity, debt and SAFE securities (see Table 8). All three security types are offered frequently; the

*Table 5c. Panel C. Product types and number of investors (135 Offerings)*

| *Product Type* | *Mean* | *Median* | *Standard Deviation* | *N* |
|---|---|---|---|---|
| *Consumer Products and Services* | *352.83* | *199.00* | *455.005* | *29* |
| *Education* | *70.40* | *47.00* | *45.577* | *5* |
| *Energy* | *106.00* | *106.00* | *.* | *1* |
| *Entertainment and Media* | *508.38* | *237.00* | *685.754* | *21* |
| *Food and Drink* | *315.08* | *271.00* | *209.199* | *37* |
| *Health Products and Services* | *293.73* | *151.00* | *240.433* | *15* |
| *Professional Services* | *439.91* | *291.00* | *428.646* | *11* |
| *Real Estate* | *163.50* | *163.50* | *6.364* | *2* |
| *Information Technology* | *238.71* | *245.00* | *117.219* | *7* |
| *Transportation* | *581.29* | *324.00* | *570.002* | *7* |
| *Total* | *358.04* | *236.00* | *415.597* | *135* |

*Notes: The product types are defined in Table 1. Product types are binary variables.*The focus is on the impact of each of the three intermediaries most frequently selected by management as fixed effects: StartEngine.com, SeedInvest.com and Wefunder.com (Table 6). Each provides an adequate sample size. When the three are added to Model 2 (Table 4), Model 3 indicates only Wefunder is significantly associated (p=.048) with a higher likelihood of achieving a successful offering (consistent with H5). One reason for the portal's significant performance is that Wefunder has the largest number of Food and Drink offerings (25 of 87) with 19 being successful; StartEngine has 6 with 4 being successful and SeedInvest has 1 offering that also is successful. Wefunder also has the lowest average fee (3.35%), a high overall funding success percentage (74.7%), and substantial average total funding ($306,107). The high funding percentage is notable given a high average level of minimum funding ($83,392). Wefunder offerings include a larger percentage of SAFE securities[5] than do the other two intermediaries, i.e., 45/87 = 51.7%, versus 4/49 = 8.2% for StartEngine and zero for SeedInvest. Wefunder remains significant in the final model, p=.032 (Model 4).

number of offerings is equity (121), debt (80) and SAFE (76). A logistic regression (untabulated) with funding success as the dependent variable and equity and SAFE securities as binary predictors plus the two control variables indicates that the equity security type is not significant (p=.269) nor is the SAFE security type (p=.143). The corresponding OLS regression for total funding achieved yields similar results.

## Offering Duration Period

Issuer management determines the duration of the funding period for raising of the minimum amount and any additional funding. A different aspect of Reg. CF regulation relative to other countries is that the initial duration period can be extended multiple times by management with the agreement of current investors. The mean (median) actual duration period for successful offerings is 128 days (101 days) with a standard deviation of 83.33, and a minimum (maximum) of 28 days (533 days). By

*Table 6. Performance of funding intermediaries*

| 1) Portal or Platform | 2) Number of Offerings Listed | 3) Number (%) of Successful Offerings | 4) Average Fee: $ Percentage of Offering | 5) Average Fee: % of Securities/ # of Offerings | 6) Average Minimum Funding (277 total) | 7) Average Total Funding (155 total) |
|---|---|---|---|---|---|---|
| DreamFunded Marketplace LLC | 14 | 0(0%) | 5.00 | 2.0%/13 | $131,429 | 0 |
| First Democracy VC | 11 | 11(100%) | 6.64 | 1.5%/10 | $81,818 | $292,077 |
| NetCapital Funding Portal Inc. | 12 | 9(75%) | 4.74 | 0%/0 | $60,417 | $150,333 |
| NextSeed US LLC | 13 | 13(100%) | 9.16 | 0%/0 | $169,231 | $285,200 |
| Republic | 10 | 10(100%) | 4.60 | 2.0%/10 | $53,500 | $122,364 |
| SeedInvest | 29 | 13(44%) | 5.95 | 5.0%/28 | $127,586 | $371,764 |
| StartEngine Capital LLC | 49 | 28(57%) | 5.45 | 0%/0 | $74,645 | $356,397 |
| truCrowd | 12 | 2(17%) | 7.54 | 0%/0 | $99,422 | $26,815 |
| Wefunder Portal LLC | 87 | 65(75%) | 3.35 | 2.0%/5 | 83,392 | $306,107 |
| Other Portals | 40 | 4(10%) | 6.65 | 3.84%/23 | $145,564 | $160,503 |
| Total | 277 | 155 | 5.24 | ---- | $100,463 | $289,688 |

*Notes:* Financial fee percentage (column 4) and percent of number of securities issued (column 5) apply only if an offering is successful. Wefunder included a larger percentage of SAFE securities than the other platforms, i.e., 45/87 = 51.7%. The percentages are 4/49 = 8.2% for StartEngine and zero for SeedInvest. First Democracy VC is a funding portal resulting from a partnership between Microventures and Indiegogo. The 12 portals in the "Other Portals" category each have less than 10 listings an average of 3.33 each).

comparison, duration periods for rewards-based projects are typically much shorter, i.e., 30-60 days; Courtney et al. (2017). The correlation of duration periods with funding success is -.085, p=.086, and with total funding achieved is -.100, p=.216.

## Location of Company

In the data there is the typical uneven distribution of locations of companies making offerings (e.g., Mollick, 2014). California (CA) has the largest number of offerings (107 of the 277), consistent with the historic level of entrepreneurial activity in Silicon Valley (Agrawal et al., 2014). Second and third are New York and Texas with, respectively, 22 and 19 offerings. However, the association between a binary

*Table 7. Regression models of total funding achieved by successful offerings (155 of 277)*

| Variable | Model 1: Business Attributes | Model 2: +Financial Risks | Model 3 +Intermediaries | Model 4 Final Model |
|---|---|---|---|---|
| **Intercept** | ***3.837 | ***3.837 | ***2.442 | ***2.604 |
| **Food and Drink** | ***.570(.189) | ***.581(.192) | ***.545(192) | **.302(.150) |
| **Entertainment/Media** | ***.626(.214) | ***.650(.216) | ***.565(.196) | **.327(.157) |
| **Consumer Prod./Serv.** | .297(.204) | *.332(.200) | .216(.192) | |
| **Professional Services** | ***.866(.231) | ***.908(.237) | ***.960(.249) | ***.672(.214) |
| **Health Prod./Services** | **.540(.253) | **.555(.256) | .*408(.244) | |
| **Transportation** | ***1.200(.324) | ***1.238(.317) | ***.893(.349) | **.657(.320) |
| **Startup Experience** | -.067(.125) | -.059(.128) | -.143(.120) | |
| **No Revenue/Profit** | | -.024(.129) | .007(.122) | |
| **Need More Capital** | | -.084(.128) | -.179(.131) | |
| **Accountant's Report** | | .001(.178) | -.095(.175) | |
| **StartEngine.com** | | | ***.880(.227) | **.762(.219) |
| **Wefunder.com** | | | ***.349(.120) | **.292(.119) |
| **SeedInvest.com** | | | *.412(.231) | |
| **Log (Target Amount)** | ***.689(.083) | ***.690(.089) | ***.813(.083) | ***.806(.067) |
| **Log (# of Employees)** | ***.160(.059) | ***.157(.060) | *.108(.061) | *.114(.061) |
| **Significance (all p<001)** | F(9,145)= 14.92 | F(12,142)= 11.03 | F(15,139)=11.01 | F(8.146)=19.57 |
| **Adjusted R2** | .449 | .439 | .494 | .491 |

*Notes:* Linear regression models are applied using robust standard errors. The dependent variable is the log of the total funding achieved. Cell entries are coefficient and standard error. ***p<.01, **p<.05 and *p<.10. The product types are binary variables and are defined in Table 1. Startup Experience measures whether one or more members of senior management indicate experience with a startup company on SEC Form C. No Revenue/Profit and Need More Capital are financial risks reported by management on Form C. Accountant's Report indicates availability of an independent review (or audit) versus management certification of financial statements. StartEngine.com, Wefunder.com and SeedInvest.com are funding intermediaries. The control variables are (1) (log of) the targeted level of necessary minimum funding and (2) (log of) Number of Employees as a measure of company size. Model 1 focuses on product types and management business risk. Model 2 adds reported financial risks and availability of an independent CPA's review (or audit) report. Model 3 adds the three funding intermediaries with large market shares (see Table 6). Model 4 is the final model.

CA location variable and funding success is not significant (chi-square= 2.319, p=.128); having a company (and offering) located in CA does not affect the likelihood of successful funding.

## ADDITIONAL ANALYSIS: TOTAL CAMPAIGN FUNDING

The funding intermediary may continue to accept investments after the minimum funding amount has been achieved up to the maximum funding authorized by issuer management on Form C. Mollick (2014) reports that successful rewards-oriented projects on Kickstarter.com fund by small margins; such is not the case for successful Reg. CF investments. The mean (median) additional funding beyond the minimum amount is $206,257 ($100,000) for the 155 successful offerings. Therefore, the total amount raised is substantial with mean (median) funding of $289,760 ($189,229). Total funding is higher for the 79 early-stage companies vs. the 76 startup companies, $318,234 versus $260,163, but the difference is not statistically significant. Fifteen campaigns raised $1,000,000 or more.

*Table 8a. Types of investment securities offered Panel A: Security types and two investment phases for 277 offerings*

| Security Type | Startup | Early-Stage | Total |
|---|---|---|---|
| Common Stock | 49 | 32 | 81 |
| Convertible Note | 6 | 6 | 12 |
| Crowd Safe | 1 | 0 | 1 |
| Debt | 30 | 32 | 62 |
| LLC Units | 10 | 9 | 19 |
| Preferred Stock | 8 | 13 | 21 |
| Revenue Sharing Note | 5 | 1 | 6 |
| Simple Agreement for Future Equity SAFE) | 37 | 38 | 75 |
| Total | 146 | 131 | 277 |

## FUTURE RESEARCH DIRECTIONS

SEC rules cause intermediaries to play a pivotal role in Reg. CF funding campaigns (Ibrahim, 2017b; SEC, 2015a). Among the three most frequently chosen intermediaries, Wefunder is most likely to improve the odds of successful funding (Tables 4 and 7). A research issue is why managements of intermediaries produce different results. Possibilities are that the services offered to issuers differ in their perceived quality, or that some intermediaries are more effective at curating possible offerings (Cumming et al., 2019). Another possibility is investor response to, and reliance placed on, the "look and feel" of information presentations made by intermediaries, e.g., Dey, Duff, Karahalios, and Fu (2017). This is interesting because the representation of

*Table 8b. Panel B. Security types and two investment phases for 155 successful offerings*

| Security Type | Startup | Early-Stage | Total | |
|---|---|---|---|---|
| | Common Stock | 20 | 20 | 40 |
| | Convertible Note | 4 | 4 | 8 |
| | Debt | 20 | 14 | 34 |
| | LLC Units | 2 | 4 | 6 |
| | Preferred Stock | 4 | 8 | 12 |
| | Revenue Sharing Note | 2 | 1 | 3 |
| | Simple Agreement for Future Equity SAFE) | 24 | 28 | 52 |
| Total | 76 | 79 | 155 | |

*Notes:* Companies in the "startup" phase of funding do not report any revenue; companies in the "early-stage" phase report revenue. The eight types of securities offered and issued are aggregated into three categories for analysis purposes: equity (121), debt (80) and SAFE (76) securities. The equity category includes 81 common stock, 21 preferred stock, and 19 LLC securities. The debt category includes 62 debt securities, 12 convertible notes and 6 revenue sharing notes. The SAFE category includes 75 SAFE and one Crowd Safe security.Models 1-4 reported in Table 7 test for the impact of company and intermediary characteristics on the magnitudes of total successful funding[6]. Model 1 tests for the impact of product types and startup experience including both the log of the minimum funding amount and the log of the number of employees as control variables. Product types dominate levels of total funding (Table 5, Panels A and B). Model 1 indicates that five of the six product types are significantly associated with total funding. Availability of startup experience is not significant. Model 2 adds the two reported financial risks and availability of an independent accountant's review/audit opinion versus management certification of financial statements. None of the three are significant. Model 3 adds the three most prominent intermediaries. Two of the three intermediaries (StartEngine.com and Wefunder.com) are associated with significantly higher total funding levels (Table 7). While SeedInvest.com is not significant (p=.139), it has the highest mean total funding, $371,764. The final model 4 includes four significant product types and the two funding intermediaries (Table 7). Model 4 has an adjusted R2 of .491.

company information by the intermediaries is very different, e.g., the more visual and vivid offering presentations at Wefunder.com compared with the more textual and formal presentations at SeedInvest.com.

Although the focus has been on the use of information from Form C and the operation of intermediaries, investors may utilize additional sources of investment information. Among them would be social media. Although the previous literature presents inconsistent results for social media (Ahlers et al., 2015; Lukkarinen et al., 2016), there may be an incremental impact of social media messages on investor funding decisions (Mollick, 2014). Further research into how investors apply the use of "hard" (financial) versus "soft" (social media) information (Bertomeu & Marinovic, 2016; Knyazeva & Ivanov, 2017) in their decision making is warranted.

There are opportunities to better understand the impact of cognitive and social attributes of investors, as well as additional contextual effects of a security-based offering, especially for non-accredited investor decisions. An example is application of the Elaboration Likelihood Model to better understand use of issue-relevant information versus peripheral (affective) cues on CF decision-making (Allison, Davis, Webb & Short, 2017). More broadly, while evidence indicates that investors understand the investment process (Estrin et al., 2018), Drover, Busenitz, Matusik, Townsend Anglin and Dushnitsky (2017) conclude that investor decision-making processes are opaque and evolving, especially for less sophisticated investors. Additionally, Hoegen et al. (2018) conclude that an inability to conduct the necessary financial analysis may be an impediment for some crowdfunding investors. How, and how well, investors use information when making their crowdfunding investment decisions is an especially worthwhile topic for future research.

## CONCLUSION

This study reports associations of issuer business attributes, financial risks and offering characteristics with funding success for the first year of Regulation Crowdfunding. The year is successful with 56% (155 of 277) of offerings being funded. This is a relatively high success rate for security-based CF offerings (e.g., Lukkarinen et al., 2016). By comparison, a success rate for rewards-based CF offerings on Kickstarter is 36% (Allison et al., 2017). Also, a significant amount of total funding was achieved. For the 155 successful offerings, the mean total amount raised is $289,760, relative to a mean minimum funding requirement of $83,503. In fact, some companies were very successful at raising funding including 15 offerings that achieved the maximum total funding permitted of, or in excess of, $1,000,000. More broadly, given the uncertainty of investing in privately-held firms, these first-year Reg. CF results, combined with efforts to increase the Reg. CF funding limit to as much as $5-20 million (e.g., Alois, 2018ab; Torris, 2018), suggest that crowdfunding may eventually provide a viable funding alternative to VC and Angel investing (Barbi & Mattioli, 2019; Belleflamme, Lambert, & Schwienbacher, 2014; Vulkan et al., 2016).

Highly relevant for investor funding decisions is the type of product (or product idea) offered to customers. Two product types, "Food and Drink" and "Health Products and Services," achieved the highest success rates (Table 3, Panel B). As noted earlier, previous research has not looked closely at varying product types and their impact on investor interest and level of funding (Lukkarinen et al., 2016). This research demonstrates that product type is a relevant characteristic for success. In addition to the product type, other business attributes that are relevant for funding success include one or more senior managers having startup experience and the magnitude of the minimum funding requested by issuer management.

Investors' funding decisions indicate that Form C serves two purposes intended by the SEC, i.e., provision of relevant information and reduction of information asymmetry (SEC, 2015b). Regarding accounting risk measures, we make the distinction between companies that do, and do not, report revenue, an important private company milestone (Halt et al., 2017). While accounting data are limited for the 146 startup firms without any revenue, several accounting-based measures of risk are relevant for the 131 companies that have operational value chains and report revenue. For example, the magnitude of revenue is significantly higher for the 79 successful versus the 52 unsuccessful offerings that did not achieve the minimum funding amount, i.e., \$913,601 versus \$310,451, $p=.011$, while the level of financial liquidity (cash plus accounts receivable) is also higher, \$233,574 versus \$77,790, $p=.025$, including an adjustment for the scale of the business. This distinction between companies that do, and do not, earn revenue may explain why previous Reg. CF research (e.g., Abrams, 2017; Knyazeva and Ivanov, 2017) has not found an overall impact of accounting information on Reg. CF funding results. Finally, while SEC guidelines call for independent CPA reviews (or audits) for offerings greater than \$100K/107K, 20% (42 of 201) were not provided in a timely manner or were not provided at all, resulting in a lower likelihood of funding success (Table 4).

The results confirm the pivotal role of a funding intermediary intended by the SEC (2015a, 2016b), i.e., a funding portal or a broker-dealer platform (Tables 4 and 6). Intermediaries offer services to help curated offerings succeed—and they do so competitively. In addition to curation, services performed include advising on necessary legal and filing documents, processing transactions and preparation of the company's presentation on the intermediary's site. Competitive success is indicated for three intermediaries that achieved large market shares of offerings during the year, i.e., SeedInvest.com, StartEngine.com and Wefunder.com (Table 6). Wefunder.com is the most successful intermediary (Tables 4 and 6) (consistent with H5). Wefunder.com has a high funding success percentage (74.7%), even with a high average minimum for funding success (\$83,392), and substantial average total funding (\$306,107). Wefunder.com remains significant in the final funding model, $p=.032$ (Model 4). An aspect of Wefunder's success is its controversial use of a larger percentage of SAFE securities than the other two intermediaries (e.g., Green & Coyle, 2016; SEC, 2017b).

## ACKNOWLEDGMENT

We hereby acknowledge excellent research assistance provided by Hannah Yattoni. Helpful comments on this research were received from participants in the Management Accounting Reading Group at University of Illinois at Urbana-Champaign and at our session at the 2019 Annual Meeting of the American Accounting Association. Also helpful are comments received from Clara Chen, Ryan Hudgins, Joe Mahoney, Kristin Stack (discussant) and Dan Zhou.

This research did not receive a grant from any funding agency in the public, commercial, or not-for-profit sectors.

## REFERENCES

Abrams, E. (2017). *Securities crowdfunding: More than family, friends and fools?* Unpublished paper. University of Chicago. doi:10.2139srn.2902217

Agrawal, A., Catalini, C., & Goldfarb, A. (2014). Some simple economics of crowdfunding. *Innovation Policy and the Economy*, *14*, 63–97. doi:10.1086/674021

Ahlers, G. K. C., Cumming, D., Gunther, C., & Schweizer, D. (2015). Signaling in equity crowdfunding. *Entrepreneurship Theory and Practice*, *39*(4), 955–980. doi:10.1111/etap.12157

Allison, T. H., Davis, B. C., Webb, J. W., & Short, J. C. (2017). Persuasion in crowdfunding; An elaboration likelihood model of crowdfunding performance. *Journal of Business Venturing*, *32*(6), 707–725. doi:10.1016/j.jbusvent.2017.09.002

Alois, J. D. (2018a, August 6). Petition the SEC: Raise the crowdfunding limit to $20 million. *Crowdfund Insider*. Retrieved from http://www.crowdfundinsider.com

Alois, J. D. (2018b, July 23). Prominent group of fintech leaders send letter to SEC chair Jay Clayton demanding an increase in regulation crowdfunding to $20 million. *Crowdfund Insider.* Retrieved from http://www.crowdfundinsider.com

Bapna, S. (2019). Complementarity of signals in early-stage equity investment decisions: Evidence from a randomized field experiment. *Management Science*, *65*(2), 933–952. doi:10.1287/mnsc.2017.2833

Barbi, M., & Mattioli, S. (2019). Human capital, investor trust and equity crowdfunding. *Research in International Business and Finance*, *49*, 1–12. doi:10.1016/j.ribaf.2019.02.005

Baum, J. A., & Silverman, B. S. (2004). Picking winners or building them? Alliance, intellectual, and human capital as selection criteria in venture financing and performance of biotechnology startups. *Journal of Business Venturing, 19*(3), 411–436. doi:10.1016/S0883-9026(03)00038-7

Belleflamme, P., Lambert, T., & Schwienbacher, A. (2014). Crowdfunding: Tapping the right crowd. *Journal of Business Venturing, 29*(5), 585–609. doi:10.1016/j.jbusvent.2013.07.003

Bentley, K. A., Omer, T. C., & Sharp, N. Y. (2013). Business strategy, financial reporting irregularities, and audit effort. *Contemporary Accounting Research, 30*(2), 780–817. doi:10.1111/j.1911-3846.2012.01174.x

Bertomeu, J., & Marinovic, I. (2016). A theory of hard and soft information. *The Accounting Review, 91*(1), 1–20. doi:10.2308/accr-51102

Casadesus-Masanell, R., & Ricart, J. E. (2010). From strategy to business models and onto tactics. *Long Range Planning, 43*(2-3), 195–215. doi:10.1016/j.lrp.2010.01.004

Connelly, B. L., Certo, S. T., Ireland, R. D., & Reutzel, C. R. (2011). Signaling theory: A review and assessment. *Journal of Management, 37*(1), 39–67. doi:10.1177/0149206310388419

Cordova, A., Dolci, J., & Gianfrate, G. (2015). The determinants of crowdfunding success: Evidence from technology projects. *Procedia: Social and Behavioral Sciences, 181*, 115–124. doi:10.1016/j.sbspro.2015.04.872

Courtney, C., Dutta, S., & Li, Y. (2017). Resolving information asymmetry: Signaling, endorsement, and crowdfunding success. *Entrepreneurship Theory and Practice, 41*(2), 265–290. doi:10.1111/etap.12267

Cumming, D., Johan, S., & Zhang, Y. (2019). The role of due diligence in crowdfunding platforms. *Journal of Banking & Finance, 108*(C), 105661. Advance online publication. doi:10.1016/j.jbankfin.2019.105661

Davila, A., Foster, G., & Li, M. (2009). Reasons for management control systems adoption: Insights from product development systems choice by early-stage entrepreneurial companies. *Accounting, Organizations and Society, 34*(3-4), 322–347. doi:10.1016/j.aos.2008.08.002

Davis, B. C., Hmieleski, K. M., Webb, J. W., & Coombs, J. E. (2017). Funders' positive affective reactions to entrepreneurs' crowdfunding pitches: The influence of perceived product creativity and entrepreneurial passion. *Journal of Business Venturing, 32*(1), 90–106. doi:10.1016/j.jbusvent.2016.10.006

Dey, S., Duff, B., Karahalos, K., & Fu, W.-T. (2017). The art and science of persuasion: Not all crowdfunding campaign videos are the same. *Proceedings of the 2017 ACM Conference on Computer Supported Cooperative Work and Social Computing*, 755-769. 10.1145/2998181.2998229

Drinker Biddle. (2017). Drinker Biddle crowdfunding report. *Drinker Biddle & Reath LLP*. Retrieved from www.faegredrinker.com

Drover, W., Busenitz, L., Matusik, S., Townsend, D., Anglin, A., & Dushnitsky, G. (2017). A review and road map of entrepreneurial equity financing research: Venture capital, corporate venture capital, angel investment, crowdfunding, and accelerators. *Journal of Management, 43*(6), 1820–1853. doi:10.1177/0149206317690584

Estrin, S., Gozman, D., & Khavul, S. (2018). The evolution and adoption of equity crowdfunding: Entrepreneur and investor entry into a new market. *Small Business Economics, 51*(2), 425–439. doi:10.100711187-018-0009-5

Green, J. M., & Coyle, J. F. (2016). Crowdfunding and the not-so-safe SAFE. *Virginia Law Review Online, 102*, 168–182.

Hage, J. (2018). *Yes! Crowdfunding is working for medical devices*. Retrieved from http://www.medicaldevicesgroup.net

Halt, G. B. Jr, Donch, J. C. Jr, Stiles, A. R., & Fesnak, R. (2017). Sources of company funding. In *Intellectual Property and Financing Strategies for Technology Startups* (pp. 11–33). Springer International Publishing AG. doi:10.1007/978-3-319-49217-9_2

Hanks, S. (2017). Happy birthday regulation CF (shame about the compliance failures). *CrowdCheck Blog*. Retrieved from www.crowdcheck.com

Hervé, F., & Schwienbacher, A. (2018). Crowdfunding and innovation. *Journal of Economic Surveys, 32*(5), 1–17. doi:10.1111/joes.12274

Hoegen, A. D., Steininger, M., & Veit, D. (2018). How do investors decide? An interdisciplinary review of decision-making in crowdfunding. *Electronic Markets, 28*(3), 339–365. doi:10.100712525-017-0269-y

Hornuf, L., & Schmitt, M. (2017). *Does a local bias exist in equity crowdfunding?* Unpublished paper. *Max Planck Institute for Innovation and Competition Research Paper No.* 16-07.

Hornuf, L., & Schwienbacher, A. (2018). Market mechanisms and funding dynamics in equity crowdfunding. *Journal of Corporate Finance, 50*, 556–574. doi:10.1016/j.jcorpfin.2017.08.009

Huelsbeck, D. P., Marchant, K. A., & Sandino, T. (2011). On testing business models. *The Accounting Review*, *86*(5), 1631–1654. doi:10.2308/accr-10096

Ibrahim, D. M. (2017a). *Crowdfunding signals*. Unpublished paper, William & Mary Law School, Research Paper No. 09-369.

Ibrahim, D. M. (2017b, June). Crowdfunding without the crowd. *North Carolina Law Review*, *95*(5), 1.

Jegeleviciute, S., & Valanciene, L. (2015). Comparative analysis of the ways crowdfunding is promoted. *Procedia: Social and Behavioral Sciences*, *213*, 268–274. doi:10.1016/j.sbspro.2015.11.536

Knyazeva, A., & Ivanov, V. I. (2017). *Soft and hard information and signal extraction in securities crowdfunding*. Paper presented at 2nd Emerging Trends in Entrepreneurial Finance Conference, Hoboken, NJ. 10.2139srn.3051380

Leach, J. C., & Melicher, R. W. (2018). *Entrepreneurial finance* (6th ed.). Cengage Learning.

Li, J., Chen, X.-P., Kotha, S., & Fisher, G. (2017). Catching fire and spreading it: A glimpse into displayed entrepreneurial passion in crowdfunding campaigns. *The Journal of Applied Psychology*, *102*(7), 1075–1098. doi:10.1037/apl0000217 PMID:28333500

Lukkarinen, A., Teich, J. E., Wallenius, H., & Wallenius, J. (2016). Success drivers of online equity crowdfunding campaigns. *Decision Support Systems*, *87*, 26–38. doi:10.1016/j.dss.2016.04.006

Madsen, J., & McMullin, J. L. (2020, July 01). Economic consequences of risk disclosures: Evidence from crowdfunding. *The Accounting Review*, *95*(4), 331–363. Advance online publication. doi:10.2308/accr-52641

Mollick, E. (2014). The dynamics of crowdfunding: An exploratory study. *Journal of Business Venturing*, *29*(1), 1–16. doi:10.1016/j.jbusvent.2013.06.005

Mollick, E., & Nanda, R. (2016). Wisdom or madness? Comparing crowds with expert evaluation in funding the arts. *Management Science*, *62*(6), 1533–1553. doi:10.1287/mnsc.2015.2207

Osiyevskyy, O., Chernenko, M., & Biloshapka, V. (2018). The role of business models in the early-stage of new technology-based firms. Technology Entrepreneurship: Insights in New Technology-Based Firms, Research Spin-Offs and Corporate Environments. 49-68.

Palepu, K. G., & Healy, P. M. (2013). *Business analysis & valuation using financial statements Text and cases* (5th ed.). South-Western Cengage Learning.

Piva, E., & Rossi-Lamastra, C. (2017). Human capital signals and entrepreneurs' success in equity crowdfunding. *Small Business Economics*, *51*(3), 667–686. doi:10.100711187-017-9950-y

Porter, M. E. (1980). *Competitive strategy: Techniques for analyzing industries and competitors*. The Free Press.

Schmitt, M. (2017). *Equity crowdfunding: Local bias, capital structure, and venture performance* (Unpublished doctoral dissertation). University of Trier, Trier, Germany.

Securities and Exchange Commission (SEC). (2015a). *Crowdfunding: Final Rules*. SEC.

Securities and Exchange Commission (SEC). (2015b). *Form C under the Securities Act of 1933*. SEC.

Securities and Exchange Commission (SEC). (2016a). *Regulation Crowdfunding: A Small Entity Compliance Guide for Issuers*. SEC.

Securities and Exchange Commission (SEC). (2016b). *Regulation Crowdfunding: A Small Entity Compliance Guide for Crowdfunding Intermediaries*. SEC.

Securities and Exchange Commission (SEC). (2017a). *Updated Investor Bulletin: Crowdfunding for Investors*. SEC.

Securities and Exchange Commission (SEC). (2017b). *Investor Bulletin: Be Cautious of SAFEs in Crowdfunding*. SEC.

Securities and Exchange Commission (SEC). (2019). *Report to the Commission: Regulation Crowdfunding*. Washington, DC: SEC.

Short, J. C., Ketchen, D. J. Jr, McKenny, A. F., Allison, T. H., & Ireland, R. D. (2017). Research on crowdfunding: Reviewing the (very recent) past and celebrating the present. *Entrepreneurship Theory and Practice*, *41*(2), 149–160. Advance online publication. doi:10.1111/etap.12270

Spence, M. (1973). Job market signaling. *The Quarterly Journal of Economics*, *87*(3), 355–374. doi:10.2307/1882010

Teece, D. J. (2010). Business models, business strategy and innovation. *Long Range Planning*, *43*(2-3), 172–194. http://www.elsevier.com/locate/lrp. doi:10.1016/j.lrp.2009.07.003

Torris, T. (2018, June 29). Germany raises the equity crowdfunding limit to ∈8 million. *Crowdfund Insider*. Retrieved from crowdfundinsider.com

Vera-Muñoz, S. C., Shackell, M., & Buehner, M. (2007). Accountants' usage of causal business models in the presence of benchmark data: A note. *Contemporary Accounting Research*, *24*(3), 1015–1038. doi:10.1506/car.24.3.12

Vismara, S. (2018a). Information cascades among investors in equity crowdfunding. *Entrepreneurship Theory and Practice*, *42*(3), 467–497. doi:10.1111/etap.12261

Vismara, S. (2018b). Signaling to overcome inefficiencies in crowdfunding markets. In D. Cumming & L. Hornuf (Eds.), The Economics of Crowdfunding: Startups, Portals and Investor Behavior. Palgrave MacMillan. doi:10.1007/978-3-319-66119-3_3

Vulkan, N., Astebro, T., & Sierra, M. F. (2016). Equity crowdfunding: A new phenomena. *Journal of Business Venturing Insights*, *5*, 37–49. doi:10.1016/j.jbvi.2016.02.001

Warnick, B., Murnieks, C., McMullen, J. S., & Brooks, W. T. (2018). Passion for entrepreneurship or passion for the product: A conjoint analysis of angel and VC decision-making. *Journal of Business Venturing*, *33*(3), 315–332. doi:10.1016/j.jbusvent.2018.01.002

Younkin, P., & Kashkooli, K. (2016). What problems does crowdfunding solve? *California Management Review*, *58*(2), 20–43. doi:10.1525/cmr.2016.58.2.20

## ENDNOTES

1 Title II of the Act permits accredited investors to purchase securities over the Internet (starting in 2013); Title III adds non-accredited investors. A non-accredited investor does not meet the requirements for an accredited investor under the Securities & Exchange Commission's Rule 501 of Regulation D.

2 Under the Securities Act of 1933, the offer and sale of securities must be registered unless an exemption from registration is available. Title III of the JOBS Act added Securities Act Section 4(a)(6) that provides such an exemption for certain crowdfunding transactions (SEC 2016a).

31 The limits as of April 5, 2017 are "If either your annual income or your net worth is less than $107,000, then during any 12-month period, you can invest up to the greater of either $2,200 or 5% of the lesser of your annual income or net worth. If both your annual income and your net worth are equal to or more than $107,000, then during any 12-month period, you can invest up to 10% of

annual income or net worth, whichever is lesser, but not to exceed $107,000." (SEC 2017a).

4 Compliance with the SEC's rules is an issue during the first year of Reg. CF; e.g., Hanks (2017); SEC (2019). Twenty-eight of 210 issuers expected to include an independent accountant's review (or audit) did not do so. In addition, 14 submitted a delinquent report. Three submitted a review (and an amended Form C) within eight days of their Form C filing and 11 summited a review 2.5-6 months later. Given the great importance of investor decision-making during the first week of a Reg. CF campaign (Abrams 2017; Vulkan et al. 2016), the 14 delinquent reviews are coded as report omissions. If the three delinquent reviews are included in Model 2 (Table 4), the impact of a review report remains significant but the exponentiated coefficient decreases from 4.249 to 3.928, indicating a dilutive impact of the three delinquent reviews. If only the 28 missing reports are included in Model 2, the exponentiated coefficient increases to 6.448.

5 A SAFE security provides a *potential opportunity* to convert into equity when a preferred round of equity funding occurs. A SAFE security has no maturity date and there is no guarantee that a preferred round will occur. As a result, it is possible that a SAFE security will never convert to equity and there is no requirement that the investment be returned (Green & Coyle 2016).

6 Management authorizes a maximum amount of total funding on Form C. Many managements apparently arbitrarily selected the maximum permitted by the SEC, i.e., $1M ($1.07M after April 5, 2017). Therefore, there are many extremely low ratios of total funding relative to the maximum authorized, e.g., 49.6% less than or equal to .20, hindering any analysis of relative total funding.

# Chapter 8
# The Power of Words in Crowdfunding

**Yuanqing Li**
*Dominican University, USA*

**Sibin Wu**
https://orcid.org/0000-0001-7761-5132
*University of Texas Rio Grande Valley, USA*

## ABSTRACT

*In this chapter, the authors first provide an overview of the crowdfunding phenomenon. Through the literature review of crowdfunding success factors in the four models, the authors then summarize that the current entrepreneurial research focused on success factors has failed to sufficiently examine how the power of words would affect crowdfunding. Therefore, the authors propose that non-verbal and verbal cues are crucial to entrepreneurial financing success. Based on the insufficient research related with those cues, especially the non-verbal ones, the authors open an area of study on non-verbal and verbal cues in the entrepreneurial financing process by conducting and writing this chapter.*

## INTRODUCTION

Crowdfunding has emerged in recent years as an alternative platform to traditional financing sources and it has caught the attention of many researchers (Mollick, 2014). So far, current crowdfunding literature has examined the phenomenon from two aspects. First, it has shown the key factors that may affect crowdfunding investment decisions. They include rewards (Gerber et al. 2012; Lee et al. 2015; Ryu

DOI: 10.4018/978-1-7998-3226-3.ch008

& Kim, 2016), financial incentives (Cholakova & Clarysse, 2015), philanthropic and support causes (Amara et al. 2014; Gerber et al. 2012; Pearson et al. 2016), altruism (Gerber et al. 2012; Bretschneider et al. 2014; Steigenberger, 2017), interpersonal relationship (Amara et al. 2014; Vedantam, 2015), involvement (Steigenberger, 2017) in the community (Gerber et al. 2012), social media (Amara et al. 2014), fun (Bretschneider et al. 2014; Ryu & Kim, 2016), enjoyment (Lee et al. 2015; Pearson et al. 2016), curiosity (Bretschneider et al. 2014; Vedantam, 2015), recognition (Ryu & Kim, 2016) or identification with the team (Bretschneider et al. 2014) as well as familiarity (Lee et al. 2015).

Second, crowdfunding research has attempted to understand why certain projects are successful. Research has demonstrated that crowdfunding success is found to be related with number of backers and percent of early target capital pledged (Colombo et al. 2015), intellectual capital (Ahlers et al. 2015), individual social capital (Giudici et al, 2012; Colombo et al. 2015), entrepreneur's social network ties (Zheng et al. 2014), amount of highest bid (Wu et al. 2015), funding goal and project duration (Cordova et al. 2015), intrinsic motivation (Cholakova & Clarysse, 2015), national culture (Zheng et al. 2014), and founder investment and firm size (Eddleston et al. 2015). The authors intend to extend the success research stream by examining the impact of words and expressions (especially non-verbal and verbal communication) on crowdfunding success.

Non-verbal cues, which account for more than 60% of communication in interpersonal interaction, are particularly effective in evoking the perception of social presence in computer-mediated communication (Short et al. 1976). Language and message (Hosman, 2002) is a necessary factor in persuasion, and thus affects crowdfunding success (Allison, et al., 2015; Ciuchta & O'Toole, 2016). Entrepreneurs could potentially increase their crowdfunding performance and effectiveness by emphasizing several factors such as non-verbal or verbal cues, which impact their overall project attractiveness. Therefore, it is very important to conduct a study on the power of words in crowdfunding. In this chapter, the authors will do just that. The chapter is structured like the following. The authors first give an overview of the crowdfunding phenomenon. It is then followed by a literature review of crowdfunding success factors in the four models. Then the effect of verbal and non-verbal cues on crowdfunding is explored and summarized. Lastly, the chapter is concluded by discussions and future research directions.

## BACKGROUND

Crowdfunding has seen a tremendous growth over the past decade (Mollick, 2014). According to the crowdfunding industry statistics, the total amount of financial support increased about 50 folds in 5 years (from 1.5 billion in 2011 to 73.9 billion in 2016). The crowdfunding industry is predicted to reach the total volume of over $300 billion by 2025 (CFX Alternative Investing Crowdfunding Statistics, 2016). It is therefore not surprising that many researchers have started to study the phenomenon. Nonetheless, crowdfunding research is still at its infancy stage, and so research has still been evolving. The earliest definition about crowdfunding could be traced back to an online article in 2006. Howe (2006) defines the phenomenon as "crowdsourcing" by illustrating an image-sharing project----Istockphoto. Belleflamme, Schwienbacher and Larralde (2010, P.7) believe the concept of crowdfunding is embedded in crowdsourcing, and could be defined as involving "an open call, essentially through the Internet, for the provision of financial resources either in form of donation or in exchange for some form of reward and/or voting rights."

More recently, Mollick (2014, P.2) defines crowdfunding as "the efforts by entrepreneurial individuals and groups (cultural, social and for-profit) to fund their ventures by drawing on relatively small contributions from a relatively large number of individuals using the Internet, without standard financial intermediaries". The authors adopt this dominant definition in the chapter.

Some researchers study crowdfunding by its processes. Crowdfunding may be categorized by the three parties that are involved in the process: investors who make monetary contributions on crowdfunding, intermediaries that provide crowdfunding platforms like kickstarter.com, and entrepreneurs who seek financing through crowdfunding (Valanciene & Jegeleviciute, 2013). Macht and Weatherston (2015) argue that crowdfunding undergoes two phases in the process: pre-investment and post-investment. Haas, Blohm and Leimeister (2014) regard crowdfunding as a two-side market, which links the investors and entrepreneurs through the crowdfunding intermediary. And they further describe the crowdfunding process as exchanges between capital givers (funders) and project initiators (founders). They state that through the intermediates of crowdfunding platforms, funders and founders seek mutual returns.

In addition, crowdfunding also is categorized by models based on the types of rewards or returns that are distributed to the crowd. Lambert and Schwienbacher (2010) regard crowdfunding investment as either pure-donations (22%), passive investments (60%), or active investments (32%). Hemer (2011) lists five categories of crowdfunding forms: crowd donation, crowd sponsoring, crowd pre-selling, crowd lending and crowd equity. From a legal perspective, Bradford (2012) categorizes crowdfunding platforms into five types: donation, rewards, pre-ordering, lending, and equity. Based on Bradford (2012)'s classification, Massolution (2013) offers a four types of crowdfunding platforms: crowd supporting, crowd lending, crowd investing and crowd donating. Haas et al. (2014) identify three types of crowdfunding— hedonism, altruistic and for profit. Based on the above analyses, the authors conclude that there are four models of crowdfunding: donation-based, equity-based, lending-based and reward-based. Next the authors summarize the success factors for each of those four models:

## Donation-based Crowdfunding Success Factors

Donation based crowdfunding is similar to charity funding and has emerged as a new way for individuals and nonprofit organizations to raise funds. Various theories and frameworks have been applied under this model to explain why people donate. Such theories include social comparison theory (Tan, Lu and Tan, 2016), unified theory of acceptance and use of technology research model (Li et al. 2018), self-system theory (Zhong and Lin, 2018) and stimulus-organism-response framework (Liu, Suh and Wagner, 2018).

Tan, Lu and Tan (2016) investigate how the reputation incentive design, peer effects, and popularity effects impact fundraising performance. They find that peer effects have positive impact while higher visibility of donors' contributions may have negative impact on fundraising. They also suggest to put more fundraising efforts on the crowding-out group to reduce the popularity effect and alleviate the rich-get-richer problem. Project description, pictures and founders' credibility significantly impact the likelihood of donation-based project success (Qian & Lin, 2017). Through the analysis of 109 nonprofit campaigns on Tencent Philanthropy, Zhou and Ye (2018) find that organization's legal status does not affect the crowdfunding outcome much. Demonstrated organizational competence, concrete personal stories, and low-risk solutions (such as in-kind assistance and direct cash) are key factors determining the crowdfunding outcomes. Collecting 1,389 green crowdfunding projects from Tencent Lejuan, Yang, Liu and Yin (2019) find a non-linear effect of goal setting and project duration on project success. That is, a higher goal is positively related with the project success while the impact of lower and moderate goals is not always significant. Long duration of the project is likely to have a positive impact on project success while the influence of short and moderate duration is not always significant.

## Equity-based Crowdfunding Success Factors

The rapid development of equity crowd-funding plays an important role in solving the difficulties of financing in innovative companies and small or micro enterprises. Based on a total of 649 completed online questionnaires collected from Angelcrunch and Zhongchou, Kang et al. (2016) identify the investing behavior from funder's perspective. They propose that trust (calculus and relationship) mediates the positive relationships of fundraiser-related (social interaction ties), project-related (network externality and perceived informativeness) and platform-related (perceived accreditation and third-party seal) factors and funder's willingness to invest. Li et al. (2016) find that the quality of entrepreneurial team information (such as the ratio of full-time staff, staff number and enterprise business age), entrepreneurs' behaviors (like posting project updates and video), lead investor information (credibility, percentage of investment, identity certification, investment experience and comments for projects) are all influencing factors of crowdfunding project performance. With a sample of 499 backers under a German equity crowdfunding platform, Hornuf and Neuenkirch (2017) find that campaign characteristics, funding progress, investor sophistication, herding behavior, and stock market volatility increase the backers' willingness of investment while the distance between backer and start-up, learning effects, and sniping don't have significant effect on funding performance. Financing objectives, assignment of shares, and the number of inquiries are found to be positively related with the investors' funding intention (Li, Cao and Zhao, 2018). Specifically, the number of inquiries and the minimum initial investment amount will impact the financing efficiency, which in turn influences the successful financing of projects. Li, Cao and Zhao (2018) further mention that the herding effect influences the equity crowdfunding outcomes by affecting the decision-making behavior of later investors through the early investments. Tan and Han (2017) confirm that the ratio of leading investment amount (strongest among all the factors), ratio of the transfer of shares, the number of favorite projects, founder education level and investors number (weakest) are the determining factors which significantly impact the financing efficiency of private equity financing. Zheng et al. (2015) state that project updates, valuation, numbers of staff and stakeholder are significantly influencers of the equity crowdfunding success.

## Lending-based Crowdfunding Success Factors

Lending-based crowdfunding has developed rapidly over the last decade as a complementary and flexible financing alternative to the banking industry. Herding behavior and creditworthiness of borrowers have been found to be related with lending success (e.g., Herzenstein, Dholakia, & Andrews, 2011; Zhang & Liu, 2012). The empirical results of Li et al. (2011)'s study reveal that borrowers' decisions such as loan amount, interest rate will determine the lending success. Based on 3,148 lending transactions from Renrendai, Chen and Ning (2013) find that the basic information of the borrower's loan deal has a significant effect on the lending success of the borrower. Cai et al. (2016) discover that the borrowing amount and borrower's lending history (successful borrowing requests) are positively and significantly related to the likelihood of successful funding, but this relationship varies from the first-time borrowing and repeated borrowing model. Han, Xiao and Su (2019) conduct a nationally representative survey and find that financing knowledge and risk attitude are two key factors influencing the consumer behavior of P2P borrowing. Mi and Zhu (2017) find that the self-initiated financial innovation improves the credit availability using the Difference-In-Differences (DID) approach and the loan transaction data collected from a Peer-to-Peer (P2P) platform. Chen, Huang and Ye (2018) find that the usage of punctuation, which affects the readability of the text and borrowers' trust, will negatively impact the borrowing rate and funding probability. Li et al. (2015) demonstrate significant impact of multidimensional (structural, relational and cognitive) friendship networks on P2P lending outcomes. They find that quantity and quality of friendship ties will affect the borrower's likelihood of being funded and interest rates. Feng, Fan and Yoon (2015) examine the impact of funding success, number of bids, and funding time on lenders' bidding strategies. They find that borrowers who have more expertise tend to propose a loan at a lower cost and that a larger loan amount and good interest rate could increase the probability of funding and attract more lenders.

## Reward-based Crowdfunding Success Factors

Crowdfunding research has seen an upper trend in exploring the drivers of successfully crowdfunded projects, especially under reward-based crowdfunding platforms (Kuppuswamy & Bayus, 2015). Mollick (2013) hypothesizes the past successful crowdfunding experiences, third party endorsements and preparedness are positively related to the crowdfunding success, with the moderating effect of geographical location and gender. Extracted 2,101 crowdfunded projects from Kickstarter, he finds that the evidence of past success, external endorsements and a prepared demonstration affect project success. However, crowdfunding seems less subject to gender and geographic biases than venture capital.

Mollick (2014) conducts a study on exploring the current situations of crowdfunding: what factors make the success or failure of a crowdfunding project. Drawing the data collected from more than 48,500 projects, he concluded that personal networks (measured by the numbers of facebook friends of founders), project quality (measured by pitch video, updates within three days of launch and spelling errors in descriptions) as well as geographic factors (examined by Nearstat and Geocode) influence the success of crowdfunding. He also collects the information of post-investment behaviors of the crowdfunding project, and finds that majority of the crowdfunded projects delay in delivering the promised goods.

Cumming, Leboeuf and Schwienbacher (2014) compare the two models in Reward-based crowdfunding campaigns----Keep it all (Indiegogo) and All-or-Nothing (Kickstarter). They propose that All-or-Nothing model has to take more risk but higher chance of success, while Keep it all model has lower chance of success with lower risk. In order to test their propositions, Cumming and associates (2014) collect 22,850 projects from the Indiegogo platform from 2011-2013. Their results show that Keep it all model fits the projects that are small and scalable, while All-or-Nothing model are suitable for projects that are large and non-scalable. Overall, Keep it all models are less successful than All-or-Nothing campaigns in achieving their funding goals. Therefore, crowdfunding models affect the funding success, with the moderation of funding goals and project size.

Kuppuswamy and Bayus (2015) find that backers support crowdfunding projects that follow a U-shaped pattern, compared with the herding patterns in equity and lending-based crowdfunding (Herzenstein, et al. 2011; Zhang & Liu, 2012) and crowding-out patterns in donation-based crowdfunding (Burtch, et al. 2013). They suggest that social information plays an important role in crowdfunding success. Project creators tend to increase their project updates towards the deadline in order to reach their funding goal. Based on two years (May 2009-February 2012) of daily data of 25,058 projects from kickstarter website, they conclude the reason for U-shaped pattern as the reduced diffusion of responsibility and positive influence of project updates towards the final stages of funding, especially for projects that have already reached their funding goals.

Colombo, Franzoni and Rossi-Lamastra (2015) conduct an empirical study through 669 Kickstarter projects to test the existence of the self-reinforcing pattern. They find that the number of early backers and the percent of target capital pledged early in the crowdfunding campaign are positively related with the crowdfunding success. Internal social capital is important for campaign success, but this relationship is moderate in the early days of the campaign.

Drawing 78,061 projects from Kickstarter.com created prior to March 2013, Zvilichovsky, Inbar and Barzilay (2015) discover that project creator's backing history could increase the crowdfunding success. Applying network exchange theory, they believe that if the entrepreneurs have previously supported others, they are going to have higher success rates, and attract more backers and hence funds. They further explain that this results from the direct (backing received from the project founders that they supported) and indirect reciprocity (backing received from the online community) forces in the context of crowdfunding.

Analyzing 762 projects from Kickstarter.com crowdfunding platform, Koch and Siering (2015) examine the factors that influence the success of crowdfunding projects. Based on media richness theory and the concept of reciprocity, they propose that project-specific factors such as depth of project description, the utilization of images, the provision of video material, project updates, small pledging goals, as well as founder-specific factors such as project creating experience and reciprocity in funding are positively related with the success of funding, with the control of funding period, number of Facebook friends and project categories. Their results show that description, images and videos on the project and founder's previous backing experience influence their funding success. However, the previous project creating experience of the entrepreneur has no significant influence on the funding result.

Cordova, Dolci and Gianfrate (2015) explore the success factors of crowdfunding through 1,127 technology projects posted on four different reward-based crowdfunding platforms: 97 successful projects on Ulule; 9 projects on Eppela; 597 successful projects on Kickstarter and 424 projects on Indiegogo. Consistent with the reinforcement model, they find that project funding goal is negatively related with the funding success, that is, the higher the funding goal, the lower probability and extent of project success. They measure the success and the overfunding of the projects as dependent variables. Their results show that project duration and the dollar amount contributed per day are positively related with project success. Therefore, the target value, project duration and contribution frequency will affect the crowdfunding success. The conclusion is that contribution breeds more contributions.

Applying the signaling theory, Wu, Wang and Li (2015) study the success factors of crowdfunding under the Chinese context. They collect data from a sample of 192 projects collected from demohour.com, a Chinese crowdfunding platform. They find that frequency of announcements and the amount of the highest bid are positively related to the crowdfunding success. And this relationship is moderated by the industry effect. In details, highest bid and frequency of announcements affect more on high–tech industry than on movie/music industries.

Greenberg and Mollick (2017) develop the concept of activist choice homophily from theories of choice homophily, based on the comparison of interpersonal choice homophily and induced homophily. Then they explore how the interpersonal choice homophily and activist choice homophily relate to gender in crowdfunding. They propose that individuals are more likely to support people who are similar with them, and this relationship is influenced by gender and industry. This paper argues that like attracts like, which likes could be generated from race, age, education, and occupation of the person. First, they conduct an experiment of 399 students to test the similarity and gender effect. Then they collect the real-world data from Kickstarter with 1,250 projects of gaming, technology, film, fashion and children's books five categories. Their results show that female founders prefer to found projects in fashion and publishing than technology and games. Projects created by female have 40% greater success rate than male. Female founders are more likely to succeed in the industries that they are underrepresented and traditionally male-gender-typed, such as technology.

Kuppuswamy and Bayus (2015) compare the effectiveness of the four crowdfunding models and conclude that reward-based crowdfunding grows faster and has a much larger number of platforms than other models of crowdfunding (Masssolution, 2015). Studies show that rewards are one of the most important motivations for participating in crowdfunding (Gerber, et al. 2012). 76.5% of the crowd-funders offer a reward to their crowd-funders (Lambert & Schwienbacher, 2010). According to Mollick (2014)'s study, research on reward-based crowdfunding is very rare, especially in the perspective of social information effect (Kuppuswamy & Bayus, 2015). In addition, reward-based crowdfunding facilitates entrepreneurial organizational legitimacy construction and exchange resources needed for a start-up (Frydrych et al. 2014). It usually requires at least a product prototype type ready when posting their crowdfunding projects and pre-sells the product or service as tangible rewards (Belleflamme et al., 2014), which stimulate the idea of entrepreneurship.

Thus far, the authors have reviewed the major success factors that appear in recent crowdfunding literature into three categories----Project Characteristics, Founder Characteristics and Funder Characteristics. And they list the success factors filling each category into Figure 1 below:

*Figure 1.*

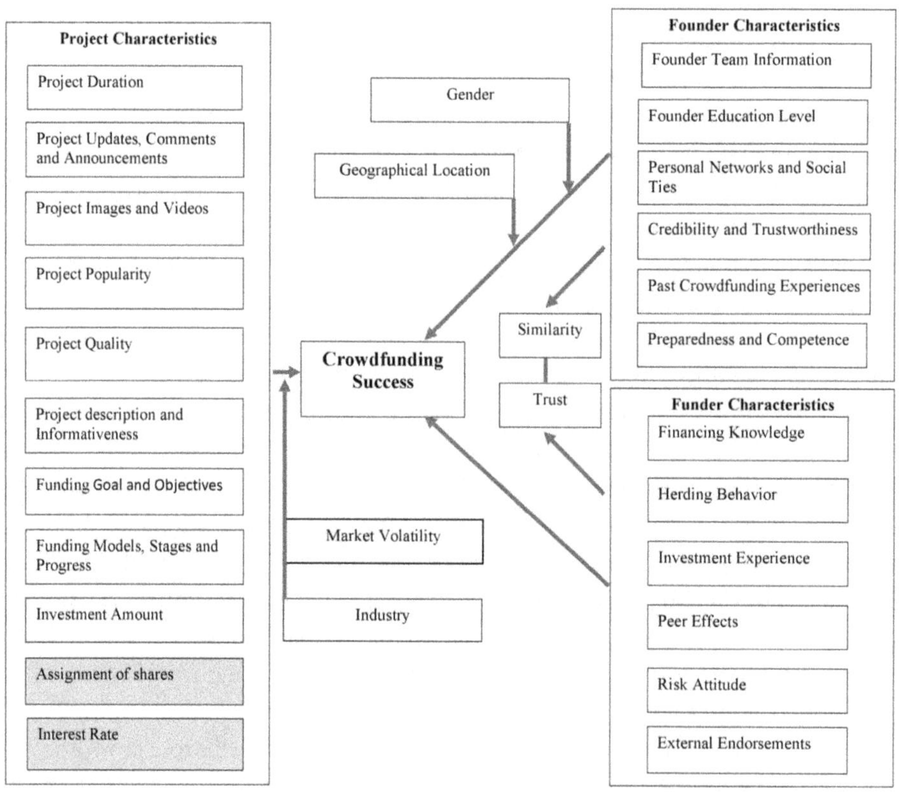

As stated earlier, studies that directly explore the impact of words and expressions on crowdfunding performance are rare. Therefore, the current chapter proposes a relationship between founders' behaviors (especially non-verbal and verbal cues) with the crowdfunding success. The authors propose that non-verbal and verbal behaviors of entrepreneurs may positively influence the crowdfunding outcome. In the following, the authors explore the current research on the roles of non-verbal and verbal behaviors in crowdfunding.

## NON-VERBAL COMMUNICATION

Non-verbal communication has been defined as behaviors other than words that create meaning in interaction (Hale, 2003). This may include expressions, gesture or symbolic behavior that conveys meaning (Burleson, 2003), intentional behavior that conveys an idea symbolically (Canary, 2003) and actions to which meaning may be attached such as a wink, a wave of hand, facial expression, dress and so on (Adejimola, 2008). Most interpersonal information is communicated by non-verbal communication (Mehrabian & Ferris, 1967).

Non-verbal communication exerts its influence through six key characteristics. It pervades every communicative act (omnipresent); can be part of every communication purpose (multifunctional); may be used and understood by world over such as smiling, crying, etc. (universal); is the first form of communication in the history between species (phylogenetic primacy), in the early lifespan of individuals (ontogenetic primacy) and in the opening minutes of human interactions (interaction primacy) (Burgoon, Guerrero, & Floyd, 2016).

Gabbott and Hogg (2001) point out that non-verbal communication transcends the written or spoken word. Non-verbal communication expresses what verbal communication cannot. Whenever there is a contradiction between non-verbal and verbal cues, people tend to believe what's communicated non-verbally rather than the verbal message (Burgoon, Guerrero, & Floyd, 2016). Non-verbal and verbal cues may conjunct with each other during the communication process. Audiences often elaborate on the non-verbal cues before comprehending the verbal message (Sundaram, & Webster, 2000). Affections are communicated faster through non-verbal communication (Noller, 1985). Grahe and Bernieri (1999) conclude that non-verbal behavior would be more important than verbal behavior when expressing a spontaneous affect or rapport and viewing brief slices of an interaction.

Two-thirds of the meaning of interactions is derived from non-verbal cues (Philpott, 1983). Non-verbal cues largely contribute to the success of communication (Burgoon, Guerrero, & Floyd, 2016). Cook (1971) divides the non-verbal cues into two broad categories: static non-verbal cues, which are related to face, physique, physical appearance, clothes, makeup and so on and dynamic non-verbal cues, which are related to gestures, facial expressions, gaze direction, space, distance, tone of voice, and the amount and fluency of speech. Sundaram and Webster (2000) specify non-verbal cues as kinesics (facial and body movements), paralanguages (vocal pitch, loudness, pauses, fluency), proxemics (distance and touch), and physical appearance. Gabbott and Hogg (2001) further categorize non-verbal cues into four broad areas: proxemics (the use of personal space and distance); kinesics (body postures and movement); oculesics (the communicative aspects of eye behavior such as gaze and movement) and vocalics (para-language such as vocal tone and intonation). DeGroot and Gooty (2009) classify three categories towards non-verbal cues: dynamic cues (facial and body movements), static cues (demographic and physical characteristics) and paralinguistic cues (speech rate and volume, vocal tone, pausing).

## NON-VERBAL COMMUNICATION AND CROWDFUNDING

Previous literature on non-verbal communication mainly appears in sociology, psychology and communication fields (Sundaram & Webster, 2000). Most of the studies argue non-verbal cues influence people's first impression and thus persuasion (Webster, 1965). Non-verbal cues have been found to influence the patients' satisfaction of a physician (Mast, 2007); interviewer's perception of applicants' qualifications (Parsons & Liden, 1984), trust and likability (DeGroot & Motowidlo,1999); customers' rapport (Lin et al. 2017) and perceptions of friendliness, credibility, trustworthiness and competence towards the service employees (Sundaram & Webster, 2000); and student engagement in an online course (Dixson et al. 2017). Cade, Koonce and Ikuta (2017) find that non-verbal cues in the video disclosure associated with investor's judgment of uncertainty. They further suggest that the choice of disclosure medium affects investors' judgment. Specifically, investors react more negatively towards the uncertainty that they perceive through video than through written text.

Videos posted on crowdfunding platforms, as the medium of entrepreneurs' non-verbal behavior disclosure, affect their crowdfunding success. Strickler (2009) suggests that crowdfunding video is a demonstration of effort from the entrepreneurs and a good predictor of success. Compared with the projects without videos (39%), crowdfunding projects with videos have a much higher success rate (54%) (Byrom, 2017). The use of video or image signals the preparedness of the entrepreneurs. Therefore, it mitigates information asymmetry between entrepreneurs and funders, as well as increases investors' perception of project quality and founder credibility in crowdfunding (Courtney, Dutta, & Li, 2017). Mollick (2014) emphasized the importance of using a video as the criteria to evaluate the crowdfunding project quality. Project presentation on the crowdfunding platform is positively related to the crowdfunding success (Beier & Wagner, 2015). A video within the project presentation can increase investors' funding motivation and funding success of a crowdfunding project (Kuppuswamy & Bayus 2013).

However, little research has examined how non-verbal cues in the video affect crowdfunding success. Here are the few exceptions. Pope and Sydnor (2011) find that race impacts the lending performance. Using data from Prosper.com, they find that African Americans' chance of receiving a loan reduces by 25-35% compared to whites with similar credit backgrounds. They further explain that the loan postings without pictures or with pictures but contain the image of black or older borrowers and unhappy emotions will be strongly discriminated. Therefore, the characteristics of borrowers displayed in the pictures and descriptions significantly influence their lending outcome.

Duarte, Siegel and Young (2012) test the relationship between borrowers' appearance and perceived trustworthiness under peer-to-peer lending site. They collect listings of 5,950 loans with 3,291 initial loans photographs, and then they employ Amazon's Mechanical Turk (MTurk) service to rate the trustworthiness and will-pay based on borrowers' photographs. Their result shows that borrowers will have higher probabilities of receiving a loan with lower interests, if their appearances are perceived as more trustworthy.

Ravina (2012) examines whether personal characteristics and presentation of founders affects lenders' decision. Based on data collected from 7,321 borrowers in an online lending market, they find that borrowers' appearance and race affect lenders' preferences and perception. If the borrowers' appearance is above average, their possibility of getting a loan would increase 1.44% with the interest rate decrease by 81 bps. Black borrowers need to pay 139-146 bps more interest rates than White borrowers. They also argue for the existence of similarity effect between borrowers and lenders on their ethnicity, residence, gender, interests and experiences. The results show that lenders prefer borrowers who are similar to them in ethnicity, residence, gender and entrepreneurial experience.

Plummer, Allison and Connelly (2016) explore the effect of entrepreneur's characteristics and actions in pursuing the initial external capital. Borrowing from the sense-making literature, they argue that entrepreneur's characteristics such as managerial experiences, as well as actions such as product introduction and commercial property operation will increase their probability of receiving the external capital. From a sample of 986 startups between 1995 and 2010 in Oklahoma, they find that affiliating with a third party is the most essential success factor for early stage financing. Entrepreneur's characteristics and actions will increase the possibility of receiving external capital, only if they are combined with a third-party affiliation.

Anderson and Saxton (2016) argue that facial expression, especially smiling behavior can influence the lending decisions. They collect 323 funding projects by women entrepreneurs from Asia on the Kiva.org crowdfunding platform. They analyze the smile of borrowers from their photo using the Facial Action Coding System. Compared with the previous research finding that Duchenne smile could increase trustworthiness, this research does not show a statistically significant relationship between Duchenne smile and trust or faster prosocial funding behavior. Therefore, they conclude that genuine enjoyment smile has no impact on increasing of trust.

Concluding the current literature of non-verbal cues in crowdfunding, we find that most of them focus on the entrepreneurs' characteristics such as race and gender (Ravina, 2012; Pope & Sydnor, 2011), dynamic cues such smiles, and physical appearance (e.g., Duarte et al. 2012)'s effect on crowdfunding outcome. In order to better illustrate the impact of non-verbal cues on crowdfunding, here we list examples of crowdfunding project from Kickstarter:

*Figure 2.*

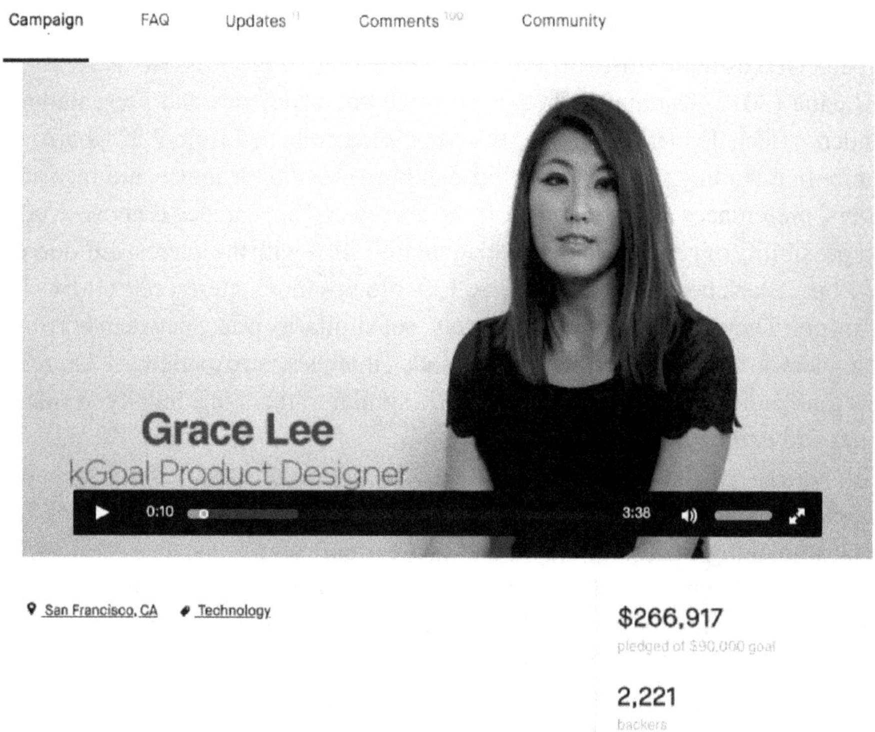

*Figure 3.*

Figures 2 and 3 show an example of Kickstart crowdfunding project. Kickstarter is the most cited, analyzed and the largest reward-based crowdfunding community (Kuppuswamy & Bayus, 2014; Kraus, 2016). Usually, a Kickstarter crowdfunding project contains basic information of the entrepreneur and the funding request, which includes the target dollar amount requested, the length of the project, number of backers, the entrepreneur's name, company and location, an image or video of the project, supports and rewards in different categories and a written description of the business idea. On their crowdfunding page, the entrepreneur needs to persuade the backers whom they don't know much or never met before to support their project. Therefore, the written description (verbal) and the photo or video (non-verbal) of the entrepreneur became relatively important for the funders to make a funding decision (Anderson & Saxton, 2016). As can be seen from the two figures, Project 1 attracts much more backers and funding than project 2, due to the entrepreneur is women with a smile appears in the video.

## VERBAL COMMUNICATION

Verbal communication has been referred to as speech communication (Adejimola, 2008) or language (Krauss, 2002). Language is very important in social gatherings or business transacxtions (Adejimola, 2008). It could be used as a resource for creating social causes of verbal power (Ng, & Bradac, 1993). The semanticity, generativity, and displacement properties of language generate an unlimited number of meaningful novel messages, which faciliate effective and versatile human communication (Krauss, 2002).

Previous research of verbal communication concentrates in the fields of sociology, psychology and communication (Parhankangas & Renko, 2017). Researchers believe that the use of words represents people's mental, social and psychological states (Pennebaker, Mehl, & Niederhoffer, 2003). The use of verbal communication has shown importance in taking care of critically ill patients (Elliott, & Wright, 1999), operating surgical team performance (Dankelman, et al, 2017), motivating students to learn (Downs, Javidi, & Nussbaum, 1988), course performance (Robinson et al., 2013), connecting individual's mood (Zajonc, 2000), appealing to communicator's audience (Parhankangas and Renko, 2017), improving firm performance (Patelli and Pedrini, 2014) and receiving funding from an angel network (Parhankangas and Ehrlich, 2014).

Krauss (2002) categorizes verbal communication as two kinds of signals: signs and symbols. Signs are related to the message we convey by nature. Symbols are the implications of social conventions. He believes that both signs and symbols are involved in the verbal communication process. Hosman (2002) points out the two elements of language: the structural element and the use element. The structural element focuses on the phonology, syntax and lexicon of the texts or narratives. The use element emphasizes the pragmatics, speech style and language varieties across different region or countries. Derived from the LIWC dimensions, Abe (2011) proposes three types of language cues: psychological distancing, cognitive complexity, and positive emotionality. Psychological distancing is associated with the distance of leaving or joining the topic being discussed. Cognitive complexity refers to the precise distinction and integration of words. Positive emotionality relates to the negative and positive emotion words.

Based on previous literature, Toma and D'Angelo (2015) study two categories of linguistic cues: function words (used for binding sentences, content-free parts with not much meaning) and social and psychological concerns (affection, cognitive and sensory process). For example, Parhankangas and Renko (2017) use two kinds of linguistic cues in their research: content words and style words. Content words represent the adjectives, nouns and verbs which contain lots of meaning while the style words concentrate on how the meaning is expressed. Research has found that 55% of the words we frequently apply are style words, even they accounts for only 0.04% of the amount of all words (Pennebaker, 2011).

Keyton et al. (2013) concludes that verbal communication behaviors perform four essential functions in workplace: information sharing, relational maintenance, expressing negative emotion, and organizing communication behaviors. Robbins and Hunsaker (2011) mention that using multiple channels (both verbal and non-verbal) and making the message complete, specific, responsible, congruent and simple could generate effective verbal communication.

However, a debate exists as to which of the two, non-verbal or verbal communication, is more important. Some argue that verbal communication provides more accurate judgments than non-verbal cues (Archer & Akert, 1977). Berry et al. (1997) contend that verbal content conveys the same amount of information as non-verbal behavior does. It would be beneficial to know how verbal and non-verbal cues interact with each other in conducting the meaning of the words or messages under different circumstances.

## VERBAL COMMUNICATION AND CROWDFUNDING

Previous research has demonstrated the important role of verbal communication content and styles in crowdfunding success. Herzenstein, Sonenshein and Dholakia (2011) argue that borrower's narratives influence lender's decision. They collect 1,493 loan listings posted by borrowers on Prosper.com in June 2006 and June 2007 and find six identity claims in their narratives: trustworthy, economic hardship, hardworking, successful, moral, and religious. They find that the more identity claims used in narratives, the more funding will be obtained, but the less pay back will be received from the borrowers. In addition, they find that narratives that emphasize trustworthy or successful identity turn out to be more effective. Therefore, it is important to emphasize several identity claims under uncertain conditions in order to obtain positive funding decisions.

Allison, McKenny and Short (2013) apply warm-glow theory (funding motivation for feeling good) to suggest that use of language influences the speed of funding decision on Kiva. From 6,051 narratives they conclude that narratives with more blame and present rhetoric lead to faster funding while narratives with more accomplishment, tenacity, and variety rhetoric have slower funding. Therefore, the characteristics of rhetoric affect the funding success of lending based crowdfunding.

Drawing from cognitive evaluation theory, Allison et al. (2015) argue that the linguistic cues (intrinsic or extrinsic) have impact on funder's funding motivation. They collect data through a lending based crowdfunding platform They measure intrinsic language with the rhetorical analysis of human interest language and diversity language, and extrinsic language with the content analysis of profit language and risk taking language. Their results show that funders invest more on the projects that they perceive as an opportunity to help others (using human interest and diversity language) rather than a business opportunity (using more profit and risk taking language).

Gorbatai and Nelson (2015) examine the role of language (linguistic content) on crowdfunding success. More specifically, they believe that the use of vivid language, positive emotion and inclusive (relational) language increases crowdfunding success while money-related language decreases the success. Gender can also affect the use of those languages and thus on funding success. It is found that women apply more vivid language, positive emotion and inclusive (relational) language and less money-related language than men do. Using a sample of 9,943 campaigns in Indiegogo, they explain why women are favored than men in receiving funding and support under crowdfunding context.

With the sample of 729 loan requests from prosper.com, Ciuchta and O'Toole (2016) suggest that non-verbal cue (physical attractiveness) and verbal cue (positive word) interact with each other in establishing "the beauty is good effect" and influencing the funding result. The "beauty is good effect" refers to the situation that attractive people are usually ascribed positive qualities simply because of their good looks (Dion, Berscheid, & Walster, 1972). They also find the use of positive word is more influential on impression formation and resource acquisition.

Siering, Koch and Deokar (2016) suggest that static and dynamic communication is useful in detecting fraudulent behavior on crowdfunding platforms. Using data from 652 projects (326 projects are suspended because of fraud while 326 are not suspended) on Kickstarter.com, they show that content based and linguistic cues extracted from static and dynamic communication are important classifiers in analyzing fraudulent behaviors. They conclude that the linguistic cues based approach is a better way for fraud detection, compared with the machine learning and economic evaluation.

Applying language expectancy theory, Parhankangas and Renko (2017) argue that the content of entrepreneurs' message on the crowdfunding platform matters. The word they choose and the story they tell will affect the crowdfunding result significantly. In details, with the data extracted from 656 crowdfunding campaigns (411 commercial and 245 social) listed on Kickstarter, they find that linguistic styles which are more understandable and relatable have higher success rate, and the relationship is moderated by the types of campaigns. Social campaigns (new ventures) are influenced by the linguistic styles more than the commercial campaigns (established category).

In summary, the current literature of verbal communication in crowdfunding mainly explores the impact of the contents of the language (e.g. money-related or human prosocial, negative or positive) on crowdfunding success. So far, no research has focused on how the expression of its language such as whether the project description is simple or complex, emotional or flat can affect crowdfunding outcome. Here the authors provide two project examples to illustrate the importance of verbal impact.

*Figure 4.*

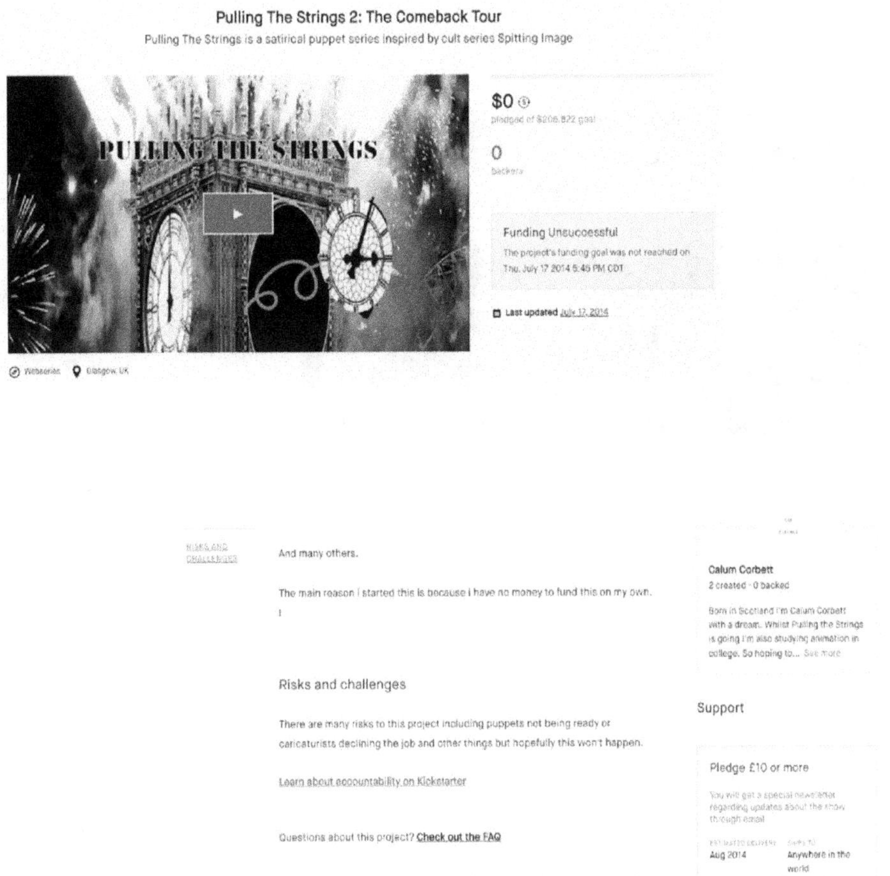


Figure 4 and Figure 5 demonstrate the different funding outcome driven by the text complexity and text readability of its project description (focused on the "risks and challenges"). The authors applied the online text analysis tool----Textalyser to calculate the readability and complexity score. Textalyaser is a text analysis software that allows entry of text or a website and displays readability analysis. After entering the content from the crowdfunding website in this software, complexity scores (measured by Lexical density formula) and readability scores (measured by Gunning fog index formula) are yielded.

As shown in Figure 4, it can be seen that Project 3: Pulling The Strings 2: The Comeback Tour has a long sentence in its "risks and challenges" description and an incomplete sentence with one word "I", turned out to be high in text complexity

*Figure 5.*

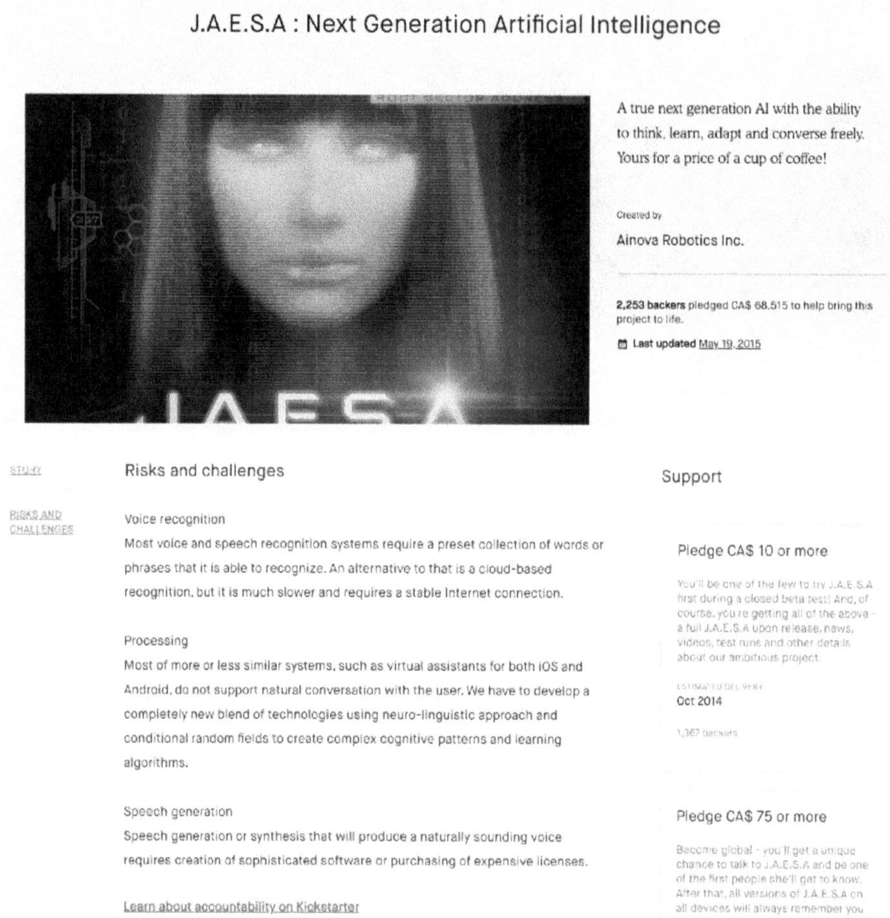


(scored 100) and moderate in text readability (scored 13.5). Project 4: J.A.E.S.A: Next Generation Artificial Intelligence with a less text complexity (scored 87.1) and more text readability (scored 14.7) is well received by the backers. Compared with Project 4's success (2253 backers supported CA$ 68,515), Project 3 did not receive any funding from any backer for the project.

## DISCUSSION AND FUTURE RESEARCH DIRECTIONS

Our literature review of the success factors among the four models of crowdfunding reveals that current research suffers two shortcomings: First, most of them focus on how crowdfunding project characteristics such as project quality (Mollick, 2014), project updates (Kuppuswamy & Bayus, 2015), description, images and videos on the project (Koch & Siering 2015), funding goals (Cumming, Leboeuf & Schwienbacher, 2014; Cordova, Dolci & Gianfrate, 2015), project duration and contribution frequency (Cordova, Dolci & Gianfrate, 2015), frequency of announcements and the amount of the highest bid (Wu, Wang & Li, 2015) effect crowdfunding success. Given the importance of entrepreneur in the entrepreneurial process (Shane & Venkataraman, 2000), researchers need to pay more attention on how entrepreneur's characteristics may affect funding success.

Second, current literature emphasizes the importance of the personal networks (Mollick, 2014), backing experiences (Koch & Siering, 2015; Zvilichovsky, Inbar & Barzilay, 2015) and social capital (Colombo et al. 2015) of the entrepreneurs, rather than the real personality or traits of them. Few researches have examined the actual founders' behavior on crowdfunding success, especially the non-verbal or verbal behaviors of them. Even through Anderson and Saxton (2016) examine the power of non-verbal behaviors on crowdfunding, they are not able to generate significant results on this effect. We also find there is a limit scope of verbal communication research in crowdfunding. Hereby the authors have integrated previous research into Figure 6 where it demonstrates the current research on non-verbal and verbal cues in crowdfunding. The authors further illustrate the findings of literature and future research directions in the following.

The summary of non-verbal-crowdfunding literature reveals the limited scope of current research. As the authors listed above, most of the current literature focus on the impact of the entrepreneur's physical characteristics (especially physical appearance) on crowdfunding outcome. However, physical characteristics are only one part of static non-verbal cues. Non-verbal communication also contains many other cues such as dynamic cues and paralinguistic cues, which has not been tested yet under crowdfunding context. Besides, most of the non-verbal-crowdfunding research is conducted under the lending-based platforms. Due to the limited literature towards the non-verbal cues' effect under crowdfunding context, especially under reward-based platforms, the authors thus call for more studies in exploring the relationship between non-verbal communication and reward-based crowdfunding success.

Compared with the limited literature associated with non-verbal cues and crowdfunding outcome, the studies of verbal cues on crowdfunding are more fruitful and various. It has been studied under both lending based crowdfunding platforms such as Kiva and Prosper, as well as the reward based crowdfunding platforms

*Figure 6.*

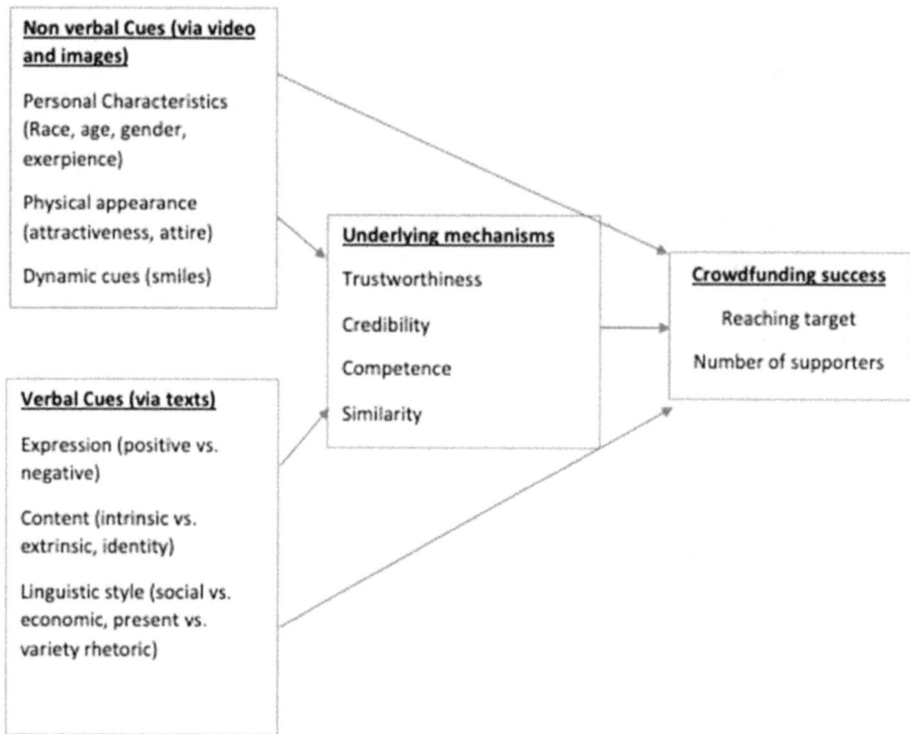


like Kickstarter and Indiegogo. However, the main theme of those researches still narrowly focused on exploring the effect of the contents of the language (e.g. money-related or human prosocial, negative or positive) on crowdfunding success. Since language acts both in terms of content and expression, it would be beneficial to explore some other aspects of verbal communication such as language styles (e.g. simple or complex; emotional, social or psychological) in crowdfunding context for future research.

## CONCLUSION

Successful entrepreneurial financing requires entrepreneurs' powerful persuasion ability (Chen, Yao, and Kotha, 2009). Language and the presentation of one's message as well as non-verbal behaviors are believed to be the critical elements of persuasion (Hosman, 2002). The current entrepreneurial research focused on success factors has been fruitful, but has failed to sufficiently examine how the verbal and non-verbal cues would affect crowdfunding (Allison, et al., 2015). The authors propose non-verbal and verbal cues are crucial to entrepreneurial financing success. Based on the insufficient research related with those cues, especially the non-verbal ones, the authors opened an area of study on non-verbal and verbal cues in the entrepreneurial financing process by conducting and writing this book chapter.

## REFERENCES

Abe, J. A. A. (2011). Changes in Alan Greenspan's language use across the economic cycle: A text analysis of his testimonies and speeches. *Journal of Language and Social Psychology*, *30*(2), 212–223. doi:10.1177/0261927X10397152

Adejimola, A. S. (2008). Language, communication and information flow in entrepreneurship. *African Journal of Business Management*, *2*(11), 201–208.

Ahlers, G. K., Cumming, D., Günther, C., & Schweizer, D. (2015). *Signaling in equity*. Academic Press.

Allison, T. H., Davis, B. C., Short, J. C., & Webb, J. W. (2015). Crowdfunding in a prosocial microlending environment: Examining the role of intrinsic versus extrinsic cues. *Entrepreneurship Theory and Practice*, *39*(1), 53–73. doi:10.1111/etap.12108

Allison, T. H., McKenny, A. F., & Short, J. C. (2013). The effect of entrepreneurial rhetoric on microlending investment: An examination of the warm-glow effect. *Journal of Business Venturing*, *28*(6), 690–707. doi:10.1016/j.jbusvent.2013.01.003

Amara, M., Ben Cheikh, A., & Abdellatif, T. (2014). *Crowdfunding: Determinants and Motivations of the Contributors to the Crowdfunding Platforms*. Academic Press.

Anderson, K. B., & Saxton, G. D. (2016). Smiles, Babies, and Status Symbols: The Persuasive Effects of Image Choices in Small-Entrepreneur Crowdfunding Requests. *International Journal of Communication*, *10*, 22.

Archer, D., & Akert, R. M. (1977). Words and everything else: Verbal and nonverbal cues in social interpretation. *Journal of Personality and Social Psychology*, *35*(6), 443–449. doi:10.1037/0022-3514.35.6.443

Beier, M., & Wagner, K. (2015). *Crowdfunding Success: A Perspective from Social Media and E-Commerce*. Academic Press.

Belleflamme, P., Lambert, T., & Schwienbacher, A. (2010, June). *Crowdfunding: An industrial organization perspective*. Prepared for the workshop Digital Business Models: Understanding Strategies, Paris, France.

Belleflamme, P., Lambert, T., & Schwienbacher, A. (2014). Crowdfunding: Tapping the right crowd. *Journal of Business Venturing, 29*(5), 585–609. doi:10.1016/j.jbusvent.2013.07.003

Berry, D. S., Pennebaker, J. W., Mueller, J. S., & Hiller, W. S. (1997). Linguistic bases of social perception. *Personality and Social Psychology Bulletin, 23*(5), 526–537. doi:10.1177/0146167297235008

Blikkendaal, M. D., Driessen, S. R., Rodrigues, S. P., Rhemrev, J. P., Smeets, M. J., Dankelman, J., van den Dobbelsteen, J. J., & Jansen, F. W. (2017). Surgical flow disturbances in dedicated minimally invasive surgery suites: An observational study to assess its supposed superiority over conventional suites. *Surgical Endoscopy, 31*(1), 288–298. doi:10.100700464-016-4971-1 PMID:27198548

Bradford, C. S. (2012). Crowdfunding and the federal securities laws. *Colum. Bus. L. Rev.*, 1.

Bretschneider, U., Knaub, K., & Wieck, E. (2014). *Motivations for Crowdfunding: What Drives the Crowd to Invest in Start-Ups?* Academic Press.

Burgoon, J. K., Guerrero, L. K., & Floyd, K. (2016). *Nonverbal communication*. Routledge. doi:10.4324/9781315663425

Burtch, G., Ghose, A., & Wattal, S. (2013). An empirical examination of the antecedents and consequences of contribution patterns in crowd-funded markets. *Information Systems Research, 24*(3), 499–519. doi:10.1287/isre.1120.0468

Byrom. (2017). *Get In on the Action: The Best Videos Used in Crowdfunding*. https://www.business.com/articles/get-in-on-the-action-the-best-videos-used-in-crowdfunding/

Cade, N. L., Koonce, L., & Ikuta, K. (2017). *Text versus Video Disclosure of Forward-Looking Information: The Effect of Non-Verbal Cues on Investors' Judgments*. Academic Press.

Cai, S., Lin, X., Xu, D., & Fu, X. (2016). Judging online peer-to-peer lending behavior: A comparison of first-time and repeated borrowing requests. *Information & Management, 53*(7), 857–867. doi:10.1016/j.im.2016.07.006

Canary, D. J. (2003). Managing interpersonal conflict: A model of events related to strategic choices. Handbook of communication and social interaction skills, 515-549.

Chen, J. Z., & Ning, X. (2013). Empirical research on the influence of personal information on P2P lending's success rate—Evidence from Renrendai. *Accounting and Finance, 6*(3).

Chen, X., Huang, B., & Ye, D. (2018). The role of punctuation in P2P lending: Evidence from China. *Economic Modelling*, *68*, 634–643. doi:10.1016/j.econmod.2017.05.007

Chen, X. P., Yao, X., & Kotha, S. (2009). Entrepreneur passion and preparedness in business plan presentations: A persuasion analysis of venture capitalists' funding decisions. *Academy of Management Journal*, *52*(1), 199–214. doi:10.5465/amj.2009.36462018

Cholakova, M., & Clarysse, B. (2015). Does the possibility to make equity investments in crowdfunding projects crowd out reward–based investments? *Entrepreneurship Theory and Practice*, *39*(1), 145–172. doi:10.1111/etap.12139

Ciuchta, M. P., & O'Toole, J. (2016). Looks and linguistics: Impression formation in online exchange marketplaces. *The Journal of Social Psychology*, *156*(6), 648–663. doi:10.1080/00224545.2016.1152218 PMID:26864921

Colombo, M. G., Franzoni, C., & Rossi-Lamastra, C. (2015). Internal social capital and the attraction of early contributions in crowdfunding. *Entrepreneurship Theory and Practice*, *39*(1), 75–100. doi:10.1111/etap.12118

Cook, S. A. (1971, May). The complexity of theorem-proving procedures. In *Proceedings of the third annual ACM symposium on Theory of computing* (pp. 151-158). 10.1145/800157.805047

Cordova, A., Dolci, J., & Gianfrate, G. (2015). The determinants of crowdfunding success: Evidence from technology projects. *Procedia: Social and Behavioral Sciences*, *181*, 115–124. doi:10.1016/j.sbspro.2015.04.872

Courtney, C., Dutta, S., & Li, Y. (2017). Resolving information asymmetry: Signaling, endorsement, and crowdfunding success. *Entrepreneurship Theory and Practice*, *41*(2), 265–290. doi:10.1111/etap.12267

Cumming, D. J., Leboeuf, G., & Schwienbacher, A. (2014, December). Crowdfunding models: Keep-it-all vs. all-or-nothing. In Paris December 2014 finance meeting EUROFIDAI-AFFI paper (Vol. 10). Academic Press.

DeGroot, T., & Gooty, J. (2009). Can nonverbal cues be used to make meaningful personality attributions in employment interviews? *Journal of Business and Psychology*, *24*(2), 179–192. doi:10.100710869-009-9098-0

DeGroot, T., & Motowidlo, S. J. (1999). Why visual and vocal interview cues can affect interviewers' judgments and predict job performance. *The Journal of Applied Psychology*, *84*(6), 986–993. doi:10.1037/0021-9010.84.6.986

Dion, K., Berscheid, E., & Walster, E. (1972). What is beautiful is good. *Journal of Personality and Social Psychology*, *24*(3), 285–290. doi:10.1037/h0033731 PMID:4655540

Dixson, M. D., Greenwell, M. R., Rogers-Stacy, C., Weister, T., & Lauer, S. (2017). Nonverbal immediacy behaviors and online student engagement: Bringing past instructional research into the present virtual classroom. *Communication Education*, *66*(1), 37–53. doi:10.1080/03634523.2016.1209222

Downs, V. C., Javidi, M. M., & Nussbaum, J. F. (1988). An analysis of teachers' verbal communication within the college classroom: Use of humor, self-disclosure, and narratives. *Communication Education*, *37*(2), 127–141. doi:10.1080/03634528809378710

Duarte, J., Siegel, S., & Young, L. (2012). Trust and credit: The role of appearance in peer-to-peer lending. *Review of Financial Studies*, *25*(8), 2455–2484. doi:10.1093/rfs/hhs071

Elliott, R., & Wright, L. (1999). Verbal communication: What do critical care nurses say to their unconscious or sedated patients? *Journal of Advanced Nursing*, *29*(6), 1412–1420. doi:10.1046/j.1365-2648.1999.01028.x PMID:10354236

Feng, Y., Fan, X., & Yoon, Y. (2015). Lenders and borrowers' strategies in online peer-to-peer lending market: An empirical analysis of PPDAI. com. *Journal of Electronic Commerce Research*, *16*(3), 242.

Frydrych, D., Bock, A. J., Kinder, T., & Koeck, B. (2014). Exploring entrepreneurial legitimacy in reward-based crowdfunding. *Venture Capital*, *16*(3), 247–269. doi:10.1080/13691066.2014.916512

Gabbott, M., & Hogg, G. (2001). The role of non-verbal communication in service encounters: A conceptual framework. *Journal of Marketing Management*, *17*(1-2), 5–26. doi:10.1362/0267257012571401

Gerber, E. M., Hui, J. S., & Kuo, P. Y. (2012, February). Crowdfunding: Why people are motivated to post and fund projects on crowdfunding platforms. In *Proceedings of the International Workshop on Design, Influence, and Social Technologies: Techniques, Impacts and Ethics* (*Vol. 2*, p. 11). Academic Press.

GiudiciG.NavaR.Rossi LamastraC.VerecondoC. (2012). Crowdfunding: The new frontier for financing entrepreneurship? *Available at* SSRN 2157429. doi:10.2139srn.2157429

Gorbatai, A., & Nelson, L. (2015). *The Narrative Advantage: Gender and the Language of Crowdfunding*. Haas School of Business UC Berkeley. Research Papers.

Grahe, J. E., & Bernieri, F. J. (1999). The importance of nonverbal cues in judging rapport. *Journal of Nonverbal Behavior, 23*(4), 253–269. doi:10.1023/A:1021698725361

Greenberg, J., & Mollick, E. (2017). Activist choice homophily and the crowdfunding of female founders. *Administrative Science Quarterly, 62*(2), 341–374. doi:10.1177/0001839216678847

Griffin, Z. J. (2012). Crowdfunding: Fleecing the American masses. *Case W. Res. JL Tech. & Internet, 4*, 375.

Haas, P., Blohm, I., & Leimeister, J. M. (2014). *An empirical taxonomy of crowdfunding intermediaries*. Academic Press.

Han, L., Xiao, J. J., & Su, Z. (2019). Financing knowledge, risk attitude and P2P borrowing in China. *International Journal of Consumer Studies, 43*(2), 166–177. doi:10.1111/ijcs.12494

Hemer, J. (2011). *A snapshot on crowdfunding* (No. R2/2011). Working papers firms and region.

Herzenstein, M., Dholakia, U. M., & Andrews, R. L. (2011). Strategic herding behavior in peer-to-peer loan auctions. *Journal of Interactive Marketing, 25*(1), 27–36. doi:10.1016/j.intmar.2010.07.001

Herzenstein, M., Sonenshein, S., & Dholakia, U. M. (2011). Tell me a good story and I may lend you money: The role of narratives in peer-to-peer lending decisions. *Journal of Marketing Research, 48*(SPL), S138-S149.

Hornuf, L., & Neuenkirch, M. (2017). Pricing shares in equity crowdfunding. *Small Business Economics, 48*(4), 795–811. doi:10.100711187-016-9807-9

Hosman, L. A. (2002). Language and persuasion. *The persuasion handbook: Developments in theory and practice*, 371-390.

Howe, J. (2006). The Rise of Crowdsourcing. *Wired, 14*(6). Available online at: https://www.wired.com/wired/archive/14.06/crowds.html

Kang, M., Gao, Y., Wang, T., & Zheng, H. (2016). Understanding the determinants of funders' investment intentions on crowdfunding platforms: A trust-based perspective. *Industrial Management & Data Systems, 116*(8), 1800–1819. doi:10.1108/IMDS-07-2015-0312

Keyton, J., Caputo, J. M., Ford, E. A., Fu, R., Leibowitz, S. A., Liu, T., ... Wu, C. (2013). Investigating verbal workplace communication behaviors. *The Journal of Business Communication (1973), 50*(2), 152-169.

Kickstarter Stats. (2020). Accessed on May 23rd, 2020. https://www.kickstarter.com/help/stats?ref=about_subnav

Koch, J. A., & Siering, M. (2015). *Crowdfunding success factors: The characteristics of successfully funded projects on crowdfunding platforms*. Academic Press.

Kraus, S., Richter, C., Brem, A., Cheng, C. F., & Chang, M. L. (2016). Strategies for reward-based crowdfunding campaigns. *Journal of Innovation & Knowledge, 1*(1), 13–23. doi:10.1016/j.jik.2016.01.010

Krauss, R. M. (2002). *The psychology of verbal communication. In International Encyclopaedia of the Social and Behavioral Sciences*. Elsevier.

Kuppuswamy, V., & Bayus, B. L. (2013). *Crowdfunding Creative Ideas: the Dynamics of Projects Backers in Kickstarter*. SSRN Working Paper.

Lambert, T., & Schwienbacher, A. (2010). An empirical analysis of crowdfunding. *Social Science Research Network, 1578175*, 1–23.

Lee, C. R., Lee, J. H., & Shin, D. Y. (2015). Factor Analysis of the Motivation on Crowdfunding Participants: An Empirical Study of Funder Centered Reward-type Platform. *Journal of Society for e-Business Studies, 20*(1).

Li, S., Lin, Z., Qiu, J., Safi, R., & Xiao, Z. (2015). How friendship networks work in online P2P lending markets. *Nankai Business Review International, 6*(1), 42–67. doi:10.1108/NBRI-01-2014-0010

Li, S., Qiu, J., Lin, Z., & Qiu, J. (2011, June). Do borrowers make homogeneous decisions in online P2P lending market? an empirical study of PPDai in China. In ICSSSM11 (pp. 1-6). IEEE.

Li, X., Tang, Y., Yang, N., Ren, R., Zheng, H., & Zhou, H. (2016). The value of information disclosure and lead investor in equity-based crowdfunding: An exploratory empirical study. *Nankai Business Review International, 7*(3), 301–321. doi:10.1108/NBRI-01-2016-0002

Li, Y., Cao, H., & Zhao, T. (2018). Factors Affecting Successful Equity Crowdfunding. *Journal of Mathematical Finance, 8*(02), 446–456. doi:10.4236/jmf.2018.82028

Lin, C. Y., Lin, C. Y., Lin, J. S. C., & Lin, J. S. C. (2017). The influence of service employees' nonverbal communication on customer-employee rapport in the service encounter. *Journal of Service Management*, *28*(1), 107–132. doi:10.1108/JOSM-08-2015-0251

Liu, L., Suh, A., & Wagner, C. (2018). Empathy or perceived credibility? An empirical study on individual donation behavior in charitable crowdfunding. *Internet Research*, *28*(3), 623–651. doi:10.1108/IntR-06-2017-0240

Macht, S. A., & Weatherston, J. (2015). Academic Research on Crowdfunders: What's Been Done and What's To Come? *Strategic Change*, *24*(2), 191–205. doi:10.1002/jsc.2010

Massolution, C. F. (2013). *The crowdfunding industry report*. Academic Press.

Mast, M. S. (2007). On the importance of nonverbal communication in the physician–patient interaction. *Patient Education and Counseling*, *67*(3), 315–318. doi:10.1016/j.pec.2007.03.005 PMID:17478072

Mehrabian, A., & Ferris, S. R. (1967). Inference of attitudes from nonverbal communication in two channels. *Journal of Consulting Psychology*, *31*(3), 248–252. doi:10.1037/h0024648 PMID:6046577

Mi, J. J., & Zhu, H. (2017). Can funding platforms' self-initiated financial innovation improve credit availability? Evidence from China's P2P market. *Applied Economics Letters*, *24*(6), 396–398. doi:10.1080/13504851.2016.1197358

Mollick, E. (2014). The dynamics of crowdfunding: An exploratory study. *Journal of Business Venturing*, *29*(1), 1–16. doi:10.1016/j.jbusvent.2013.06.005

Mollick, E. R. (2013). *Swept away by the crowd? Crowdfunding, venture capital, and the selection of entrepreneurs*. Academic Press.

Ng, S. H., & Bradac, J. J. (1993). *Power in language: Verbal communication and social influence*. Sage Publications, Inc.

Noller, P. (1985). Video primacy—A further look. *Journal of Nonverbal Behavior*, *9*(1), 28–47. doi:10.1007/BF00987557

Parhankangas, A., & Ehrlich, M. (2014). How entrepreneurs seduce business angels: An impression management approach. *Journal of Business Venturing*, *29*(4), 543–564. doi:10.1016/j.jbusvent.2013.08.001

Parhankangas, A., & Renko, M. (2017). Linguistic style and crowdfunding success among social and commercial entrepreneurs. *Journal of Business Venturing*, *32*(2), 215–236. doi:10.1016/j.jbusvent.2016.11.001

Parsons, C. K., & Liden, R. C. (1984). Interviewer perceptions of applicant qualifications: A multivariate field study of demographic characteristics and nonverbal cues. *The Journal of Applied Psychology*, *69*(4), 557–568. doi:10.1037/0021-9010.69.4.557

Patelli, L., & Pedrini, M. (2014). Is the optimism in CEO's letters to shareholders sincere? Impression management versus communicative action during the economic crisis. *Journal of Business Ethics*, *124*(1), 19–34. doi:10.100710551-013-1855-3

Pearson, A., Johdet, J.,, & Näselius, M. (2016). *Understanding The Crowd: A quantitative study on investor motivation in equity crowdfunding*. Academic Press.

Pennebaker, J. W. (2011). The secret life of pronouns. *New Scientist*, *211*(2828), 42–45. doi:10.1016/S0262-4079(11)62167-2

Pennebaker, J. W., Mehl, M. R., & Niederhoffer, K. G. (2003). Psychological aspects of natural language use: Our words, our selves. *Annual Review of Psychology*, *54*(1), 547–577. doi:10.1146/annurev.psych.54.101601.145041 PMID:12185209

Philpott, J. S. (1983). *The relative contribution to meaning of verbal and nonverbal channels of communication: A meta-analysis* (Unpublished master's thesis). University of Nebraska, Lincoln.

Plummer, L. A., Allison, T. H., & Connelly, B. L. (2016). Better together? Signaling interactions in new venture pursuit of initial external capital. *Academy of Management Journal*, *59*(5), 1585–1604. doi:10.5465/amj.2013.0100

Pope, D. G., & Sydnor, J. R. (2011). What's in a Picture? Evidence of Discrimination from Prosper. com. *The Journal of Human Resources*, *46*(1), 53–92. doi:10.3368/jhr.46.1.53

Qian, Y., & Lin, J. (2017). Antecedents of project success in donation-based crowdfunding-based on Tencent LeJuan platform in China. *Proceedings of Science, ISCC*.

Ravina, E. (2012). *Love & loans: The effect of beauty and personal characteristics in credit markets*. Academic Press.

Robbins, S., & Hunsaker, P. L. (2011). Training in interpersonal skills: Tips for managing people at work. Pearson Higher Ed.

Robinson, R. L., Navea, R., & Ickes, W. (2013). Predicting final course performance from students' written self-introductions: A LIWC analysis. *Journal of Language and Social Psychology*, *32*(4), 469–479. doi:10.1177/0261927X13476869

Ryu, S., & Kim, Y. G. (2016). A typology of crowdfunding sponsors: Birds of a feather flock together? *Electronic Commerce Research and Applications*, *16*, 43–54. doi:10.1016/j.elerap.2016.01.006

Shane, S., & Venkataraman, S. (2000). The promise of entrepreneurship as a field of research. *Academy of Management Review*, *25*(1), 217–226. doi:10.5465/amr.2000.2791611

Short, J., Williams, E., & Christie, B. (1976). *The social psychology of telecommunications*. John Wiley and Sons.

Siering, M., Koch, J. A., & Deokar, A. V. (2016). Detecting Fraudulent Behavior on Crowdfunding Platforms: The Role of Linguistic and Content-Based Cues in Static and Dynamic Contexts. *Journal of Management Information Systems*, *33*(2), 421–455. doi:10.1080/07421222.2016.1205930

Steigenberger, N. (2017). Why supporters contribute to reward-based crowdfunding. *International Journal of Entrepreneurial Behaviour & Research*, *23*(2), 336–353. doi:10.1108/IJEBR-04-2016-0117

Strickler, Y. (2009). *The importance of video*. Retrieved July 12th, 2017 from https://www.kickstarter.com/blog/the-importance-of-video

Sundaram, D. S., & Webster, C. (2000). The role of nonverbal communication in service encounters. *Journal of Services Marketing*, *14*(5), 378–391. doi:10.1108/08876040010341008

Tan, L., & Han, J. Y. (2017). Research on the Influence Factors of the Financing Efficiency of Internet Private Equity Financing Platform in China. *Journal of Natural Science of Hunan Normal University*, (3), 12.

Tan, X., Lu, Y., & Tan, Y. (2016). Why should I donate? Examining the effects of reputation, peer influence, and popularity on charitable giving over social media platforms. *Examining the Effects of Reputation, Peer Influence, and Popularity on Charitable Giving Over Social Media Platforms.*

Toma, C. L., & D'Angelo, J. D. (2015). Tell-tale words: Linguistic cues used to infer the expertise of online medical advice. *Journal of Language and Social Psychology*, *34*(1), 25–45. doi:10.1177/0261927X14554484

Valanciene, L., & Jegeleviciute, S. (2013). Valuation of crowdfunding: Benefits and drawbacks. *Economics and Management, 18*(1), 39–48. doi:10.5755/j01.em.18.1.3713

Vedantam, L. (2015). *Toward a Typology of Crowdfunding Motivations. Strategic Approaches to Successful Crowdfunding*. Academic Press.

Webster, J. C. (1965). Speech communications as limited by ambient noise. *The Journal of the Acoustical Society of America, 37*(4), 692–699. doi:10.1121/1.1909395 PMID:14288280

Wu, S., Wang, B., & Li, Y. (2015). How to attract the crowd in crowdfunding? *International Journal of Entrepreneurship and Small Business, 24*(3), 322–334. doi:10.1504/IJESB.2015.067465

Yang, J., Liu, L., & Yin, C. (2019). A Non-Liner Decision Model for Green Crowdfunding Project Success: Evidence from China. *International Journal of Environmental Research and Public Health, 16*(2), 187. doi:10.3390/ijerph16020187 PMID:30634654

Yuan, H., Lau, R. Y., & Xu, W. (2016). The determinants of crowdfunding success: A semantic text analytics approach. *Decision Support Systems, 91*, 67–76. doi:10.1016/j.dss.2016.08.001

Zhang, J., & Liu, P. (2012). Rational herding in microloan markets. *Management Science, 58*(5), 892–912. doi:10.1287/mnsc.1110.1459

Zheng, H., Huang, Y., Wang, T., & Chen, D. (2015). Antecedents of Equity-based Crowdfunding Success for Innovation Projects. *China Soft Science, 2015*(1), 130–138.

Zheng, H., Li, D., Wu, J., & Xu, Y. (2014). The role of multidimensional social capital in crowdfunding: A comparative study in China and US. *Information & Management, 51*(4), 488–496. doi:10.1016/j.im.2014.03.003

Zhong, Z. J., & Lin, S. (2018). The antecedents and consequences of charitable donation heterogeneity on social media. *International Journal of Nonprofit and Voluntary Sector Marketing, 23*(1), e1585. doi:10.1002/nvsm.1585

Zhou, H., & Ye, S. (2018). Legitimacy, worthiness, and social network: An empirical study of the key factors influencing crowdfunding outcomes for nonprofit projects. *Voluntas*, 1–16.

Zvilichovsky, D., Inbar, Y., & Barzilay, O. (2015). *Playing both sides of the market: Success and reciprocity on crowdfunding platforms*. Academic Press.

## ADDITIONAL READING

Allison, T. H., Davis, B. C., Short, J. C., & Webb, J. W. (2015). Crowdfunding in a prosocial microlending environment: Examining the role of intrinsic versus extrinsic cues. *Entrepreneurship Theory and Practice*, *39*(1), 53–73. doi:10.1111/etap.12108

Allison, T. H., Davis, B. C., Webb, J. W., & Short, J. C. (2017). Persuasion in crowdfunding: An elaboration likelihood model of crowdfunding performance. *Journal of Business Venturing*, *32*(6), 707–725. doi:10.1016/j.jbusvent.2017.09.002

Anderson, K. B. (2016). *Let me tell you a story: An exploration of the compliance-gaining effects of narrative identities in online crowdfunding textual appeals* (Doctoral dissertation, State University of New York at Buffalo).

Gafni, H., Marom, D., & Sade, O. (2019). Are the life and death of an early-stage venture indeed in the power of the tongue? Lessons from online crowdfunding pitches. *Strategic Entrepreneurship Journal*, *13*(1), 3–23. doi:10.1002ej.1293

Gorbatai, A., & Nelson, L. (2015). *The narrative advantage: Gender and the language of crowdfunding*. Haas School of Business UC Berkeley. Research Papers.

Kim, J., Cho, D., & Lee, B. (2016). The mind behind crowdfunding: An empirical study of speech emotion in fundraising success.

Lagazio, C., & Querci, F. (2018). Exploring the multi-sided nature of crowdfunding campaign success. *Journal of Business Research*, *90*, 318–324. doi:10.1016/j.jbusres.2018.05.031

Li, J. J., Chen, X. P., Kotha, S., & Fisher, G. (2017). Catching fire and spreading it: A glimpse into displayed entrepreneurial passion in crowdfunding campaigns. *The Journal of Applied Psychology*, *102*(7), 1075–1090. doi:10.1037/apl0000217 PMID:28333500

Siering, M., Koch, J. A., & Deokar, A. V. (2016). Detecting fraudulent behavior on crowdfunding platforms: The role of linguistic and content-based cues in static and dynamic contexts. *Journal of Management Information Systems*, *33*(2), 421–455. doi:10.1080/07421222.2016.1205930

## KEY TERMS AND DEFINITIONS

**Crowdfunding:** A method of financing by collecting small amounts of contributions from a large crowd of people, usually through the internet.

**Donation-Based Crowdfunding:** A crowdfunding model that is similar to charity funding, which investors just donate for goodwill and acknowledgement.

**Equity-Based Crowdfunding:** A crowdfunding model in which funders are treated as equity stakeholders with profit sharing in return of their investments.

**Lending-Based Crowdfunding:** A crowdfunding model that investors offer funds through small loans and earn the returns through interest payments from the borrowers.

**Non-Verbal Cues:** Communication among people that do not involve a direct verbal translation. It contains dynamic cues such as body movements and facial expressions, static cues such as demographic and physical characteristics and paralinguistic cues such as speech volume and vocal tone.

**Reward-Based Crowdfunding:** A crowdfunding model offers funders with pre-ordering product, services, or some incentives as the return of backers' investments.

**Success Factor:** A management term for an element that is essential and necessary to achieve the crowdfunding project funding goal.

**Verbal Cues:** Communication delivered through speech and language. It could be divided into content cues which contain lots of meaning and the style cues concentrating on how the meaning is expressed.

# Chapter 9
# Is Crowdfunding One Way to Pay Education?

**Isabel Pimentel Maia**
*Faculdade de Economia da Universidade de Coimbra, Portugal*

## ABSTRACT

*Crowdfunding is an innovative, creative tool of distance collaborative funding, which can galvanise an optimal number of people to various potentials, including education. The aim is to understand crowdfunding and its implementation in Portugal, focusing on successful projects and exploring its potential use in literacy and educational projects, as an alternative to resources perceived as 'classical'. Successful Portuguese projects in education are still underused and under-reported, despite being great allies to innovative, creative educational entrepreneurs requiring swift responses in a post-pandemic future. Is crowdfunding a way to change education?*

## INTRODUCTION

The new global economic crisis derives from a health crisis, unlike global financial crises such as the one that took place in 2008.

Covid19 democratized this new crisis and halted economies worldwide, a situation from which nothing and nobody is exempt. The production and consumption of goods, as well as distance training and education have become a priority. A great battle is now being fought against an unknown actor (a virus), which hinders the connection between people and 'normal' life as it was known. Geographically close people became as physically distant as those geographically apart. This levelling in distancing appears to enable more democratic opportunities, regardless of individuals

DOI: 10.4018/978-1-7998-3226-3.ch009

and the area they are in, but this might not be the case: we were not ready for this, and inequality remains stark.

Now more than ever, Information and Communication Technology (ICT) is an indispensable ally in social and economic recovery in various areas of activity. In the present and in a post-pandemic future, ways to overcome barriers and counteract new threats need to be (re)invented so that the world can carry on growing and developing with a better prepared 'normal' life.

Collective and/or collaborative funding (crowdfunding, or Cf) is an innovative way to leverage development in moments such as these, especially for financing projects that promote sustainable recovery, adjusted to immediate future needs. Crowdfunding presents itself as a response which can quickly surpass the advantages of micro credit - it is a contractual proposal disseminated on the internet and using new technologies, often emerging before State and bank funding, since it resorts to the available liquidity of the general public for quick, non-bureaucratic financial help. In every moment of crisis, new opportunities for financial innovation arise and this tool may gain more potential if properly developed (Valancience & Jegeleviciute, 2014).

Given the lack of literature, especially on the analysis of projects in education, the present chapter sets out to encourage the study and development of the subject. The barriers imposed by unequal opportunities in education, which exist regardless of any unexpected changes and notably during Covid19, must be overcome. Digital education and mass availability of distance education/training is a very recent, important subject. Before a common, poorly-understood enemy, a new reality was forced upon society, exposing existing inequalities. The analyses presented herein address the way network relations and platform technologies operate in current online collaborative environments, in order to make funding alternatives through Cf available to all and to help overcome socio-economic inequalities in areas such as education, in which the right to equality must be prioritised.

## 1. What is Crowdfunding

Crowdfunding is a model founded in the beginning of the 21st century to fund multiple projects from various areas in a simple, fast way. As the word implies, Crowdfunding is an innovative funding system through which an entrepreneur in any sector or a proposed beneficiary requests small individual sums from the general public through online platforms. These projects are usually considered too high risk, despite the small amounts requested, to be directly funded by the traditional channels, such as banks.

Authors such as Forbes and Schaefer (2017) define Cf as 'a process in which a project or business can be realised, by collecting the necessary funding from a large group of people willing to take part in that investment'. Like Schwienbacher and Larralde (2010) they use an interesting image: 'an open call, essentially via the Internet, to raise financial resources, in various ways - donation, reward exchange or voting rights, with a view to supporting initiatives with specific purposes'.

Besides its main funding purpose, Cf also can also help in other areas, for example: broadening networks; reaching more clients; safer negotiations; and obtaining better terms and conditions. This exchange of information and privileged contacts has a low-to-zero cost, because it happens online. Authors such as (Mollick, 2014; Pril, 2015) explain the low cost compared to other media differently: through Cf., individuals or businesses, social, and cultural organisations, as well as not-for-profits, which have to carry out their activity and projects directly through the collaboration of a great number of people, can avoid paying intermediaries and other associated costs.

Various platforms have emerged in Portugal. To some extent, Cf has helped provide more support to less privileged creators, especially in the Third Sector, albeit insufficiently to meet current demand.

In very general terms, the way Cf works is very straightforward: the mentor who has a funding idea must present it as clearly as possible to the public, usually through a platform, specifying the budgeted amount necessary to develop the project and a deadline. People interested in the project are directed to a website, where the project is presented in various possible ways, and decide whether or not to contribute. The hosting platform receives a commission (in Portugal, usually around 5%), in case the target is achieved before the deadline. If the target amount is not reached, the entrepreneur receives nothing, regardless of the amount received.

Valancience and Jegeleviciute (2014) highlight Cf as a creative, innovative and global funding option, thus presenting itself as an alternative to other types of funding. Digital marketing is essential for disseminating Cf.

According to Catarino (2018) the Cf phenomenon is an environmental refraction which translates as a return to 'small is beautiful', from the perspective of raising small sums to launch new projects not only in the Third Sector, realising social and cultural projects which promote equality and equal opportunities, but also in other sectors, of which start-ups are a good example. The millennium generation – 18 to 37-year-olds – comprises over 86 million people and only approximately 28% of Cf investors are over 50 (Catarino, 2018). It is a nonconformist, creative generation which dislikes slow responses to change. The 2008 financial crisis discredited many of the traditional agents who brokered financial processes, seen as classical. The banking and parabanking system became discredited by the general opinion, who felt the damaging effects of the crisis, partly caused by this sector. For this reason, there is a considerable desire to reduce the influence of intermediaries in this new future. Various authors place the origin of Cf in crowdsourcing1, given its propensity for philanthropy, especially for funding art as well as less privileged emerging sectors.

## 2. The Crowdfunding Model

Cf base model is very simple and easy to operate in the digital world. As mentioned above, it does not require so many intermediaries when compared to other ways of financing credit, only requiring three elements or actors to implement the process: i) the intermediary (platform); ii) the investor (public); iii) and the beneficiary (entrepreneur).

i) The computer platform serves as the only intermediary, that is, a company manages the Cf operations through new technologies and the internet. The funding object is presented in these platforms, which make technical, material and human resources available to connect 'willingness' between investors and beneficiaries;
ii) the investor or the general public decides whether or not to invest in the project. At this stage, transparency and clarity of information will ensure the necessary protection, which is is all the more important, if the aim of the Cf is either capital or a loan;
iii) the beneficiary, that is, whoever seeks funding to implement an idea or business.

The above three main actors can always be supported by other actors for various types of services, such as legal aid, marketing, accounting, etc. Nevertheless the base model is as simple as this.

## 3. Types of Crowdfunding in Portugal

Cf has been regulated in Portugal since 2015, under Law No.102/2015. As in most countries, the law provides for four types of collaborative funding, based on returns: i) donation-based, the recipient receives the amount raised; ii) reward-based, the recipient is obliged to deliver a product or service, in return for the funding2; iii) equity, the recipient remunerates the donor through shareholding, distribution of dividends or profits and iv) crowdlending, the recipient rewards through interest https://economiafinancas.com/.

Each type of Cf is usually aimed at sectors/niches or investors with specific characteristics.

i) Crowdfunding through donations

The recipient receives a donation without a direct delivery of non-monetary compensation to the investors. These initiatives have a social focus, usually promoted by Non-Governmental Organisations (NGOs), Social Solidarity Private Institutions

(SSPI) or not-for-profit associations. They are mostly used by the Third Sector. eSolidar and Novo Banco Co-Crowdfunding are two examples of platforms used in this type of financing.

ii) Reward-based Crowdfunding

Within this mechanism, the recipient is obliged to 'reward' or make an exchange with the investors, which can materialise as follows: funded product and/or service, in return for the sum obtained – the investors receive gadgets, an album, a miniaturised replica, a book or another token symbolising the product they funded, etc. PPL is an example of a platform used for crowdfunding reward, with great implementation in the Portuguese market This type of crowdfunding became well known worldwide, thanks to platforms such as Indiegogo and Kickstarter. Many of these initiatives serve mostly to test market interest in new products.

iii) Equity Crowdfunding

The recipient rewards the investor by giving shares, thus granting him/her the right to receive dividends and/or share profits. Seedrs is an example of these platforms At the initial stage, the proposal is presented on the platform, specifically the projects and/or businesses which need financing and the rewards available, usually proportionate to the contributions.

iv) Crowdlending

Similar to other market alternatives, the recipient rewards the investor by paying fixed interest set at the time of the funding. Raize is one of these platforms. A great number of small and medium-size businesses which for various reasons have not been able to borrow money from banks have used crowdlending. Interest rates vary between 5 and 9%, but without guarantee of invested capital, which requires assessing the risk of non-compliance by the financed companies.

The latter two types of Cf bypass the banking system and the financial markets (Bernardes & Lucian, 2015; Catarino, 2018).

## 4. Advantages and Disadvantages of Crowdfunding

Since the 2008 crisis, Cf has been clearly growing both in Portugal and abroad. Triggered by the financial sector, this crisis overloaded banks with regulations and bureaucracy, in order to minimise risk and increase trust, while hindering the dynamism and the amount of bank support in sectors where fast response is a priority. Bureaucracy, slowness and risk barriers in banking have a negative impact on businesses, especially small new companies and entrepreneurs who find themselves increasingly removed from innovative, creative deals. Cf has exploited and grown into this gap According to a study by Catarino (2018), in times of more restrictive granting of credit and/or financial crisis, unemployment rates go up, especially in small businesses, thus attracting funding alternatives such as Cf.

With regards to alternative funding, Cf presents advantages to both investors and recipients, such as: i) more democratic ease of access; ii) quickness in response; iii) community-building; iv) generating new opportunities.

i) Democratisation and ease of access – the internet, a well-known 'open window' of global opportunities, facilitates access to funding or investment to any individual with a bank account or payment card. Crowdlending and Equity Cf may face national legal restrictions or constraints. But for the most part, most countries are open and flexible to operations in any part of the globe.
ii) Speed of response – any funding request process in banking and parabanking is usually very slow and bureaucratic. The simplicity of the Cf model and application makes the process run quicker, thus requiring a specific timeline for the rigorous planning of the project. Besides removing all the bureaucracy associated to the most common traditional bank credit, Cf does not require highly meticulous business budgeting; instead, it places emphasis on the idea and its implementation, thus attracting more creative projects.
iii) Community-building – the interaction between those interested in investing leads to the creation of a network/community in which ideas and experiences (successful or unsuccessful) are exchanged. Information exchange usually entails considerable planning costs. However, with Cf this type of information flows easily and transparently at a low cost. One single campaign is enough to show the reliability and transparency in Cf, regardless of the degree of success or failure of previous experience, which is testimony to the continuous participation of platform users in fundraising campaigns.
iv) Generating new opportunities – success in a Cf campaign leads to a snowball effect, thanks to the trustworthiness generated in a network of investors who wish to carry on supporting successful projects, thus providing new campaign opportunities and deals in the short and medium term, besides more adequate, privileged information.

However, disadvantages in the mechanism underlying Cf have been identified. Return is not guaranteed; there are fees and tax consequences; intellectual property issues and absence of liability.

v) Non-guaranteed return – regardless of the work put into a Cf campaign with or without dedicated marketing, there is no guarantee of return. Indeed the initiator or entrepreneur may receive nothing, But that can depend on the terms of the platform or platform channel, if opting for 'all-or-nothing'. In a reward-based campaign, while clear this rule should be carefully considered, in order to avoid decisions being affected by bias.
vi) Fees and tax consequences – platforms offering this option charge commissions on the fundraising process, to which fees of sometimes over 10% are added (though usually around 5% of credit card processing, paid into the participation of an investor in a campaign). However, if the investment collected rates as revenue, it will obviously be subject to tax. All these elements entail variables and costs, and will play a role in decision making.
vii) Intellectual Property – while still at the stage of funding an idea, intellectual property only appears to be a minor detail. But later on it can become more significant before or after implementation, as a reasonable number of difficulties and bitter experiences throughout the world have shown. On occasion, successful campaigns which carelessly are not registered beforehand for financial reasons run the risk of losing their ideas to others by the end of the campaign. Despite the possibility of monitoring, total control is often impossible given the possibility of quick dissemination and multiplication.
viii) Different types of project assessment and absence of liability – in Cf platforms, campaign assessment is mostly focused on ideas and their potential, not so much on credit and risk analyses with detailed financial/economic indicators. Even capital transactions are not regulated or advised by specific guidelines for mentors to present and develop projects. Decision-making is thus constrained for investors and equity holders, even when faced with management difficulties and mismanagement during business implementation.

Despite the interest in challenging this balance between advantages and disadvantages, the dynamics brought by Cf are very tempting, offering an alternative to the inertia of the economy for lack of financial resources. New generations do not wait and Cf enables an interesting motivation so that a new idea does not disappear without being explored, even if it happens in a small niche. It would be wasteful not to take advantages of the exponential development of the internet and the platforms hosting this new type of social interaction faithful to an ever-increasing (Jenkins, Purushotma, Weigel, Clinton, & Robison, 2009) network Even the media offer these collective actions, similarly to a snow ball through their own campaigns of digital, social and creative marketing, which is needed to attract more interest. Indeed, networks in which resources are shared include people committed to maintaining their freedom of intervention and participation without being bound to any obligation or sacrifice — these are characteristics found in this new generation which is keen to go further (Botsman & Rogers, 2011).

## 5. Information and Communication Technologies (ICT) and Crowdfunding

ICT has contributed greatly to solutions in this new innovative, fast-moving world. Creativity coupled with problem-solving though information technologies has become an increasingly real connection. The speed with which relations and new connections happen in networks create a new reality, which necessarily transforms our day-to-day lives. The word 'network' is commonly used in today's language — those who are not in the network are either excluded or non-existent.

But what is this truth, what is a network? It comes from the Latin word rete, a structure with a distinctive pattern (Cambridge B.E.D., 2011). According to Castells (2001), a 'network is a set of interconnected nodes'3. Intranet, the internet or even local network are examples of the technological basis of this system of interconnected 'nodes'.

Indeed, when referring to a network we know that it is a set of points joined in a way that is very mutable, flexible and adaptable to what joins them. This new way of connecting by moulding solutions to the needs of an ever-changing world addresses numerous unexpected possibilities of increasingly distant worldwide connections. And these 'connecting points' or 'nodes' make us largely dependent, both as human beings and organisations (Castells, 2007).

The development of Cf cannot be disassociated from that of ICT, especially the platforms which serve as the basis for all. When faced with existing disadvantages, banks and parabanks are good funding alternatives with ICT solutions. As explained, the greatest difference lies in risk assessment. Naturally, crowdlending and equity Cf campaigns have more similarities with financial products offered by the financial market and pose greater competition than donation-based and reward-based Cf. The last two are aimed at not-for-profit organisations in the Third Sector, similar to community collections though wider and faster. However, recently banks have begun offering this type of social responsibility product (donations), as a response to the growing strength of Cf (Méric, bouaiss, & Maque, 2014).

So why aren't Cf operations more quickly disseminated?

On one hand, there is a long way to go in literacy, but especially in disseminating a new financial culture and the use of new technologies among the Portuguese population. And although 'necessity is the mother of invention', the use of online communication and distant ICT is still low for the major part of the Portuguese population. The new generation is ready for that giant leap, but it needs resources.

Education and lifelong learning must contribute more proactively to this giant leap in ICT. Times such as those in which we live today and in a post-pandemic future must be used for encouraging new funding solutions, such as Cf. Who knows if the future will bring the massification of Cf, starting with education and training? Despite many European countries having requested restrictions in Cf leverage, the banking system is endeavouring to include Cf as a product offered in their branches associated to various existing platforms (Bouaiss, Maque, & Meric, 2014)– 'if you can't beat them, join them.".

## 6. Crowdfunding Platforms in Portugal

PPL (People) is a Portuguese platform which emerged in 2011.

PPL's mission is to promote entrepreneurship and help develop the economy through leveraging the profile of the Portuguese population for joint collaboration within the network. This highly popular platform supports a variety of projects in different channels organised by subject, alongside social causes for which it is well-known (Leal, 2016). It focuses on cultural and technological products. PPL moved over 4 720 878 euros in fundraisers, and has approximately 158 220 members and 138 590 supporters.

In times of greater need, and as a solution to a financial crisis during which liquidity in small companies and entrepreneurs is scarce, the use of Cf through PPL – especially the channel PPL Causes – has developed and grown. Humanitarian causes in the Third Sector, with or without voluntary and/or social intervention programmes, are all supported and developed on the platform. In an area as important as education, projects include tuition fees payments for students facing economic difficulties and/or to further their studies in other levels of education; scholarship programmes for studying abroad; support for educational/voluntary projects in underdeveloped countries, especially Portuguese-speaking countries; or technical and material support for online learning.

PPL follows the basic Cf model, by simply providing the fundraising campaign of either the total sum sought by the mentors, or more for each project. In the case of an unsuccessful fundraising campaign, that is, when the necessary sum is not raised, the rule determines that no funding is given ('all- or-nothing' rule), and the money is given back to the 'investors'. In spite of this, some exceptions are allowed – in the case of PPL Causes –, in which investors donate the amount initially raised, even if the promoter/institution is unable to reach 100% of the necessary funding.

The way PPL operates, with its various channels and areas, is similar to that of the majority of Cf platforms: the entrepreneur/mentor uploads the project on to the platform with a written and video presentation, sets the target sum and a deadline (up to 90 days), and in the case of reward-based Cf (such as PPL's), describes the type of reward that the investor gets in return according to the amounts of the contribution. Paypal is the commonly most used payment method and a 35-cent fee is charged, plus 3.4% of the sum raised (in general).

Some of the most popular examples of campaigns in education were Ecobook (a reusable 40-pages A4 notebook with a very noble environmental purpose) and A Academia une todos à distância (The Academy unites all online), which in the midst of the Covid 19 pandemic collected funds to help online learning. The funds were used to buy urgent IT equipment and pay internet connections for students with financial difficulties, thus helping education became more equal in parts of Portugal

Another example of a Portuguese platform, which also emerged in 2011, is MassiveMov, which was also an alternative to traditional funding of innovative projects with added value, aimed at entrepreneurs and enterprises with a view to developing entrepreneurship. Many bands have recorded albums, since this platform was largely dedicated to reward-based cultural projects – in the case of these albums, usually the reward was recorded music. This platform worked as crowdsourcing with an 80% system. Mentors were given the option to present their projects on the platform, without any costs. If the specified value had been achieved within 90 days - a minimum of 80% of that sum – the project was validated, that is, the entrepreneur earned the collected amount. Otherwise, the project was not considered and the payment was not carried out. No fee was charged over values in this platform, although a 1.9 to 3.4% fee was charged for using Paypal. There has not been registered activity on this platform since 2016 and the web domain is for sale.

Of the current Portuguese platforms some are aimed at companies and entrepeneurs, devoted to equity Cf and crowdlending, such as: Raize; eSolidar; Novo Banco Crowdfunding and Portugalcrowd. Gofundme, Kickstarter, Indiegogo, Mintos, Seedrs are some of the foreign platforms operating in Portugal.

Kickstarter is, perhaps, the most well-known worldwide. This platform supports all types of projects of an artistic nature (for example, design, music, illustration) and operates as donation-based Cf. The platform also uses the 'all-or-nothing' system and gives clients 1 to 60 days to raise the set sum for the project. For each validated project, the platform charges a 5% fee over the raised sum, as well as Amazon's transaction fees, which vary from 3% to 5%. Unsuccessful projects are not subject to fees.

Indiegogo is another leading platform in Cf. It works with a wide range of projects, from fundraising campaigns for producing albums (by professional and amateur musicians), personal financial needs, various charitable projects, surprises and tributes. Anything in fact, other than investments. What makes it different from Kickstarter is the greater variety of projects. This platform allows longer deadlines (up to 120 days) to achieve the intended sum and even if the project fails to reach this number, the mentor receives whichever amount is raised. IndieGoGo deducts

4% of the raised sum if the campaign succeeds. Otherwise, the mentor of the project keeps the amount raised deducted from 9% of the total to the platform.

Crowdfunder is a platform for companies, with an increasing network of investors, technological startups, small companies and Third Sector organisations. Crowdfunder includes donations with investment based on Cf by individuals and business angels4.

However, for funding projects in education, there is more activity in the platform PPL.

## 7. Analysis of PPL in Campaigns for Education in Portugal

As explained above, the first Cf platforms went online in Portugal in 2011, with PPL and MassiveMov. The initial legal void was reported and an intervention was requested in subsequent years, since this activity needed regulation.

PPL is a well-known reward-based platform. As of June 2nd, 2020, it had registered on its website a total of 4 720 878 Euros raised, 158 220 members, 138 590 supporters – of whom 20 486 had contribute to more than one campaign. In total, 1 162 campaigns were funded with a 44% success rate. Campaigns last last on average 48 hours, with a fundraising rate of 120% (3 528 euros).

PPL's website states that 'Crowdfunding (or collaborative funding) is a simple, straightforward way of raising funds for a project through an online community sharing the same interests. PPL is a platform that hosts a network of promoters and their supporters'. This type of text reflects the intention of combining common goals which go beyond fundraising by promoting a dedicated network of shared interests (Vasylieva, 2018). It is, without doubt, a meeting point of synergies which turn risk into success, minimizing effort and risk to both parties.

The legal framework for crowdfunding (RJFC) was only established in 2015, with Law No. 102/2015 (August 24th). After some degree of pressure from the market due to a legal loophole, the legal document was changed by Law No. 3/2018 (February 9th). Persistent legal loopholes still generate criticism. Portuguese regulators are designated according to the model of Cf: Equity Cf or Crowdlending are regulated by the Portuguese Securities Market Commission (CMVM); but donation or reward-based CF are regulated by the Economic and Food Safety Authority (ASAE).

PPL has various channels, as illustrated by Figure No. 1, including one for Education usually under the PPL Causes area.

For this study, the campaigns in Education belonging to PPL Causes were analysed. The applications under PPL Causes aim to raise funds for voluntary actions with or without humanitarian intervention; tuition fees for furthering education or purchasing learning materials; supporting sports teams or organisations; cofunding medical expenses; acquiring equipment for social institutions; supporting animal welfare organisations, etc. The channel operates on a 'all-or-nothing' basis, that is, either the requested sum is achieved or exceeded within the due date or the raised sum is returned to the donors and the project will not be funded. However, supporters may decide to support a cause unconditionally, that is, transferring their donation even if the promoters/organisation is unable to achieve the target sum in its entirety.

The chart on Figure 1 shows various categories of PPL campaigns, including Education.

*Figure 1. PPL Fundraiser per category.*

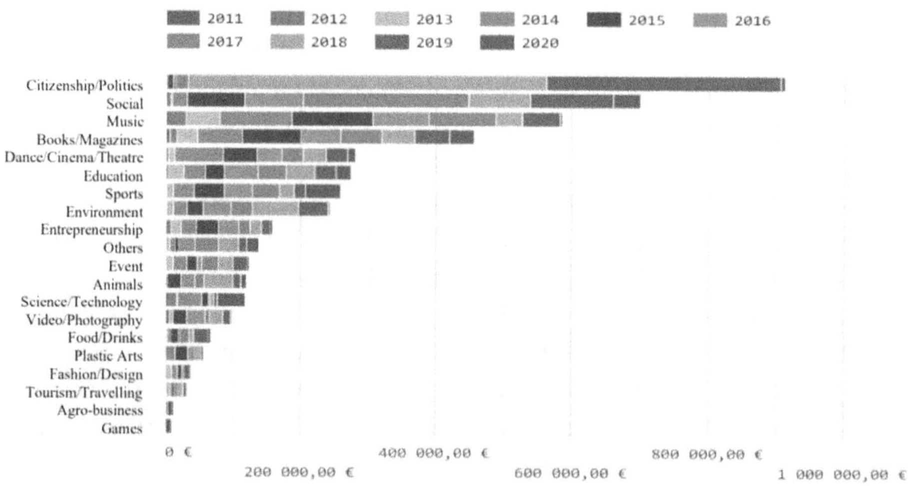


Of all the different categories distributed by the channels, Education placed 6/20 regarding the total amount raised between 2011 and 2020.

## 8. Crowdfunding for Education in Portugal

With the Covid19 pandemic and the emergent demand for online teaching, which includes both IT equipment and digital learning materials, the demand for funds to rapidly cover these costs increased, given the lack of existing resources felt by schools and families.

The health crisis triggered and brought to light a social crisis, revealing less noticeable inequalities in this aspect of education.

Portuguese State education is compulsory until the 12th year, with practically 100% in-class lessons. From one moment to the next, Portugal had to close schools and plan a new way of distance learning in record time. Lack of training was overcome by improvisation through video calls or recorded lessons, but the lack of technical means had to be quickly resolved, through families and organisations buying IT equipment on credit or via loans.

This emergency brought quick, simplified alternative funding to the forefront. Cf offered adequate responses, as seen in PPL's records, (figure1), for example.

With teachers working from home and students confined therein, the need for large-scale use of technologies increased overnight Besides the existing public health problem, education became a priority of political and social responsibility

In Portugal, the State was immediately called to intervene by the people and schools. However, the response was neither efficient, nor universal. Civil society united to help the under-privileged, families who needed IT equipment so that parents could work and children study simultaneously. There were various informal community campaigns to collect IT equipment in the media, as well as to raise money through various channels to buy equipment, and to pay internet suppliers for formal basic and higher education. Cf campaigns were once again amongst the most popular. And once more the rapidity of response in these campaigns was a success. With this pandemic, the need for simple, non-bureaucratic solutions for funding projects brought Cf to the fore.

Most of the proposals presented on Cf platforms in education are not direct alternatives to traditional bank funding. In some cases, for example, scholarships and purchase of IT equipment, funding could have been obtained through micro-credit given to families and small organisations. Community and social responsibility projects tend to be the causes for which collaborative collection is more commonly opted. Collaborative collections have always been common in small communities, with their prize draws, raffles, and auctions. It could even be said that the most widely used Cf in education is donation and reward-based. Crowdlending is less widespread. This type of Cf is more common in other countries for purchasing equipment for private schools.

Undoubtedly, speed and particularly the range of donors in donation and reward-based Cf are significantly greater than in the usual collections within restricted groups and communities.

The alternative to Cf in education is reduced to micro-credit to individuals, which for underprivileged families is simply another form of unaffordable, ineffective debt.

The Portuguese platform that hosts the greatest number of campaigns in education, specifically donation or reward-based Cf is PPL. At present, various identical products associated to banks working with PPL are offered, as in the case of Novo Banco. One of the first Portuguese platforms, PPL survives and thrives in the financial market, and this fact deserves our attention. In the last few months, PPL received applications (which are still ongoing) for campaigns to support education and ICT for education. One of the prerequisites for preparing for the new academic year after the first wave of Covid19 is the provision of resources for distance learning: groups of young people, not-for-profits and schools have launched projects on Cf platforms.

The highest bidding campaign in education until now was 'a class room (9th year) for Jardim do Monte Waldorf School' (2017), which earned 122 supporters and raised 12 903 euros, followed by 'Distance Learning for all in Portela and Moscavide' (2020), with 12 315 euros and 253 supporters (https://ppl.pt/apoiar/educacao).

Conversely, the lowest achievement was 'A Kind of Workshop in Mafra Business Factory', which raised 60 euros from seven donors (120% of the requested amount) in 2017 (https://ppl.pt/vaquinha/mbf-crowdfunding).

As seen in the chart of Figure 2, 2016 and 2018 were the years with the most successful campaigns in education (45 124 and 42 034 euros, respectively). As for the average percentage of funds raised, 2016 reached 131%, followed by 2017 and 2013 (116%) and lastly 2018 (115%).

*Figure 2. Average % of funds raised in education per annum in PPL (chart by the authors)*

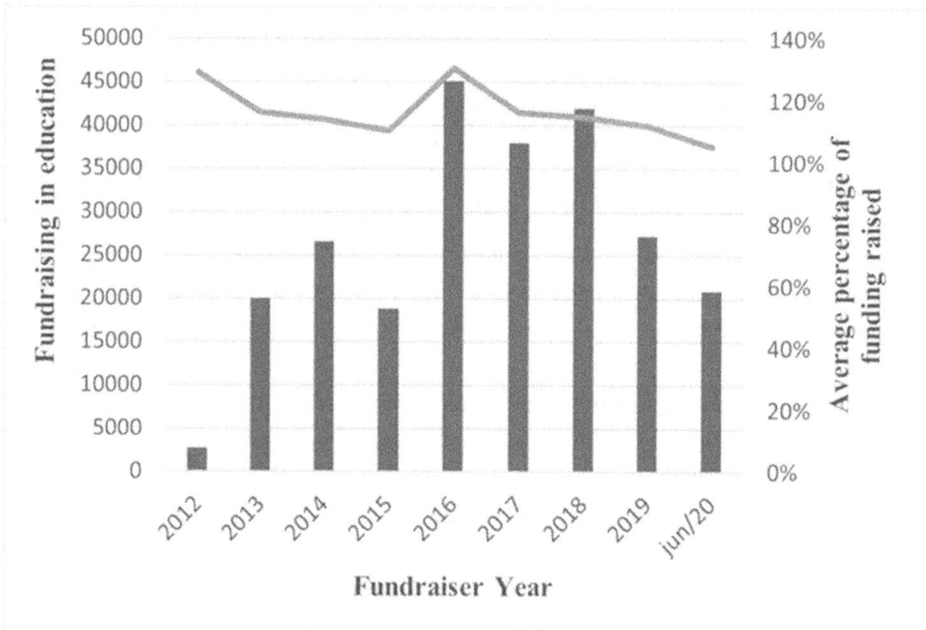


In its eight years of activity, education in PPL hosted a wide range of projects, although every year campaigns for volunteering in Portuguese-speaking countries share one element. On careful analysis, in 2013 PPL supported a digital project in education for the first time which was the creation of a database of Portuguese history books, an idea which ended up being replicated to other similar databases.

Interestingly, according to Figure 4 education projects were only funded by anonymous supporters/investors in 2015, when legislation was implemented.

The chart also shows how in 2018 effective members were engaged in the platform, evidencing the loyalty of investors not only to PPL, but also to the growing network of active members and recurrent supporters. PPL has succeeded not only in maintaining its activity but also in increasing the number of participants, the average amounts per campaign and the number of new supporters. Over these last eight years, the majority of participants have remained active.

Despite the differences in processes, both crowdlending and Equity Cf have striking resemblances with financial instruments made available by banks and financial markets, which might confuse users. However, donation-based platforms are mostly aimed at not-for-profits, such as projects in art, culture, education or charity (Bouaiss et al., 2014).

For the sustainable growth of Cf in Portugal, the future must bring accurate, disseminated information on this funding method and its advantages, so that the general public feels more comfortable not only with internet security, but also with the straightforwardness of online processes. In some European countries, there seem to be constraints regarding Cf, evidenced by the demand for more regulation and limited access to platforms. Concurrently, banks come up with very similar products often associated to existing platforms, such as the association of Novo Banco and PPL, Raize and Seedrs (Bouaiss et al., 2014).

## 9. Funding Needs in Distance Education in Portugal

It is widely acknowledged that technologies of the New Digital Era have not always been fully supported by governments. With regards to education, ten years ago the government attempted to make access to computers universal among primary school students, but the programme was discontinued. But the Covid19 pandemic in 2020 brought greater awareness of the need and importance of technologies regardless of the level of education.

The interest generated around the purchase of IT equipment for distance learning has been reflected in the government's budget albeit very moderately. However, funding is often allocated to other areas prioritised by the governments, according to budgetary assessment reports in education.

Despite the increase of internet portals and websites dedicated to learning support, especially to children with special educational needs (SEN), the truth is that many families are not able to afford adequate IT equipment for their children's education.

*Figure 3. Table of successful projects in education in PPL over the years.*

| PPL - Education Campaign | fundraiser | funds raised | %funds raised | new supporters | recurrent supporters | anonymous supporters | PPL members | end date |
|---|---|---|---|---|---|---|---|---|
| A Academia Une Todos à Distância | 500 | 5 600 | 112% | 62 | 5 | 13 | 67 | 01/06/2020 |
| Ensino à distância para todos na Portela e Moscavide | 12000 | 12 315 | 103% | 220 | 33 | 75 | 253 | 29/04/2020 |
| Ajuda-nos a criai um pré-escolar para as crianças da ilha do Príncipe | 3000 | 3 025 | 101% | 61 | 34 | 32 | 95 | 29/01/2020 |
| Um livro infantil que te vai levar ao Mundo Mágico das Emoções | 2300 | 2 660 | 116% | 74 | 17 | 16 | 91 | 27/12/2019 |
| Ana Raquel - from Kibera With Love (Quénia) | 1000 | 1 108 | 111% | 22 | 16 | 14 | 38 | 15/10/2019 |
| Instalação de Painéis solares na Escola de Binte - Guiné Bissau | 1100 | 1 210 | 110% | 27 | 38 | 31 | 65 | 23/08/2019 |
| Kanfya - São Tomé e Príncipe | 1000 | 1 035 | 104% | 23 | 9 | 9 | 32 | 19/08/2019 |
| Dá aí uma mãozinha | 500 | 570 | 114% | 21 | 18 | 15 | 39 | 16/08/2019 |
| Dançamos em Amsterdão? | 1000 | 1 245 | 125% | 36 | 30 | 27 | 66 | 08/08/2019 |
| Sebê Nón-Educar para a Igualdade | 3500 | 3 546 | 101% | 74 | 22 | 35 | 96 | 08/08/2019 |
| Conheça o Projeto Príncipe 2019 | 2500 | 2 552 | 102% | 99 | 31 | 64 | 130 | 15/07/2019 |
| Artzeri competition | 1000 | 1 000 | 100% | 36 | 8 | 7 | 44 | 14/05/2019 |
| Estúdio de vídeo na Escola Aldeia de Cem Soldos | 5000 | 5 785 | 116% | 105 | 29 | 42 | 134 | 05/04/2019 |
| 0 mês de voluntariado no Butterfly Educational Centre (BEC) | 500 | 516 | 103% | 11 | 5 | 6 | 16 | 13/03/2019 |
| "Crescer em Força(s)": um jogo para semear forças nos mais novos | 3000 | 3 754 | 125% | 75 | 38 | 16 | 113 | 14/02/2019 |
| Olimpíadas de Economia | 1000 | 1 171 | 117% | 63 | 6 | 23 | 69 | 25/01/2019 |
| A Aurora da Educação | 931 | 1 139 | 122% | 24 | 5 | 7 | 29 | 22/01/2019 |
| "Montessori:a Arte de Educar pela Mão da Criança" | 3200 | 3 742 | 117% | 54 | 21 | 9 | 75 | 17/12/2018 |
| Carbo para todos - gere a tua diabetes no dia-a-dia | 3000 | 3 051 | 102% | 70 | 14 | 26 | 84 | 16/11/2018 |
| Sala aberta - (Fasardi - Centro sagrada família) | 10000 | 10 050 | 101% | 10 | 2 | 4 | 12 | 16/11/2018 |
| O Capitão Perneta! | 5000 | 5 077 | 102% | 152 | 35 | 77 | 187 | 03/09/2018 |
| Finalista - sala da Bé | 500 | 510 | 102% | 18 | 7 | 7 | 25 | 14/08/2018 |
| Projeto Kêlê | 1000 | 1 250 | 125% | 41 | 7 | 17 | 48 | 13/07/2018 |
| Projeto Príncipe 2018 | 2500 | 2 717 | 109% | 57 | 27 | 44 | 84 | 29/06/2018 |
| Ajuda-me a voar para a Austrália | 5500 | 6 245 | 114% | 24 | 10 | 17 | 34 | 18/06/2018 |
| Desafia-te com NTS | 500 | 502 | 100% | 15 | 10 | 12 | 2515 | 15/06/2018 |
| 231km do IRONMAN Frankfurt=500 euros para a Escola de Pediatria do IPO Lx | 500 | 1 030 | 206% | 18 | 28 | 19 | 46 | 30/04/2018 |
| Livros Escolares para Crianças Nepalesas | 1250 | 1 280 | 102% | 38 | 12 | 15 | 50 | 13/04/2018 |
| Projeto Darte para 16 crianças | 2880 | 2 980 | 103% | 34 | 18 | 29 | 52 | 16/03/2018 |
| Mundubila - Educação de nova geração | 2500 | 3 100 | 124% | 32 | 25 | 25 | 57 | 15/01/2018 |
| Academia - Escola de Formação | 500 | 500 | 100% | 12 | 3 | 4 | 15 | 02/01/2018 |
| A um passo do sonho de ser harpista | 6000 | 6 000 | 100% | 44 | 20 | 20 | 64 | 10/11/2017 |
| Uma sala de aula (9°ano) para a Escola Waldorf Jardim do Monte | 12650 | 12 903 | 102% | 90 | 32 | 38 | 122 | 25/08/2017 |
| Direção:Limerick leva a Marta à 38th Choral Conducting Summer School da AOHC | 800 | 864 | 108% | 16 | 7 | 10 | 23 | 25/08/2017 |
| Um dia po Mandela - Mandela Day (Lisboa) | 600 | 600 | 100% | 14 | 4 | 10 | 18 | 31/07/2017 |
| Implementação São Tomé. Combate ao abandono escolar | 550 | 875 | 159% | 36 | 10 | 9 | 46 | 25/07/2017 |
| Projeto Príncipe 2017 | 2500 | 2 575 | 103% | 61 | 32 | 38 | 93 | 30/06/2017 |
| Educar para a Felicidade (Science of Happiness) | 1000 | 1 570 | 157% | 59 | 7 | 13 | 66 | 16/06/2017 |
| Casa Cultural Rafael Pombo - Colômbia | 600 | 768 | 128% | 10 | 3 | 3 | 13 | 22/05/2017 |
| Projeto Bang - The Best Arm for the Next Generation is Education | 3500 | 3 535 | 101% | 18 | 7 | 6 | 25 | 03/04/2017 |
| Uma dúzia ao oitavo | 3000 | 3 210 | 107% | 55 | 32 | 45 | 87 | 24/03/2017 |
| Camila Castigo na Universidade | 1455 | 1 601 | 110% | 18 | 47 | 34 | 65 | 28/02/2017 |
| Uma espécie de Workshop na Mafra Business Factory | 50 | 60 | 120% | 5 | 2 | 2 | 7 | 17/01/2017 |
| Curso de Son-Rise para o futuro do Enzo | 1400 | 1 932 | 138% | 21 | 9 | 10 | 38 | 10/11/2016 |
| Projeto + Coaching de mãos dadas com as escolas | 5000 | 5 001 | 100% | 25 | 9 | 12 | 34 | 21/10/2016 |
| Vamos dar asas às Crianças Butterfly no Cambodja | 1500 | 1 771 | 118% | 9 | 3 | 6 | 12 | 30/09/2016 |
| Sonho frequência Summer School | 1513 | 1 540 | 102% | 78 | 11 | 29 | 89 | 11/08/2016 |
| Darte Mais | 6000 | 6 000 | 100% | 30 | 22 | 21 | 52 | 18/08/2016 |
| Mestre Né - Pagamento de propinas de um mestrado | 1210 | 1 514 | 125% | 19 | 36 | 30 | 55 | 25/07/2016 |
| Projeto Príncipe 2016 | 2500 | 2 735 | 109% | 58 | 29 | 37 | 87 | 22/07/2016 |
| Creche/JI/ATL 24h/365 dias | 1000 | 1 000 | 100% | 8 | 0 | 2 | 8 | 30/06/2016 |
| Mimi at Sea - Aprender no mar | 3612 | 3 621 | 100% | 12 | 1 | 7 | 13 | 27/06/2016 |
| Guitarra precisa-se para projeto infantil | 500 | 520 | 104% | 20 | 9 | 14 | 29 | 20/05/2016 |
| Medicina mais perto: Moçambique 2016 | 3500 | 3 535 | 101% | 36 | 24 | 23 | 60 | 09/05/2016 |
| Dias do Pão - Espetáculo de marionetas com sessão pedagógica | 2100 | 2 478 | 118% | 48 | 14 | 24 | 62 | 02/05/2016 |
| Educa Mussapadæ | 3500 | 3 970 | 113% | 26 | 24 | 23 | 50 | 19/02/2016 |
| Escolinha nas Roças | 2500 | 2 855 | 114% | 40 | 17 | 20 | 57 | 12/02/2016 |
| To Kibera With Love | 1600 | 6 652 | 416% | 121 | 50 | 49 | 171 | 11/01/2016 |
| Uma Harpa Nacional | 850 | 850 | 100% | 13 | 7 | 8 | 20 | 26/11/2015 |
| Escola + | 1104 | 1 145 | 104% | 11 | 1 | 4 | 12 | 20/11/2015 |
| À descoberta dos transportes fora dos Açores | 750 | 753 | 100% | 7 | 1 | 3 | 8 | 20/11/2015 |
| Projeto Príncipe 2015 | 2500 | 2 804 | 112% | 71 | 47 | 0 | 118 | 15/07/2015 |
| Projeto Be Equal | 500 | 810 | 162% | 13 | 1 | 0 | 14 | 30/06/2015 |
| Medicina mais perto: Moçambique 2015 | 3000 | 3 296 | 110% | 25 | 20 | 0 | 45 | 22/05/2015 |
| Para um coberto de sonho | 2000 | 2 086 | 104% | 83 | 7 | 0 | 90 | 27/04/2015 |
| Right to na Education | 2000 | 2 067 | 100% | 36 | 14 | 0 | 50 | 27/02/2015 |
| Ginástica dos Afetos para incluir com ternura | 5000 | 5 042 | 101% | 27 | 16 | 0 | 43 | 14/02/2015 |
| Sementes de Palavras: das histórias à motivação para a leitura | 550 | 625 | 114% | 11 | 5 | 0 | 16 | 23/12/2014 |
| Coziubarte | 1500 | 1 629 | 109% | 15 | 6 | 0 | 21 | 22/12/2014 |
| A loja do Wood - Brinquedos educativos de madeira | 550 | 575 | 105% | 10 | 10 | 0 | 20 | 10/12/2014 |
| Projetos Salus - Combate à obesidade desde a infância | 2500 | 2 562 | 102% | 43 | 15 | 0 | 58 | 17/10/2014 |
| Aumentador de Asas - Manual de educação para o voluntariado | 3500 | 3 500 | 100% | 56 | 17 | 0 | 73 | 15/10/2014 |
| Uma cozinha para a nossa "casa" | 2000 | 2 000 | 100% | 9 | 4 | 0 | 13 | 11/09/2014 |
| Realing - Plataforma online de reabilitação da linguagem | 1500 | 1 545 | 103% | 11 | 11 | 0 | 22 | 11/08/2014 |
| Sonha, Faz e Acontece - Projeto Príncipe 2014 | 2200 | 2 725 | 124% | 70 | 36 | 0 | 106 | 18/07/2014 |
| Caracol ao Sol - construção de um chão de madeira | 1005 | 1 520 | 151% | 18 | 13 | 0 | 31 | 02/06/2014 |
| Medicina mais perto: Moçambique 2014 | 2500 | 3 200 | 128% | 35 | 34 | 0 | 69 | 05/05/2014 |
| Peninha: aprender com a natureza e a História | 3500 | 4 583 | 131% | 63 | 28 | 0 | 91 | 07/04/2014 |
| Livro de exercícios " Narrar en El Pasado. Los Tiempos de Pasado en Espanol" | 2100 | 2 115 | 101% | 11 | 1 | 0 | 12 | 02/01/2014 |
| Voluntariado em Kathmandu no Nepal | 1400 | 1 140 | 103% | 25 | 9 | 0 | 34 | 20/09/2013 |
| Formação Intensiva Templo Taoista | 2572 | 3 465 | 135% | 76 | 41 | 0 | 117 | 09/09/2013 |
| Projeto Príncipe 2013 - Reconstrução de Creche da Ponta do Sol | 1000 | 1 410 | 141% | 35 | 24 | 0 | 59 | 26/07/2013 |
| Ticket to Canada | 1000 | 1 084 | 108% | 32 | 25 | 0 | 57 | 25/07/2013 |
| Lura - aprender naturalmente | 5000 | 5 020 | 100% | 18 | 9 | 0 | 27 | 15/07/2013 |
| Crescer com afeto - Ateliers Psicopedagógicos | 1250 | 1 255 | 100% | 28 | 13 | 0 | 41 | 15/07/2013 |
| Medicina mais perto: Moçambique | 2000 | 2 724 | 136% | 46 | 33 | 0 | 79 | 08/06/2013 |
| Sebas.pt | 1900 | 1 900 | 100% | 57 | 15 | 0 | 72 | 20/05/2013 |
| Free Your Mind | 702 | 902 | 128% | 14 | 5 | 0 | 19 | 17/03/2013 |
| BiblioHistória - base de dados literária | 1000 | 1 120 | 112% | 35 | 20 | 0 | 55 | 15/02/2013 |
| Suporte para a Grande Transição | 2111 | 2 720 | 129% | 24 | 19 | 0 | 43 | 12/07/2012 |

*Figure 4. Type of PPL/education supporters (numbers on average)*

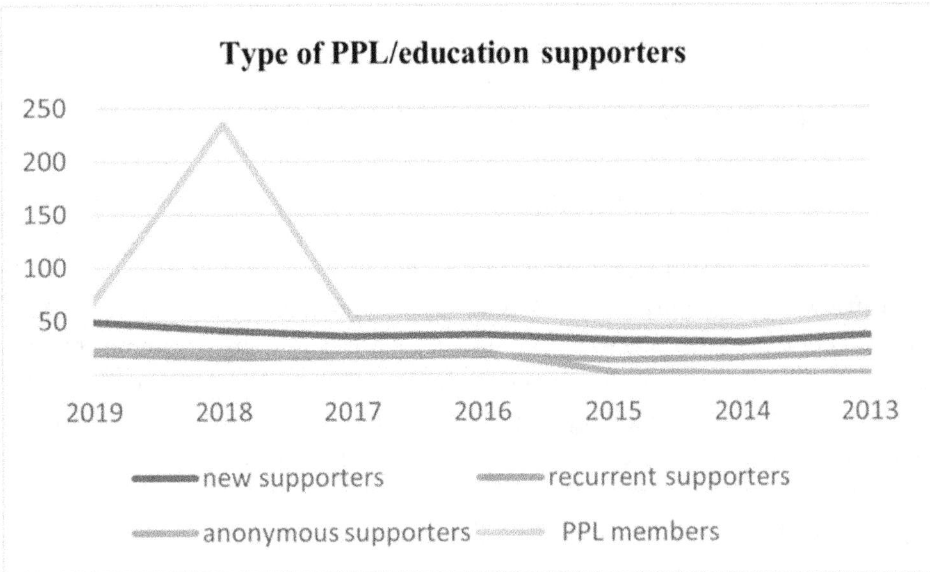


As shown by the table in Figure 3, of the three projects concluded in the beginning of 2020 in PPL, two were for purchasing distance learning equipment, with a further four ongoing.

Scholarships are still the main focus for Cf campaigns5, especially for funding higher education outside Portugal. In addition, voluntary projects for the less privileged in Portugal and in under developed Portuguese-speaking countries (PALOPS), as well as projects for funding distance education are currently very popular in Cf, both on PPL and other platforms.

## 10. Final Thoughts

In times of crisis or recovery, public funding must prioritise education, as well as health. In circumstances such as the current pandemic, the need for greater investment in these areas is clear. Social development can only be achieved and sustained when balancing health and education.

Social inequalities are not exclusively a product of our times, but can be more or less noticeable. School reveals these differences from an early age, showing that students do not enjoy the same opportunities for making their choices freely during school years.

In critical periods of crisis of great technological changes, social and economic differences deepen. Making funding available can help overcome barriers in the short term, and have a positive impact on people, organisations, communities and even countries in the future. The educational system must be ready for and able to adapt to any sudden change for whatever reason. This year's sudden outbreak of Covid19 proved exactly that, since one of the first measures to stop its spread was school closures. But learning cannot be 'closed' indefinitely and online solutions had to emerge quickly.

It is undoubtedly important to innovate and create. But without funding set aside for unexpected circumstances, only through creative, quick solutions can individuals and organisations obtain loans and donations.

In many cases, the urgency of 'doing' is incompatible with the long waiting periods imposed by classical ways of funding, such as bank loans The more creative and innovative the project, the riskier the level of funding and the more delayed the analysis of credit, hindering or preventing the implementation of important ideas and changes. Cf presents itself as an innovative, quick simplified solution, as it splits the risk between many actors, responds in record time, and facilitates a greater number of donations received. In case of education, Cf can help schools prepare prevention, and not defence.

One of the lessons drawn from this pandemic is the importance of preventive investment in education. This includes not only equipment, but also training for teachers and students in new ICT for online education.

In the aftermath of the pandemic, an economic crisis is likely to happen and public investment may be inefficient, without carefully considering a greater need for adequate means in education.

We cannot ensure progress while ignoring the lessons drawn from this pandemic.

Without replacing the State, civil society initiatives can make a difference in preventing inequalities by delivering training for all and acquiring adequate equipment. Cf offers the advantages of transparency and speed in implementing new ideas.

If this pandemic changed conventional training in the future, it also rapidly showed that the general use of technologies is needed for development. Alternatives such as Cf for educational projects may become an important resource to reduce current inequalities, which only worsened with the pandemic.

It is likely that Cf may become an inspirational alternative that will bring back hope to funding more technological projects in education which, despite its greater initial risk, will bring social classes closer through online education. Social projects will undoubtedly increase the demand for Cf, as they are closely linked to education and crises: Cf did not appear and grow after a major financial crisis purely by chance.

In the aftermath of the pandemic, an economic crisis is likely to happen and public investment may be inefficient, without carefully considering a greater need for adequate means in education.

We cannot ensure progress while ignoring the lessons drawn from this pandemic.

Without replacing the State, civil society initiatives can make a difference in preventing inequalities by delivering training for all and acquiring adequate equipment. Cf offers the advantages of transparency and speed in implementing new ideas.

If this pandemic changed conventional training in the future, it also rapidly showed that the general use of technologies is needed for development. Alternatives such as Cf for educational projects may become an important resource to reduce current inequalities, which only worsened with the pandemic.

It is likely that Cf may become an inspirational alternative that will bring back hope to funding more technological projects in education which, despite its greater initial risk, will bring social classes closer through online education. Social projects will undoubtedly increase the demand for Cf, as they are closely linked to education and crises: Cf did not appear and grow after a major financial crisis purely by chance.

## REFERENCES

Bernardes, B., & Lucian, R. (2015). Comportamento de consumidores brasileiros e portugueses em plataformas de «crowdfunding». Revista Portuguesa e Brasileira de Gestão, 26–36.

Botsman, R., & Rogers, R. (2011). What's Mine Is Yours: How Collaborative Consumption is Changing the Way We. Collins.

Bouaiss, K., Maque, I., & Meric, J. (2014). More than three's a crowd...in the best interest of companies! Crowdfunding as Zeitgeist or ideology? Society and Business Review, 10(1), 23-39.

Brabham, D. C. (2016). Crowdsourcing in the Public Sector (Public Management and Change). Georgetown University Press.

Cambridge Business English Dictionary. (2011). Cambridge University Press.

Campos, K. (2008). Crowdsourcing e a revolução na tomada de decisões empresariais. Waggl.

Castells, M. (2001). A sociedade em rede. In A era da informação: Economia, sociedade e cultura (5.ª ed., Vol. 1, pp. 15-80). São Paulo: Paz e Terra.

Castells, M. (2007). A sociedade em rede (T. R. V. Majer, Trans.). In A era da informação: Economia, sociedade e cultura (6.ª ed., Vol. 1, pp. 15-80). São Paulo: Paz e Terra.

Catarino, L. G. (2018). Crowdfunding e crowdinvestment: o Regresso ao Futuro? CEDIPRE - Faculdade de Direito da Universidade de Coimbra, (32), 1-66.

Forbes, H., & Schaefer, D. (2017). Guidelines for Successful Crowdfunding. Procedia CIRP, (60), 398-403.

Gonçalves, J. G. P., & Carvalho, P. d. M. (2018). Análise do Crowdfunding e seus impactos no Brasil. Revista Estudos Eleitorais, 2(4), 1-87.

Jenkins, H., Purushotma, R., Weigel, M., Clinton, K., & Robison, A. J. (2009). Confronting the Challenges of Participatory Culture: Media Education for the 21st Centur. The MIT Press. doi:10.7551/mitpress/8435.001.0001 doi:10.7551/mitpress/8435.001.0001

Leal, G. F. C. (2016). Crowdfunding em Portugal: estudo de caso da plataforma PPL. ISEG, 1-47.

Mollick, E. (2014). The dynamics of crowdfunding: An exploratory study. Journal of Business Venturing, 29(1), 1-16.

Pril, P. (2015). Crowdfunding. A study about the composition of investors in crowdfunding projects on Crowd About Now. Universiteit van Amsterdan, 1-35.

Schwienbacher, A., & Larralde, B. (2010). Crowdfunding of Small Entrepreneurial Ventures. The Oxford Handbook of Entrepreneurial Finance, 1-23.

Strausz, R. (2017). A Theory of Crowdfunding: A Mechanism Design Approach with Demand Uncertainty and Moral Hazard. American Economic Review, 107(6), 1430-1476.

Valancience, L., & Jegeleviciute, S. (2014). Crowdfunding for creating value: stakeholder approach. Procedia - Social and Behavioral Sciences, (156), 599-604.

Vasylieva, N. (2018). How to start an education crowdfunding website: essential features and functionality. Justcoded, 1-13.

## ENDNOTES

1. Crowdsourcing is a collective contribution phenomenon for problem solving and online production models (Brabham, 2016). According to data from Crowdsourcing.org. – an organisation founded in 2010 dedicated to studying and implementing Crowdsourcing. There are approximately 789 services based on crowdsourcing worldwide, but the greatest is the digital encyclopaedia Wikipedia. There are many examples, such as Netflix which used the crowdsourcing strategy in 2012 to develop an algorithm to improve the process of film suggestions by 10% between the platform and the user (Campos, 2008).

To a certain extent, crowdfunding actually means crowdsourcing a financing problem, that is, collective funding (Strausz, 2017).

2 As a matter of interest, in 1885 the Statue of Liberty - gifted by France to the USA – did not have a plinth. At the time, the journalist and press mogul Joseph Pulitzer, had the idea of a fundraiser not via a platform, but in the New York World, asking for 1-dollar donations, in exchange for a model statue and the publication of the donors' names in the newspaper.(Gonçalves & Carvalho, 2018)Fundraising networks, therefore, have been used for much of history, but now have a new configuration through technology, which only amplifies its efficacy. A Portuguese example to illustrate this occurred on October 4th, 1980, when an airplane carrying the Prime Minister Francisco de Sá Carneiro crashed in Camarate (outside Lisbon), causing his death. The newspaper 'O Dia' launched a Cf to erect a statue in his honour in Lisbon, a campaign not dissimilar to the New York World's. The seeds of Cf, as we know it, were being sowed (Catarino, 2018).

3 Petilson's experiment in 1940 can serve as an example - through a teletype machine, he sent instructions of his Model K from Dartmouth College, in New Hampshire, to his calculator in New York, thus achieving results through this very system – a network (Catarino, 2018) .

4 A business angel is an individual with high net worth who is available to support small companies or start-ups financially. In general, business angels hope to get share capital. They are known for focusing more on growth rather than profit, which differentiates them from venture capitalists

5 Recently, a young Portuguese student living in the UK featured in the international press. Vitória Mário, 18, dreams of completing a Master's degree in Mathematics at the University of Warwick, but she needs 40 thousand pounds. On the brink of giving up after many attempts, including several direct requests to some of the UK's wealthiest people, a friend suggested using Cf via the platform GoFundMe. To her astonishment, not only was the total requested amount quickly raised, but also the North-American singer Taylor Swift contributed with the largest share.

# Chapter 10
# Crowdfunding:
## A New Funding Source for NGOs

**Majdi Hassen**
*University of Tunis, Tunisia*

**Ibtissem Ouertatani**
*University of Tunis, Tunisia*

## ABSTRACT

*In this chapter, the research deals with NGOs and their current weight in state's development and public conditions improvement. The researcher also goes to connect the financial challenging faced by NGOs and how the use of crowdfunding platform is important specifically to solicit funding to start, continue, and expand its works. The chapter will highlight the crowdfunding models suitable for NGOs specifically crowdfunding and NGOs in developing countries with describing crowdfunding policies and regulations. Through that, the researcher helps in shaping best practices based on NGO success stories. This chapter will also review previous studies and statistics as a guide for the researcher to present crowdfunding as a tool for the non-profit sector.*

## INTRODUCTION

In the last decade, crowdfunding began to increase exponentially (Dushnitsky, 2016). in 2012, the total worldwide crowdfunding volume reached $2.7 billion; the following year, the volume increased to $6.1 billion and in 2014 the amount of money collected through crowdfunding topped $16.2 billion. the predicted volume for 2015 is estimated at $34.4 billion dollars (Marketwired, 2015). The annual increase in raised

DOI: 10.4018/978-1-7998-3226-3.ch010

funds and the development of new fields for crowdfunding applications (e.g., civic crowdfunding) shows that the financing method has become a trustworthy way for potential funders to contribute and for founders to raise funds in an alternative way.

The variation of crowdfunding applications (e.g., collecting funds for start-ups, existing companies, donating or lending money to individuals in need of investing in companies' equities) creates the potential for financing third sector organizations where the problem of lack resources still remains. crowdfunding can be used as an additional source of raising funds. (e.g., smith et al., 2014, bog et al., 2012).

The objective of this thesis is to bring a new and innovative approach to using crowdfunding as an alternative source of funding for NGOs. I will first shed the light on the NGO's different specificities, their main intervention to developing countries. by going through the different conventional and non-conventional funding sources of NGOs, and analyzing its financial sustainability challenges. the thesis includes a deep understanding of how the crowdfunding will contribute to NGO sustainability by raising funds through a crowdfunding platform.

## BACKGROUND

During the last decade, there has been a notable rise of non-governmental organizations (NGOs) not only in the developing but has sustained itself suitably in the developed, world, triggering off an "associational revolution". Clarke (1998). Despite this significant growth, there has been a relatively minor contribution to the sphere of contemporary NGO literature. Salamon (1994) highlighted this gap as the following:

"A striking upsurge is underway around the globe in…the creation of private, nonprofit or non-governmental organizations…Indeed, we are in the midst of a global `associational revolution' that may prove to be as significant to the latter twentieth century as the rise of the nation-state was to the latter nineteenth."

## MAIN FOCUS OF THE CHAPTER[1]

### Issues, Controversies, Problems

This chapter emphasizes on the crucial role of NGOs, which is to support the Government and the private sector when they are unable to gill the community's needs.

''Theory of Government failure/ Market failure"

However, to fully achieve this noble role, NGOs need to be independent and possess the required resources to reach its financial sustainability.

While most of the NGO funding is derived from foreign sources (grants, government /private sector support) they found themselves governed by the interests of the contributors among donors and volunteers who decide on their own priorities, rather than having the beneficiaries setting these priorities.

Indeed, NGO leaders perceive government, private sector and, donors' support as an essential funding source for the NGO's financial viability, while at the same time, they recognize that there are challenges associated with reliance on grants and other sources of external funding.

This challenge is heightened by the aforementioned tendency on the part of the donors to cease or limit funding of NGOs. In fact, the sustainability of funding is not always guaranteed, which puts NGOs with no other source of funding under the risk of going bankrupt.

## SOLUTIONS AND RECOMMENDATIONS

Nowadays, Crowdfunding is one of the relatively non-traditional funding sources that took root immediately after the global financial crisis when traditional financing sources ceased to operate. On the other hand, the traditional way always received criticism from entrepreneurs and Business holders due to its rigidity and its modal. As consequence, a difficulty to securing a funding from these sources is not likely to be successful.

In fact, the motivation behind needing capital comes from six obvious reasons: expanding awareness of one's work, maintaining creative control over the outcome, measuring supporter interest in the project, making longer-term connections with customers, gaining approval and confidence in the project, and to learn more about business and fundraising ((Gerber et al. (2012)).

Belleflamme et al. (2012) finds that, at least when offering product pre-orders via crowdfunding, it is the high-value customers that are most likely to contribute to a crowdfunding project, thus suggesting that the connections made with customers through crowdfunding are likely to be high-value.

Furthermore, crowdfunding provides benefits for communities through both local and global means. Kitchens and Torrence (2012) state that if crowdfunding is going to be a tool for people to invest in their own communities and this will help to create sustainable economic health.

Moreover, Gobble (2012) draws attention to the fact, that getting financing through crowdfunding is easier, in comparison to venture capital- in addition to money. Sometimes such help can be crucial for small NGOs to survive.

NGOs and startups who succeeded in raising funds through the crowdfunding platform demonstrate that crowdfunding is increasingly recognized as a feasible vehicle to market flourish.

## FUTURE RESEARCH DIRECTIONS

Non-profit organizations have always been inclined to seek traditional ways of funding based on the domain in which they operate. And nowadays, these traditional ways are less and less and NGOs should identify diversified sources and based on the digital and the public empathy. To do so, many of them have successfully migrated to the online crowdfunding.

It is true that this innovative funding model has answered to what entrepreneurs and business seek when it comes to raising funds. And we can assume will provide to NGOs all the right answers to their questions pertaining to its time and cost-effectiveness and is fast positioning itself as a go-to source for raising funds. Research still minimalist when it comes to the efficiency of crowdfunding in the NGO life cycle. However, the question to answer in the next few years is: What impact the crowdfunding will have on the NGO sustainability?

## CONCLUSION

Crowdfunding has been praised for its sustainability to businesses that search for an additional option to raise capital. Crowdfunding also addresses fundraising needs for other than for-profit activities. It has opened a new source of funding for non-profit organizations that may " analyze the potential of crowdfunding for non-profit or non-governmental organizations. Current literature tends to focus on direct donations through online portals (Saxton & Wang, 2011; Smith et al., 2014; Bog et al., 2012). A non-profit field, which recently received attention from researchers, is civic projects. Davies (2014, p.29) described civic projects as those, "which produce goods that can be enjoyed by all members of a community equally and without regard to their contribution".

## REFERENCES


Aldashev, G., & Navarra, C. (2018). Development NGOs: Basic facts. *Annals of Public and Cooperative Economics*, *89*(1), 125–155. doi:10.1111/apce.12188

Anheier, H. K. (2014). *Nonprofit Organizations theory, management, policy*. Routledge. doi:10.4324/9781315851044

Boli, J., & Thomas, G. M. (1999). *Constructing World Culture: International Nongovernmental Organizations since 1875*. Stanford University Press.

Bouncken, R. B., Komorek, M., & Kraus, S. (2015). Crowdfunding: The Current State Of Research. *International Business & Economics Research Journal*, *14*(3), 407.

Bromideh, A. A. (2011). The widespread challenges of NGOs in developing countries: Case studies from Iran. *International NGO Journal*, *6*(9), 197–202. doi:10.5897/NGOJ11.014

Clarke, G. (1998). Non-governmental organizations (NGOs) and politics in the developing world. *Political Studies*, *46*(1), 36–52. doi:10.1111/1467-9248.00128

Cornwall, A. (2007). Buzzwords and fuzzwords: Deconstructing development discourse. *Development in Practice*, *17*(4–5), 471–484. doi:10.1080/09614520701469302

Gerber, E. M., Hui, J. S., & Kuo, P.-Y. (2012). Crowdfunding: Why people are motivated to post and fund projects on crowdfunding platforms. *Proc. of the International Workshop on ...*, 10.

Hailey, J. (2000). Indicators of identity: NGOs and the strategic imperative of assessing core values. *Development in Practice*, *10*(3–4), 402–407. doi:10.1080/09614520050116550

Howard, M. M., Mendelson, S. E., Glenn, J. K., & Howard, M. M. (2002). The Power and Limits of NGOs: A Critical Look at Building Democracy in Eastern Europe and Eurasia. *Slavic Review*.

Lindblom, A. K. (2006). *Non-Governmental organisations in international law. Non-Governmental Organisations in International Law*. Cambridge University. doi:10.1017/CBO9780511494406

Omeri, K. L. (2015). Factors Influencing Financial Sustainability of Non-Goverment Organizations: A Survey of NGOs in Nakuru County, Kenya. *International Journal of Economics. Commerce and Management*, *3*(9), 704–743.

Ramani, J. (2019). *Real Estate Crowdfunding: A Guide on Facts, Benefits and Platforms*. Academic Press.

Salamon, L. M. (1994). The Rise of the Nonprofit Sector. *Foreign Affairs*, *73*(4), 109.

Salamon, L. M. (2016). Market Failure. In The Nature of the Nonprofit Sector (3rd ed., pp. 119-120). Boulder: Westview Press.

Stemler, A. R. (2013, May). The JOBS Act and crowdfunding: Harnessing the power-and money-of the masses. *Business Horizons*, *56*(3), 271–275. doi:10.1016/j.bushor.2013.01.007

Thomas, G. M., Chhetri, N., & Hussaini, K. (2008). Legitimacy and the Rise of NGOs: The Global and Local in South Asia. *Journal of Civil Society*, *4*(1), 31–42. doi:10.1080/17448680802051139

Tvedt, T. (2006). Policy arena: The international aid system and the non-governmental organisations: A new research agenda. Journal of International Development, 18(5), Vakil, A. C. (1997). Confronting the classification problem: Toward a taxonomy of NGOs. *World Development*, *25*(12), 2057–2070. doi:10.1016/S0305-750X(97)00098-3

Valanciene, L., & Jegeleviciute, S. (2013). Valuation of crowdfunding. *Economics and Management*, *18*(1), 39–48.

World Bank. (n.d.). *Defining Civil Society*. http://go.worldbank.org/4CE7W046K0

# Compilation of References

Abe, J. A. A. (2011). Changes in Alan Greenspan's language use across the economic cycle: A text analysis of his testimonies and speeches. *Journal of Language and Social Psychology*, *30*(2), 212–223. doi:10.1177/0261927X10397152

Abigail, Scharf, & Smith. (2014). *Online Fundraising-The Perfect Ask?* Competitive Advantage In the Global Economy (CAGE).

Abrams, E. (2017). *Securities crowdfunding: More than family, friends and fools?* Unpublished paper. University of Chicago. doi:10.2139srn.2902217

Adejimola, A. S. (2008). Language, communication and information flow in entrepreneurship. *African Journal of Business Management*, *2*(11), 201–208.

Afsaneh, B., Hasti, C., & Ashkan, E. (2019). Crowdfunding motivations: A focus on donors' perspectives. *Technological Forecasting and Social Change*, *146*, 218–232. doi:10.1016/j.techfore.2019.05.002

Agrawal, Christian, & Avi. (2011). *The geography of crowdfunding*. National Bureau of Economic Research.

Agrawal, A., Catalani, C., & Goldfarb, A. (2015). Crowdfunding: Geography, social networks, and the timing of investment decisions. *Journal of Economics & Management Strategy*, *24*(2), 253–274.

Agrawal, A., Catalini, C., & Goldfarb, A. (2014). Some simple economics of crowdfunding. *Innovation Policy and the Economy*, *14*, 63–97. doi:10.1086/674021

Agrawal, A., Catalini, C., & Goldfarb, A. (2015). Crowdfunding: Geography, Social Networks, and the Timing of Investment Decisions. *Journal of Economics & Management Strategy*, *24*(2), 253–274. doi:10.1111/jems.12093

Agrawal, A., Catalini, C., & Goldfarb, A. (2015). Crowdfunding: Geography, Social Networks, and the Timing of Investment Decisions. *Journal of Economics & Management Strategy*, *24*, 253–274.

Ahlers, G. K., Cumming, D., Günther, C., & Schweizer, D. (2015). *Signaling in equity*. Academic Press.

Ahlers, G. K. C., Cumming, D., Günther, C., & Schweizer, D. (2015). Signaling in Equity Crowdfunding. *Entrepreneurship Theory and Practice*, *39*(4), 955–980. doi:10.1111/etap.12157

Aidan, H., & Sweetman, A. (2004). Microfinance and famine: The Irish loan funds during the great famine. *World Development*, *32*(9), 1509–1523. doi:10.1016/j.worlddev.2004.04.002

Aitamurto, T. (2011). The Impact of Crowdfunding on Journalism: Case study of Spot.Us, a platform for community-funded reporting. *Journalism Practice*, *5*(4), 429–445.

Akula, V. (2010). *A Fistful of Rice: My Unexpected Quest to End Poverty Through Profitability*. Harvard Business Press.

Alain, C. (2008). *Il Terzo Paradigma: Antropologia Filosofica Del Dono*. Bollati Boringhieri.

Aldashev, G., & Navarra, C. (2018). Development NGOs: Basic facts. *Annals of Public and Cooperative Economics*, *89*(1), 125–155. doi:10.1111/apce.12188

Alderfer, C. P. (1969). An empirical test of a new theory of human needs. *Organizational Behavior and Human Performance*, *4*(2), 142–175.

Aldrich, H. E. (2014). The democratization of entrepreneurship? Hackers, makerspaces, and crowdfunding. *Annual Meeting of the Academy of Management*. 10.5465/ambpp.2014.10622symposium

Al-Fadhli, S. (2008). Students' perceptions of E-learning in Arab society: Kuwait University as a case study. *E-Learning and Digital Media*, *5*(4), 418–428.

Alijani, S., Assadi, D., & Ashta, A. (2016). Can Social Dynamics Be Channeled from Offline to Online Communities? Commitment, Compliance and Cooperation from Microfinance to Crowdfunding. In D. Assadi (Ed.), *Strategic Approaches to Successful Crowdfunding* (pp. 210–227). IGI Global.

Allison, T. H., Davis, B. C., Short, J. C., & Webb, J. W. (2015). Crowdfunding in a prosocial microlending environment: Examining the role of intrinsic versus extrinsic cues. *Entrepreneurship Theory and Practice*, *39*(1), 53–73. doi:10.1111/etap.12108

Allison, T. H., Davis, B. C., Webb, J. W., & Short, J. C. (2017). Persuasion in crowdfunding: An elaboration likelihood model of crowdfunding performance. *Journal of Business Venturing*, *32*(6), 707–725. doi:10.1016/j.jbusvent.2017.09.002

Allison, T. H., McKenny, A. F., & Short, J. C. (2013). The effect of entrepreneurial rhetoric on microlending investment: An examination of the warm-glow effect. *Journal of Business Venturing*, *28*(6), 690–707. doi:10.1016/j.jbusvent.2013.01.003

Alois, J. D. (2018a, August 6). Petition the SEC: Raise the crowdfunding limit to $20 million. *Crowdfund Insider*. Retrieved from http://www.crowdfundinsider.com

Alois, J. D. (2018b, July 23). Prominent group of fintech leaders send letter to SEC chair Jay Clayton demanding an increase in regulation crowdfunding to $20 million. *Crowdfund Insider.* Retrieved from http://www.crowdfundinsider.com

Amara, M., Ben Cheikh, A., & Abdellati, T. (2014). *Crowdfunding: Determinants and motivations of the contributors to the crowdfunding platforms*. Retrieved from https://papers.ssrn.com/sol3/papers.cfm?abstract_id=2552168

Amara, M., Ben Cheikh, A., & Abdellatif, T. (2014). *Crowdfunding: Determinants and Motivations of the Contributors to the Crowdfunding Platforms*. Academic Press.

Anderson, A. J., & Vingrys, A. J. (2001). Small samples: Does size matter? *Investigative Ophthalmology & Visual Science*, *42*(7), 1411–1413. PMID:11381039

Anderson, K. B., & Saxton, G. D. (2016). Smiles, Babies, and Status Symbols: The Persuasive Effects of Image Choices in Small-Entrepreneur Crowdfunding Requests. *International Journal of Communication*, *10*, 22.

André, K., Bureau, S., Gautier, A., & Rubel, O. (2017). Beyond the Opposition Between Altruism and Self-interest: Reciprocal Giving in Reward-Based Crowdfunding. *Journal of Business Ethics*, *146*(2), 313–332. doi:10.100710551-017-3652-x

Angwin J. (2009), *Stealing MySpace: The Battle to Control the Most Popular Website in America*. Random House.

Anheier, H. K. (2014). *Nonprofit Organizations theory, management, policy*. Routledge. doi:10.4324/9781315851044

Arborio, A. M., Fournier, P., de Singly, F., & Fournier, P. (2015). l'observation directe. Armand Colin.

Archer, D., & Akert, R. M. (1977). Words and everything else: Verbal and nonverbal cues in social interpretation. *Journal of Personality and Social Psychology*, *35*(6), 443–449. doi:10.1037/0022-3514.35.6.443

Ariely, D., Bracha, A., & Meier, S. (2009). Doing good or doing well? Image motivation and monetary incentives in behaving prosocially. *The American Economic Review*, *99*(1), 544–555.

Armand, M. (2002). *Storia Della Società Dell'informazione*. Einaudi.

Armendáriz de Aghion, B., & Morduch, J. (2005). *The Economics of Microfinance*. The MIT Press.

Armin, S., & Larralde, B. (2010). Crowdfunding of small entrepreneurial ventures. In *Handbook of entrepreneurial finance*. Oxford University Press.

Asch, S. E. (1951). Effects of Group Pressure on the Modification and Distortion of Judgments. In H. Guestzkow (Ed.), *Groups, Leadership, and Men*. Carnegie Press.

Ashta, A., & Assadi, D. (2009). Do Social Cause and Social Technology Meet? Impact of Web 2.0 Technologies on peer-to-peer lending transactions in general and microfinance in particular. *Proceedings of the The First European Research Conference on Microfinance.*

Ashta, A., & Dayson, K. (2013). Microcredit as a Social Innovation. In The International Handbook on Social Innovation. Edward Elgar.

Ashta, A., Demay, I., & Couchoro, M. (2016). The Role of Stakeholders in the Historical Evolution of Microfinance in Togo. *Economic History of Developing Regions, 31*, 303–344.

Assadi, D. (2004). *Les 7 modèles économiques d'Internet: pour vendre sur Internet en gagnant de l'argent.* Gualino éd.

Assadi, D. (2016). In search of crowdfunding business models. In D. Assadi (Ed.), Strategic Approaches to Successful Crowdfunding (pp. 1-33). IGI Global.

Assadi, D. (2004). *Les 7 modèles économiques sur Internet.* Gualino Editions.

Assadi, D., & Ashta, A. (2014). Innovative Transposition of Trust Mechanisms in Social Lending Groups from Offline to Online Strategic Change. *Briefings in Entrepreneurial Finance, 23*, 461–480.

Attuel-Mendès, L. (2017). The different ways of collaboration between a retail bank and crowdfunding. *Strategic Change: Briefings in Entrepreneurial Finance, 26*, 213–225.

Attuel-Mendès, L., Caseau, C., & Bonescu, M. (2014). Brand identity process of financial cooperatives: An Austrian case. *Strategic Change: Briefings in Entrepreneurial Finance, 23*, 493–506.

Audretsch, D. B., & Fritsch, M. (1994). The geography of firm births in Germany. *Regional Studies, 28*(4), 359–359. doi:10.1080/00343409412331348326

Auerswald, P. E. (2009). Creating social value. *Stanford Social Innovation Review*, 51–55.

Autorité de Contrôle Prudentiel. (2013). *Guide du financement participatif (crowdfunding) à destination du grand public.* Retrieved from https://www.economie.gouv.fr/vous-orienter/entreprise/numerique/crowdfunding-tout-savoir-pour-se-lancer

Bagheri, A., Chitsazan, H., & Ebrahimi, A. (2019). Crowdfunding motivations: A focus on donors' perspectives. *Technological Forecasting and Social Change, 146*, 218–232.

Bain and Company. (2009). *Management tools and Trends.* http://www.bain.com/management_tools/home.asp

Baltača, B., & Mavrenko, T. (2009). Financial Cooperation As A Low-Cost Tool For Effective Microfinancing. *Journal of Business and Management*, 56–64.

Bannerman, S. (2013). Crowdfunding Culture. *Journal of Mobile Media, 7*(1).

Bapna, S. (2019). Complementarity of signals in early-stage equity investment decisions: Evidence from a randomized field experiment. *Management Science*, *65*(2), 933–952. doi:10.1287/mnsc.2017.2833

Barbi, M., & Mattioli, S. (2019). Human capital, investor trust and equity crowdfunding. *Research in International Business and Finance*, *49*, 1–12. doi:10.1016/j.ribaf.2019.02.005

Barral, L. M., & Barral, L. M. (2014). ¿Por qué la Gente Financia Proyectos Vía Crowdfunding? Investigación realizada entre la Comunidad de Mecenas de Lánzanos. Ed. Two much Research studio, Madrid.

Batson, C. D. (1987). Prosocial motivation: Is it ever truly altruistic? *Advances in Experimental Social Psychology*, *20*, 65–122.

Baumgardner, T., Neufeld, C., Huang, P., Sondhi, T., Mursalin, F., & Talha, A. (2017). Crowdfunding as a Fast-Expanding Market for the Creation of Capital and Shared Value. *Thunderbird International Business Review*, *59*(1), 115–126. doi:10.1002/tie.21766

Baum, J. A., & Silverman, B. S. (2004). Picking winners or building them? Alliance, intellectual, and human capital as selection criteria in venture financing and performance of biotechnology startups. *Journal of Business Venturing*, *19*(3), 411–436. doi:10.1016/S0883-9026(03)00038-7

Beaulieu, T., Sarker, S., & Sarker, S. (2015). A Conceptual Framework for Understanding Crowdfunding. *Communications of the Association for Information Systems*, *37*, 1–31. doi:10.17705/1CAIS.03701

Beck, T., & Demirguc-Kunt, A. (2006). Small and Medium-size Enterprises: Access to Finance as a Ggrowth Constraint. *Journal of Banking & Finance*, *30*(11), 2931–2943. doi:10.1016/j.jbankfin.2006.05.009

Beier, M., & Wagner, K. (2015). *Crowdfunding Success: A Perspective from Social Media and E-Commerce*. Academic Press.

Bellavitisa, C., Filatotchev, I., Kamuriwob, D., & Vanackerd, T. (2017). Entrepreneurial finance: New frontiers of research and practice. *Venture Capital*, *19*(1-2), 1–16. doi:10.1080/13691066.2016.1259733

Belleflamme, Lambert, & Schwienbacher. (2012). Crowdfunding: Tapping the Right Crowd. Academic Press.

Belleflamme, P., Lambert, T., & Schwienbacher, A. (2010, June). *Crowdfunding: An industrial organization perspective*. Prepared for the workshop Digital Business Models: Understanding Strategies, Paris, France.

Belleflamme, P., Lambert, T., & Schwienbacher, A. (2013). Individual crowdfunding practices. *Venture Capital*, *15*(4), 313–333. doi:10.1080/13691066.2013.785151

Belleflamme, P., Lambert, T., & Schwienbacher, A. (2014). Crowdfunding: Tapping the right crowd. *Journal of Business Venturing*, *29*(5), 585–609. doi:10.1016/j.jbusvent.2013.07.003

Belleflamme, P., Omrani, N., & Peitz, M. (2015). The economics of crowdfunding platforms. *Information Economics and Policy*, *33*, 11–28. doi:10.1016/j.infoecopol.2015.08.003

Bellihi & Berachid. (2018). Perceiving Success among Shariah Compliant Crowdfunding Social Entrepreneurs. *Revue de Gestion et d"Économie*, *6*(3), 264-293.

Ben Slimane, F., & Rousselet, E. (2016). Plateformes de financement participatif et acteurs historiques: Pourquoi les partenaires se multiplient-ils? *Revue Banque*, *795*, 62–64.

Bentley, K. A., Omer, T. C., & Sharp, N. Y. (2013). Business strategy, financial reporting irregularities, and audit effort. *Contemporary Accounting Research*, *30*(2), 780–817. doi:10.1111/j.1911-3846.2012.01174.x

Berger, S., & Gleisner, F. (2009). *Emergence of Financial Intermediaries on Electronic Markets: The Case of Online P2P Lending*. http://www.business-research.org/early_view/berger_gleisner_preview.pdf

Berger, A., & Udell, G. (1995). Relationships Lending and Lines of Credit in Small Firm finance. *The Journal of Business*, *68*(3), 351–381. doi:10.1086/296668

Berglin, H., & Strandberg, C. (2013). *Leveraging customers as investors: The driving forces behind crowdfunding* (Unpublished bachelor's thesis). Uppsala University.

Bernardes, B., & Lucian, R. (2015). Comportamento de consumidores brasileiros e portugueses em plataformas de «crowdfunding». Revista Portuguesa e Brasileira de Gestão, 26–36.

Bernardino, S., & Freitas Santos, J. (2018). Unleashing the Intelligence of Cities by Social Innovation and Civic Crowdfunding: An Exploratory Study. *International Journal of Technology and Human Interaction*, *14*(2), 54–68. doi:10.4018/IJTHI.2018040104

Bernardino, S., Freitas Santos, J., & Cadima Ribeiro, J. (2016). Social Crowdfunding: A New Model for Financing Regional Development? *Journal of Urban and Regional Analysis*, *8*(2), 97–115.

Berry, D. S., Pennebaker, J. W., Mueller, J. S., & Hiller, W. S. (1997). Linguistic bases of social perception. *Personality and Social Psychology Bulletin*, *23*(5), 526–537. doi:10.1177/0146167297235008

Bertomeu, J., & Marinovic, I. (2016). A theory of hard and soft information. *The Accounting Review*, *91*(1), 1–20. doi:10.2308/accr-51102

Bessiere, V., & Stephany, E. (2014). *Le Crowdfunding: Fondements et Pratiques*. Deboeck.

Best, J., Neiss, S., & Swart, R. (2013). *Scaling innovation: Crowdfunding's potential for the developing world*. Information for Development Program, The World Bank.

Birch, D. L. (1987). *Job creation in America: How our smallest companies put the most people to work*. The Free Press.

Blikkendaal, M. D., Driessen, S. R., Rodrigues, S. P., Rhemrev, J. P., Smeets, M. J., Dankelman, J., van den Dobbelsteen, J. J., & Jansen, F. W. (2017). Surgical flow disturbances in dedicated minimally invasive surgery suites: An observational study to assess its supposed superiority over conventional suites. *Surgical Endoscopy, 31*(1), 288–298. doi:10.100700464-016-4971-1 PMID:27198548

Blohm, I., Leimeister, J.-M., Wenzlaff, K. & Gebert, M. (2013). *Crowdfunding Studie 2013/2014*. Berlin: epubli.

Bogost, I. (2012). *Kickstarter, Crowdfunding Platform Or Reality Show?* Fast Company. Www. Fastcompany.Com/1843007/Kickstarter-Crowdfunding-Platform-Or-Reality-Show

Boli, J., & Thomas, G. M. (1999). *Constructing World Culture: International Nongovernmental Organizations since 1875*. Stanford University Press.

Bornstein, D. (2007). *How to change the world: Social entrepreneurs and the power of new ideas*. Oxford University Press.

Botsman, R., & Rogers, R. (2011). What's Mine Is Yours: How Collaborative Consumption is Changing the Way We. Collins.

Bouaiss, K., Maque, I., & Meric, J. (2014). More than three's a crowd...in the best interest of companies! Crowdfunding as Zeitgeist or ideology? Society and Business Review, 10(1), 23-39.

Bouaiss, K., Maque, I., & Méric, J. (2015). More than Three's a Crowd… in the Best Interest of Companies! Crowdfunding as Zeitgeist or Ideology? *Society and Business Review, 10*, 23–39.

Bouman, F. J. A. (1983). Indigenous savings & credit societies in the developing world. In A. D. Von Pischke (Ed.), *Rural Financial Markets in the Developing World*. World Bank.

Bouncken, R. B., Komorek, M., & Kraus, S. (2015). Crowdfunding: The Current State Of Research. *International Business & Economics Research Journal, 14*(3), 407.

Boxenbaum, E., & Battilana, J. (2005). Importation as innovation: Transposing managerial practices across fields. *Strategic Organization, 3*, 355–383.

Brabham, D. C. (2016). Crowdsourcing in the Public Sector (Public Management and Change). Georgetown University Press.

Bradford, C. S. (2012). Crowdfunding and the federal securities laws. *Colum. Bus. L. Rev.*, 1.

Bradford, C. S. (2012). *Crowdfunding and the Federal Securities Laws*. Working paper.

Bretschneider, U., Knaub, K., & Wieck, E. (2014). *Motivations for Crowdfunding: What Drives the Crowd to Invest in Start-Ups?* Academic Press.

Bretschneider, U., Knaub, K., & Wieck, E. (2014). Motivations for crowdfunding: what drives the crowd to invest in start-ups? *Twenty Second European Conference on Information Systems, Research in Progress, Tel Aviv 2014*.

Bretschneider, U., & Leimeister, J. M. (2017). Not just an ego-trip: Exploring backers' motivation for funding in incentive-based crowdfunding. *The Journal of Strategic Information Systems*, *26*(4), 246–260.

Bromideh, A. A. (2011). The widespread challenges of NGOs in developing countries: Case studies from Iran. *International NGO Journal*, *6*(9), 197–202. doi:10.5897/NGOJ11.014

Brown S., Tilton A., Woodside D. (2002). *The case for on-line communities*. McKinsey Quarterly.

Brown, T. E., Boon, E., & Pitt, L. F. (2017). Seeking funding in order to sell: Crowdfunding as a marketing tool. *Business Horizons*, *60*(2), 189–195. doi:10.1016/j.bushor.2016.11.004

Bruton, G., Khavul, S., Siegel, D., & Wright, M. (2015). New financial alternatives in seeding entrepreneurship: Microfinance, crowdfunding, and peer-to-peer innovations. *Entrepreneurship Theory and Practice*, *39*(1), 9–26. doi:10.1111/etap.12143

Bugg-Levine, A., & Emerson, J. (2011). Impact investing: Transforming how we make money while making a difference. *Innovations*, *6*, 9–18.

Burgoon, J. K., Guerrero, L. K., & Floyd, K. (2016). *Nonverbal communication*. Routledge. doi:10.4324/9781315663425

Burnkrant, R., & Alain, C. (1975). Informational and Normative Social Influence in Buyer Behavior. *The Journal of Consumer Research*, 206–215.

Burt S. (2010). Always On. *London Review of Books*.

Burtch, G., Ghose, A., & Wattal, S. (2013). An Empirical Examination of the Antecedents and Consequences of Contribution Patterns in Crowd-funded Markets. *Information Systems Research*, *24*(3), 499–519. doi:10.1287/isre.1120.0468

Burtch, G., Ghose, A., & Wattal, S. (2015). The Hidden Cost of Accommodating Crowdfunder Privacy Preferences: A Randomized Field Experiment. *Management Science*, *61*(5), 949–962. doi:10.1287/mnsc.2014.2069

Butticè, V., Colombo, M. G., & Wright, M. (2017). Serial Crowdfunding, Social Capital, and Project Success. *Entrepreneurship Theory and Practice*, *41*(2), 183–207. doi:10.1111/etap.12271

Byrom. (2017). *Get In on the Action: The Best Videos Used in Crowdfunding*. https://www.business.com/articles/get-in-on-the-action-the-best-videos-used-in-crowdfunding/

Cade, N. L., Koonce, L., & Ikuta, K. (2017). *Text versus Video Disclosure of Forward-Looking Information: The Effect of Non-Verbal Cues on Investors' Judgments*. Academic Press.

Cai, S., Lin, X., Xu, D., & Fu, X. (2016). Judging online peer-to-peer lending behavior: A comparison of first-time and repeated borrowing requests. *Information & Management*, *53*(7), 857–867. doi:10.1016/j.im.2016.07.006

Cai, Z., Zhang, P., & Han, X. (2020). *The inverted U-shaped relationship between crowdfunding success and reward options and the moderating effect of price differentiation*. China Finance Review International. doi:10.1108/CFRI-11-2019-0152

Calder, B., & Burnkrant, R. (1977). Interpersonal Influence on Buyer Behavior: An Attribution Theory Approach. *The Journal of Consumer Research*, 29–38.

Cambridge Business English Dictionary. (2011). Cambridge University Press.

Cambridge Dictionary. (2019). *Cambridge Dictionary: English Dictionary*. Retrieved 13 07 2019, from Cambridge University Press https://dictionary.cambridge.org/pt/dicionario/ingles/corporate-governance

Campos, K. (2008). Crowdsourcing e a revolução na tomada de decisões empresariais. Waggl.

Canary, D. J. (2003). Managing interpersonal conflict: A model of events related to strategic choices. Handbook of communication and social interaction skills, 515-549.

Carè, S., Trotta, A., Carè, R., & Rizzello, A. (2018). Crowdfunding for the Development of Smart Cities. *Business Horizons*, *61*(4), 501–509. doi:10.1016/j.bushor.2017.12.001

Casadesus-Masanell, R., & Ricart, J. E. (2010). From strategy to business models and onto tactics. *Long Range Planning*, *43*(2-3), 195–215. doi:10.1016/j.lrp.2010.01.004

Cassar, A., Crowley, L., & Wydick, B. (2007). The Effect Of Social Capital On Group Loan Repayment: Evidence From Field Experiments. *Economic Journal (London)*, *117*, F85–F106.

Cassar, G. (2004). The Financing of Business Start-ups. *Journal of Business Venturing*, *19*(2), 261–283. doi:10.1016/S0883-9026(03)00029-6

Castells, M. (2001). A sociedade em rede. In A era da informação: Economia, sociedade e cultura (5.ª ed., Vol. 1, pp. 15-80). São Paulo: Paz e Terra.

Castells, M. (2007). A sociedade em rede (T. R. V. Majer, Trans.). In A era da informação: Economia, sociedade e cultura (6.ª ed., Vol. 1, pp. 15-80). São Paulo: Paz e Terra.

Catarino, L. G. (2018). Crowdfunding e crowdinvestment: o Regresso ao Futuro? CEDIPRE - Faculdade de Direito da Universidade de Coimbra, (32), 1-66.

Cecere, G., Le Guel, F., & Rochelandet, F. (2017). Crowdfunding and social influence: An empirical investigation. *Applied Economics*, *49*(57), 5802–5813.

Chabaud, D., & Germain, O. (2006). La réutilisation de données qualitatives en sciences de gestion: un second choix? *M@ n@ gement*, *9*(3), 199-221.

Chan, H. F., Moy, N., Schaffner, M., & Torgler, B. (2019). The effects of money saliency and sustainability orientation on reward based crowdfunding success. *Journal of Business Research*. Advance online publication. doi:10.1016/j.jbusres.2019.07.037

Chemla, G., & Tinn, K. (2016). *Learning through Crowdfunding*. Working paper.

Chen, A., Cumming, D., & Hughes, A. (2009). Outside Entrepreneurial Capital. *Economic Journal (London), 119*(540), 1494–1533. doi:10.1111/j.1468-0297.2009.02270.x

Chen, J. M. (2016). *Finance and the Behavioral Prospect*. Palgrave Macmillan.

Chen, J. Z., & Ning, X. (2013). Empirical research on the influence of personal information on P2P lending's success rate—Evidence from Renrendai. *Accounting and Finance*, *6*(3).

Chen, X. P., Yao, X., & Kotha, S. (2009). Entrepreneur passion and preparedness in business plan presentations: A persuasion analysis of venture capitalists' funding decisions. *Academy of Management Journal, 52*(1), 199–214. doi:10.5465/amj.2009.36462018

Chen, X., Huang, B., & Ye, D. (2018). The role of punctuation in P2P lending: Evidence from China. *Economic Modelling, 68*, 634–643. doi:10.1016/j.econmod.2017.05.007

Chinese Academy of Cyberspace Studies. (Ed.). (2019). *World Internet Development Report 2017*. Springer.

Chiteji, N. S. (2002). Promises kept: Enforcement and the role of rotating savings and credit associations in an economy. *Journal of International Development, 14*, 393–411.

Chiu, C.-M., Hsu, M.-H., & Wang Eric, T. G. (2006). Understanding Knowledge Sharing In Virtual Communities: An Integration Of Social Capital And Social Cognitive Theories. *Decision Support Systems, 42*(3), 1872–1888. doi:10.1016/j.dss.2006.04.001

Cholakova, M., & Clarysse, B. (2015). Does the possibility to make equity investments in crowdfunding projects crowd out reward-Based investments? *Entrepreneurship Theory and Practice, 39*(1), 145–172.

Cholakova, M., & Clarysse, B. J. E. T. (2015). Does the Possibility to Make Equity Investments in Crowdfunding Projects Crowd Out Reward–Based Investments? *Entrepreneurship Theory and Practice, 39*(1), 145–172. doi:10.1111/etap.12139

Cho, M., & Kim, G. (2017). A cross-cultural comparative analysis of crowdfunding projects in the United States and South Korea. *Computers in Human Behavior, 72*, 312–320. doi:10.1016/j.chb.2017.03.013

Chris, A. (2006). The Long Tail. *Wired*. https://Archive.Wired.Com/Wired/Archive/12.10/Tail_Pr.Html

Ciuchta, M. P., & O'Toole, J. (2016). Looks and linguistics: Impression formation in online exchange marketplaces. *The Journal of Social Psychology, 156*(6), 648–663. doi:10.1080/00224545.2016.1152218 PMID:26864921

Clarke, G. (1998). Non-governmental organizations (NGOs) and politics in the developing world. *Political Studies, 46*(1), 36–52. doi:10.1111/1467-9248.00128

Colombo, M. G., Franzoni, C., & Rossi–Lamastra, C. (2015). Internal social capital and the attraction of early contributions in crowdfunding. *Entrepreneurship Theory and Practice, 39*(1), 75–100. doi:10.1111/etap.12118

Comisión Europea. (2016). *Una Agenda Europea para la Economía Colaborativa*. Author.

Comley, P. (2008). Online research communities. *International Journal of Market Research, 50*, 679–694.

Connelly, B. L., Certo, S. T., Ireland, R. D., & Reutzel, C. R. (2011). Signaling theory: A review and assessment. *Journal of Management, 37*(1), 39–67. doi:10.1177/0149206310388419

Cook, S. A. (1971, May). The complexity of theorem-proving procedures. In *Proceedings of the third annual ACM symposium on Theory of computing* (pp. 151-158). 10.1145/800157.805047

Cordova, A., Dolci, J., & Gianfrate, G. (2015). The Determinants of Crowdfunding Success: Evidence from Technology Projects. *Procedia: Social and Behavioral Sciences, 181*, 115–124. doi:10.1016/j.sbspro.2015.04.872

Cornwall, A. (2007). Buzzwords and fuzzwords: Deconstructing development discourse. *Development in Practice, 17*(4–5), 471–484. doi:10.1080/09614520701469302

Courtney, C., Dutta, S., & Li, Y. (2017). Resolving Information Asymmetry: Signaling, Endorsement, and Crowdfunding Success. *Entrepreneurship Theory and Practice, 41*(2), 265–290. doi:10.1111/etap.12267

Cruz, J. (2018). Beyond financing: Crowdfunding as an informational mechanism. *Journal of Business Venturing, 33*(3), 371–393. doi:10.1016/j.jbusvent.2018.02.001

CSESS. (2011). *Rapport de synthèse du Groupe de travail Innovation Sociale*. Conseil supérieur de l'économie sociale et solidaire, Téléchargé le 25 octobre 2017 sur http://www.avise.org/sites/default/files/atoms/files/20140204/201112_CSESS_GTIS_Synthese.pdf

Cumming, D. J., Leboeuf, G., & Schwienbacher, A. (2014, December). Crowdfunding models: Keep-it-all vs. all-or-nothing. In Paris December 2014 finance meeting EUROFIDAI-AFFI paper (Vol. 10). Academic Press.

Cumming, D. J., Leboeuf, G., & Schwienbacher, A. (2020). Crowdfunding models: Keep-It-All vs. All-Or-Nothing. *Financial Management, 49*(2), 331–360. doi:10.1111/fima.12262

Cumming, D., Johan, S., & Zhang, Y. (2019). The role of due diligence in crowdfunding platforms. *Journal of Banking & Finance, 108*(C), 105661. Advance online publication. doi:10.1016/j.jbankfin.2019.105661

Cumming, D., Leboeuf, G., & Schwienbacher, A. (2014). *Crowdfunding Models: Keep-it-all vs. All-or-nothing* (Vol. 10). Paris Finance Meeting EUROFIDAI-AFFI Paper.

Cumming, D., & Zhang, Y. (2016). Alternative Investments in Emerging Markets: A Review and New Trends. *Emerging Markets Review, 29*, 1–23. doi:10.1016/j.ememar.2016.08.022

Dai, H., & Zhang, D. J. (2019). Prosocial goal pursuit in crowdfunding: Evidence from Kickstarter. *JMR, Journal of Marketing Research, 56*(3), 498–517.

Danmayr, F. (2013). Archetypes of Crowdfunding Platforms: A Multidimensional Comparison. Springer Science & Business Media.

Datta, P.B., & Gailey, R. (2012). Empowering Women Through Social Entrepreneurship: Case Study of a Women's Cooperative in India. *Entrepreneurship Theory and Practice, 36*, 569–587.

Davidson, R., & Poor, N. (2014). "The Barriers Facing Artists" use of Crowdfunding Platforms: Personality, Emotional Labor, and Going to the Well One too many Times. *New Media & Society, 17*(2), 289–307. doi:10.1177/1461444814558916

Davila, A., Foster, G., & Li, M. (2009). Reasons for management control systems adoption: Insights from product development systems choice by early-stage entrepreneurial companies. *Accounting, Organizations and Society, 34*(3-4), 322–347. doi:10.1016/j.aos.2008.08.002

Davis, B. C., Hmieleski, K. M., Webb, J. W., & Coombs, J. E. (2017). Funders' positive affective reactions to entrepreneurs' crowdfunding pitches: The influence of perceived product creativity and entrepreneurial passion. *Journal of Business Venturing, 32*(1), 90–106. doi:10.1016/j.jbusvent.2016.10.006

De Falco, S. E., Vargas-Sánchez, A., & Cucarini, N. (2015). *Social Innovation Practices: Focus on Success Factors for Crowdfunding.* Available at: www.naplesforumonservice.it/uploads/files/EspositoDeFalco

Deci Edward, L., & Ryan Richard, M. (1985). The General Causality Orientations Scale: Self-Determination In Personality. *Journal of Research in Personality, 19*(2), 109–134. doi:10.1016/0092-6566(85)90023-6

Deci Edward, L., & Ryan Richard, M. (2000). Self-determination theory and the facilitation of intrinsic motivation, social development, and well-being. *The American Psychologist, 55*(1), 68–78. doi:10.1037/0003-066X.55.1.68 PMID:11392867

Deci, E. L., & Ryan, R. M. (1985). *Intrinsic motivation and self-determination in human behavior.* Plenum.

DeGroot, T., & Gooty, J. (2009). Can nonverbal cues be used to make meaningful personality attributions in employment interviews? *Journal of Business and Psychology, 24*(2), 179–192. doi:10.100710869-009-9098-0

DeGroot, T., & Motowidlo, S. J. (1999). Why visual and vocal interview cues can affect interviewers' judgments and predict job performance. *The Journal of Applied Psychology, 84*(6), 986–993. doi:10.1037/0021-9010.84.6.986

Dejardin, M., & Fritsch, M. (2011). Entrepreneurial dynamics and regional growth. *Small Business Economics, 36*(4), 377–382. doi:10.100711187-009-9258-7

Demirguc-Kunt, A., Klapper, L., Singer, D., & Oudheusden, P. V. (2015). *The Global Findex Database 2014: Measuring Financial Inclusion around the World*. Policy Research Working Paper 7255. World Bank.

Demirguc-Kunt, A., Klapper, L., Singer, D., Ansar, S., & Hess, J. (2018). *The Global Findex Database 2017: Measuring financial inclusion and the fintech revolution*. The World Bank. Retrieved May 5, 2020 on https://globalfindex.worldbank.org/

Dey, S., Duff, B., Karahalos, K., & Fu, W.-T. (2017). The art and science of persuasion: Not all crowdfunding campaign videos are the same. *Proceedings of the 2017 ACM Conference on Computer Supported Cooperative Work and Social Computing*, 755-769. 10.1145/2998181.2998229

Dion, K., Berscheid, E., & Walster, E. (1972). What is beautiful is good. *Journal of Personality and Social Psychology*, *24*(3), 285–290. doi:10.1037/h0033731 PMID:4655540

Dixson, M. D., Greenwell, M. R., Rogers-Stacy, C., Weister, T., & Lauer, S. (2017). Nonverbal immediacy behaviors and online student engagement: Bringing past instructional research into the present virtual classroom. *Communication Education*, *66*(1), 37–53. doi:10.1080/03634523.2016.1209222

Don, T., & Williams, A. D. (2007). Innovation In The Age Of Mass Collaboration. *Business Week*, 1.

Downs, V. C., Javidi, M. M., & Nussbaum, J. F. (1988). An analysis of teachers' verbal communication within the college classroom: Use of humor, self-disclosure, and narratives. *Communication Education*, *37*(2), 127–141. doi:10.1080/03634528809378710

Drinker Biddle. (2017). Drinker Biddle crowdfunding report. *Drinker Biddle & Reath LLP*. Retrieved from www.faegredrinker.com

Drover, W., Busenitz, L., Matusik, S., Townsend, D., Anglin, A., & Dushnitsky, G. (2017). A review and road map of entrepreneurial equity financing research: Venture capital, corporate venture capital, angel investment, crowdfunding, and accelerators. *Journal of Management*, *43*(6), 1820–1853. doi:10.1177/0149206317690584

Duarte, J., Siegel, S., & Young, L. (2012). Trust and credit: The role of appearance in peer-to-peer lending. *Review of Financial Studies*, *25*(8), 2455–2484. doi:10.1093/rfs/hhs071

Dushnitsky, G., Guerini, M., Piva, E., & Rossi-Lamastra, C. (2016). Crowdfunding in Europe: Determinants of Platform Creation across Countries. *California Management Review*, *58*(2), 44–71. doi:10.1525/cmr.2016.58.2.44

Eisenhardt, K. (1989). Building theories from case study research. *Academy of Management Review*, *14*(4), 532–550. doi:10.5465/amr.1989.4308385

Ellerman, D. (2005). *Helping people help themselves*. University of Michigan Press.

Elliott, R., & Wright, L. (1999). Verbal communication: What do critical care nurses say to their unconscious or sedated patients? *Journal of Advanced Nursing*, *29*(6), 1412–1420. doi:10.1046/j.1365-2648.1999.01028.x PMID:10354236

Eloranta, V., & Turunen, T. (2016). Platforms in service-driven manufacturing: Leveraging complexity by connecting, sharing, and integrating. *Industrial Marketing Management, 55*, 178–186.

Emerson, R. M., Fretz, R. I., & Shaw, L. L. (2011). Writing Ethnographic Fieldnotes. University of Chicago Press.

Escalas, J.E., & Bettman, J.R. (2005). Self-construal, reference groups, and brand meaning. *The Journal of Consumer Research, 32*, 378–389.

Estrin, S., Gozman, D., & Khavul, S. (2018). The evolution and adoption of equity crowdfunding: Entrepreneur and investor entry into a new market. *Small Business Economics, 51*(2), 425–439. doi:10.100711187-018-0009-5

Etang, A., Fielding, D., & Knowles, S. (2011). Trust and ROSCA membership in rural Cameroon. *Journal of International Development, 23*, 461–475.

Ethan, M. (2013). The dynamics of crowdfunding: An exploratory study. *Journal of Business Venturing, 29*(1), 1–16.

European Commission. (2014). *Unleashing the potential of Crowdfunding in the European Union.* Communication from the Commission to the Parliament, the Council, the European Economic and Social Committee and the Committee of the Regions. Brussels, 27.3.2014 COM(2014) 172 final.

European Commission's Capital Market Union. (2016). *Report on Crowdfunding in the EU Capital Markets Union.* Brussels: Author.

European Crowdfunding Network AISB. (2017). *Identifying Market and Regulatory Obstacles to Cross-border Development of Crowdfunding in the EU.* Brussels: European Commission.

Feng, Y., Fan, X., & Yoon, Y. (2015). Lenders and borrowers' strategies in online peer-to-peer lending market: An empirical analysis of PPDAI. com. *Journal of Electronic Commerce Research, 16*(3), 242.

Financement Participatif France. (2014). *Observatoire du Crowdfunding chez les Français.* Available at: https://financeparticipative.org/

Financement Participatif France. (2015). *Baromètre du Crowdfunding.* Available at: https://www.gartner.com/en

Financement Participatif France. (2016). *Baromètre du crowdfunding 2015.* Retrieved from http://financeparticipative.org/barometre-du-crowdfunding-2015/

Financement Participatif France. (2018). *Baromètre du crowdfunding 2017, en collaboration avec KPMG.* Retrieved from http://financeparticipative.org/wp-content/uploads/2018/01/Barometre-CrowdFunding-2017_KPMG-FPF_page-%C3%A0-page.pdf

Financement Participatif France. (2019). *Baromètre du crowdfunding en France 2018 réalisé par KPMG pour Financement Participatif France*. Retrieved from https://financeparticipative.org/wp-content/uploads/2019/01/Barom%C3%A8tre-du-crowdfunding-KPMG-et-FPF-%C3%A9dition-2018.pdf

Fischer, M. M., & Nijkamp, P. (2009). *Entrepreneurship and regional development*. Working Paper: Serie Research Memoranda 0035. VU University Amsterdam, Faculty of Economics, Business Administration and Econometrics. Amsterdam.

Fischer, E., Bristor, J., & Gainer, B. (1996). Creating or Escaping Community? An Exploratory Study of Internet Consumers' Behaviors. *Advances in Consumer Research. Association for Consumer Research (U. S.)*, *23*, 178–182.

Flamant, N. (2005). Observer, analyser, restituer. Conditions et contradictions de l'enquête ethnologique en entreprise. *Terrain, Anthropologies & Sciences Humaines*, *44*, 137-152. https://journals.openedition.org/terrain/2505

Forbes, H., & Schaefer, D. (2017). Guidelines for Successful Crowdfunding. Procedia CIRP, (60), 398-403.

Francesca, C. (2010). *Networked Sociability*. Academic Press.

Freedman, S., & Jin, G.Z. (2008). *Do Social Networks Solve Information Problems for Peer to-Peer Lending? Evidence from Prosper*. Retrieved at: http://www.fas.nus.edu.sg/ecs/events/seminar-papers/12Mar09.pdf

Frey, B. S. (1997). *Not just for money. An economic theory of personal motivation*. Edgar Elgar.

Frydrych, D., Bock, A. J., Kinder, T., & Koeck, B. (2014). Exploring entrepreneurial legitimacy in reward-based crowdfunding. *Venture Capital*, *16*(3), 247–269. doi:10.1080/13691066.2014.916512

Gabbott, M., & Hogg, G. (2001). The role of non-verbal communication in service encounters: A conceptual framework. *Journal of Marketing Management*, *17*(1-2), 5–26. doi:10.1362/0267257012571401

Gadja, O., & Walton, J. (2013). *Review of crowdfunding for development initiatives. IMC Worldwide for Evidence on Demand*. UK Department for International Development. doi:10.12774/eod_hd061.jul2013.gadja;walton

Gafni, H., Marom, D., & Sade, O. (2019). Are the life and death of an early-stage venture indeed in the power of the tongue? Lessons from online crowdfunding pitches. *Strategic Entrepreneurship Journal*, *13*(1), 3–23. doi:10.1002ej.1293

Gagne, M., & Deci, E. L. (2005). Self-determination theory and work motivation. *Journal of Organizational Behavior*, *26*(4), 331–362.

Galloway. I. (2009). *Peer-toPeer Lending and Community Development Finance*. Working Paper, Community Development Center, Federal Reserve of San Francisco. Retrieved on frbsf.org/cdinvestments

Gartner Group. (2013). Available at: https://www.gartner.com/en

Geert, L. (2016). *Social Media Abyss. Critical Internet Cultures And The Force Of Negation.* Polity Press.

George, S. (1950). *The Sociology Of Georg Simmel* (Vol. 92892). Simon and Shuster.

Georg, S. (1903), *Die Großstädte Und Das Geistesleben.* Dresden: Petermann.

Gerber Elizabeth, M., & Hui, J., S., & Kuo, P.-Y. (2012). Crowdfunding: Why People Are Motivated To Post And Fund Projects On Crowdfunding Platforms. *ACM Conference On Computer Supported Cooperative Work.*

Gerber, E. M., Hui, J. S., & Kuo, P. Y. (2012, February). Crowdfunding: Why people are motivated to post and fund projects on crowdfunding platforms. In *Proceedings of the International Workshop on Design, Influence, and Social Technologies: Techniques, Impacts and Ethics* (*Vol. 2*, p. 11). Academic Press.

Gerber, E. M., Hui, J. S., & Kuo, P.-Y. (2012). Crowdfunding: Why people are motivated to post and fund projects on crowdfunding platforms. In *Proceedings of the International Workshop on Design, Influence, and Social Technologies: Techniques, Impacts and Ethics* (*vol. 2*). Academic Press.

Gerber, E. M., Hui, J. S., & Kuo, P. Y. (2012). Crowdfunding: Why People are Motivated to Post and Fund Projects on Crowdfunding Platforms. *Proceedings of the International Workshop on Design, Influence, and Social Technologies: Techniques, Impacts and Ethics*, *2*, 11-21.

Gerber, E. M., Hui, J. S., & Kuo, P.-Y. (2012). Crowdfunding: Why people are motivated to post and fund projects on crowdfunding platforms. *Proc. of the International Workshop on ...*, 10.

Ghatak, M. (1999). *Group lending, local information and peer selection.* Academic Press.

Gianturco. (2004). *L'intervista Qualitativa.* Guerini Studio.

GiudiciG.NavaR.Rossi LamastraC.VerecondoC. (2012). Crowdfunding: The new frontier for financing entrepreneurship? *Available at* SSRN 2157429. doi:10.2139srn.2157429

Godbout, J. T., & Alain, C. (1998). *Il Linguaggio Del Dono.* Bollati Boringhieri.

Gonçalves, J. G. P., & Carvalho, P. d. M. (2018). Análise do Crowdfunding e seus impactos no Brasil. Revista Estudos Eleitorais, 2(4), 1-87.

Gorbatai, A., & Nelson, L. (2015). *The Narrative Advantage: Gender and the Language of Crowdfunding.* Haas School of Business UC Berkeley. Research Papers.

Grahe, J. E., & Bernieri, F. J. (1999). The importance of nonverbal cues in judging rapport. *Journal of Nonverbal Behavior*, *23*(4), 253–269. doi:10.1023/A:1021698725361

Granovetter, M. (2005). The Impact of Social Structure on Economic Outcomes. *The Journal of Economic Perspectives*, *19*, 33–50.

Granovetter, M. S. (1973). *The Strength of Weak Ties. American Journal of Sociology, 78*, 1360–1380.

Grant, A. M. (2008). Does intrinsic motivation fuel the prosocial fire? Motivational synergy in predicting persistence, performance, and productivity. *The Journal of Applied Psychology, 93*(1), 48–58. PMID:18211134

Greenberg, J., & Mollick, E. (2017). Activist choice homophily and the crowdfunding of female founders. *Administrative Science Quarterly, 62*(2), 341–374. doi:10.1177/0001839216678847

Greenberg, M. D., Hui, J., & Gerber, E. (2013). *Crowdfunding: A Resource Exchange Perspective. In CHI"13 Extended Abstracts on Human Factors in Computing Systems*. ACM. doi:10.1145/2468356.2468514

Green, J. M., & Coyle, J. F. (2016). Crowdfunding and the not-so-safe SAFE. *Virginia Law Review Online, 102*, 168–182.

Griffin, Z. J. (2012). Crowdfunding: Fleecing the American masses. *Case W. Res. JL Tech. & Internet, 4*, 375.

Griffin, Z. J. (2012). Crowdfunding: Fleecing the American Masses. *Case W. Res. JL Tech. & Internet, 4*, 375.

Guan-Cheng, L. (2019). *Kickstarter Structured Relational Database*. Harvard Dataverse., doi:10.7910/DVN/EOYBXM

Haas, P., Blohm, I., & Leimeister, J. M. (2014). *An empirical taxonomy of crowdfunding intermediaries*. Academic Press.

Hage, J. (2018). *Yes! Crowdfunding is working for medical devices*. Retrieved from http://www.medicaldevicesgroup.net

Hailey, J. (2000). Indicators of identity: NGOs and the strategic imperative of assessing core values. *Development in Practice, 10*(3–4), 402–407. doi:10.1080/09614520050116550

Halt, G. B. Jr, Donch, J. C. Jr, Stiles, A. R., & Fesnak, R. (2017). Sources of company funding. In *Intellectual Property and Financing Strategies for Technology Startups* (pp. 11–33). Springer International Publishing AG. doi:10.1007/978-3-319-49217-9_2

Hampton, K., & Wellman, B. (2002). Neighboring in Netville: How the Internet supports community and social capital in a wired suburb. *City & Community, 2*(3), 277–311.

Hanks, S. (2017). Happy birthday regulation CF (shame about the compliance failures). *CrowdCheck Blog*. Retrieved from www.crowdcheck.com

Han, L., Xiao, J. J., & Su, Z. (2019). Financing knowledge, risk attitude and P2P borrowing in China. *International Journal of Consumer Studies, 43*(2), 166–177. doi:10.1111/ijcs.12494

HarmsM. (2007). *What drives motivation to participate financially in a crowdfunding community?* (Unpublished master's thesis). Vrije Universiteit Amsterdam. Retrieved from http://ssrn.com/abstract=2269242

Harrer, T., Lehner, O. M., & Weber, C. (2019). Do(n't) Trust This! –A Longitudinal Exploration of Institutional Trust in Crowdfunding. *BAM2019 Conference Proceedings*. Retrieved from https://www.bam.ac.uk/sites/bam.ac.uk/files/contribution212.pdf

Harrison, R. (2013). Crowdfunding and the revitalisation of the early stage risk capital market: Catalyst or chimera? *Venture Capital*, *15*(4), 283–287. doi:10.1080/13691066.2013.852331

Hellmann, T. (2007). Entrepreneurs and the Process of Obtaining Resources. *Journal of Economics & Management Strategy*, *16*(1), 81–109. doi:10.1111/j.1530-9134.2007.00133.x

Hemer, J. (2011). *A snapshot on crowdfunding* (No. R2/2011). Working papers firms and region.

Hemer, J. (2011). A snapshot on crowdfunding. Working papers firms and region, No. R2/2011. *Site Econstor*.Retrieved from http://hdl.handle.net/10419/52302

Henry, J., Ito, M., & Boyd, D. (2015). Participatory Culture In A Networked Era: A Conversation On Youth, Learning, Commerce, And Politics. John Wiley & Sons.

Henry, J. (2006). *Cultura Convergente*. Apogeo.

Herrero-Lopez, S. (2009). Social Interactions in P2P Lending. *Proceedings of the 3rd workshop on Social Network Mining and Analysis (SNA), International Conference on Knowledge Discovery and Data Mining*. Retrieved at: http://www.snakdd.com/AcceptedPapers/snakdd2009_submission_5.pdf

Hervé, F., & Schwienbacher, A. (2018). Crowdfunding and innovation. *Journal of Economic Surveys*, *32*(5), 1–17. doi:10.1111/joes.12274

Herzberg, F., Mausner, B., & Bloch Snyderman, B. (1959). *The motivation to work*. John Wiley & Sons, Inc.

Herzenstein, M., Andrews, R., Dholakia, U., & Lyandres, E. (2008). *The Democratization of Personal Consumer Loans? Determinants of Success in Online Peer-to-Peer Lending Communities*. Retrieved at: http://www.rice.edu/nationalmedia/multimedia/online

Herzenstein, M., Sonenshein, S., & Dholakia, U. M. (2011). Tell me a good story and I may lend you money: The role of narratives in peer-to-peer lending decisions. *Journal of Marketing Research, 48*(SPL), S138-S149.

Herzenstein, M., Dholakia, U. M., & Andrews, R. L. (2011). Strategic herding behaviour in peer-to-peer loan auctions. *Journal of Interactive Marketing*, *25*(1), 27–36. doi:10.1016/j.intmar.2010.07.001

Hoegen, A. D., Steininger, M., & Veit, D. (2018). How do investors decide? An interdisciplinary review of decision-making in crowdfunding. *Electronic Markets, 28*(3), 339–365. doi:10.100712525-017-0269-y

Homans, G. (1961). *Social Behavior: Its Elementary Forms*. Harcourt.

Hornuf, L., & Schmitt, M. (2017). *Does a local bias exist in equity crowdfunding?* Unpublished paper. *Max Planck Institute for Innovation and Competition Research Paper No.* 16-07.

Hornuf, L., & Neuenkirch, M. (2017). Pricing shares in equity crowdfunding. *Small Business Economics, 48*(4), 795–811. doi:10.100711187-016-9807-9

Hornuf, L., & Schwienbacher, A. (2018). Market mechanisms and funding dynamics in equity crowdfunding. *Journal of Corporate Finance, 50*, 556–574. doi:10.1016/j.jcorpfin.2017.08.009

Hosman, L. A. (2002). Language and persuasion. *The persuasion handbook: Developments in theory and practice*, 371-390.

Hossain, M. (2015). A Review of Literature on Open Innovation in Small and Medium-sized Enterprises. *Journal of Global Entrepreneurship Research, 5*(1), 1–12. doi:10.118640497-015-0022-y

Hossain, M., & Oparaocha, G. O. (2017). Crowdfunding: Motives, definitions, typology and ethical challenges. *Entrepreneurship Research Journal, 7*(2), 1–14. doi:10.1515/erj-2015-0045

Howard, M. M., Mendelson, S. E., Glenn, J. K., & Howard, M. M. (2002). The Power and Limits of NGOs: A Critical Look at Building Democracy in Eastern Europe and Eurasia. *Slavic Review*.

Howe, J. (2006). *Crowdsourcing: A Definition*. Retrieved from https://crowdsourcing.typepad.com/cs/2006/06/crowdsourcing_a.html

Howe, J. (2006). The Rise of Crowdsourcing. *Wired, 14*(6). Available online at: https://www.wired.com/wired/archive/14.06/crowds.html

Huelsbeck, D. P., Marchant, K. A., & Sandino, T. (2011). On testing business models. *The Accounting Review, 86*(5), 1631–1654. doi:10.2308/accr-10096

Hui, J. S., Greenberg, M. D., & Gerber, E. M. (2014). Understanding the role of community in crowdfunding work. In *Proceedings of the 17th ACM conference on Computer supported cooperative work & social computing* (pp. 62-74). ACM. 10.1145/2531602.2531715

Hulme, M., & Wright, C. (2006). *Internet Based Social Lending: Past, Present and Future*. Social Futures Observatory.

Hu, M., Li, X., & Shi, M. (2015). Product and pricing decisions in crowdfunding. *Marketing Science, 34*(3), 331–345. doi:10.1287/mksc.2014.0900

Ibrahim, D. M. (2017a). *Crowdfunding signals*. Unpublished paper, William & Mary Law School, Research Paper No. 09-369.

Ibrahim, D. M. (2017b, June). Crowdfunding without the crowd. *North Carolina Law Review*, *95*(5), 1.

Ibrahim, N., & Verliyantina. (2012). The Model of Crowdfunding to Support Small and Micro Businesses in Indonesia through a Web-based Platform. *Procedia Economics and Finance*, *4*, 390–397. doi:10.1016/S2212-5671(12)00353-X

IDEO.ORG. (2015). *The Field Guide to Human-Centered Design*. Téléchargé le 25 octobre 2017 sur http://www.designkit.org//resources/1

Iikuza, M. (2014). *Le Crowdfunding: Les Rouages du Financement Participatif-édition 2015*. E. Editions, Ed..

Iyer, R. I., K.A., Luttmer, E.F.P., & Shue, K. (2009). *Screening in New Credit Markets: Can Individual Lenders Infer Borrower Creditworthiness in Peer-to-Peer Lending?* NBER Working Paper No. 15242. Retrieved at: http://www.nber.org/papers/w15242

Jegeleviciute, S., & Valanciene, L. (2015). Comparative analysis of the ways crowdfunding is promoted. *Procedia: Social and Behavioral Sciences*, *213*, 268–274. doi:10.1016/j.sbspro.2015.11.536

Jenkins, H., Purushotma, R., Weigel, M., Clinton, K., & Robison, A. J. (2009). Confronting the Challenges of Participatory Culture: Media Education for the 21st Centur. The MIT Press. doi:10.7551/mitpress/8435.001.0001 doi:10.7551/mitpress/8435.001.0001

Jonathan, M. (1999). The microfinance promise. *Journal of Economic Literature*, *37*(4), 1569–1614. doi:10.1257/jel.37.4.1569

Josefy, M., Dean, T. J., Albert, L. S., & Fitza, M. A. (2017). The Role of Community in Crowdfunding Success: Evidence on Cultural Attributes in Funding Campaigns to "Save the Local Theater". *Entrepreneurship Theory and Practice*, *41*(2), 161–182. doi:10.1111/etap.12263

Joshi, M. (2018). Crowdfunding for Startups in India. *WEshkar*, *24*(1), 37–48.

Kahneman, D., & Tversky, A. (1979). Prospect theory: An analysis of decision under risk. *Econometrica*, 263–291.

Kang, M., Gao, Y., Wang, T., & Zheng, H. (2016). Understanding the determinants of funders' investment intentions on crowdfunding platforms: A trust-based perspective. *Industrial Management & Data Systems*, *116*(8), 1800–1819. doi:10.1108/IMDS-07-2015-0312

Kapoor, A. (2007). The SEWA way: Shaping another future for informal labour. *Futures*, *39*, 554–568.

Kathrine, C., & Daniel, S. (2016). Crowdsourcing for a better world. *Information Technology & People*, *29*(1), 221–247. doi:10.1108/ITP-09-2014-0215

Keyton, J., Caputo, J. M., Ford, E. A., Fu, R., Leibowitz, S. A., Liu, T., ... Wu, C. (2013). Investigating verbal workplace communication behaviors. *The Journal of Business Communication (1973), 50*(2), 152-169.

Khelladi, I., Castellano, S., & Bertaud, A. (2018). Les déterminants de la confiance de l'internaute dans le contexte d'une collecte de crowdfunding. *Innovations, 2*(56), 117–140. doi:10.3917/inno.pr1.0040

Kickstarter Stats. (2020). Accessed on May 23rd, 2020. https://www.kickstarter.com/help/stats?ref=about_subnav

Kim, K., & Hann, I. H. (2014). *Crowdfunding and the Democratization of Access to Capital: a Geographical Analysis.* Robert H. Smith School Research Paper.

Kim, K., & Hann, I.-H. (2019). Crowdfunding and the Democratization of Access to Capital—An Illusion? Evidence from Housing Prices. *Information Systems Research, 30*(1), 276–290. doi:10.1287/isre.2018.0802

Kitch, E. W. (2013). Crowdfunding and an Innovator's Access to Capital. *Geo. Mason L. Rev., 21*, 887.

Kitchens & Torrence. (2012). The JOBS Act-crowdfunding and beyond. *Economic Development Journal, 11*(4), 42.

Klein, D. B. (1997). *Reputation: Studies in the Voluntary Elicitation of Good Conduct.* University of Michigan Press.

Knyazeva, A., & Ivanov, V. I. (2017). *Soft and hard information and signal extraction in securities crowdfunding.* Paper presented at 2nd Emerging Trends in Entrepreneurial Finance Conference, Hoboken, NJ. 10.2139srn.3051380

Koch & Siering. (2015). *Crowdfunding Success Factors: The Characteristics of Successfully Funded Projects on Crowdfunding Platforms.* Academic Press.

Koch, J. A., & Siering, M. (2015). *Crowdfunding success factors: The characteristics of successfully funded projects on crowdfunding platforms.* Academic Press.

Koch, J.-A., & Siering, M. (2015). *Crowdfunding success factors: the characteristics of successfully funded projects on crowdfunding platforms.* Paper presented at the Twenty-Third European Conference on Information Systems (ECIS) 2015.

Kozinets, R. V. (2002). The field behind the screen: Using netnography for marketing research in online communities. *JMR, Journal of Marketing Research, 39*, 61–72.

Kraus, S., Richter, C., Brem, A., Cheng, C. F., & Chang, M. L. (2016). Strategies for reward-based crowdfunding campaigns. *Journal of Innovation & Knowledge, 1*(1), 13–23. doi:10.1016/j.jik.2016.01.010

Krauss, R. M. (2002). *The psychology of verbal communication. In International Encyclopaedia of the Social and Behavioral Sciences*. Elsevier.

Kuan, T. S. (1996). Life on the Net: The Reconstruction of Self and Community. Advances in Consumer Research 23 Association of Consumer Research.

Kuppuswamy & Bayus. (2015). *Crowdfunding Creative Ideas: The Dynamics of Project Backers in Kickstarter.* Academic Press.

Kuppuswamy, V., & Bayus, B. L. (2013). *Crowdfunding Creative Ideas: the Dynamics of Projects Backers in Kickstarter*. SSRN Working Paper.

Kuppuswamy, V., & Bayus, B. L. (2018b). A review of crowdfunding research and findings. In Handbook of Research on New Product Development (pp. 361-373). Edward Elgar Publishing. doi:10.4337/9781784718152.00028

Kuppuswamy, V., & Bayus, B. L. (2017). Does my contribution to your crowdfunding project matter? *Journal of Business Venturing*, *32*(1), 72–89. doi:10.1016/j.jbusvent.2016.10.004

Kuppuswamy, V., & Bayus, B. L. (2018a). Crowdfunding Creative Ideas: The Dynamics of Project Backers. In D. Cumming & L. Hornuf (Eds.), *The Economics of Crowdfunding: Startups, Portals and Investor Behavior* (pp. 151–182). Springer International Publishing. doi:10.1007/978-3-319-66119-3_8

Kuti, M., & Madarasz, G. (2014). Crowdfunding. *Public Finance Quarterly*, *59*(3), 355–366.

La Loi, E. S. S. (2014). *LOI n° 2014-856 du 31 juillet 2014 relative à l'économie sociale et solidaire*. In NOR: ERNX1315311L, Téléchargé le 25 octobre 2017 sur https://www.legifrance.gouv.fr/affichTexte.do?cidTexte=JORFTEXT000029313296&categorieLien=id

Labrecque, L., Krishen, A., & Grzeskowiak, S. (2011). Exploring social motivations for brand loyalty: Conformity versus escapism. *Journal of Brand Management*, *18*, 457–472.

Lakhani KarimR. (2003), *Why Hackers Do What They Do: Understanding Motivation and Effort in Free/Open Source Software Projects*. doi:10.2139srn.443040

Lambert, T., & Schwienbacher, A. (2010). An empirical analysis of crowdfunding. *Social Science Research Network*, *1578175*, 1–23.

Laurence. (2016). Crowdfunding and Crowdmicrofinance, an Evolution of Models for Entrepreneurship of the Poor. *Open Access Library Journal*, *3*(12), 1.

Lawont, J.J., & N'Guessan, T. (2000). *Group lending with adverse selection*. Academic Press.

Lea Stephen, E. G. (2006). Money As Tool, Money As Drug: The Biological Psychology Of A Strong Incentive. *Behavioral and Brain Sciences*, *29*(2), 161–209. doi:10.1017/S0140525X06009046

Leach, J. C., & Melicher, R. W. (2018). *Entrepreneurial finance* (6th ed.). Cengage Learning.

Leal, G. F. C. (2016). Crowdfunding em Portugal: estudo de caso da plataforma PPL. ISEG, 1-47.

Lederer, E. (2015). *La finance participative accélère son incroyable expansion*. Retrieved from https://www.lesechos.fr/31/03/2015/LesEchos/21909-119-ECH_la-finance-participative-accelere-son-incroyable-expansion.htm

Lee, C. R., Lee, J. H., & Shin, D. Y. (2015). Factor Analysis of the Motivation on Crowdfunding Participants: An Empirical Study of Funder Centered Reward-type Platform. *Journal of Society for e-Business Studies, 20*(1).

Lee, R., & Barry, W. (2012). *Networked: The New Social Operating System*. MIT Press.

Lehner, O. M. (2013). Crowdfunding Social Ventures: A Model and Research Agenda. *Venture Capital, 15*(4), 289–311. doi:10.1080/13691066.2013.782624

Lehner, O. M., & Nicholls, A. (2014). Social finance and crowdfunding for social enterprises: A public-private case study providing legitimacy and leverage. *Venture Capital, 16*(3), 271–286. doi:10.1080/13691066.2014.925305

Lelo de Larrea, G., Altin, M., & Singh, D. (2019). Determinants of success of restaurant crowdfunding. *International Journal of Hospitality Management, 78*, 150–158. doi:10.1016/j.ijhm.2018.10.003

Leonard, H., Beauvais, L., & Scholl, W. (1999). Work Motivation: The Incorporation of Self-Concept-Based Process. *Human Relations, 52*(8), 969-998.

Li & Duan. (2014). *Dynamic Strategies for Successful Online Crowdfunding*. Academic Press.

Li, S., Qiu, J., Lin, Z., & Qiu, J. (2011, June). Do borrowers make homogeneous decisions in online P2P lending market? an empirical study of PPDai in China. In ICSSSM11 (pp. 1-6). IEEE.

Liam, C., & Yannis, P. (2012). *The venture crowd: crowdfunding equity investment into business*. NESTA.

Li, G., & Wang, J. (2019). Threshold effects on backer motivations in reward-based crowdfunding. *Journal of Management Information Systems, 36*(2), 546–573. doi:10.1080/07421222.2019.1599499

Li, J., Chen, X.-P., Kotha, S., & Fisher, G. (2017). Catching fire and spreading it: A glimpse into displayed entrepreneurial passion in crowdfunding campaigns. *The Journal of Applied Psychology, 102*(7), 1075–1098. doi:10.1037/apl0000217 PMID:28333500

Lin, Y., Boh, W. F., & Goh, K. H. (2014). *How different are crowdfunders? Examining archetypes of crowdfunders and their choice of projects*. Retrieved from https://papers.ssrn.com/sol3/papers.cfm?abstract_id=2397571

Lin, C. Y., Lin, C. Y., Lin, J. S. C., & Lin, J. S. C. (2017). The influence of service employees' nonverbal communication on customer-employee rapport in the service encounter. *Journal of Service Management, 28*(1), 107–132. doi:10.1108/JOSM-08-2015-0251

Lindblom, A. K. (2006). *Non-Governmental organisations in international law. Non-Governmental Organisations in International Law*. Cambridge University. doi:10.1017/CBO9780511494406

Lin, M., & Viswanathan, S. (2014). *Home Bias in Online Investments: an Empirical Study of an Online Crowd Funding Market*. Mimeo.

Li, S., Lin, Z., Qiu, J., Safi, R., & Xiao, Z. (2015). How friendship networks work in online P2P lending markets. *Nankai Business Review International*, *6*(1), 42–67. doi:10.1108/NBRI-01-2014-0010

Liu, L., Suh, A., & Wagner, C. (2018). Empathy or perceived credibility? An empirical study on individual donation behavior in charitable crowdfunding. *Internet Research*, *28*(3), 623–651. doi:10.1108/IntR-06-2017-0240

Li, X., Tang, Y., Yang, N., Ren, R., Zheng, H., & Zhou, H. (2016). The value of information disclosure and lead investor in equity-based crowdfunding: An exploratory empirical study. *Nankai Business Review International*, *7*(3), 301–321. doi:10.1108/NBRI-01-2016-0002

Li, Y., Cao, H., & Zhao, T. (2018). Factors Affecting Successful Equity Crowdfunding. *Journal of Mathematical Finance*, *8*(02), 446–456. doi:10.4236/jmf.2018.82028

Luke, B., & Eve, C. (2000). *Le Nouvel Esprit Du Capitalisme*. Gallimard.

Lukkarinen, A., Wallenius, J., & Seppälä, T. (2019). *Investor motivations and decision criteria in equity crowdfunding*. Retrieved from https://papers.ssrn.com/sol3/papers.cfm?abstract_id=3263434

Lukkarinen, A., Teich, J. E., Wallenius, H., & Wallenius, J. (2016). Success drivers of online equity crowdfunding campaigns. *Decision Support Systems*, *87*, 26–38. doi:10.1016/j.dss.2016.04.006

Macht, S. A., & Weatherston, J. (2015). Academic Research on Crowdfunders: What's Been Done and What's To Come? *Strategic Change*, *24*(2), 191–205. doi:10.1002/jsc.2010

Madsen, J., & McMullin, J. L. (2020, July 01). Economic consequences of risk disclosures: Evidence from crowdfunding. *The Accounting Review*, *95*(4), 331–363. Advance online publication. doi:10.2308/accr-52641

Mahadevan, B. (2000). Business models for Internet-based e-commerce: An anatomy. *California Management Review*, *42*, 55–69.

Malecki, E. J. (1997). Entrepreneurs, networks, and economic development. *Advances in Entrepreneurship, Firm, Emergence, and Growth*, *3*, 57–118.

Mamonov, S., & Malaga, R. (2018). Success factors in Title III equity crowdfunding in the United States. *Electronic Commerce Research and Applications*, *27*, 65–73. doi:10.1016/j.elerap.2017.12.001

Manuel, C. (2002). La Nascita Della Società. In *Rete*. Università Bocconi.

Marcell, M. (1925). Essai Sur Le Don. Forme Et Raison De L'échange. In *Les Sociétés*. Ristampato Da Einaudi.

Marco, A., & Anna, C. (2010). *Il Dono Al Tempo Di Internet*. Einaudi.

Marconatto, D. A. B., Barin-Cruz, L., & Pedrozo, E. (2016). Lending groups and different social capitals in developed and developing countries. *Revista de Administração Contemporânea*, *20*, 651–672.

Maroco, J. (2007). Análise estatística com utilização do SPSS (3rd ed.). Lisboa: Edições Sílabo.

Martin, R. L., & Osberg, S. (2007). Social entrepreneurship: The case for definition. *Stanford Social Innovation Review*, 5.

Marx, M. T., & Seibel, H. D. (2012). The Evolution Of Financial Cooperatives In Nigeria:Do They Have A Place In Financial Intermediation? In Cooperative Finance in Developing Economies. Soma Prints Limited.

Massimo, R. (2001). La Solidarietà Nelle Società Complesse. In Solidarietà In Questione. Contributi Teorici E Analisi Empiriche. Meltemi.

Massolution, C. F. (2013). *The crowdfunding industry report*. Academic Press.

Massolution. (2013). *The Crowdfunding Industry Report, 2013CF.* Academic Press.

Massolution. (2015). *The Crowdfunding Industry Report, 2015CF.* Academic Press.

Mast, M. S. (2007). On the importance of nonverbal communication in the physician–patient interaction. *Patient Education and Counseling*, *67*(3), 315–318. doi:10.1016/j.pec.2007.03.005 PMID:17478072

Matthews, J., & Vachet, J. (2014). Le Crowdsourcing et le Crowdfunding Culturels dans le Web Collaborative. La Culture par les Foules, 28-39.

Mcclelland, D. C. (1961). *The achieving society*. doi:10.1037/14359-000

McKenny, A. F., Allison, T. H., Ketchen, D. J. Jr, Short, J. C., & Ireland, R. D. (2017). How Should Crowdfunding Research Evolve? A Survey of the Entrepreneurship Theory and Practice Editorial Board. *Entrepreneurship Theory and Practice*, *41*(2), 291–304. doi:10.1111/etap.12269

Mehrabian, A., & Ferris, S. R. (1967). Inference of attitudes from nonverbal communication in two channels. *Journal of Consulting Psychology*, *31*(3), 248–252. doi:10.1037/h0024648 PMID:6046577

Meyer, T. (n.d.). *Financial services 2.0: How social computing and P2P activity are changing financial research and lending*. Deutsche Bank Research. Retrieved on www.dbresearch.com

Mihaly. (1975). *Beyond Boredom And Anxiety: Experiencing Flow In Work And Play*. San Francisco: Jossey-Bass.

Mi, J. J., & Zhu, H. (2017). Can funding platforms' self-initiated financial innovation improve credit availability? Evidence from China's P2P market. *Applied Economics Letters*, *24*(6), 396–398. doi:10.1080/13504851.2016.1197358

Mollick, E. (2014). The dynamics of crowdfunding: An exploratory study. Journal of Business Venturing, 29(1), 1-16.

Mollick, E. R. (2013). *Swept away by the crowd? Crowdfunding, venture capital, and the selection of entrepreneurs*. Academic Press.

Mollick, E. (2014). The dynamics of crowdfunding: An exploratory study. *Journal of Business Venturing*, *29*(1), 1–16. doi:10.1016/j.jbusvent.2013.06.005

Mollick, E., & Nanda, R. (2016). Wisdom or madness? Comparing crowds with expert evaluation in funding the arts. *Journal Management Science*, *62*(6), 1533–1553. doi:10.1287/mnsc.2015.2207

Moreau, F., & Nicolas, Y. (2018). *Financement Participatif: une Voie d"avenir pour la Culture? Lectures, Publications Reçues*. M. de la Culture, Ed.

Moritz, A., Block, J. H., & Lutz, E. (2014). *Investor communication in crowdfunding: A qualitative-empirical study*. Retrieved from https://papers.ssrn.com/sol3/papers.cfm?abstract_id=2462282

Muhammad. (1999). *Banker To The Poor: Micro-Lending And The Battle Against World Poverty*. New York: Public Affairs.

Müller, S. (2013). *Entrepreneurship and regional development: on the interplay between agency and context* (Unpublished PhD Thesis). Business and Social Sciences of Aarhus University.

Muller, M., Geyer, W., Soule, T., Daniels, S., & Cheng, L.-T. (2013). Crowdfunding inside the enterprise: employee-initiatives for innovation and collaboration. *Proceedings of the SIGCHI conference on human factors in computing systems*. 10.1145/2470654.2470727

Müller, S. (2016). A progress review of entrepreneurship and regional development: What are the remaining gaps? *European Planning Studies*, *24*(6), 1133–1158. doi:10.1080/09654313.2016.1154506

Muniz, A.M., & O'Guinn, T.C. (2001). Brand community. *The Journal of Consumer Research*, *27*, 412–432.

Muzellec, L., Ronteau, S., & Lambkin, M. (2015). Two-sided Internet platforms: A business model lifecycle perspective. *Industrial Marketing Management*, *45*, 139–150.

Nadiya, M., & Laurence, A.-M. (2015). Can Microfinance Crowdfunding Reduce Financial Exclusion? Regulatory Issue. *International Journal of Bank Marketing*, *33*(5), 624–636. doi:10.1108/IJBM-06-2014-0080

Negrão, C. S. V. (2018). Impact of E-Commerce on Agricultural Business Success. In L. dall'Acqua & D. Lukose (Eds.), Improving Business Performance Through Effective Managerial Training Initiatives (pp. 223-253). Hershey, PA: IGI Global.

Negrão, C. S. V. (2020). Impact of Managers on Agricultural Business Success. *Journal of Information Technology Research, 13*(3), 126–141. doi:10.4018/JITR.2020070108

Ng, S. H., & Bradac, J. J. (1993). *Power in language: Verbal communication and social influence.* Sage Publications, Inc.

Nguyen, S. (2019, May 6). *The 8 Best Crowdfunding Sites of 2019.* Retrieved from https://www.thebalancesmb.com/best-crowdfunding-sites-4580494

Niemand, T., Angerer, M., Thies, F., Kraus, S., & Hebenstreit, R. (2018). Equity Crowdfunding across Borders: A Conjoint Experiment. *International Journal of Entrepreneurial Behaviour & Research, 24*(4), 911–932. doi:10.1108/IJEBR-07-2017-0256

Niklas, L. (1986). The Autopoiesis Of Social Systems. Sociocybernetic Paradoxes, 6(2), 172-192.

Noller, P. (1985). Video primacy—A further look. *Journal of Nonverbal Behavior, 9*(1), 28–47. doi:10.1007/BF00987557

OECD, European Commission. (2014). *Pallier la Pénurie d"entrepreneurs: Politiques d"entrepreneuriat Inclusif en Europe*. OECD Publishing. . doi:10.1787/9789264188211-fr

OECD. (1998). *Fostering entrepreneurship - the OECD jobs strategy*. OECD.

OECD. (2006). *Reestructuring the regions: analysis, policy model and prognosis*. OECD.

Okleshen, C., & Grossbart, S. (1988). Unset Groups, Virtual Community and Consumer Behavior. In J. W. Alba & J. W. Hutchinson (Eds.), *Advances in Consumer Research 25* (pp. 276–282). Association of Consumer Research.

Omeri, K. L. (2015). Factors Influencing Financial Sustainability of Non-Goverment Organizations: A Survey of NGOs in Nakuru County, Kenya. *International Journal of Economics. Commerce and Management, 3*(9), 704–743.

Onnée, S., & Renault, S. (2014). Crowdfunding: Vers une compréhension du rôle joué par la foule. *Management et Avenir, 8*, 117–133.

Onnee, S., & Renault, S. (2014). Crowdfunding: Vers une compréhension du rôle joué par la foule. *Revue Management & Avenir, 74*(8), 117–133. doi:10.3917/mav.074.0117

Ordanini, A., Miceli, L., Pizzetti, M., & Parasuraman, A. J. J. (2011). Crowd-funding: Transforming customers into investors through innovative service platforms. *Journal of Service Management, 22*(4), 443–470. doi:10.1108/09564231111155079

Osiyevskyy, O., Chernenko, M., & Biloshapka, V. (2018). The role of business models in the early-stage of new technology-based firms. Technology Entrepreneurship: Insights in New Technology-Based Firms, Research Spin-Offs and Corporate Environments. 49-68.

Palacios, M., Martinez-Corral, A., Nisar, A., & Grijalvo, M. (2015). Crowdsourcing and Organizational Forms: Emerging Trends and Research Implications. *Journal of Business Research, 69*(5), 1834–1839. doi:10.1016/j.jbusres.2015.10.065

Palepu, K. G., & Healy, P. M. (2013). *Business analysis & valuation using financial statements Text and cases* (5th ed.). South-Western Cengage Learning.

Parhankangas, A., & Ehrlich, M. (2014). How entrepreneurs seduce business angels: An impression management approach. *Journal of Business Venturing, 29*(4), 543–564. doi:10.1016/j.jbusvent.2013.08.001

Parhankangas, A., & Renko, M. (2017). Linguistic style and crowdfunding success among social and commercial entrepreneurs. *Journal of Business Venturing, 32*(2), 215–236. doi:10.1016/j.jbusvent.2016.11.001

Parsons, C. K., & Liden, R. C. (1984). Interviewer perceptions of applicant qualifications: A multivariate field study of demographic characteristics and nonverbal cues. *The Journal of Applied Psychology, 69*(4), 557–568. doi:10.1037/0021-9010.69.4.557

Paschen. (2017). Choose wisely: Crowdfunding through the stages of the startup life cycle. *Business Horizons, 60*, 179-188.

Paschen, J. (2017). Choose Wisely: Crowdfunding through the Stages of the Startup Life Cycle. *Business Horizons, 60*(2), 179–188. doi:10.1016/j.bushor.2016.11.003

Passebois-Ducros, J., & Pulh, M. (2015). *Vers un modèle conceptuel des facteurs explicatifs de la participation et de la réussite d'une opération de crowdfunding dans le secteur culturel non marchand.* Retrieved from https://www.researchgate.net/profile/Mathilde_Pulh/publication/281554469_Vers_un_modle_conceptuel_des_facteurs_explicatifs_de_la_participation_et_de_la_russite_d%27une_opration_de_crowdfunding_dans_le_secteur_culturel_non_marchand/links/55ed869108ae21d099c75cbb.pdf

Patelli, L., & Pedrini, M. (2014). Is the optimism in CEO's letters to shareholders sincere? Impression management versus communicative action during the economic crisis. *Journal of Business Ethics, 124*(1), 19–34. doi:10.100710551-013-1855-3

Pearson, A., Johdet, J., & Näselius, M. (2016). *Understanding The Crowd: A quantitative study on investor motivation in equity crowdfunding*. Academic Press.

Pearson, A., Johdet, J., & Näselius, M. (2016). *Understanding the crowd: A quantitative study on investor motivation in equity crowdfunding*. Retrieved October 2, 2019 on http://www.diva-portal.org/smash/record.jsf?pid=diva2%3A932955&dswid=6652

Peneff, J. (2009). *Le goût de l'observation. Comprendre et pratiquer l'observation participante en sciences sociales*. Paris: La Découverte/Grands repères.

Pennebaker, J. W. (2011). The secret life of pronouns. *New Scientist, 211*(2828), 42–45. doi:10.1016/S0262-4079(11)62167-2

Pennebaker, J. W., Mehl, M. R., & Niederhoffer, K. G. (2003). Psychological aspects of natural language use: Our words, our selves. *Annual Review of Psychology, 54*(1), 547–577. doi:10.1146/annurev.psych.54.101601.145041 PMID:12185209

Phillips, J. R. (2005). Monovision slows juvenile myopia progression unilaterally. *The British Journal of Ophthalmology*, *89*(9), 1196–1200. doi:10.1136/bjo.2004.064212 PMID:16113381

Phills, J. A., Deiglmeier, K., & Miller, D. T. (2008). Rediscovering social innovation. *Stanford Social Innovation Review*, *6*, 34–43.

Philpott, J. S. (1983). *The relative contribution to meaning of verbal and nonverbal channels of communication: A meta-analysis* (Unpublished master's thesis). University of Nebraska, Lincoln.

Pierluigi, G., & Cristina, M. (2008). *L'interpretazione Dello Spirito Del Dono*. Francoangeli.

Piva, E., & Rossi-Lamastra, C. (2017). Human capital signals and entrepreneurs' success in equity crowdfunding. *Small Business Economics*, *51*(3), 667–686. doi:10.100711187-017-9950-y

Plummer, L. A., Allison, T. H., & Connelly, B. L. (2016). Better together? Signaling interactions in new venture pursuit of initial external capital. *Academy of Management Journal*, *59*(5), 1585–1604. doi:10.5465/amj.2013.0100

Pope, D. G., & Sydnor, J. R. (2011). What's in a Picture? Evidence of Discrimination from Prosper. com. *The Journal of Human Resources*, *46*(1), 53–92. doi:10.3368/jhr.46.1.53

Porter, M. E. (1980). *Competitive strategy: Techniques for analyzing industries and competitors*. The Free Press.

Pril, P. (2015). Crowdfunding. A study about the composition of investors in crowdfunding projects on Crowd About Now. Universiteit van Amsterdan, 1-35.

Prpić, J., Shukla, P., Roth, Y., & Lemoine, J. F. (2015). *A geography of participation in IT-mediated crowds*. Retrieved from https://papers.ssrn.com/sol3/papers.cfm?abstract_id=2494537

Prpić, J., Shukla, P. P., Kietzmann, J. H., & McCarthy, I. P. (2015). How to Work a Crowd: Developing Crowd Capital through Crowdsourcing. *Business Horizons*, *58*(1), 77–85. doi:10.1016/j.bushor.2014.09.005

Pytkowska, J. (2006). Is Commercial Financing a Growth Engine for Microfinance Institutions? *Finance & the Common Good/Bien Commun*, 101-104.

Qian, Y., & Lin, J. (2017). Antecedents of project success in donation-based crowdfunding-based on Tencent LeJuan platform in China. *Proceedings of Science, ISCC*.

Ramani, J. (2019). *Real Estate Crowdfunding: A Guide on Facts, Benefits and Platforms*. Academic Press.

Ravina, E. (2012). *Love & loans: The effect of beauty and personal characteristics in credit markets*. Academic Press.

Rayskin, V. (2016). Dynamics of Two-Sided Markets. *Review of Marketing Science*, *14*, 1–19.

Reisinger, M. (2014). Two-part Tariff Competition between Two-sided Platforms. *European Economic Review*, *68*, 168–180. doi:10.1016/j.euroecorev.2014.03.005

Renault, S. (2014). Crowdsourcing: La nébuleuse des frontières de l'organisation et du travail. *RIMHE: Revue Interdisciplinaire Management, Homme & Entreprise*, 23-40.

Riccardo, P. (1998). *Le Radici Fiduciarie Del Legame Sociale*. Franco Angeli.

Ries, J. (2014). *A Few Concerns with Crowdfunding*. Retrieved from http://blog.hbs.edu/dighbs/a-few-concerns-with-crowdfunding/

Robbins, S., & Hunsaker, P. L. (2011). Training in interpersonal skills: Tips for managing people at work. Pearson Higher Ed.

Roberts, E. B. (1991). *Entrepreneurs in High Technology*. Oxford University Press. doi:10.1093/acprof:oso/9780195067040.001.0001

Rob, G., & Joseph, F. (2016). Does heart or head rule donor behaviors in charitable crowdfunding markets? *International Journal of Electronic Commerce*, *20*(4), 499–524. doi:10.1080/10864415.2016.1171975

Robinson, R. L., Navea, R., & Ickes, W. (2013). Predicting final course performance from students' written self-introductions: A LIWC analysis. *Journal of Language and Social Psychology*, *32*(4), 469–479. doi:10.1177/0261927X13476869

Rochet, J. C., & Tirole, J. (2003). Platform competition in two-sided markets. *Journal of the European Economic Association*, *1*(4), 990–1029.

Rochet, J. C., & Tirole, J. (2006). Two-sided Markets: A Progress Report. *The RAND Journal of Economics*, *37*(3), 645–667. doi:10.1111/j.1756-2171.2006.tb00036.x

Rochet, J. C., & Tirole, J. (2006). Two-sided markets: A progress report. *The RAND Journal of Economics*, *37*, 645–667.

Roggan, J. (2015). *Motivation of German entrepreneurs to seek equity via crowdfunding: An exploratory study* (Doctoral dissertation). Retrieved October 2, 2019 on https://bibliotecadigital.fgv.br/dspace/bitstream/handle/10438/13623/John%20Roggan_Master%20Thesis_EAESP_2015_Final.pdf

Ross, L., & Bierbrauer, G. S. H. (1976). The Role of Attribution Processes in Conformity and Dissent. *The American Psychologist*, 148–157.

Ross, S. A. (1978). Some Notes on Financial Incentive-signalling Models, Activity Choice and Risk Preferences. *The Journal of Finance*, *33*(3), 777–792. doi:10.1111/j.1540-6261.1978.tb02018.x

Rubinton, B. J. (2011). *Crowdfunding: Disintermediated Investment Banking*. Academic Press.

Ryan, J. (2012). The Digital Graveyard. In Human no more: Digital subjectivities, unhuman subjects, and the end of anthropology. University Press of Colorado.

Ryan, J., Reuk, K., & Wang, C. (2007). *To Fund or Not To Fund: Determinants Of Loan Fundability in the Prosper.com Marketplace*. Stanford Graduate School of Business. Retrieved at: http://www.prosper.com/about/academics.aspx

Ryu, S., Kim, K. & Kim, Y. (2016). Reward versus philanthropy motivation in crowdfunding behaviour. *PACIS 2016 Proceedings, 87.*

Ryu, S., & Kim, Y. G. (2016). A typology of crowdfunding sponsors: Birds of a feather flock together? *Electronic Commerce Research and Applications, 16*, 43–54. doi:10.1016/j.elerap.2016.01.006

Sa-Dhan. (2016). The Bharat Microfinance Report 2016. Sa-Dhan.

Salamon, L. M. (2016). Market Failure. In The Nature of the Nonprofit Sector (3rd ed., pp. 119-120). Boulder: Westview Press.

Salamon, L. M. (1994). The Rise of the Nonprofit Sector. *Foreign Affairs, 73*(4), 109.

Sartre-Canelas, E. (2016). Reward Based Cultural Crowdfunding in Spain: Opinions of Project Promoters. Lillehammer: Knowledge Works National Centre for Cultural industries.

Schmidt, R. H., Seibel, H. D., & Thomes, P. (2016). From Microfinance to Inclusive Finance: Why Local Banking Works. Wiley-VCH Verlag.

Schmitt, M. (2017). *Equity crowdfunding: Local bias, capital structure, and venture performance* (Unpublished doctoral dissertation). University of Trier, Trier, Germany.

Schwienbacher, A., & Larralde, B. (2010). Crowdfunding of Small Entrepreneurial Ventures. The Oxford Handbook of Entrepreneurial Finance, 1-23.

SchwienbacherA.LarraldeB. (2010). Crowdfunding of small entrepreneurial ventures. doi:10.2139srn.1699183

Schwienbacher, A., & Larralde, B. (2010). *Crowdfunding of Small Entrepreneurial Ventures. Handbook of Entrepreneurial Finance. Academic Press.*

Schwienbacher, A., & Larralde, B. (2012). Crowdfunding of small entrepreneurial ventures. In D. Cumming (Ed.), *The Oxford Handbook of Entrepreneurial Finance* (pp. 369–392). Oxford University Press.

Securities and Exchange Commission (SEC). (2015a). *Crowdfunding: Final Rules*. SEC.

Securities and Exchange Commission (SEC). (2015b). *Form C under the Securities Act of 1933*. SEC.

Securities and Exchange Commission (SEC). (2016a). *Regulation Crowdfunding: A Small Entity Compliance Guide for Issuers*. SEC.

Securities and Exchange Commission (SEC). (2016b). *Regulation Crowdfunding: A Small Entity Compliance Guide for Crowdfunding Intermediaries*. SEC.

Securities and Exchange Commission (SEC). (2017a). *Updated Investor Bulletin: Crowdfunding for Investors*. SEC.

Securities and Exchange Commission (SEC). (2017b). *Investor Bulletin: Be Cautious of SAFEs in Crowdfunding*. SEC.

Securities and Exchange Commission (SEC). (2019). *Report to the Commission: Regulation Crowdfunding*. Washington, DC: SEC.

Sergio, B. (1999). Individuo E Bene Comune Nella Società Complessa. *Acta Philosophica*, *8*, 7–22.

Shane, S., & Venkataraman, S. (2000). The promise of entrepreneurship as a field of research. *Academy of Management Review*, *25*(1), 217–226. doi:10.5465/amr.2000.2791611

Shirley, A. (1964). The comparative study of rotating credit associations. *The Journal of the Royal Anthropological Institute of Great Britain and Ireland*, *94*(2), 201–229. doi:10.2307/2844382

Shneor, R., & Munim, Z. H. (2019). Reward crowdfunding contribution as planned behaviour: An extended framework. *Journal of Business Research*, *103*, 56–70. doi:10.1016/j.jbusres.2019.06.013

Short, J. C., Ketchen, D. J. Jr, McKenny, A. F., Allison, T. H., & Ireland, R. D. (2017). Research on Crowdfunding: Reviewing the (Very Recent) past and Celebrating the Present. *Entrepreneurship Theory and Practice*, *41*(2), 149–160. doi:10.1111/etap.12270

Short, J., Williams, E., & Christie, B. (1976). *The social psychology of telecommunications*. John Wiley and Sons.

Siering, M., Koch, J. A., & Deokar, A. V. (2016). Detecting Fraudulent Behavior on Crowdfunding Platforms: The Role of Linguistic and Content-Based Cues in Static and Dynamic Contexts. *Journal of Management Information Systems*, *33*(2), 421–455. doi:10.1080/07421222.2016.1205930

Simpson, M., Padmore, J., & Newman, N. (2012). Towards a new model of success and performance in SMEs. *International Journal of Entrepreneurial Behaviour & Research*, *18*(3), 264–285. doi:10.1108/13552551211227675

Solesvik, M. (2016). Crowdfunding and Entrepreneurial Finance. *International Journal of Entrepreneurial Behaviour & Research*, *22*(1), 175–177. doi:10.1108/IJEBR-09-2015-0206

Sørensen Inge, E. (2015). Go Crowdfund Yourself: Some Unintended Consequences Of Crowdfunding For Documentary Film And Industry In The UK. In Moneylab Reader, An Intervention In Digital Economy. Institute Of Network Cultures.

Spain Parliament. (2015). *Ley del Fomento de la Financiación Empresarial* (Ley 5/2015). Madrid: BOE.

Spence, M. (1973). Job market signaling. *The Quarterly Journal of Economics*, *87*(3), 355–374. doi:10.2307/1882010

Stake, R. (1995). *The art of case research*. Sage Publications.

Statista. (2018). *Value of funds raised through Crowdfounding worldwide from 2014-2016*. Retrieved from: https://www.statista.com/statistics/360512/funds-raised-via-crowdfunding-globally/

Statista. (2019). *Amount of funding delivered via alternative finance platforms in selected European countries as of 2017*. Retrieved from https://www.statista.com/statistics/412372/europe-alternative-finance-funding-amounts-country/

Stefano, E. (2007). *Appunti Sul Rapporto Tra Media E Reti*. Http://Blogstefanoepifani.It

Steigenberger, N. (2017). Why Supporters Contribute to Reward-based Crowdfunding. *International Journal of Entrepreneurial Behaviour & Research*, *23*(2), 336–353. doi:10.1108/IJEBR-04-2016-0117

Stemler, A. R. (2013). The JOBS Act and Crowdfunding: Harnessing the Power- and Money- of the Masses. *Business Horizons*, *56*(3), 271–275. doi:10.1016/j.bushor.2013.01.007

Strausz, R. (2017). A Theory of Crowdfunding: A Mechanism Design Approach with Demand Uncertainty and Moral Hazard. American Economic Review, 107(6), 1430-1476.

Strickler, Y. (2009). *The importance of video*. Retrieved July 12th, 2017 from https://www.kickstarter.com/blog/the-importance-of-video

Sundaram, D. S., & Webster, C. (2000). The role of nonverbal communication in service encounters. *Journal of Services Marketing*, *14*(5), 378–391. doi:10.1108/08876040010341008

Tan, X., Lu, Y., & Tan, Y. (2016). Why should I donate? Examining the effects of reputation, peer influence, and popularity on charitable giving over social media platforms. *Examining the Effects of Reputation, Peer Influence, and Popularity on Charitable Giving Over Social Media Platforms*.

Tan, L., & Han, J. Y. (2017). Research on the Influence Factors of the Financing Efficiency of Internet Private Equity Financing Platform in China. *Journal of Natural Science of Hunan Normal University*, (3), 12.

Tapscott, D., Lowy, A., & Ticoll, D. (2000). *Digital capital: Harnessing the power of business webs*. Harvard Business Press.

Tasque, S. (2011). La lutte contre l'exclusion bancaire des particuliers. Une perspective franco-américaine. *La Revue de l'Ires*, (3), 61-88. Retrieved May 5, 2020 on https://www.cairn.info/revue-de-l-ires-2011-3-page-61.htm#

Teece, D. J. (2010). Business models, business strategy and innovation. *Long Range Planning*, *43*(2-3), 172–194. http://www.elsevier.com/locate/lrp. doi:10.1016/j.lrp.2009.07.003

Teresa, C. M., & Piol, A. (2013). Tech and the city Startup a New York un modello per l'Italia. Guerini e associate.

The Crowd Funding Center. (2018). *The Crowd Data Center*. Retrieved from https://www.thecrowdfundingcenter.com/data

Thomas & Bernard. (2017). *Sustainability and the reconstruction of academic finance*. Academic Press.

Thomas, G. M., Chhetri, N., & Hussaini, K. (2008). Legitimacy and the Rise of NGOs: The Global and Local in South Asia. *Journal of Civil Society*, *4*(1), 31–42. doi:10.1080/17448680802051139

Tito, M. (2012). *Il Circolo Della Gratuità – Il Paradosso Del Dono E La Reciprocità Sociale*. Tangram Edizioni Scientifiche.

Toma, C. L., & D'Angelo, J. D. (2015). Tell-tale words: Linguistic cues used to infer the expertise of online medical advice. *Journal of Language and Social Psychology*, *34*(1), 25–45. doi:10.1177/0261927X14554484

Tomczak, A., & Brem, A. (2013). A conceptualized investment model of crowdfunding. *Venture Capital*, *15*(4), 335–359. doi:10.1080/13691066.2013.847614

Torris, T. (2018, June 29). Germany raises the equity crowdfunding limit to ∈8 million. *Crowdfund Insider*. Retrieved from crowdfundinsider.com

Turan, M. T. (2008). *Measuring and/or estimating social value creation: Insights into eight integrated cost approaches: The Gats Foundation Website*. Téléchargé le 25 octobre 2017 sur https://docs.gatesfoundation.org/documents/wwl-report-measuring-estimating-social-value-creation.pdf

Tvedt, T. (2006). Policy arena: The international aid system and the non-governmental organisations: A new research agenda. Journal of International Development, 18(5), Vakil, A. C. (1997). Confronting the classification problem: Toward a taxonomy of NGOs. *World Development*, *25*(12), 2057–2070. doi:10.1016/S0305-750X(97)00098-3

Ulrich, B., & Leimeister, J. M. (2017). Not just an ego-trip: Exploring backers' motivation for funding in incentive-based crowdfunding. *The Journal of Strategic Information Systems*, *26*(4), 246–260. doi:10.1016/j.jsis.2017.02.002

Unger, J. M., Rauch, A., Frese, M., & Rosenbusch, N. (2011). Human capital and entrepreneurial success: A meta-analytical review. *Journal of Business Venturing*, *26*(3), 341–358. doi:10.1016/j.jbusvent.2009.09.004

Valancience, L., & Jegeleviciute, S. (2014). Crowdfunding for creating value: stakeholder approach. Procedia - Social and Behavioral Sciences, (156), 599-604.

Valanciene, L., & Jegeleviciute, S. (2013). Valuation of crowdfunding. *Economics and Management*, *18*(1), 39–48.

Valanciene, L., & Jegeleviciute, S. (2013). Valuation of crowdfunding: Benefits and drawbacks. *Economics and Management*, *18*(1), 39–48. doi:10.5755/j01.em.18.1.3713

Valanciene, L., & Jegeleviciute, V. (2014). Crowdfunding for creating value: Stakeholder approach. *Procedia: Social and Behavioral Sciences*, *156*, 599–604. doi:10.1016/j.sbspro.2014.11.248

Van Wingerden, R., & Ryan, R. (2011). *Fighting for funds: An exploratory study into the field of crowdfunding*. Degree Project in International Marketing and Brand Management, Lund University School of Economics and Management. Retrieved from http://lup.lub.lu.se/luur/download?func=downloadFile&recordOId=1982630&fileOId=2436193

Vasylieva, N. (2018). How to start an education crowdfunding website: essential features and functionality. Justcoded, 1-13.

Vedantam, L. (2015). *Toward a Typology of Crowdfunding Motivations. Strategic Approaches to Successful Crowdfunding*. Academic Press.

Venkatesan, M. (1966). Experimental Study of Consumer Behavior Conformity and Independence. *JMR, Journal of Marketing Research, 3*, 384–387.

Vera-Muñoz, S. C., Shackell, M., & Buehner, M. (2007). Accountants' usage of causal business models in the presence of benchmark data: A note. *Contemporary Accounting Research, 24*(3), 1015–1038. doi:10.1506/car.24.3.12

Vik, E. (2010). In Numbers We Trust: Measuring Impact or Institutional Performance? *Perspectives on Global Development and Technology, 9*, 292–326.

Vismara, S. (2018b). Signaling to overcome inefficiencies in crowdfunding markets. In D. Cumming & L. Hornuf (Eds.), The Economics of Crowdfunding: Startups, Portals and Investor Behavior. Palgrave MacMillan. doi:10.1007/978-3-319-66119-3_3

Vismara, S. (2016). Equity retention and social network theory in equity crowdfunding. *Small Business Economics, 46*(4), 579–590. doi:10.100711187-016-9710-4

Vismara, S. (2016). Information Cascades among Investors in Equity .Crowdfunding. *Entrepreneurship Theory and Practice.*

Vismara, S. (2018a). Information cascades among investors in equity crowdfunding. *Entrepreneurship Theory and Practice, 42*(3), 467–497. doi:10.1111/etap.12261

Vissak, T. (2010). Recommendations for using the case study method in international business research. *Qualitative Report, 15*(2), 370–388.

Vohs Kathleen, D., Mead Nicole, L., & Goode Miranda, R. (2006). *The Psychological Consequences Of Money. Science, 314*(5802), 1154–1156. PMID:17110581

von Neumann & Oskar. (1944). *Theory Of Games And Economic Behavior*. Princeton University Press.

Vulkan, N., Astebro, T., & Sierra, M. F. (2016). Equity crowdfunding: A new phenomena. *Journal of Business Venturing Insights, 5*, 37–49. doi:10.1016/j.jbvi.2016.02.001

Wardrop, R., Zhang, B., Rau, R., & Gray, M. (2015). Moving Mainstream, The European Alternative Finance Benchmarking Report. Cambridge Centre for Alternative Finance.

Wardrop, R., Zhang, B., Rau, R., & Gray, M. (2015). *Moving Mainstream. The European alternative finance benchmarking report*. University of Cambridge.

War, J.C., & Reingen, P.H. (1990). Socioconitive Analysis of Group Decision Making among Consumers. *The Journal of Consumer Research, 17*, 245–261.

Warnick, B., Murnieks, C., McMullen, J. S., & Brooks, W. T. (2018). Passion for entrepreneurship or passion for the product: A conjoint analysis of angel and VC decision-making. *Journal of Business Venturing, 33*(3), 315–332. doi:10.1016/j.jbusvent.2018.01.002

Watkins, C. (2009). *The Young and the Digital: What the Migration to Social Network Sites, Games and Anytime, Anywhere Media Means for Our Future*. Beacon Press.

Weber, M. (2006). *Considerazioni Intermedie. Il Destino Dell'occidente*. Armando Editore.

Webster, J. C. (1965). Speech communications as limited by ambient noise. *The Journal of the Acoustical Society of America, 37*(4), 692–699. doi:10.1121/1.1909395 PMID:14288280

Wechsler, J. (2013). *Know your crowd: The drivers of success in reward based crowdfunding* (Unpublished master's thesis). University of Fribourg Department of Mass Media and Communication Research Master of Arts in Business Communication. Retrieved from https://crwdfnd.files.wordpress.com/2013/07/know-your-crowd-jonaswechsler.pdf

Wennekers, S., & Thurik, R. A. (1999). Linking Entrepreneurship and Economic Growth. *Small Business Economics, 13*(1), 27–55. doi:10.1023/A:1008063200484

Wheat, R. E., Wang, Y., Byrnes, J. E., & Ranganathan, J. (2013). Raising Money for Scientific Research through Crowdfunding. *Trends in Ecology & Evolution, 28*(2), 71–72. doi:10.1016/j.tree.2012.11.001 PMID:23219380

Williamson, O. E. (2000). The New Institutional Economics: Taking Stock, Looking Ahead. *Journal of Economic Literature, 38*, 595–613.

Wilson & Testoni. (2014). *Improving the Role of Equity Crowdfunding in Europe's Capital Markets* (No. 2014/09). Bruegel Policy Contribution.

Witt, R. E., & Bruce, G. D. (1972). Group Influence and Brand Choice. *JMR, Journal of Marketing Research, 9*, 440–443.

World Bank. (2013). *Crowdfunding's Potential for the Developing World*. Finance and Private Sector Development Department.

World Bank. (n.d.). *Defining Civil Society*. http://go.worldbank.org/4CE7W046K0

Wuillaume, A., Jacquemin, A., & Janssen, F. (2018). The Right Word for the Right Crowd: An Attempt to Recognize the Influence of Emotions. *International Journal of Entrepreneurial Behaviour & Research*. Advance online publication. doi:10.1108/IJEBR-10-2017-0412

Wu, S., Wang, B., & Li, Y. (2015). How to attract the crowd in crowdfunding? *International Journal of Entrepreneurship and Small Business, 24*(3), 322–334. doi:10.1504/IJESB.2015.067465

Xia, W., Chunling, Y., & Yujie, W. (2012). Social Media Peer Communication and Impacts on Purchase Intentions: A Consumer Socialization Framework. *Journal of Interactive Marketing, 26*, 198–208.

Xu, L. Z. (2018). Will a Digital Camera Cure your Sick Puppy? Modality and Category Effects in Donation-based Crowdfunding. *Telematics and Informatics, 35*(7), 1914–1924. doi:10.1016/j.tele.2018.06.004

Yang & Lai. (2010). Motivations Of Wikipedia Content Contributors. *Computers in Human Behavior, 26*(6), 1377–1383.

Yang, J., Liu, L., & Yin, C. (2019). A Non-Liner Decision Model for Green Crowdfunding Project Success: Evidence from China. *International Journal of Environmental Research and Public Health*, *16*(2), 187. doi:10.3390/ijerph16020187 PMID:30634654

Yin, R. (1994). *Case study research: Design and methods*. Sage Publishing.

Yochai, B. (2007). *La Ricchezza Della Rete: La Produzione Sociale Trasforma Il Mercato E Aumenta Le Libertà*. Egea.

Yochai, B. (2011). *The Penguin And The Leviathan: How Cooperation Triumphs Over Self-Interest*. Crown Business.

Younkin, P., & Kashkooli, K. (2016). What problems does crowdfunding solve? *California Management Review*, *58*(2), 20–43. doi:10.1525/cmr.2016.58.2.20

Yuan, H., Lau, R. Y., & Xu, W. (2016). The determinants of crowdfunding success: A semantic text analytics approach. *Decision Support Systems*, *91*, 67–76. doi:10.1016/j.dss.2016.08.001

Yunus, M. (1994). *Grameen Bank, as I See it*. Grameen Bank.

Yunus, M. (1999). *Banker to the Poor: Micro-Lending and the Battle Against World Poverty*. PublicAffairs.

Yunus, M. (2007). *Creating A World without Poverty: Social Business and The Future Of Capitalism*. Public Affairs.

Yunus, M. (2010). *Building Social Business: The New Kind of Capitalism that Serves Humanity's Most Pressing Needs*. Public Affairs.

Yu, S., Johnson, S., Lai, C., Cricelli, A., & Fleming, L. (2017). Crowdfunding and regional entrepreneurial investment: An application of the CrowdBerkeley database. *Research Policy*, *46*(10), 1723–1737. doi:10.1016/j.respol.2017.07.008

Zhang, J., & Liu, P. (2012). Rational herding in microloan markets. *Management Science*, *58*(5), 892–912. doi:10.1287/mnsc.1110.1459

Zhao, Q., Chen, C. D., Wangand, J. L., & Chen, P. C. (2017). "Determinants of Backers" Funding Intention in Crowdfunding: Social Exchange Theory and Regulatory Focus. *Telematics and Informatics*, *34*(1), 370–384. doi:10.1016/j.tele.2016.06.006

Zheng, H., Huang, Y., Wang, T., & Chen, D. (2015). Antecedents of Equity-based Crowdfunding Success for Innovation Projects. *China Soft Science*, *2015*(1), 130–138.

Zheng, H., Li, D., Wu, J., & Xu, Y. J. I. (2014). The role of multidimensional social capital in crowdfunding: A comparative study in China and US. *Information & Management*, *51*(4), 488–496. doi:10.1016/j.im.2014.03.003

Zhong, Z. J., & Lin, S. (2018). The antecedents and consequences of charitable donation heterogeneity on social media. *International Journal of Nonprofit and Voluntary Sector Marketing*, *23*(1), e1585. doi:10.1002/nvsm.1585

Zhou, H., & Ye, S. (2018). Legitimacy, worthiness, and social network: An empirical study of the key factors influencing crowdfunding outcomes for nonprofit projects. *Voluntas*, 1–16.

Ziegler, T., Shneor, R., Garvey, K., Wenzlaff, K., Yecolemou, N., Hao, R., & Zhang, B. (2018). *Expanding horizons, The 3rd European alternative finance industry benchmarking report.* University of Cambridge. Retrieved from https://www.jbs.cam.ac.uk/fileadmin/user_upload/research/centres/alternative-finance/downloads/2018-02-ccaf-exp-horizons.pdf

Zvilichovsky, D., Inbar, Y., & Barzilay, O. (2015). *Playing both sides of the market: Success and reciprocity on crowdfunding platforms*. Academic Press.

Zygmunt, B. (2000). *Liquid Modernity*. Polity Press.

Zygmunt, B. (2001). Community. Seeking Safety. In *An Insecure World*. Polity Press.

# About the Contributors

**Arvind Ashta** is professor of Accounting, Finance and Law at CEREN, EA 7477, Burgundy School of Business - Université Bourgogne Franche-Comté in Dijon, France. His main research interest is microfinance. He has recently authored "Microfinance: Battling a Wicked Problem" and "A Realistic Theory of Social Entrepreneurship: A lifecycle analysis of microfinance."

**Djamchid Assadi** is an Associate Professor and Researcher in Higher Education at the Burgundy School of Business (BSB). He has written and coordinated several books in French and English. He is also the author of several articles and a member of several editorial committees. His research concerns the impact of technological and social innovations on the reduction of transaction costs and the formation of the spontaneous order among peers intermediation of the political organs. Crowdfunding, FinTechs, mobile telephony and the information system are part of the technological innovation that he studies. In the field of social innovation, he is particularly interested in group loans and social guarantees based on social ties. It also questions the identification of the conditions under which the market for the excluded, for example banking, would be profitable for financial institutions. Djamchid Assadi is no less interested in the impact of non-economic factors such as music, religion and storytelling on buying behavior and strategic behavior.

**Laurence Attuel-Mendès** is Director Institutional Relations & Governance, professor of Law at Burgundy School of Business after being a lecturer at University in Paris and Dijon (1999-2004). She is member of the Board of Trustees of COMUE UBFC (public institution that merges universities higher education entities at a regional scale). She holds a PhD in Law from the University of Paris 2 (Panthéon-Assas) and is an expert on legal aspects of business. Dr. Attuel-Mendès is referee for management journals. Author of two books, one about consent and contracts (LexisNexis Group) and another on company director's liability, she authored very numerous articles in national law journals. In addition, she co-authored several articles in international journals and book chapters in crowdfunding, microfinance and marketing. Her field of research covers mainly crowdfunding and legal aspects of marketing about banking on the Internet as well.

**Susana Bernardino** is an adjunct professor of Management at the Polytechnic of Porto - Institute of Accounting and Administration (ISCAP), S. Mamede de Infesta, Portugal, and researcher at CEOS.PP/ISCAP. She completed her under-graduation degree in Management at the Faculty of Economics of the University of Porto, where also obtained the curricular part of the master's course in Finance. She got her PhD in Management in 2014 from the Portucalense University. Her research interests focus on social entrepreneurship, entrepreneurship, social and solidarity economy, smart cities, urban and regional development. and crowdfunding.

**Amaya Erro-Garcés**, assistant professor. Doctor in Economy. Master in Business Administration. Postgraduate at ESADE Business School, Deusto Business School, Harvard University and University of Columbia. Professor in "Organizational Design and Behavior", "Operations Management", "Business Economics"... Worked as General Manager in the Chamber of Commerce and Industry of Navarre from 2011 to 2014. Technical manager from 2003 to 2010, and technical staff from1999 to 2003. Research award, 2003. Award for Economic Degree, 1999. Publications in refereed journals: Journal Electronic Commerce in Organizations (JECO), Tijdschrift voor Economische en Sociale Geografie, International Journal of Entrepreneurship and Small Business (IJESB)... Research interests areas: open innovation, business strategy, entrepreneurship, teleworking, economic growth.

**Majdi Hassen** holds an M.A. in Finance, an M.A in management and a Ph.D. in finance about "The explanation of the overreaction in financial markets: Behavioral approach". Dr. Majdi is a professor in the High School of Business Studies and Economics of Tunis and in Tunis Business School. He's also responsible for M.A of NGO management which is the first master program in the MENA region addressed to enable young professionals and students to develop key management and competencies required in leadership and management positions in NGOs. During his educational career and till now, Majdi always synchronizes between his practical and theoretical knowledge and spread his expertise to his students. Majdi's researches and studies are used as references to raising awareness on the national level and a governmental level and this by pinpointing the deficiencies of the economy, and by tackling sensitive areas such as private-public dialogue, economic reforms, and governance. In addition to his successful career in teaching. Majdi Hassen is a seasoned leader with 20 years of experience in managing projects with social and economic impact, entrepreneurship, governance, advocacy, and private-public dialogue. Due to his high level of expertise, he became an expert shifting seamlessly between overseeing strategies' implementation and supervising projects from an executive level. As an accredited trainer with the UNIDO and Mentor in Forsa Mentoring program, Majdi strengths his capacity building in entrepreneurship and economic policymaking processes. Majdi is the Executive Director of the Arab Institute of Business Leaders and leader of more than 17 successful projects with big International NGOs and foreign agencies such as GIZ, CIPE, OXFAM, MEPI, and SPARK.

**Yuanqing Li** is an Assistant Professor of Entrepreneurship at Dominican University. She graduated with a Doctor of Philosophy in Business Administration (Entrepreneurship Focus) at University of Texas Rio Grande Valley (UTRGV). Her undergraduate degree in English Education (Henan Normal University, 2010) and master degrees in both Teaching Chinese to Speakers of Other Languages (Minzu University of China, 2012) and Management (MBA UTRGV, 2015) have prepared her to teach and conduct research in diverse interests (including Entrepreneurship especially in crowdfunding, cross cultural communication and organizational behavior). Her publications have appeared in such journals as International Journal of Entrepreneurship and Small Business and International Journal of Entrepreneurial Behavior & Research.

**Francesca Moretti** holds a bachelor and a master degree in Communication Studies from La Sapienza – Università di Roma. In February 2019, Francesca has completed her three year PhD course at the Coris department (La Sapienza) with a dissertation focused on the study of crowdfunding for the Belgian, Italian and American film industry. During the years she has participated to numerous conferences and she has published papers with Italian and international journals.

**Ibtissem Ouertatani** holds a Bachelor degree in Marketing, a M.A. in digital economy and entrepreneurship and a M.A in NGOs management. She had volunteered for over two years with the Red Crescent, and with ENACTUS for three years, where she had the chance to oversee all financial aspects of the operation, supervised the membership process, planned major fundraising events, and participated in marketing activities. Ibtissem also participated in Young Arab Voices, a debating program focused on equipping young Tunisians with skills to promote peace and tolerance in post-revolutionary Tunisia through debates. As a freelance marketing consultant, she worked with small associations to develop their marketing strategies, their notoriety. Helped students, and NGO members to build their communication techniques with providing training and workshops in universities. Ibtissem then joined the Arab Institute of Business Leaders, as IACE business developer and works on preparing grant proposals and monitoring and documenting the grant-making workflow processes.

**Silsa Raymond** is a consultant. She focuses on helping companies solve strategic and organizational problems, particularly those related to the development of innovative products and business models in a disruptive environment.

**J. Freitas Santos** is a Professor of International Business at the Polytechnic of Porto - Institute of Accounting and Administration (ISCAP), and researcher at CEOS.PP- Centre for Organisational and Social Studies of P. Porto. He obtained his PhD in 1997 from the Minho University. His research interests include tourism, regional development, social entrepreneurship, internationalisation and digital marketing. Besides presentations on these topics at various conferences in Portugal and foreign countries, his articles have been published in several domestic and international journals.

**Begoña Urien** is an Assistant Professor. PhD in Psychology (Teams at work and team efficacy: A study on the automotive sector). From 1986 to 2013, she hold several management positions in consultancy firms, the regional government and a mobility company. From 2002 to 2013 guest lectured. Since 2014, full time lecturer. Her research interests include the following topics: team work and team efficacy, ethical decision making. She published in several journals such as the Journal of Management Psychology, Revista del Trabajo y de las Organizaciones, or the Journal of Work and Organizational Psychology, among others.

**Margaret M. Wright** is a Clinical Assistant Professor at the Gies College of Business, University of Illinois, Urbana-Champaign. She teaches primarily in the field of Business Law, including corporate law and legal issues in entrepreneurship. Margaret is a graduate of Pepperdine Law School where she received her J.D. and New York University where she received her LL.M. in corporation law. Margaret has been with the Securities and Exchange Commission, served as in house-counsel in Washington D.C. and in private practice both in Illinois and California. Professor Wright is a member of the California, Illinois and District of Columbia bar associations. Her area of research involves crowdfunding in the United States.

**William F. Wright** is a Zimmerman Scholar at the Geis School of Business, University of Illinois at Urbana-Champaign. He has also held an academic position at the University of Waterloo, University of California, Irvine and Stanford University, among others. His research interests are applying data analytics for performance evaluation in managerial accounting and auditing contexts, and aspects of entrepreneurship. His Ph.D. is from the University of California, Berkeley.

**Sibin Wu** is Professor of Management at the University of Texas Rio Grande Valley. He earned his PhD from the University of Wisconsin-Milwaukee School of Business Administration in 2004. His current research interests include strategic decision making, international entrepreneurship, and behaviors of nascent entrepreneurs. His works have appeared in journals such as the Academy of Management Journal, Information and Management, Journal of Business Research, International Business Review, and Management and Organization Review. Professor Wu was the recipient of the John Jack Award at the United States Association of Small Businesses and Entrepreneurship in 2015.

# Index

## G



## I



## K



## L



## M



## N



## O



## P



## R

www.ingramcontent.com/pod-product-compliance
Lightning Source LLC
LaVergne TN
LVHW081334300926
849161LV00008B/1971
* 9 7 8 1 7 9 9 8 3 2 2 6 3 *